FIGURES OF
SOUTHEAST
ASIAN
MODERNITY

FIGURES OF SOUTHEAST ASIAN MODERNITY

Edited by **JOSHUA BARKER, ERIK HARMS,** *and* **JOHAN LINDQUIST**

UNIVERSITY OF HAWAI'I PRESS

Honolulu

18   17   16   15   14   13   6   5   4   3   2   1

Library of Congress Cataloging-in-Publication Data
Figures of Southeast Asian modernity / edited by Joshua
Barker, Erik Harms, and Johan Lindquist.
       pages   cm
  Includes bibliographical references and index.
   ISBN 978-0-8248-3646-7 (alk. paper)—ISBN 978-0-
8248-3741-9 (pbk. : alk. paper)
  1. Southeast Asia—Social conditions—21st century. 2.
Southeast Asia—Social life and customs—21st century.
3. Southeast Asia—Biography. I. Barker, Joshua,
editor of compilation. II. Harms, Erik, Ph. D., editor of
compilation. III. Lindquist, Johan, editor of compilation.
  HN690.8.A8F54 2013
  305.800959—dc23

2012029391

Designed by Julie Matsuo-Chun
Printed by Sheridan Books, Inc.

CONTENTS

ACKNOWLEDGMENTS

This book is the product of a set of dialogues that began at Stockholm University in 2006, continued on a panel at the annual meeting of the American Anthropological Association in 2008, and reached fruition at a workshop at Yale University in 2010. We are grateful to all the people who contributed to these dialogues. We are especially thankful to Rosalind Morris, Xiang Biao, Joe Errington, and Ben Kiernan, all of whom provided incisive comments that shaped our thinking just as our plans for the book were beginning to take shape. Mike McGovern provided invaluable comments on the introduction, and Andrew Carruthers and two anonymous reviewers gave us many helpful suggestions for improving the entire manuscript. At the University of Hawai'i Press we would like to thank Pamela Kelley for her ongoing enthusiasm and support for the project, Cheri Dunn for managing the transformation of the manuscript into a book, and Lee S. Motteler for careful copyediting.

The dialogues that underpin the book were made possible through the support of a number of funding agencies and institutions, including the Swedish School of Advanced Asia Pacific Studies, the Yale University Council on Southeast Asian Studies, the Social Sciences and Humanities Research Council of Canada, the Swedish Foundation for International Cooperation in Research and Higher Education, and the Edward J. and Dorothy Clarke Kempf Fund administered by the MacMillan Center for International and Area Studies at Yale. We thank Quang Phu Van, Indriyo K. Sukmono, Michael Dove, Kristine Mooseker, and Yale graduate students for helping to make the Yale Workshop the success that it was. We are also grateful to Behzad

Sarmadi and Jean Chia, who worked on the index and helped prepare the final manuscript for submission.

Finally, we are indebted to Cornell Southeast Asia Publications for permission to republish portions of an earlier article that helped set the stage for this book: Joshua Barker, Johan Lindquist, et al., "Figures of Indonesian Modernity," *Indonesia* 87 (April 2009): 35–72.

PROLOGUE

ULF HANNERZ

My visits to Southeast Asia have been rather few and far between, but as the manuscript of *Figures of Southeast Asian Modernity* comes into my hands, I am reminded of some particular moments and experiences. My first encounter with the region was in early May 1975, when I arrived in Bangkok—and it was only a few days after Saigon had (as the common term had it) "fallen," and the long war in Vietnam was finally over. According to the widely accepted "domino theory," it would be Bangkok next. That prospect was anxiously debated in at least some quarters of the city those days. A little later, in Penang, I made my first acquaintance with an important Southeast Asian institution, the food court—at the time not yet so common elsewhere in the world, but to my mind a sort of tropical megaversion of a smorgasbord—and I also had my first taste of the durian fruit.

Then in 1987, I happened to arrive in Manila just a few days after a coup attempt by a dashing young colonel, "Gringo" Honasan. It was not yet quite clear whether the attempt was really over. There were soldiers behind sandbags here and there in the streets. Nobody seemed quite sure where "Gringo" was: still in the city? In the forest? On an American gunboat, outside the harbor? The so-called mosquito press, tabloids in black-and-red print that had emerged after the fall of the Marcos regime, seemed to spread rumors and speculations efficiently. And then Corazon Aquino, still president despite "Gringo's" endeavor, went on television to speak to the nation. She started out, spectacles on, speaking in English, reading from a manuscript. Then she made a very brief pause, took her glasses off, looked straight into the camera, and continued speaking in Pilipino—at which point, of course, I was lost. A couple of months later, when I was in Kuala Lumpur, there was the moment when Prime Minister Mohathir Mohamad targeted a varied set of people whom he defined as adversaries, placing them in detention, in what became known as Operation Lalang. (In Khoo Gaik Cheng's account of Malaysian political satire in this volume, we are reminded in passing of this event.)

Recently in Singapore (2011), I found public attention focused on a new book featuring an interview with Lee Kuan Yew, father of the city-state, by a set of local journalists. Lee, now in his late eighties, still with a unique official position as minister mentor (abbreviated MM in the media), apparently as self-confident as ever and still a man of strong opinions, had offered some views on the place of Muslims (in this context, basically meaning Malays) in society, and then the current prime minister, who also happens to be the minister mentor's son, had to display his capacity for damage control.

In a study I did of news media foreign correspondents some time ago, I noted that there is a type known in the trade as "parachutists" or "firemen."[1] These are the newspeople who hurry in to a place briefly, mostly to report on some crisis, and then depart just as quickly. This is in contrast to the correspondents who are based for some considerable time in a single place or region and have a chance to acquire a great deal of local knowledge. With regard to Southeast Asia, I have been if anything a sort of parachute anthropologist, showing up very occasionally and briefly. (But then, these visits are mostly not in moments of real crisis, so there the parallel with the newspeople breaks down; and in fact I have tended not to do much reporting on these occasions either.) As with these other parachutists, however, it may turn out that when I come back to a place, it is after a fairly long time. (Parachutists are often veterans.) And so I notice the changes.

Consequently when I read this book, which is very much a document of early twenty-first-century Southeast Asia, I am struck by one thing: Even though Southeast Asia includes metropoles exhibiting great affluence as well as pockets of both urban and rural misery, it has now become a single region in a single world. We are reminded occasionally, by those with a sense of history, that the notion of "Southeast Asia" was in large part a strategically useful product of the period after World War II. Mostly, before then, Western scholarship had tended to keep the area divided into the parts belonging to three—or even four—European empires. But then as it began to turn into that entity with one regional identity, Southeast Asia was again dramatically divided. Those days of my first visit to Bangkok, the times of domino theory, were in the climactic period of that divide. What some now refer to as World

War III was, in much of the world, only a Cold War. For a long stretch of time, it was particularly in Southeast Asia that it was a real hot war. And the Bamboo Curtain may have sounded rather more idyllic than an Iron Curtain, but it was nonetheless a matter of a real divide.

Now, as these portrayals of twenty-first-century Southeast Asians show us, there is a lively flux of people—or at least of ideas—across boundaries in an interconnected region, as well as beyond. You can read in this book about Huong, aka Kat, a student in Hanoi, with her e-mail address hellokittysmile1988@yeehaw.com, and her ambition to seek higher education somewhere in one of the best universities of the United States (although she cannot even afford the postage to send in her application). I see this for myself on a Sunday afternoon at the Lucky Plaza shopping center, Orchard Road, Singapore, when Filipina domestic workers congregate to have a snack, chat, and send their remittances to their families at home. Then too, of course, in response to globalization rhetoric with too shallow a time perspective, scholars remind us that certain things are really not so new. This is a region with very old transnational connections, not least across the Indian Ocean and the Arabian Sea.[2] It is also true that the political allegiances of the fairly recent past can occasionally be glimpsed and brought into the present, as in the story of a Soviet-trained Vietnamese veterinary scientist. As an ingredient of continuity, moreover, I notice here and there in republican Southeast Asia the durable, or at least on-and-off, prominence of members of political families—not only Lee Kuan Yew and Lee Hsien Loong. In the chapters that follow, we also encounter Cory Aquino's son Benigno Aquino III, "Noynoy," president like his mother; and Aung San Suu Kyi, daughter of a Burmese independence hero and martyr. (Fairly briefly, there was also Megawati Sukarnoputri, daughter of Indonesia's founding father and then herself president.)

Over the years, there has been much in Southeast Asia to nourish the anthropological imagination—"involution," "cultural brokers," and "moral economy" are among the key concepts that have been intimately although not always uniquely connected with Southeast Asian studies. As the editors note in their introduction to this book, around the mid-twentieth century, in the late colonial period, the British colonial civil servant Furnivall set the idea of the "plural society" in circulation, based on his experience in this region. Then, crossing into anthropology, it became a traveling concept, employed not least in Africa and in the Caribbean.[3] Here was an ambitious macroconcept, aiming at capturing the nature of an entire social order. In its Southeast Asian version, it typically depicted a colonial society that was also a plantation society, to a fairly great extent made up of populations with long-distance migrations in their history. The theoretical point to which plural society thinkers were inclined to return was that this was not, as the mainstream social theorists of the day usually had it, about "societies" generally, an entity based on consensus and shared values. Essentially, separate peoples met mostly in the market place; and at the top, over all that, was the colonial power.

In the early twenty-first century, "plural society" is not a term so frequently heard anymore. In the general vocabulary in much of the world, "multiculturalism" does some of its work.[4] At home in Southeast Asia, that is to a degree also true, but more importantly society has come half a century or more away from colonialism, and in very considerable part it has left the plantation behind as a main arena of economy and society. The present-day habitat is one of shopping malls, no-frills airlines, high-rise public housing, and expansive transnational knowledge industries, as well as of hill farms and paddy fields.[5] Perhaps "modernity" is a term that can cover all this, but otherwise it would be difficult to find a single conceptual umbrella. Yet if the original "plural society" involved a particular colonial organization of ethnicity, it is clear that ethnic categories continue to be salient in Southeast Asian society. It is not only the old minister mentor, who could himself no doubt remember the times of old-style pluralism, who thinks and talks in such terms. In Singapore there are still Chinese, Malays, and Indians. There is, too, the assistant professor of accounting at the national university who chooses to return to his Yemeni family business heritage and becomes a restaurateur and community activist in Arab Street. The particular makeup of national populations varies from one country to the next. Yet here as elsewhere in the world, one may sense that top-down multiculturalism, depending on sharp, stable borders for large-scale policy and administrative measures, often works less than perfectly. In the Philippines, Richard Chu points out in his contribution to the book that it may not be widely understood how many important figures in the history of the country were actually "Chinese mestizos." In Singapore, again, the Chinese are supposed to speak Mandarin, despite the fact that most of them arrived there speaking Hokkien; and it seems they respond in part by making up a "Singlish" patois. And one of the nicest museums in town is the Peranakan Museum, celebrating the cultural history of a group emerging from ethnic mixture.

To capture the real, multifaceted, polyphonic diversity of contemporary Southeast Asia with its fluidity, transgressions, and collective reflexivity, the editors of this volume have chosen the format of presenting a rich gallery of figures—shifting smoothly between particular concrete individuals and ideas of social types. It is, again, a bit like a sizeable food court, providing food for thought about the varieties of the human condition, and it is a measure of the success of this strategy that it stimulates a reader's appetite to think of further types that might also have been there. But those who are portrayed in the pages that follow take us into all kinds of nooks and crannies in regional social life. To draw on one kind of anthropological vocabulary: They involve studying down, up, and sideways.[6] We meet the gangster, the prostitute, and one transnational working man who has found a rather uncomfortable way of seeing the world (pineapples in Hawai'i, building sites in Singapore, an Israeli kibbutz, oil drilling in the Middle East, and a Korean plastics factory), before returning as indebted as ever to his Thai village. There is the journalist, the schoolteacher, even an anthropologist-musician. And as far "up" as you can get, there is one of the region's leading political figures, Malaysia's Mohathir Mohamad, "Doctor M."

Several things can be said about this format of presentation. One is that it is clearly only possible because there is such a wealth of present-day scholarship to draw on, devoted to so many aspects of Southeast Asian society. Another is that as far as I can see, it makes a remarkable contribution to ongoing experimentation in anthropological writing. (Not all the contributors to the book are anthropologists, but I believe most are, and so are all three editors.) If anthropology is itself basically a study of diversity, one might expect diversity in writing to come naturally. Yet despite tendencies toward renewal, a very large part of writing in the discipline is still one variety or other of "me-and-my-ethnography." As fieldwork in anthropology tends to be a lone-wolf pursuit, writing and publication have also mostly been individual activities. Undoubtedly the contributors to *Figures of Southeast Asian Modernity* are also capable of organizing their knowledge in the style of more conventional, specialized monographs, but here we see how well-orchestrated collaborative efforts can offer their own valuable insights and overviews.

That is one pleasing conclusion, but there is also one more somber afterthought. Mostly, after all its twentieth-century turbulence, the Southeast Asian region at this point in time seems to be one where scholars can pursue their research interests freely, safely, reasonably comfortably, and openly in a productive and relaxed mingling of expatriates and local colleagues doing "anthropology at home." Yet it appears there is one exception. There was a time when Burma could be a site for major anthropological field studies carried out along the established lines of such research.[7] For quite a long time, Burma (or Myanmar) has been a country less often heard from. Perhaps that can change again. Meanwhile, the fact that this book can still include a vivid section on modern Burmese figures tells us something about the commitment and the reporting skills of this particular set of contributors. It also reminds us, however, that field ethnography of the usual academic type is a politically vulnerable pursuit, peculiarly demanding because of its emphasis on long-term local immersion, and therefore one with a checkered history of exits and absences from particular countries and regions in the world.[8]

But, to repeat, such intensive and extended involvement with Southeast Asia—any part of it—has never been mine. Moving quickly in and out of the region at various times over the decades, and even reading this book now, I have been a parachute anthropologist, not an area specialist. Yet I also know that in parachutist journalism, the visiting newsperson, in his or her hunting and gathering efforts, is very dependent on finding one or more "fixers"—people with extensive local knowledge, not least those with a good overview of who is who in local society. A fixer is, to use again one of those anthropological terms with Southeast Asian origins, a kind of "cultural broker." Indeed, in no small part, the skill of a foreign correspondent lies in the ability to identify and make good use of the best fixers at hand. But finding such fixers is to a degree also a matter of luck. I count myself lucky, in this case, to be allowed to benefit from the insights of Joshua Barker, Erik Harms, and Johan Lindquist—and all the informants, the "sources," whom they have in their turn recruited.

INTRODUCTION

JOSHUA BARKER, ERIK
HARMS, *and* JOHAN LINDQUIST

We live in a world populated not just
by individuals but by figures—people who loom larger than life because they
alternately express and challenge conventional understandings of social types.
Such figures are important because they serve as anchors for local, national,
and transnational discourses about contemporary social life and its futures.
Like Raymond Williams' analysis of keywords in modern social thinking, an
analysis of the "key figures" of a given social formation can provide unique
insights into ideological formations and their contestations.[1]

This book considers a wide range of figures that populate the social and
cultural imaginaries of contemporary Southeast Asia—some familiar only in
particular contexts, others recognizable across the region or even globally. We
focus specifically on what we call figures of modernity, which we define quite
simply as *persons within a given social formation whom others recognize as
symbolizing modern life.* They are figures because they stand out against the
ground of everyday life. They are "of modernity" not because they are tied
to a particular historical epoch but because they encapsulate a modern ethos.
This definition, as well as terms such as "figure," "modern," "modernity," and
the seemingly benign geographical placemarker "Southeast Asia," all require
further elaboration. We therefore begin by explaining what we mean by these
terms and why we believe that the analysis of such figures of modernity offers a unique methodological window into contemporary Southeast Asia and
opens up new vistas within a broader comparative perspective.[2]

Before dwelling on explanations, however, it is important to recognize
that the figures we describe are all real people. The book thus deliberately

aims to bring life and humanity to historical processes and transformations that, in other academic contexts, are treated as abstractions. At the same time, all of the figures in this book have been chosen because they represent and give voice to something larger than themselves, offering a view into social life that is at once highly particular and general. They include such diverse figures as the NGO Worker in Indonesia, the Returning Urbanite in Malaysia, the Schoolteacher in Singapore, the Cham Modernizer in Cambodia, the Filipino Seaman, and the Vietnamese Transnational. These and other figures reveal subject positions that manifest and comment upon a particular historical moment in the complex articulation of large-scale processes that are shaping the countries of the region. With the engaging clarity of concrete human experiences, these figures reveal processes of commodification, class formation, globalization, religious change, and political conflict.

The book is organized through the nine major countries of the region: Burma (or Myanmar), Cambodia, Indonesia, Laos, Malaysia, the Philippines, Singapore, Thailand, and Vietnam. Each section begins with an introductory essay by a country editor, followed by the individual contributions. The number of figures for each country is roughly proportionate to the population size of each country, with Indonesia having the most and Laos the fewest. In total, this book brings together more than eighty scholars from a range of academic disciplines. Each author has been asked to identify and describe a specific figure of modernity in a one-thousand-word essay that offers a vivid and intimate portrait set against the background of contemporary Southeast Asia. Importantly, the invited contributors are mainly early career scholars engaged in ongoing fieldwork, thus allowing us to create a volume that combines scholarly rigor with a vivid, up-to-date description of a region of the world undergoing rapid change. Ultimately, it is the authors themselves who have—through a combination of field research experience and personal understanding of the people they describe—identified the significance of the figures they have chosen. Their understanding may not always reflect what others within the relevant locale say or have said about these figures, but ideally the contextualization and analysis they provide should account for such insider perceptions.

The Figure

A figure, in its most basic sense, refers to "a person as an object of mental contemplation." The term "figure" also refers variously to someone of rank, someone respected, or someone outlandish in some aspect.[3] In short, a figure is someone whom others recognize as standing out and who encourages reflexive contemplation about the world in which the figure lives. Importantly, in explaining why a figure stands out as meaningful, we must pay attention to the grounds from which figures emerge and from which they are distinguished.[4] As Gestalt psychologists have argued, the act of concentrating on a figure necessarily involves the establishment of a ground against which it can be perceived; it is through the totality of the figure/ground combination that meaning is constituted.[5] The analysis of a figure is thus simultaneously an exercise in trying to vividly depict the key contemplative features of the figure's form while also determining the relevant sociohistorical backgrounds that make the figure stand out in that given place and time.

We seek to make sense of the Southeast Asian figures that populate this book much like Walter Benjamin made sense of the flaneur against the ground of nineteenth-century Paris.[6] Our aim is not to compare twenty-first-century Southeast Asia to nineteenth-century Paris but to focus on the emergence, persistence, or decline of particular social figures, which like the flaneur serve to evoke both underlying historical processes and the "structures of feeling" of a particular time and place.[7] Like anthropologist Ara Wilson, we see figures as "personae that represent new modes of work and new styles of being that accompany economic modernity." They are, Wilson adds, "embodied symbols of the promise and problems of new economic realities."[8]

In short, figures are real people who also operate as "symbols" that embody the structures of feeling associated with larger, seemingly impersonal conditions of a particular time. As such, the concept of the figure differs in important ways from the sociological concept of the "social type" because figures are meant primarily neither to classify nor to define the "role" an individual plays; instead, they emphasize the symbolic work the individual performs within society. In analytical terms, the concept of the social type is primarily an instrument of classification, a description of a functional role-playing persona that fits into an ordered social typology.[9] At best, social types can map the diverse landscape of individuals populating a society and reveal the classificatory concerns of specific moments in a society, or as in Max Weber's concept of the ideal type, stress certain elements at the expense of others in order to facilitate comparison.[10] At worst, social types can collapse into ideological stereotypes.[11]

In everyday life, social types most commonly emerge from objectifying and power-laden discourses, as for instance James Siegel described criminal types appearing in tabloid newspapers during Indonesia's New Order era.[12] From this perspective, studying the emergence of a type draws attention to the capacity of discourse to constitute subject positions, particularly those of marginalized or stigmatized persons (e.g., through stereotypes), while leading to an examination of how discourses circulate and are mediated to a broader public through various kinds of mass media. For instance, some social types may circulate primarily in discourses at a very local level, such as neighborhood gossip circuits. Others may circulate primarily in national discourses or in media circuits with a global reach. As Rosalind Morris has reminded us, social types almost invariably are conceived at points where the emergence of more disruptive forces might have occurred;[13] again, as exemplified in Siegel's analysis of the criminal type as an ideological device. In this process, the deployment of marginal social types in discourse helps to anchor and define the limits of a given social order.[14]

Our approach to figures is not about making types but instead draws from ethnographic description and contextualization that attends to the lifeworlds of particular individuals. While many of the figures we discuss are shadowed by a discourse that typifies them, we are more interested in the tensions that the figures themselves feel—or that we observe through their experiences—as they struggle to define their own historical agency. This struggle tends to be particularly pronounced in cases where discourses on social types are buttressed by institutions of state power, as can be seen in cases such as the Prostitute in Vietnam, the Lawless Element in the Philippines, or the Person with HIV/AIDS in Indonesia. In such cases, a focus on figures does not preclude a consideration of the genealogy of discourses of related types, but it draws attention to how such typification is experienced and negotiated by particular individuals. An analysis of figures can offer a window into attitudes, subject positions, and worlds of meaning, while also shedding light on the specific backdrops that give them heightened significance at a given historical moment. Just as the flaneur makes sense only against the backdrop of emerging mass commodification in nineteenth-century Paris, so too do the figures in this volume make sense only once they have been set against particular backgrounds. For example, the Indonesian Street Kid appears only against the ground of a burgeoning but divided metropolis, Miss Beer Lao appears only against the ground of Laotian nationalism and the political economy of market-oriented socialism, and the Philippine Seaman appears only against the ground of globalizing trade and masculinist nationalism. In this volume, therefore, what emerges from the discussion of figures is a wide array of grounds—technological, economic, political, religious, social—that help to shed light on the ongoing figuration process in contemporary Southeast Asia.

If the social type is typically conceived of as a symptom of the times—fulfilling a role, or somehow "resulting" from the conditions particular to a social setting—figures, by contrast, may be more accurately conceived as *signs* of the times. They operate both as semiotic signs that send a message to observers about key features of social life and as "vital signs" or "signs of life" that evoke the pulse of a particular social formation. Because they are real human beings who also express seemingly idealist conceptions, the figures mediate the often elusive and fleeting notion of philosophical idealism—the so-called zeitgeist—with the material conditions of lived life and experience. Because they have complex histories and variegated life courses, figures offer a way of reading into the ethos of a particular age without reducing it to singularities or depending on elusive philosophical notions of "spirit" or reductionist notions of cultural essence. More generally, in this process the figure becomes a device that allows us to find points of mediation between the functional and the symbolic, between contemporary lifeworlds and historical processes, and between the generalizing claims of positivist social sciences and the poetic modalities of ethnography and the humanistic social sciences.[15]

The use of figures to mark historical shifts is a method evident in many of the modern classics of Southeast Asian studies. In Benedict Anderson's *Imagined Communities,* the Philippine novelist José Rizal was described as a figure whose work signified a shift toward a new form of nationalist imaginary, as the experience of temporal simultaneity—a sense of the "meanwhile"—came to define the possibilities of imagining the nation.[16] In James Siegel's *Fetish, Recognition, Revolution,* figures such as Mas Marco Kartodikromo and Tan Malaka—and their engagement with the Indonesian lingua franca—came to stand in for broader transformations and historical paths not taken as the subject of Indonesia emerged over the decades prior to the Second World War.[17] In James C. Scott's *Weapons of the Weak,* rich and stingy Haji Broom and poor dishonest Razak were descriptions of real people who nonetheless functioned, within the modernizing village of Sedaka, as symbols, "social banners," or "effective vehicles of propaganda" that embodied "a critique of things as they are as well as a vision of things as they should be."[18] In Rudolf Mrázek's history of technology and nationalism, the Indonesian dandy was seen to be loosely equivalent to Benjamin's flaneur, slowly losing his place as capitalism took shape and placed new demands on its subjects.[19] In Fenella Cannell's ethnography of the Christian Philippines, the *bakla,* or male transvestite, was shown to exemplify a widely admired capacity to effect self-transformation through mediation of global notions of glamor.[20] And in Vicente Rafael's work, the "persistent figurality" of the criminal helped to excite broad sociocultural effects, such as the production of a social geography of fear across the region.[21] All of these earlier works serve as examples and inspiration for the method we employ here, while also serving as reference points for drawing historical comparisons to the contemporary figures that are our focus.

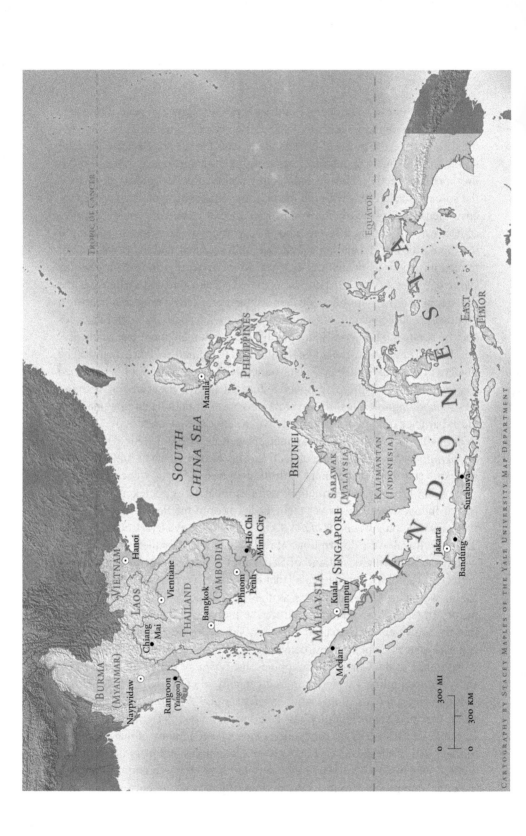

Southeast Asia

As a definable geographic region, Southeast Asia is largely a historical fiction that emerged as a relic of colonial demarcations of space, World War II military command structures, Cold War geopolitics, and the scholarly categories of academic area studies.[22] Thus, apparently similar figures appearing in different Southeast Asian nations will not likely understand each others' languages, know much about each others' histories, or even know the names of each others' national leaders. Nevertheless, all of the different countries in the region have experienced the rise of industrialization, the positive and negative effects of the agricultural green revolution, and the promise of economic growth, as well as the pains of the 1997 Asian financial crisis. The region is also rapidly becoming more urban, with the rise of mega-urban regions surrounding Manila, Jakarta, Bangkok, Ho Chi Minh City, and Kuala Lumpur, the revival of once neglected capital cities such as Phnom Penh and Hanoi, and the rise of Singapore as a "global city."[23]

Linked by shared regional experiences, Southeast Asian nations are also separated by dramatic political, economic, religious, and cultural differences, mediated by diverse histories of Dutch, British, French, Spanish—and in the case of Thailand, the absence of—colonial rule. These variable trajectories have differentially framed their postcolonial nation-building efforts, as well as their relationship with electoral democracy, socialism, and the global market. In the middle of the twentieth century, the early postcolonial economies of Southeast Asia largely depended on producing raw materials with unskilled labor, a pattern that had helped fuel industrialism in Europe and the United States during the colonial era. But beginning in the 1960s, Indonesia, Thailand, Malaysia, and Singapore experienced agricultural and industrial revolutions that transformed their economic and social base.[24] Singapore, for instance, grew to prominence with the global electronics boom in the 1970s—a time when Vietnam, Laos, and Cambodia were caught up in war or genocide—before transforming itself into a global business hub in the 1980s and 1990s. In the latter period, production moved offshore, with factories and industrial estates relocating to countries such as Indonesia, Malaysia, the Philippines, and Thailand. Historic rates of economic growth were facilitated by new relationships with global corporations, new trade and zoning practices, and the control and regulation of populations in ways that favored foreign direct investment and the accumulation of capital among well-connected elites.[25]

The ten-member Association of Southeast Asian Nations (ASEAN) now represents all of the major nation-states in the region as a powerful economic trade bloc, giving some political substance to an otherwise imagined carto-graphic shorthand.[26] But it remains important not to overstate the historical depth or validity of the designation "Southeast Asia," which is home to dra-matic economic and political differences.[27] In economic terms, Singapore is one of the richest countries in the world, while largely rural Laos is ge-nerally considered one of the poorest. In political terms, an even more va-riegated mosaic of ideologically disparate forms of governance covers the region. A military junta rules in Burma, while more open, yet still politically firm communist parties rule via "market-oriented socialism" in Vietnam and Laos. Cambodia, Malaysia, and Thailand are all constitutional monarchies. In Cambodia, a multiparty (but not quite participatory) parliamentary democracy is developing in fits and starts after years of restructuring. In Thailand, reli-gion, king, and state combine through Theravada Buddhism, while Malaysia is dominated by ethnic Malay and Islamic interests that are often posed in op-position to the Chinese, who make up more than a quarter of the population. Finally, formal secular democracies negotiate with various entrenched power interests in the "controlled democratic" parliamentary republic of Singapore, the post-Suharto Republic of Indonesia, and the Philippines, where bossism, family politics, and election violence color a state ostensibly governed by ex-ecutive, legislative, and judicial branches of government.[28] If ASEAN serves as a bloc for negotiating mutual economic interests, it is also notoriously weak if not wholly uninterested in enforcing any semblance of universal ideals, as evidenced by its hands-off policy toward political abuses in Burma and the proliferation of legal loopholes that mark its statements about human rights.[29] Officially presenting itself as the unitary voice of the region, ASEAN cannot enforce its ideals across Southeast Asia because the region itself lacks under-lying coherence.

Despite the political and cultural diversity of the region, however, there are important cross-cutting features. The various figures in this book are all animated by the advent of industrial modernity in the context of authoritarian and interventionist states and the ensuing boom-and-bust cycles of the "Asian tiger economies."[30] While Southeast Asian states increasingly promote neo-liberal business-friendly policies couched in the rhetorical language of free markets and good governance, governance on the ground is often illiberal, and well-connected and powerful actors often enjoy exceptions to laissez-faire policies.[31] The effects of neoliberalism across the region thus have been uneven. In Thailand, the collapse of the banking sector during the 1997 crisis and subsequent reforms and cutbacks have led to an unstable political land-scape characterized by populism. In Indonesia, the fall of the dictator Suharto in 1998 led to the disbanding of monopolies under the watching eye of the

International Monetary Fund and to ensuing political decentralization. In Vietnam, *đổi mới,* or "renovation," policies allowed for an opening up to foreign capital, officially dubbed "market-oriented socialism," and in Cambodia a postconflict donor industry and foreign investment have led to massive landgrabs characteristic of primitive forms of accumulation.[32] Neoliberal reforms have also created the conditions for individuals to imagine themselves and interact with state institutions in new ways.[33] Domestic and regional politics have been affected by sometimes violent forms of populism, separatism, and radical Islam (most notably in Indonesia, Malaysia, the Philippines, and Thailand). At the same time, nongovernmental organizations have become ever more pervasive, and struggles in the name of "people power," democratic reform, and individual rights and freedoms have reshaped several political landscapes.[34]

At the height of the "Asian economic miracle," young female factory workers emerged as iconic figures of modernity across the region. The entry of these women into the public sphere should not be understood only in terms of their role in industrial production but also for the way they created a new group of mass consumers, disturbed patriarchal hierarchies, and became focal points for broader anxieties about female sexuality.[35] In this book, a similar ambivalence toward working women is expressed through figures such as the Filipina Call Center Agent, the Vietnamese female Petty Trader (*tiểu thương*), and the Indonesian Career Woman (*wanita karir*). Economic growth and liberalization have also created prosperity and given rise to both a middle class and a class of new rich across Southeast Asia.[36] Although ethnic Chinese minorities continue to dominate the region's economies, wealth has increasingly spread across ethnic divides.[37] This has, however, also intensified inequalities, as markers of class and variegated levels of development are played out visibly on the streets and in city spaces.[38] While the poorest residents live in squatter housing plagued by recurrent flooding and dengue fever epidemics, ever-increasing numbers of middle- and upper-class residents live in gated communities. While the great majority of Southeast Asians move about their cities on foot, by bicycle, motorbike, bus, jeepney, or minivan, the wealthiest residents are driven through the streets by personal chauffeurs in luxury automobiles.

Inequality not only characterizes intracity forms of mobility, it also shapes patterns and qualities of flows of people between cities, between rural and urban areas, and across national boundaries. The porous borderlands between Burma and Thailand have helped to sustain informal transnational economies, but they have also given rise to more or less permanent refugee camps.[39] In Singapore and Malaysia—the region's largest importer of migrant labor—

deportation regimes and border controls have strengthened in the wake of the economic crisis and amidst anxieties about terrorism following the 9/11 attacks and the Bali bombings.[40] Both Indonesia and the Philippines are now among the world's main exporters of migrant labor, supplying not only the most successful Asian economies but also wealthy Middle Eastern oil countries.[41] For many observers, the female domestic servant has come to replace the female factory worker as iconic of the international division of gendered labor. These new mobilities are linked not only to shifts in the organization of work but also to changing patterns of consumption and leisure. The deregulation of the airline industry and the massive success of the Malaysian-based budget carrier Air Asia have made air travel increasingly affordable. Low-cost airlines not only facilitate migrant travel but also contribute to rising intraregional tourism.[42] Importantly, however, the experience of *immobility* develops together with mobility, as the majority of Southeast Asians remain in their home villages throughout their life cycle, even as they are increasingly affected by the circulation of capital, individuals, goods, and images that touch upon every part of the region.

As in other parts of the world, the dramatic rise of information technologies is having a profound impact across Southeast Asia. As of June 2011, Indonesia had the second-largest number of Facebook users in the world after the United States, the Philippines ranked seventh globally, and Singapore, one of the smallest countries in the region, had close to one million Twitter users out of a population of just five million.[43] While it is not surprising that Singapore has such a media-savvy population, it is perhaps more unexpected that developing countries such as the Philippines and Indonesia have taken new Internet platforms to heart, largely bypassing the personal computer and moving straight to the smartphone. These new technologies undoubtedly help to constitute new forms of subjectivity and are deeply symptomatic of emergent concerns with self-cultivation and self-fashioning.

If neoliberalism is a form of rule that leads the individual to cultivate and govern the self in accordance with liberal ideals,[44] then nowhere are its effects more conspicuous than in the rise of market-based solutions to higher education. Even as education continues to serve as an important means of class differentiation, it has become increasingly internationalized and has acquired critical importance as a marketplace for neoliberal self-fashioning. Dramatic improvements in literacy rates and the institutionalization of primary and secondary education have been followed by the ascent of English, computer, design, and business schools, which dot cities and provincial towns across the region. Neverthelesss, the high cost of tuition at colleges and universities continues to act as a barrier to the vast majority of people. Even those who can afford to pay face an uncertain future, since the labor market for skilled workers remains limited. The Vietnamese Aspiring Overseas Student described in this volume typifies the many Southeast Asians who hope to study abroad in Australia, Europe, or the United States. Yet it is also the case that universities in those countries increasingly see places such as Singapore and Malaysia as crucial nodes in their own internationalization efforts, as the globalization of higher education is just beginning.

The lives of the figures described in this book are all entwined with global production systems in various ways: Some work in sleek new downtown offices, others in special economic zones, and still others work in rural spaces that sometimes seem remote but are more often than not directly connected to global networks. Even seemingly noneconomic spiritual life is transformed by the economic and spatial regimes of the modern economy, as evidenced by the Lao Mobile Phone Monk, the corporate Spiritual Trainer in Indonesia, or the shift from place-based to person-based cults epitomized by the figure of the Spirit Medium in Thailand. The figures in this book live in the variegated spaces of contemporary modernity and participate in modern, outward-oriented economic activities, such as the struggle to attract foreign investments, the commercialization and industrialization of agriculture, the mass extraction of natural resources, the movement of rural people to cities and overseas, and the never-ending attempt to gain elite (and often foreign) educations. Some of the figures are members of the "New Rich," others of a rising consumer-oriented middle class, and yet others constitute a burgeoning proletariat working in industrial parks, call centers, and agro-industry. They are investors, cadres, village chiefs, or athletes; they work as domestic helpers, flight attendants, engage in sex work, or fight for workers rights as community organizers.

While scholars have long understood Southeast Asia as a dynamic space of cross-cultural encounters and hybridity, the region today is even more intensely marked by transnational connections and flows, all of which impact and guide contemporary national transformations. Writing of the great waterways and tradewinds that circulate throughout the region, historian Oliver Wolters perceptively noted that, unlike the Mediterranean, the sea has never bound Southeast Asia into a unified region characterized by cultural similarities but rather functions as a sea "in common" that has facilitated exchanges of trade goods and ideas, sometimes leading to borrowings, never leading to homogenization, and always resulting in "localization."[45] Wolters ascribes to Southeast Asia "a propensity for modernity that came from an outward-looking disposition encouraged by easy maritime communications."[46] We believe these insights also apply to the current period and that the figures in this book, despite all their differences, have "modernity in common."

Modernity

The figures in this book speak to something more recent than the postcolonial moment and more enduring than the contemporary. We call them figures of *modernity*. We might have called them figures of "postmodernity," "alternative modernities," "late modernity," "second modernity," "radicalized modernity," "high modernity," or even "the contemporary," to cite but a few of the terms social theorists have coined to describe the current era.[47] Discussions concerning the nature of modernity—at the heart of the social sciences since the industrial revolution—are notoriously complex and contentious. While these debates are important, we are primarily interested in how the figures in this book all speak to more generalizable features associated with the expansion of capitalism, the waxing and waning influence of the nation-state, the development of and challenge to particular forms of rationality associated with the rise of science and technology, and the transformation of the self—all features commonly understood as falling under the rubric of modernity. Even in cases when the figures in this book appear to dramatically extend, undermine, or otherwise transform the forces of modernity, they are nonetheless entangled in these very processes. At the same time, many of the figures highlight novel aspects of social life that appear to be transcending classic elements of modernity. They embody the increased (yet often explicitly semipermeable) porosity of national borders, the development of transnationalism and flexible citizenship, the advent of instantaneous technology, and the critique of universalisms in the face of increasing global connections.[48]

For many scholars, "modernity" refers to the forms of life and organization that emerged in Europe from the seventeenth century and that subsequently came to spread around the world.[49] Since the 1990s, however, scholars working in countries outside of North America and Europe have challenged the notion that modernity diffuses from a Western origin or strictly reproduces Western models. In this book we are not ultimately concerned with reading backwards into questions of origins, but we do value and see this book as contributing to recent conceptualizations of cosmopolitan, alternative, and multiple modernities.[50] Such work shows that the relationship between homogenizing and heterogenizing forces has become increasingly difficult to conceptualize in terms of a single telos, or end point. Despite the critique of area studies or the danger of methodological nationalism that comes through a focus on particular countries, the concern with non-Western life experiences that animate this book gives empirical basis to increasingly common assertions that modernity must be understood as emerging in particular contexts.

Our approach to the study of modernity is explicitly ethnographic and grounded in lived experience. In particular, we understand the figure as a key mediator and methodological vantage point from which it is possible to engage empirically and analytically with key themes of modernity. This approach is by no means unique in disciplines such as anthropology. Indeed, it has arguably become a norm in the ongoing struggle to describe relationships between local and global processes. By depicting more than eighty different figures, however, we have dramatically expanded the scope of the ethnographic project and created a veritable panorama of the landscape of Southeast Asian modernity.[51] Rather than attempting to categorize this landscape through the identification of a series of ideal types, we continue to work in the Geertzian tradition of "thick description," even as we disavow any reductionist attempt to compartmentalize different cultures. Instead, the possibility of comparison emerges from the constraints that have been placed on the individual essays in terms of a strict word count and general format.

While modernity has many aspects, the one that most interests us is its *ethos*. This ethos is characterized by a reflexive engagement with and embrace of a broader world that at least temporarily leads away from the identities, practices, languages, and ways of knowing that are assumed to be relatively timeless and enduring (i.e., the realm of tradition), as well as an engagement with the kinds of self-fashioning that pertain to the advent of neoliberalism.[52] As Ong and Zhang have noted, this ethos becomes an ethic of "how one should live."[53]

Anderson's work on the origins of nationalism provides a vivid illustration of such an ethos and its emergence during the colonial era.[54] According to Anderson, the spread of print capitalism—particularly in the form of the newspaper and the novel—was a critical technological development that enabled people who had never before met one another to imagine themselves belonging to the same spatially demarcated and sovereign nation. In his book on radicalism in Java during the early twentieth century, Takashi Shiraishi captures the power of this moment by referring to it as "an age in motion" in which people strike out from their usual patterns of life to establish new modes of political organization and new forms of sociality, which in turn leads them to think differently about the lives they left behind.[55] Clearly, the ethos that informs this kind of movement was not particular to the epoch that saw the rise of nationalism. Indeed, as shown by figures in this book—such as the Aspiring Overseas Student in Vietnam, the Thai Airways Flight Attendant, the Call Center Agent in the Philippines, or the World Musician in Cambodia—it is an ethos that one also finds alive and well in the first decades of this century.

Historically, modernity involved not only a radically new form of consciousness and community but also a shift in political cosmology. In Southeast

Asia, this shift was characterized by a move away from a political cosmology defined by divine kingship, "exemplary centres,"[56] and unclear territorial boundaries to one composed of homogeneous space carved up into a limited number of discrete, bounded nation-states. As Thongchai Winichakul has shown, it was a shift that required more than just the technologies of the novel and the newspaper; it also required the advent and deployment of mapping technologies, which allowed for the unambiguous delineation and representation of political boundaries.[57] In some ways, these trends continue through the most banal, everyday forms of popular culture. In other ways, however, our figures describe a world that is not seamlessly organized around the nation—neither in terms of consciousness nor technology. As Faisal Devji has argued in *Landscapes of the Jihad,* in the contemporary world the breakdown of modern (as well as traditional) forms of authority has led to an increasingly self-conscious and fragmented concern with ethics that opens up the possibility of new forms of imagining through technologies such as the Internet.[58] Devji's account thus points toward various forms of rupture in the nation-state to a crisis of authority—but also to a crisis of authenticity.

Every Southeast Asian national language has a relatively straightforward equivalent for the idea of being "modern," which is not the case for academic terms such as "postmodernity" or even "high modernity." As Mary Beth Mills has noted about Thailand, "Discourses on modernity permeate much of everyday life."[59] This is not to say that what counts as modern is at all universal throughout the region—or even within different countries. For example, while every Thai has an idea of what *tan samai* means, there will of course be great differences of opinion about what kinds of persons might rightfully be recognized as *being up-to-date.* While every Vietnamese knows what *hiện đại* means, there remains great contest over who might be considered *modern.* The terms are not fixed and are subject to both popular and academic debate. In mid-twentieth-century Java, for example, Clifford Geertz famously described a split between *modèren* and *kolot* (modern and conservative) Islam, yet recent scholarship has noted how the so-called return to doctrinaire text-based Islam is itself a modern phenomenon.[60] In such cases, the idea of modernity remains salient, though always contested and transformed.

We are thus not concerned primarily with problems of terminology but rather more specifically with empirical problems of listening to these discourses of modernity. They speak about the loss of grand narratives, an opening to the foreign, a blurring of old status and class distinctions, an embracing and intensification of capitalism and mass media, and a reworking of the politics of connection. In making concrete the contemporary, these various figures help us to sort out exactly what is at stake across Southeast Asia today.

In other words, we conceptualize figures as ethnographic sites that mediate a wide range of processes and structures that are themselves often in flux. For this reason, the term "modernity" in our title should be read not as a reference to the moment that so fascinated Benjamin but as a temporary placeholder for the constellation of forces that define the contemporary moment in at least one region of the world. As will be clear, this moment is characterized by the pervasive effects of capitalism and commodification, the refashioning of relations between the state and the self along neoliberal lines, a deep ambivalence about older figures of authority, the emergence of new claims to authority grounded in new media, and the continuing objectification of various marginalized people across the social field. By making modernity our leitmotif, we have chosen a theme that is expansive and encompassing, providing us with a way to focus our conversations without overly constraining them. It is a theme that draws attention to the contemporary moment, while also throwing aspects of history and tradition into relief. By examining modernity through the lives of particular figures, we are able to explore how people across Southeast Asia position themselves in relation to global configurations of modernity and to create a panoramic snapshot of a region in motion.

Method

Whereas Benjamin's project was fragmented in its form and his flaneur stood as an isolated figure in the Parisian urban swirl, the figures that are described in the coming pages often overlap and intersect with one another. These intersections were not planned. Each of the contributing authors was asked to choose a figure that she or he had encountered during ongoing fieldwork. The figure chosen might be an individual, but it should also be someone who is recognizable as representing modern life. What emerged was a series of figures that symbolize broader transformations across the Southeast Asian region. The initially fragmentary nature of the project was thus transformed into a revealing composite form.

Although this book describes a specific cast of key figures that pertain to contemporary Southeast Asia, we have broader methodological goals. We believe that a focus on figures—or "key figures," as Raymond Williams might have phrased it—can provide the basis for an illuminating comparative ethnographic method that could span regions and times. Many of the most enduring concepts in social theory began as social types but then went on to acquire greater significance as figures capable of illuminating larger ideas. For example, Georg Simmel's analysis of the "stranger"—the "man who comes today and stays tomorrow"—has proven productive in analyzing critical processes of modernity, most notably Zygmunt Bauman's study of the Holocaust. Max Weber's ideal type of the charismatic leader has provided ways to conceptualize and compare forms of leadership across cultures, for instance through Benedict Anderson's analysis of power in Java. These examples are more than types; they are figures. Similarly, we argue that figures like the Street Kid and the Schoolteacher can provide ways of thinking both about the generality and the specificity of contemporary social formations around the world.[61]

There are at least three reasons that the figures approach offers such great potential. First, the figure comes into focus both in terms of its own history—the shifts in meaning and in inflection over time—and in terms of its relation to other key figures. These two modes of exploring a discursive field are associated with two different kinds of reading; one that is linear and another that involves tunneling between keywords in a manner that is similar to reading hypertext. In our focus on figures, we likewise want to use them as access points to broader cultural formations.

Second, a focus on figures does not depend on drawing an artificial line between scholarly discourse and the forms of discourse we encounter among our interlocutors in the field. A study of figures involves participating in a kind of folk sociology, where social imaginaries are populated by certain recognizable social types. It is against the backdrop of these types that particular figures acquire their significance and their force.

Third, a study of figures allows for a focus on cultural and historical particularities—something that both anthropology and area studies do well—without trapping us in these particularities. Instead, it allows for an opening out into a broader comparative conversation. Indeed, what we have found over the time that we have been engaged in this project is that a discussion of a figure tends to provoke people to think about related figures in other places or times. By following through these chains of associations, we gain access to other places and other social worlds. Imagining one figure leads one to conjure up others, to populate a world of ethnographically rich, sociologically varied, interconnected figures. The prologue and epilogue of this volume are examples of how generative this notion of figures can be.

How to Read the Book

As processes of globalization have come to reshape Southeast Asia in recent decades, academic debates have intensified with regard to the withering away of the nation-state and the problematic legacy of area studies. Organizing this volume according to the region's major nation-states arguably marginalizes not only smaller countries such as East Timor or Brunei but also nonstate figures such as "insurgents" in Burma and Laos. In response to these broader issues, some influential observers have even imagined an alternative region dubbed Zomia—the massif that cuts through the region from India to China and is populated by highland groups that have largely remained outside of the control of the nation-state.[62] Yet for the great majority of the region's inhabitants, the nation-state remains the dominant organizational form of everyday life. Rather than positioning ourselves "outside" of this form, we thus attempt to map the contemporary landscape of modernity through a series of figures that primarily identify in terms of nationality rather than, for instance, ethnicity or religion. This does not mean that we take the nation-state as a given. Rather, we understand it to be a widely contested way for organizing societies and establishing collective identifications. Indeed, our hope is that our focus on key figures will open up new ways of thinking comparatively, both across the region and beyond it. We therefore encourage readers to find alternative itineraries through the volume that open up new vistas for regional understanding.

Our ambition is for this book to be used in a number of different ways. On the one hand, it can certainly be read straight through by students and a broader lay audience as a somewhat idiosyncratic introduction to contemporary Southeast Asia. On the other hand, we would also encourage our readers to find alternative ways through the book that would highlight other themes beyond a strict focus on nation-states. For instance, readers with an interest in themes such as gender, technology, and social marginality could read a grouping of essays on each of these themes. To facilitate this kind of reading, we have provided an index in which we identify a wide range of themes, each of which runs through several essays in the book. But we trust that readers will discover new itineraries inspired less by our modes of thinking than by the figures of modernity themselves. Indeed, it is precisely the idiosyncratic and disparate nature of the volume that we find so exciting. By asking so many individual authors to write about a figure of their own choosing, we have opened up the possibility that our readers might identify emergent themes in Southeast Asian studies. Our hope is that it is the cacophony of voices, the diversity of stories, and the limitless connections between these figures of modernity that ultimately serve to organize this book.

1 23456789

THE PHILIPPINES

Edited by SMITA LAHIRI
and DEIRDRE DE LA CRUZ

In a world full of exhaust-choked megacities, Metro Manila's traffic snarls are widely recognized as among the very worst around. Boredom, frustration, and anxiety overwhelm and unite Manileños as they sit cheek by jowl, for hours on end, in becalmed taxis, private cars, trucks, SUVs, jeeps, buses, vans, and tricycles. And yet it could be argued that this state offers a distorted reflection of what anthropologist Victor Turner called *communitas*—a synchronized, collective experience that brings home the commonality of shared human or social existence to its subjects.[1] Other than traffic, one would certainly be hard pressed to find an experience that cuts so clearly across the social worlds of those who live and sojourn in Metro Manila, held as they are in their distinct orbits defined by age, class, kinship, sexuality, education, occupation, ethnicity, and locality.

Metro Manila's road traffic may be, as one columnist observes, "the great equalizer,"[2] but it can also be understood as a theater of cultural performance. Against the apparently undifferentiated ground of traffic, a distinctive figure now and again emerges: for instance, the forty-something Manila executive who arrived late to an important meeting last year after getting stuck in traffic. To appreciate his significance, it must be known that the young man was no ordinary honcho but rather the country's recently elected chief executive. In July 2010, Benigno Aquino III (better known by his nicknames: Noynoy, President Noy, and the slyly hip P-Noy) fell victim to Manila traffic, arriving more than half an hour late to his own Cabinet's swearing-in ceremony. His martyrdom was self-ordained, for in his inauguration speech, delivered

19

just weeks previously, Aquino had publicly forsworn the use of *wangwang* (traffic-clearing sirens) for even official purposes, a gesture intended to condemn the increasing use of the device by private motorists for muscling their way through traffic.

Taken at face value, Aquino's stand against the *wangwang* might appear self-defeating, as indeed it did to several Philippine commentators. But one can also see his renunciation of a legitimate (some would say indispensable) prerogative of high office as a public rebuke of the country's privileged classes, a canny effort to distinguish himself from their notoriously self-serving and arrogant ranks. In short, the figure cut by Aquino as a not-so-hapless traffic victim effectively brings into focus the contested and ambiguous nature of the cityscape, closely tied as it is in equal measure to class warfare and to democratic fantasies of inclusiveness and equality. Here and especially clearly, we also see the utility of attending to a specific figure—whether a singular individual, unique yet delineable within a given social field, or alternatively, a social type, role, or category that expresses a specific sociocultural imaginary—as a point of entry into unstable hegemonies, emergent solidarities, and forms of public intimacy within the contemporary nation-state.

The sketches offered in the following pages make no pretense of offering a comprehensive portrait of the contemporary Philippines. Still, they cut across a wide swath of the social landscape, illuminating a variety of strategies—themselves shaped by historical dynamics—through which individuals negotiate the complex entanglement of local worlds within today's global order. It might be noted that our project takes on complex resonances in the context of the archipelago's protracted history of successive colonization. After all, imperial and elite power has often been exerted in the Philippines (as elsewhere) through the distillation and deployment of knowledge concerning social "types" and categories. From *costumbrismo* in the late Spanish colonial period and census-taking in the early twentieth century under U.S. rule to more recent stereotypes like *bakya* (literally a cheap wooden shoe, used idiomatically to designate a provincial person as backward), the construction of archetypal figures in the Philippines has hardly been an innocent mode of cultural politics. At the same time, typification in the Philippine context has also served playful and even counterhegemonic purposes. One instance of this is the widely used *trapo,* a sarcastic contraction of "traditional politician" (read "corrupt politico") that puns on the Spanish word for "rag." To one extent or another, each of the essays in this collection engages this ambivalent history of representation, revealing subjects who submit to, resist, negotiate, or remake subject positions that stand as sedimented products of social typification at various historical junctures.

While the figures delineated here can be fruitfully played off one another in a number of ways, our space for discussion is necessarily limited. We begin by noting that typification is simultaneously a matter of social construction and of individual agency, their respective moments variably operating in tandem or even at odds. Certain figures in this collection embody this tension with particular salience. Thus, the social category of the Chinese mestizo offers a striking example of how a seemingly transparent ethnic category has created space for individuals to negotiate the gestalt between figure and ground, ethnicized Other, and unmarked Filipino, inadvertently and at the same time reinforcing ideas of Chinese as foreigners (Chu). Significantly, while the quotidian movement between individual singularity and social image is central to typification, more often than not it goes unnoticed within the social field. In the contemporary, media-saturated moment, however, this movement (or its failure) can make for fleeting moments of high drama. The recent and widely reviled flubbing of an interview question that was posed in English and on live television to an aspiring beauty queen from humble origins illustrates this potential (Tupas).

Other essays in this collection point to the elaboration of certain figures as ideological constructs, critically interrogating their lack of fit with reality in order to tease out aspects of the contemporary social and political economic landscape that might otherwise be elided. Thus we learn that the paranoid tendency of some elements of the Philippine state to view community health workers (CHW) as underground rebels masks what is truly subversive about these figures: that they provide desperately needed information and resources related to family planning despite being for the most part disenfranchised themselves (Tacqueban). In a parallel fashion, the neoliberal fantasy of a "sunshine industry" that is bringing a whole new level of consumer citizenship within reach of its workforce is stripped away to reveal the reality of stressed and physically exhausted call center workers (Padios).

When considered together, these essays also track the work of figuration as it plays out across the metropolis and its margins, a divide that is as much imagined as it is actual. The figure of the *atsay* or domestic helper/nanny reveals the well-to-do urban home as an uneven terrain of domestic citizenship where service, affection, and loyalty are extracted in return for an uncertain claim upon family membership (Capino). And while the predominantly Muslim areas of Mindanao are sometimes regarded as a space of exception within the Philippine body politic, in fact bossism and predatory accumulation in the region looks much like dynamics seen elsewhere. Mindanao's "lawless elements" may not always answer to the law, but they do quite often respond to its text messages (de Guzman).

Let us now return briefly to traffic, whose aptness as a frame for this collection rests on two points. First, as we have seen, traffic offers a particularly clear analogy for that gestalt movement among various "figures" and "grounds" that serves as a key analytical strategy of this volume as a whole. Equally importantly, traffic stands as an emblem of movement itself, the passages and forms of circulation that give contemporary Philippine modernity its distinct character. It is worth noting that fully half of the ten figures presented here touch upon ramifications of the Philippines' position within global labor markets. Thus we glimpse the "virtual migration" of call center work (Padios), the downstream impacts of overseas labor upon agribusiness (Lukasiewicz), the neoliberal fashioning of bureaucrats into "public managers" as part of their role as regulators of overseas work (Guevarra), and the emergence of a specific field of cultural production geared to wooing Filipino men into becoming merchant sailors (Fajardo). We see too the diverse forms of code switching that take shape as, for example, *bakla* and other occupants of third-gender categories move away from and then back to the Philippines in the course of working as overseas caregivers (Manalansan).

On purely empirical grounds then, one might point to the sheer range and ubiquity of these entanglements with global labor markets as the distinctive characteristic of contemporary Philippine modernity. Such entanglements are obviously present elsewhere in Southeast Asia, although perhaps not to such a widespread and normalized degree. At the same time, it is striking that the *idea* of modernity appears to hold relatively little salience for this set of figures or the ideological formations they embody. While Filipinos seem to long acutely for many of the same things as their coregionists (transparency in government, for one), they seem less prone to identify or understand these desires and preoccupations as quintessentially "modern" (see, by comparison, the essays on Vietnam and Cambodia in this volume). We are certainly not denying that *modernism* has played an important role as an aesthetic and technocratic ideal at various junctures.[3] Rather, we simply observe that the desire for modernity as a culminating state just out of grasp—aptly captured by Dipesh Chakrabarty's image of languishing in the "imaginary waiting room of history"[4]—does not seem to loom large among Filipinos at this moment. This may be because the developmentalist nightmare that unfolded under the "New Society" of Ferdinand and Imelda Marcos is still within recent memory for many Filipinos. But as a country located among key channels of the world system since at least the sixteenth century, and as a population whose extraordinary movement in the contemporary period extends to every imaginable corner of the globe, it may simply be that Filipinos have—through voyage, trade, adoption, sojourn, and return—seen it all.

Domestic Helper
JOSÉ B. CAPINO

Janet Beating has worked for the same middle-class family for the last twenty-five years. Like most housemaids, she has no savings, having spent most of her earnings on her parents and siblings in the boondocks. She continues to nurture the dream of marrying her longtime boyfriend, Felix, who is coincidentally the namesake of her late father, younger brother, and nephew. But that dream would have to wait some more because Janet and Felix cannot envision making enough to get by on their own. Besides that, Janet, who is past childbearing age, is deeply attached to her young wards. She has spent more time with those children than their parents, who have a six-hour daily commute to and from their jobs in Manila's financial district.

In better times, a domestic helper's stint would not have lasted this long. Domestic work is ideally a way for young rural women to find their footing in the city. Preferably, the domestic helper is placed by family or neighbors in households familiar to them. These "recruiters" would then serve as the maid's support group in the city. In the course of her work, the maid gains proficiency in the national language, acquires skills, learns the basics of urban living, saves a little money, and builds relationships that will increase her social mobility. Some maids take cooking lessons or even attend college at their employer's expense. But for many domestic helpers like Janet, the scarcity of jobs and real estate and the high cost of living have put the dream of mobility out of reach. Beyond the promise of modest social security benefits and the generosity of newly affluent relatives, maids have few resources to strike out on their own. Their prospects for mobility lie in navigating the hierarchies of domestic work.

A hierarchy of domestic workers has existed in one form or another for centuries. Every social science textbook in the Philippines describes precolonial forms of indentured servitude in terms of differences in social class, type of labor, and location. The *alipin* was either a *namamahay* (servant with his or her own house) or the lowly *sagigilid* (a domestic slave).[5] Related terms such as *muchacha* and *achay* gained currency during and after the three hundred years of Spanish rule. In Mary Helen Fee's memoirs, *A Woman's Impression of the Philippines* (1904), the schoolteacher in American colonial Philippines records different types of domestic workers in her household. Fee describes a young woman whose job it was to sleep in Fee's bedroom because she was unmarried and thus, by local custom, needed a guardian for her propriety.[6] Fee also recalls a family of servants that came with the house she rented. The wife, Fee writes, "would embroider for me, or wash a garment if I needed it in a hurry," while her husband "skated my floors till they shone like mirrors."[7] To be sure, American colonial modernity influenced the "professionalization" of domestic work by impacting the status of the individual, the management of Filipino households, and the conditions of domestic labor. Over the years, new categories of domestic workers emerged, each reflecting a more efficient and humane division of labor. These categories include the *all-around,* who is responsible for most household chores except for laundering; the *yaya* (nanny), who informally doubles as a preschool teacher; and the *alalay,* who serves as a guide to the elderly or personal assistant to adults.

Moving up the hierarchy of domestic work means switching categories, attaining seniority, or sharing in the newfound prosperity of an employer. The option of changing employers, while potentially lucrative, belongs chiefly to younger maids. Seasoned domestic workers hesitate to move on because loyalty to employers comes with the informal promise of financial assistance in their old age. Such quasi-familial bonds with employers not only discourage mobility but also keep their pay low. Sometimes this long history of physical proximity, affective relations, and socioeconomic disparity leads to acrimonious and violent partings. The news teems with stories of domestics who conspire with thieves and killers and employers who punish their maids with jagged glass and laundry irons.[8]

Like many Filipina maids who find themselves "trapped" in middle-class households, Janet does not fit the profile of the globe-trotting domestic helper. Many "global" maids began at a higher social class, with college degrees and rosier dreams than hers. The Filipina *ayas* prized by middle-class families in Singapore and Hong Kong were schoolteachers or professionals in another life. Less well-off members of the global diaspora overcame the economic barriers to joining the global bandwagon by unusual means: chain migration through relatives, special visas sponsored by former employers, and so on. There is also a new generation of domestic helpers who, unlike Janet, obtained academic credentials for their trade. This new breed attended yearlong programs in "professional caregiving" run by the same trade schools that capitalize on lower-middle-class youths' dreams of becoming a global information technology professional or a nurse in a first-world country. For these "global" maids with first-world incomes, the old pipedream of moving *up* and moving *on* may still be realized.

Janet tells me in a recent phone call that she has suffered a setback. As it turns out, some years ago her brother Felix gave her an attached living space in his wooden shanty. She has filled this space with secondhand appliances and household items, including a Korean-brand TV and a karaoke machine discarded by her employers. Many of those items were stolen when an intruder broke into her place. She has already installed a stronger padlock and brought in a couple of new items.

Chinese Mestizo
RICHARD T. CHU

One day while visiting Bahay Tsinoy (the "Museum of the Chinese in Philippine Life"), I was struck by the inclusion of some "Filipinos" in the gallery featuring prominent Tsinoys. These "Filipinos" include Mariano Limjap, José Rizal, and Emilio Aguinaldo, all Chinese mestizos who, because of their involvement in the fight versus the Spanish and American colonizers, are considered "founding fathers" of the Filipino nation. Thus, I felt some confusion when I saw their portraits in a museum that was supposed to be about the Chinese in the Philippines. Another visitor, a Filipino college student, upon seeing the portraits, exclaimed, "*Pilipinas na ba ito?*" ("Is this the Philippines already?").

The Chinese mestizo of the Philippines is an important figure for those interested in the country's history of colonialism and nationalism. Its appearance as an ethnic categorization under the Spanish colonial period, subsequent disappearance under the Americans, and reappearance (in different guises) in contemporary Philippine society point us to ways dominant powers attempt to spread their hegemonic control over others. Outsider portrayals of the Chinese mestizo, turning up periodically as those at Bahay Tsinoy, do not really reveal who the Chinese mestizo really was, but rather they draw attention to the desires and/or anxieties of those deploying such characterizations.

Intermarriages and consensual unions between Chinese men and local women led to the increase in the number of Chinese mestizos during the Spanish colonial period. Spanish colonial policy classified a person as Chinese mestizo patrilineally, even after several generations. However, a Chinese mestizo could change his classification. For a Chinese mestiza, her classification depended upon her civil status. If she married a Spaniard or an *indio,* then she followed her husband's classification. But if she married a Chinese, she remained a "Chinese mestiza." By the late nineteenth century, Chinese mestizos constituted 6 percent of a total population of 5.5 million.

To impose control over its newly subjugated subjects, the Americans reclassified ethnic categorizations in the Philippines along racial-national lines. Chinese mestizos and *indios* were classified "Filipinos," while the "Chinese" were classified "aliens." Thus, the American colonial period created the "Chinese" and "Filipino" binary found in contemporary Philippine society. With the disappearance of the "Chinese mestizo" as an ethnolegal classification, to be "mestizo" in Philippine society today is to be of Caucasian-Asian mixture. Within the Chinese community, offspring of unions between Chinese and Filipinos are called *tsut-si-a* ("someone born into this world"), a term that carries negative connotations of racial impurity.

While not as prominent as Rizal and Aguinaldo, Mariano Limjap is mentioned in Philippine history textbooks for his role in the revolutions against the colonizers. Under Aguinaldo's government, he became inspector general of the railroad. After the Americans released him from prison, he remained active in helping build the Philippine nation-state. When he died in 1926, the *Tribune* bannered his passing and called him a "noted Filipino philanthropist."

Scholars have attempted to explain why many descendants of Chinese mestizo families from the Spanish colonial period are now identified as "Filipinos" and not as "Chinese." Wickberg argues that culturally, Chinese mestizos were Hispanicized and Catholicized and rejected their Chineseness.[9] This explanation makes sense to contemporary definitions of "Filipinoness," which are Hispanic and Catholic in orientation. An event in Mariano's life bears this out.

In 1891, Adriano Marcelo, an *indio,* sued Mariano. According to Adriano's affidavit, Mariano's deceased father Joaquin Limjap owed him money. However, as executor of his father's will, Mariano refused to turn the money over, leading Adriano to charge him with swindling (*estafa*). On a particular day at the court, Adriano's lawyer raised another charge against Mariano: that of misrepresenting himself. He pointed out that in the documents, Mariano had the "audacity" to identify himself as "mestizo Español" (Spanish mestizo), when "(Mariano's) face tells us that he is of pure Chinese blood, his father Don Joaquin Limjap being pure Chinese, and his mother being mestiza Chinese." The lawyer argued that this constituted a crime under the Penal Code.

But Mariano had a basis for identifying himself as "Spanish mestizo." His father was a naturalized Spanish subject. Following Spanish policy of patrilineality, Mariano could be Spanish mestizo. Also, as noted earlier, Spanish subjects in the Philippines were allowed to switch ethnolegal classifications. Furthermore, many Chinese mestizos desired to emulate and be identified with their colonizers' culture.

But a closer examination of his life shows that while Mariano was "Hispanicized" and "Catholic," he was also "Sinicized." He spoke Hokkien and often traveled to China to visit his Chinese "half-brothers," since his father Joaquin had a Chinese family.

"Chinese mestizo"? "Spanish mestizo"? "Filipino"? In his life, Mariano was not just one but all of these, either simultaneously or at different points in his life. Today, he is being resurrected as Tsinoy. Kaisa Para Sa Kaunlaran ("Unity in Progress"), which established Bahay Tsinoy, is composed of members who are Filipinos of ethnic Chinese background. In coining the term "Tsinoy," a combination of the words "Tsino" (Chinese) and "Pinoy" (Filipino), the organization wants to emphasize its members' biculturality and provide an alternative to the pejorative term "Intsik," which many Filipinos use to call the Chinese.

By including Mariano and other Chinese mestizos in the museum, is Kaisa misleading its visitors? Not quite, for Kaisa defines Tsinoy as "The Chinese who is Filipino or the Filipino who is Chinese." Hence, Mariano Limjap is Tsinoy. But while Kaisa claims him as one of its own, another group has, too. In 1993, the Beijing University Press published the *Dictionary of Overseas Chinese* and included Mariano.

A good way, then, to approach the question of Chinese mestizo identity is to examine how different groups have cast and recast this category.[10] Yet such a question also needs to take into account how individuals daily negotiate this categorization. Like many Chinese mestizos of his time, Mariano was able to "segue from one [identity] to another, experiment with alternative forms of identification, shrug in and out of identities, or evade imposed forms of identi-fication."[11] Mariano's story and those of other Chinese mestizos challenge the binaries constructed by colonialists and nationalists in their quest for position, power, and control.

Filipino Seaman
KALE BANTIGUE FAJARDO

A video tribute to Filipino seamen and overseas employment agencies, "Tagumpay Nating Lahat" ("Success for Us All") depicts a Filipino boy staring at Manila Bay with two ships in the distance. A Filipina with a high-octave voice begins to sing a patriotic Tagalog song. Two Filipino seamen approach the boy. Stressing Filipino seamen's "*bayani*-ness" (patriotic heroism), the video next moves to images of Filipino seamen in valiant, hypermasculine action on land and at sea. Filipino cadets march; a young seaman waves the Philippine flag. Other seamen are shown working and living on ships: doing office work, calcu-lating navigational maneuvers, fixing equipment, praying in their cabins, eating and drinking together. The video's lyrics also support the masculine Filipino and heroic visual imagery. The opening English subtitles, for example, read, "I have a simple dream. For my beloved country. With one united effort. Together we can reach our goals. I come from a land of heroes. A place where you can find the finest Filipino seafarers. Bring pride to the whole Nation."

The seven-minute video tribute, shown at the 2007 Philippine Manning Convention in Manila (a convention for overseas employment agencies), celebrates Filipino seamen and the hundreds of overseas employment agencies located in Manila that deploy Filipino seamen in the global maritime transportation industry. Through a handshake between manning agency executives and past Philippine president Macapagal Arroyo, the video symbolically seals the corporate-state partnership between overseas employment agencies, shipping companies, and the Philippine state. The video also seeks to highlight and construct a dominant state- and corporate-sanctioned maritime and migrant masculinity of or for Filipino seamen, one that is hypermasculine and macho, heterosexual and heteronormative, responsible and hardworking, cooperative and devoutly Catholic, and ultimately, heroically patriotic.

The video also seeks to underscore Filipino seamen's quasi-military orientation and their preferred docility (that is, preferred by the state and global capital) in the global maritime transportation industry. This reading of docility is possible precisely because the video celebrates quasi-military power hierarchies and chains of command where authority is not conventionally questioned. Recall too that the video also shows a Filipino boy at Manila Bay being interpellated (in Althusser's sense) by the two older seamen and more broadly by representatives or partners of the state and recruited into seafaring as a future sea-based overseas Filipino worker (OFW).[12] The scene near Manila Bay, therefore, reveals the unequal power dynamic among maritime migrant and seamen's labor, private overseas employment agencies, and the Philippine state. Moreover, through its use of patriotic audiovisual strategies, the tribute also evokes and taps into broader images and tropes of OFWs as *bagong bayani* (new heroes or heroines).[13]

To more fully understand the figure of the contemporary Filipino seaman, we must consider this figure in relation to other OFWs, especially female OFWs. Several feminist scholars—including Rhacel Salazar Parreñas, Nicole Constable, and Neferti X. Tadiar—have theorized the feminization of Filipino/a global migration and Filipino/a migrant labor in terms of racialized and class processes. This feminization has become particularly familiar and naturalized through well-known figures, most notably the Filipina domestic helper or "entertainer."[14] Indeed, Tadiar has even suggested that the feminization of Filipino/a migrant labor contributes to the feminization of the Philippines as a nation-state in the realm of Southeast Asian and Asia-Pacific international politics, where the most powerful nations, such as the United States, are usually gendered/sexualized as white, wealthy, heterosexual, and masculine.

This global feminization of Filipino/a labor and nation helps to account for why the figure of the masculine, heterosexual, heteronormative, and patriotic Filipino seaman has become increasingly important as a way for state actors and leaders to promote a more masculine image of the Philippine nation-state as well as of overseas workers themselves. (This is, of course, a patriarchal and capitalist cultural/economic perspective that understands or constructs femininities as less valuable than masculinities.) By narrating and visualizing the image of Filipino seamen as *bagong bayani,* the state is able to promote masculinist and nationalist maritime images of heroic masculine Filipino seamen who labor and sacrifice for the Philippine nation.

While Filipino and native sailors have clearly contributed to transpacific and global maritime trade in the past and present, what is critical to keep in mind is *how* Philippine maritime histories and figures—such as Filipino seamen—are used or manipulated by state officials and corporate elites to promote Philippine dependencies on neoliberal economics and so-called free trade or globalization; dependencies on international IMF–World Bank loans; and dependencies on OFW remittances.[15] While Filipino seamen and other OFWs do significantly contribute to the national economy (e.g., through mandatory remittances), the point that many scholars and activists seek to stress is that the aforementioned dependencies are not the only economic and political strategies available to the Philippines or Filipinos.[16] Indeed, during my fieldwork in the Ports of Manila and Oakland, many Filipino seamen revealed to me that they would prefer to work *in* the Philippines, but since their economic opportunities were limited "back home," seafaring was their "best option." Other seamen I encountered also resisted the dominant narrative and image through the practice of "jumping ship." That is, some Filipino seamen abandon their ship, leave the shipping industry, and migrate to other countries in search of less demanding work. Thus, while the video tribute highlights dominant narratives of Filipino seamen as masculine, patriotic, heteronormative, and docile, the everyday lives of Filipino seamen provocatively reveal other masculinity practices (such as jumping ship). In doing so, Filipino seamen reveal alternative productions of manhood—what we can imagine as the "crosscurrents of masculinities."[17]

Public Manager
ANNA ROMINA GUEVARRA

I sit confronted by a poster-sized photo of this man proudly posing next to former Philippine president Gloria Macapagal Arroyo.[18] His image follows me because every wall of his office is adorned with photographs of him with various state dignitaries. His assistant tells me he *knows* he is a handsome man. His day is filled with managing public queries, complaints, and trag-edies, as well as empowering the downtrodden to realize their potential, so much so that his staff must nag him about eating lunch. A group of men huddle around him adoringly, responding to his animated debriefing of his encoun-ter with representatives of a migrant nongovernmental organization whose "sharpness" posed a challenge to him. His palatial yet pristine office is me-ticulously decorated to suit a person who carries himself with such pride and self-importance. The Bible and Fabergé-like golden egg that sit prominently on his desk and Catholic religious statues that tower behind it—Santo Niño, crucifix of Jesus Christ, and the Virgin Mary—are jarring attempts to signal the presence of a spiritual figure.

This man is a labor bureaucrat, one of the hundreds of devoted disciples of the Philippine state running the country's labor export economy. They diligently develop gimmicky materials parading the added export value of Filipinos and preach to foreign employers that the Philippines is the "Home of the Great Filipino Worker."[19] Yet, they claim they are *not* promoting migra-tion. "We are *public managers,* not bureaucrats," they exclaim. Public manag-ers demand recognition as creative forces who are not mere state automatons, but who approach their work with passion and purpose. While their personal and political networks enable them to pursue such careers, they are also de-termined to make their mark. "It is so important to me to have a personal mission," one official proclaims, while explaining his feelings of frustration when his policy recommendations are stalled or ignored. Unlike a typical bureaucrat, he would rather explore alternatives and take risks than follow a program to the letter. While they see themselves as integral to the state's labor-brokering machinery, they refuse to be rendered as mere cogs.

The public manager exemplifies the neoliberal ethos reflecting the state's love affair with the market, wielding its power from a distance and govern-ing Filipinos through principles of individual responsibility and "freedom."[20] Public managers envision that they courageously manage migrants' "choic-es" to work overseas, harness their skills to cultivate entrepreneurialism, and empower them to embody an ethic of self-responsibility in order to protect themselves from abusive and violent employers. Public managers seek to give meaning to their sacrifices by grooming them to be "more than usual workers" who can turn the "Great Filipino Worker" into the country's brand-name com-modity. Meanwhile, OFWs learn to embody their global value, obediently fol-lowing public managers who coach them with this mantra as they face foreign employers: "We don't need them. They need us."

The public manager supports the Philippine state labor bureaucracy, rep-resented primarily by the Philippine Overseas Employment Administration and the Overseas Workers Welfare Administration. These institutions emerged following the 1974 labor code, which formalized the country's labor export policy. While meant to be temporary, succeeding administrations could not overlook the promising remittances that started to flood the Philippine banking channels, which by the 1980s became so noticeably striking that OFWs became the country's modern-day heroes (*bagong bayani*). But it also pushed the state to address the high price of this heroism as coffins containing bodies of OFWs began their homecoming. To appease a growing public outcry, it responded with the Migrant Workers and Overseas Filipinos Act of 1995, which outlined a multiprong promise of welfare protection. It also mirrored a change in policy paradigm that reconceptualized the country's overseas employment program as one that sought to manage labor migration. It is this framework that gave birth to the public manager who would anchor the state through this neoliberal turn, while catapulting Filipinos' dreams and aspirations for the country's economic advantage.

Public managers perform "labor diplomacy" by promoting OFWs as "internationally shared human resources" to be marketed and protected. The "charm and cheerful efficiency" that grace the brochures they disseminate in their marketing missions accompany their efforts to appease the public's persistent criticisms of the state's inability to secure workers' safe passage. Thus, the same public managers can be seen conducting spiritual awakening activities[21] or appearing on media broadcasts to espouse comforting yet cautionary messages. They also inculcate in the workers' minds that they are the country's model workers and thus have a shared responsibility in upholding this image.

The public manager consumed by his image reflects a market-driven state obsessed with fulfilling an appearance of global greatness. As I probe him about being a public manager, the religious icons that surround me continue to clash with the unexpected casualness of his appearance, in jeans and polo shirt, eagerly sipping iced coconut (*buko*) juice. "I feel that God put me in this position and that I must search for the reason why I am here," he expresses, while outlining his plan to remake OFWs into the enterprising OFIs (overseas Filipino investors). They paint themselves as the workers' "caregivers" who will not "coddle" but nurture them with information to prepare them for the perils of working overseas. Seeing workers as soldiers, they believe they must arm them with the "bullets" to survive the global battlefield. As I leave his office, exhausted after half a day waiting to interview him, his voice lingers with this sentiment: "A fully informed and fully educated Filipino national is the best protection for him [*sic*]." I wonder what the wounded and the dead would say to this.

Lawless Element
ORLANDO DE GUZMAN

I was enjoying the breathtaking view of the Sulu Archipelago from our vantage point, when Chris reminded me not to get too exposed. "The enemies are just down here," he warned, as he pointed to the cluster of sandbagged homes built on stilts over the turquoise Sulu Sea, just a few hundred feet below.

Chris, short for "Christian," spent most of his life on faraway Luzon, where he was born to a Christian Ilocano father (therefore his name) and a Tausug mother. He used to work as a security guard for Citibank in Makati, he told me, but moved back to Sulu to live with his mother, a small-time *datu* (local chief) by the name of Dayang-Dayang Haji Aminah Buclao. Today, Chris was clutching a sniper rifle and peering down through his scopes to see if his enemies were on the lookout. Near him, half a dozen young men, some in their teens, dug trenches and foxholes in anticipation of the next gun battle. They carried an assortment of assault rifles, machine guns, and grenade launchers. Unlike the legions of blue uniformed security guards of Manila, Chris and his men wore vests with red and green bandanas inscribed with spells and verses lifted from the Qur'an. "This is our bullet proof," one of Chris' men said, and he lifted his shirt to show a tiny scar above his right nipple where a rocket-propelled grenade was said to have landed.

A few days before, I hitched a boat ride to Tulayan Island with the provincial director of the Philippine National Police and about two dozen of his men. They were tasked to bring Chris and his fellow "lawless elements" into the fold of the law, first by making them agree to a ceasefire and then encouraging them to disarm. Chris did not see himself in those terms. "We are not fighting the law," Chris explained. "Our enemies are not the military, nor the police. Our enemies are fellow Tausugs."

Open any of the major dailies in the Philippines, and there are frequent references to an ambiguous category of local bad guys, the "lawless elements." The ringleaders of the lawless elements are almost never mentioned, and it is assumed they exist in areas, like parts of Mindanao, where the reach of state institutions is weak and where there is a breakdown of social order. Their existence, according to the official view, is entirely apolitical and unorganized, involved only in such criminal activity as drug dealing, kidnap for ransom, cattle rustling, and extortion.

Recent academic studies of the Philippines have given a greater appreciation to the emergence of "entrepreneurs of violence": men whose reputation for terror precedes them and whose violent work can be dispatched for political and economic gain.[22] These men—from Noberto Manero of the

Christian Ilaga vigilante group to his Muslim counterparts such as Commander Robot of the Abu Sayyaf—have attained folk hero status largely because of their capacity for terror. However, these lawless elements hardly exist outside the realm of law and politics; they are central to the projection of local power and appropriation of capital.

Recently I met one such character: Tata Uy, an ex-military officer turned cattle rustler in the Liguasan Marsh area of Maguindanao Province. Despite his criminal record and multiple arrest warrants, he is seen as a local Robin Hood, protecting farmers against land grabbing by the powerful mayors allied with the notorious Ampatuan clan.

Scholars of local politics in the Philippines have increasingly moved away from using patron-client relationships as a way to describe social relations, focusing instead on criminality and the coercive nature of local bosses in their quest for capital accumulation and political office. As Sidel has argued in his illuminating studies of bossism in Cavite and Cebu, local politicians keep the broad mass of the population in a constant state of scarcity, insecurity, and competition for resources, thus making them more pliable to predatory rule.[23]

Scarcity of resources was the overriding theme on Tulayan Island in Sulu. The island itself is less than a square mile in area. Given the size of the island, both the Buclao and the Kharfaisa clans were within earshot of each other. They would occasionally yell out obscenities to each other, which would in turn provoke gunfire and the occasional grenade tossing.

The Buclaos viewed the fight as a resource issue: The rival Kharfaisa clan was claiming a ten-hectare parcel of prime coconut groves on the island. The Kharfaisas deny this, claiming instead that the fight had its roots in politics, specifically in the defeat of the Buclao family in the last *barangay* (village) elections. But a closer look at the material (i.e., weapons, food, and ammunition) and political backing behind the small clan war reveals a larger competition between more powerful provincial bosses.

Tulayan Island's competing candidates for *barangay* captain were being fielded by rival local bosses from the first and second district of Sulu: Governor Abdusakur Tan and Congressman Munir Arbison. Village elections had to be postponed twice on Tulayan, because of the possibility of violence. The Commission on Elections eventually gave the seat to the Kharfaisa clan, but that didn't end the political stalemate.

When I arrived on Tulayan, the Buclaos held the high ground, and judging from the network of trenches they were digging, they were determined to keep it. As Chris Buclao settled into his sentry duty, the hilltop post revealed another strategic advantage: It was the only spot on the island to receive the fickle cell phone signal that came all the way from the provincial capital of Jolo. "Two bars!" he would proudly proclaim, referring to the strength of the signal. And so Chris would pass the boredom of sentry duty by sending and receiving text messages. For the Buclao clan, the phone signal was a lifeline to political authority in Jolo, where his uncle was a powerful municipal board member and backer of Sulu governor Abdusakur Tan. Chris' men were never disarmed. The provincial police chief, after all, was an appointee of Governor Tan.

Long after I left the island, I would receive occasional text messages from Chris detailing Tulayan's interclan feud. They were succinct battlefield reports, which detailed matter-of-factly the fatalities, injuries, and length of firefight. I still think of Chris, out there on the periphery of the nation's ubiquitous mobile phone network, rifle in one hand and cell phone in the other.

Agriculturalist
ADAM LUKASIEWICZ

Having just returned from a muddy tour of Mr. Ladines' farmland in the Philippine town of Lucban, Quezon Province, I shamelessly hijacked my respondent's ritual afternoon siesta to ply my questionnaire. Notwithstanding his lost nap, he gracefully accepted me into his courtyard and was just as eager to use his English as I was to practice my Filipino, so we volleyed (some might say "stumbled") between the two the rest of the afternoon. The shade of the family home offered refuge from the sharpest rays of the midday sun, while the freshly washed concrete of the driveway cooled our feet. The hired help—three young men from a neighboring town—sat on their haunches quickly forming neat piles of freshly harvested, neon green coriander. Listening in on my conversation with the landowner, they went about wrapping each bale in plastic before meticulously punching tiny holes into the inflated bags with needles to ensure just the right amount of airflow: small in scale, but the definition of a production line nonetheless. This unusual crop sparked my curiosity, as I had never seen coriander for sale in the local market, nor did I recall it ever being used in local dishes. In a town where few farmers ventured away from the staple crops of rice and coconuts, I wondered why he had bothered with such exotic produce in the first place. "Money," he put it simply. "This is how we're investing our money from Hong Kong."

For the past five years, Mr. Ladines' wife Elma had been working as a domestic helper for a Chinese family in Hong Kong, and it was there that she was introduced to cooking with coriander. She discovered a market for the crop in Manila through networks of fellow migrants, and within a few years she had convinced her husband to use her earnings to establish one of the first coriander gardens in the region. The family had made a considerable profit along the way by shipping their harvest to Manila's markets every few months. The freshly painted and by all accounts palatial house under which we sought shade that afternoon stood as a testament to this newfound wealth. How then, I thought, would I classify them in my survey of farmers? Was this a farming family? Aside from financing the operation, Mark and Elma had hired help and did little manual work themselves. Moreover, none of their three adult sons had any hand in the business. How then could the Ladines be considered peasants, I thought to myself? Was the gulf between small-scale subsistence farmers and larger-scale, market-integrated producers so great that grouping them together under the category of "farmer" became a misnomer? On this question, Mr. Ladines was glad to educate me. "We are not farmers," he clarified. "A farmer is just an old man who grows rice (*magsasaka*)—we're *agriculturalists.*"

While in much of the world an agriculturalist is more or less equated with a farmer, in this locality the term—and the identity that is attached to it—is understood as a marker for distinction. This distinction is further reinforced through language itself. While we randomly jumped between languages throughout much of our conversation that afternoon, certain words were clearly anchored in one language over another. "Farmer," for example, almost always remained in its Tagalog form of *magsasaka.* "Agriculturalist," on the other hand, would only ever be used in its English form—and in fact has no direct translation.

People like Mark and Elma Ladines are as unusual in the literature on transnational households as they are in Lucban. And there is indeed something novel about the "agriculturalist" who uses foreign remittances as capital for new farming ventures with the goal of turning that investment around for an even greater profit. This, according to Mark and many of his neighbors, is what sets Elma and himself apart from the traditional farmer, who "thinks small" and mainly in terms of direct household consumption. "We don't grow rice to eat our own rice," Mr. Ladines told me, "we grow coriander to sell to buy ten times more rice to eat than if we grew it ourselves." His next words revealed an understanding of his own family's unusually savvy response to the contemporary moment, even as they echoed, perhaps unconsciously, a language of distinction that dates at least as far back as the green revolution: "An agriculturalist like I am, like we are as a family, we're more modern than the old-style of farmers in town—we're like businessmen, they're [farmers growing traditional crops without the aid of chemical fertilizers, specialized inputs, or access to urban markets] a little lower."[24]

While classic village studies from the rural Philippines have alluded to the salience of migration to the livelihoods of Filipino families,[25] the exact impacts of ongoing labor migration on agrarian change are still uncertain.[26] The direct linkage between remittances and farming we see today embodies a particularly new form of rural modernity. The study of such translocal agriculturalist households would benefit from a transnational, multisited approach to ethnographic fieldwork. Poststructural feminist analyses have in this way been particularly innovative at shedding light on such global connections, with examples of the diverse economic activities migrants (and their families in the Philippines) are engaged in, both at home and overseas.[27] While there is still much to learn, what we can now be sure of is that novel forms of agrarian entrepreneurship in the Philippines are being seeded by remittances, and new approaches to farming fashion new, enduring forms of status and identity. While securing a decent living through any form of farming remains precarious here, labor migration affords the contingency of foreign cash to draw upon should tough times arise. Migrating for work abroad not only brings in the capital with which to start new market-oriented ventures, but—even more importantly, as the case of the Ladines family shows—it brings the *ideas* themselves. As transnational household linkages transform agrarian relations, opening up the possibility for new rural identities such as the agriculturalist to emerge, academics must be sure to keep pace. As Mr. Ladines advised me, "Maybe you should add some more columns to your questionnaire."

Bakla Returnee
MARTIN F. MANALANSAN

On June 12, 2008, Arturo (a pseudonym), one of the informants for my book *Global Divas*,[28] arrived in Manila's Ninoy Aquino International Airport after being in the United States for more than twenty years, most of which were spent as an undocumented immigrant. He waited until the Philippine immigration officer stamped his blue American passport and then he sailed through baggage claim and customs into the arms of his friends, to whom he declared, "The *bakla* has returned!" What does it mean for the *bakla* to "return"? What shifts in cultural politics and embodied experiences are enacted for this kind of return? What is the place of the *bakla* within global cultural flows?

Bakla is a Tagalog gloss for effeminacy, transvestism or cross-dressing, homosexuality, and in some cases, hermaphroditism. Another common term is *pusong babae,* or "man with a female heart." *Bakla* has been ethnologically located within the broad Southeast Asian/Pacific sex-gender complex that includes epicene and quasi-religious figures such as the *kathoey* of Thailand, the *waria* of Indonesia, and the *fa'afafine* of the various Pacific islands. All these figures, the *bakla* included, are classified within a global taxonomy that culminates in the emergence of modern gay identity. Compared to Western modern sexual identities, this wide-ranging Southeast Asian/Pacific complex of characters involves the blurring of the divisions between sex and gender. Thus, in popular discourses, these figures are no more than premodern antecedents to "gay."

Arturo, upon settling into Philippine terra firma, was engulfed in a whirl-wind of parties, dinners, and trips. Amidst all these, he intimated that while many people have chided his clear, lightened skin and his somewhat "robust" figure—markers allegedly of his being a prosperous *balikbayan* or returnee—he is somewhat circumspect about the tribulations of having lived abroad and the perils and pleasures of return. In New York City, he said, he was seen as nothing more than a fey Asian man who had feminine small features and stature. While he watched gay pride parades and attended transgender parties, he was wary of the burden of labels. When I pressed him about the question of identity, he succinctly said, "It is all about the event." Transgender, gay, or *bakla* categories, he explained, were part of the multiple landscapes he had to navigate as someone who had an undocumented status as well as a nonnormative composure (voice/accent, bodily comportment, skin color). He said, "You have to take on whatever the event demands. You have to be flexible." Such flexibility, according to Arturo, is about being able to "show" and "exhibit" the right appearance and presentation that would enable the person to survive and flourish in any situation. In other words, flexibility is legibility. For Arturo and several other Filipino *bakla* returnees I interviewed, this social legibility enables them to cross political and cultural borders. For example, they talk about how they have insisted on their own forms of social legibility in their travails as migrants in the United States, Europe, and the Middle East to varying forms and degrees of success.[29]

For Arturo, returning to the homeland has enabled him to assess the enduring questions of self and personhood with renewed intensity. He mentioned how his old friends and relatives in the Philippines have remarked on how, despite obvious signs of "aging gracefully," he has remained the same. He did not completely agree with this perception. Rather, he said, "All my life I have been all about changing myself—how I look, how I speak, but at the same time, they [meaning his friends and relatives] may be right. I may still be the same [person]." The paradox of change/transformation and stability in Arturo's life is echoed by many of my other queer informants. Such a paradox is at the center of the constitution and construction of the *bakla* vis-à-vis modernity.

The *bakla* is a figure of mobility. By "mobility," I do not mean an easy shuttling from third world to first world; rather, mobility involves the difficult jaunts between various forms of material and psychic struggles in both sites. While movement across political and gender borders is filled with insecurity, violence, and dangers, the *bakla* nevertheless can be seen as "skirting" the political ramification of his/her gender and sexual presentation. While I do not mean to create a hero/ine of this figure, I aim to highlight the ways in which their very presence in a range of transnational sites serves to "queer" the idea of globalization on the one hand and gay modernity on the other. Many would insist that *bakla* can be translated as "transgender," since the latter is sometimes seen as a transcultural umbrella category touted to encompass the variety of sex/gender systems in various cultural regions. But the recalcitrant specificity of the *bakla* defies easy translations and homologies.

Within the global traffic of queer identities, communities, and cultures, the *bakla* can be seen as an alternative way of narrating gender and sex that does not easily slip into the stories of "transition" that characterize present-day discourses about transgender and transsexual individuals. As Arturo's return shows, *bakla* is less of an identity and more of an event.[30] It is a process of being and becoming that does not easily get encased in preformed modern notions of sexuality and gender, of politics and culture, of global and local. Arturo's return highlights the idea that the return of the *bakla* is not about the championing of a vestige of some primordial Southeast Asian tradition. It is a haunting—not of a ghost of queer pasts, but rather as an insistent visitation of the unruliness and tensions of the global present and the promise of a really queer set of futures.

Call Center Agent
JAN M. PADIOS

Manila's Emerald Avenue is not as majestic as its name suggests, but on most weekends, around one in the morning, it is dotted with streetlamps, lighted store signs, and the bluish fluorescent glow of office building lobbies. Most importantly, it is alive with people: men and women in their twenties, wearing casual clothing, traversing the sidewalks, smoking cigarettes, and chatting over coffee. As taxicabs come and go along this multilane street, the activity smacks of urban nightlife, like that of any major city. Meeting me during her "lunch" break long before dawn, my informant Miah Mendez—a call center agent of seven years—appears in perfect harmony with her surroundings: Twenty-seven, sporting a black blouse and fashionable dark jeans, a mobile phone in one hand and a Starbucks cup in the other, Miah greets me with an affable smile and a smoothly delivered "How's it going?" As I walk with Miah, however, the impression of insouciance on the avenue begins to wane. People move in a distressed manner; many smoke while pacing or staring blankly into space; others throw back coffee as a defense against extreme physical and mental fatigue; and, like Miah, almost all have identification badges affixed to their clothing or hanging around their necks. The badges display the name of the business process outsourcing (BPO) firm—known more commonly as a "call center"—for which a person works. At one in the morning, Emerald Avenue is not an urban party zone but an urban work zone, where almost every office tower houses at least three or four BPO firms. In those frigidly air-conditioned offices, computer terminals hum with white noise, as thousands of Filipino workers answer a constant flow of customer service inquiries from consumers calling mostly from the United States.

Filipino call center agents cut both bright and perplexing figures of Philippine modernity. In 2009, former Philippine president Gloria Macapagal Arroyo celebrated the rapid proliferation of call centers over the previous years, referring to business process outsourcing as the country's "sunrise industry." As this official narrative goes, BPO firms draw much-needed foreign investment and jobs into the country, harness the skills of some of the most talented service workers in the world, and promise to usher the Philippines into a future of high-tech global integration. The 1-800 numbers, it seems, will connect all Filipinos to a modernity centered on urbanity, technology, consumption, and youth—ostensibly embodied by thousands like Miah. Yet, among the workers who spend nights attending to American consumers over the phone, "modernity" also feels like disrupted circadian rhythms and alienation induced by repetitive, emotional work.[31] Indeed, call center workers must contend with callers' demands—often delivered with irritation and insults—as well as management's panoptic measures of their productivity. How many calls did Ephran "resolve" on his first attempt? How quickly did Jade take the customer's payment? How much empathy did Alan display?

Between the official narrative of national progress and one of unmitigated exploitation, the Filipino call center agent indexes momentous shifts in production and consumption, both globally and locally. For example, the genealogy of the BPO firm can be traced to the industrial export-processing zones created at the behest of the neoliberal "transnational rule regime" of Marcos, the IMF, and the World Bank in the 1970s.[32] Rather than electronics and apparel, however, BPO firms export customer service and back-office support such as payroll and medical transcription—a structural arrangement made possible by even more fervent rounds of economic liberalization of the Philippine economy in the 1990s. Moreover, call centers are products of the last fifteen years of massive investments in Philippine urban development, in contradistinction to the Philippine countryside. What else can explain how a country with an average wait time of five and a half years for the installation of a landline telephone in the early 1990s[33] came to boast a multibillion-dollar telecommunications infrastructure that literally connects over 450,000 Filipino call center agents to the global service economy in the twenty-first century? At the same time, the Philippines' consumer economy too has expanded, urging Filipinos to calibrate their aspirations and social mobility against such things as cars, homes, vacations, or investments. With entry-level salaries exceeding those for certified public accountants or college professors, call center workers' remarkable purchasing power makes them newly prized members of the nation's consumer economy.

On Emerald Avenue we catch glimpses of these recent changes, but we also see that which falls outside of official narratives about call centers and Philippine modernity. With their "virtual migration" a corollary to the physical labor migration of Filipinos abroad, call center workers face precarious futures engendered by BPO firms' flexible labor practices.[34] Not all call center agents have the social and cultural capital Miah inherited through a Class-A upbringing—elite education, a debt-free existence living with mom and dad, disposable income to save and spend—traits that put one on the fast track for call center success and make for a lifestyle of comfort. Others are working parents who travel hours to their cubicles; at the end of the "day" they must eschew youth-based cultures of consumption for the unglamorous logic of more basic survival. Miah is, however, like many other workers in the industry who find sexual partners in their coworkers, a symbol of the supposed sexual proclivities of call center agents that troubles many in this majority-Catholic nation (as evidenced by at least one moral panic about call center workers contracting HIV). On the avenue, history also reminds us that Filipino call center agents are squarely situated within U.S.–Philippine colonial relations that have constituted Filipinos as racialized labor for well over a century. From the agricultural American West to American factories on former U.S. military bases to call centers in Manila's commercial hubs, Filipino workers are crucial figures within the history of American empire. At one in the morning, the agents on Emerald Avenue are somewhere between labor and leisure, between a search for pleasurable work and a fantasy of national development that characterizes them as the Philippines' "competitive advantage" on the world stage.[35]

Community Health Worker
MAI M. TAQUEBAN

"Ate" Linda is a health worker in one of Metro Manila's urban slums: a for-mer dumpsite turned village community, home to over eight hundred fami-lies, and ironically called Paradise.[36] Born into a poor family in the Bicol region, she once dreamed of getting a college degree. But life got in the way, and she was only able to complete two years of high school. Her story is fairly typical up until the events of some fifteen years ago. She was busy making a living for her family selling knickknacks, and she was the village *kubrador* (a local community bookie for an illicit numbers game) until her third pregnancy—a result, she says, of failing to avail herself of family plan-ning services.

Her predicament led her to a community clinic run by a nongovernmen-tal organization (NGO). Later, she was recruited as a clinic volunteer. After intensive training ("I cried because I was studying so hard!"), she became one of the first community health workers (CHWs) in Paradise. She tells me that it's challenging work: The local government's policy is to support only "natural" family planning methods, and there are no contraceptives available in the hospitals. Conservatives, mainly within the hierarchy of the Catholic Church and adamant about the sanctity of life, refuse to countenance any form of modern contraception. Many of the mothers have unplanned pregnancies. Some make desperate choices: self-induced abortion or abortion by a *hilot* (traditional birth attendant). Often these procedures entail the use of a clothes hanger inserted in the vagina to induce abortion.

Ate Linda feels it is her duty to help the women. Being a mother her-self, she tells me, she knows the difficulty of having many children. So she ignores the conservatives, tiptoes around the law (abortion is illegal in the Philippines), and continues to educate the women about contraceptives. And in some cases she offers a safer option for abortion.

What Ate Linda does is dangerous. On February 6, 2010, the military arrested forty-three CHWs in Rizal Province, east of the capital—not for contravening the national family policy, admittedly, but on the charge of be-ing militant rebels. One of the detained was pegged as the assassin tasked to kill retired army brigadier general Jovito Palparan, dubbed the "Butcher" by leftist militants for numerous political killings committed during his term as commander. The military also claimed, against all appearances, that the forty-three were not attending a health training under the auspices of an NGO. Instead, it said, they were being trained in bomb making. Two physicians, one nurse, one midwife, and thirty-nine community health workers, most of whom were poor farmers or workers continuing their training as paramedics and health educators, were arrested. Two of the women were pregnant.

The Community-Based Health Program (CBHP) was born during a tumultuous period in the country's history. It was the 1970s, poverty was escalating, and corruption had become the norm in government. Ferdinand Marcos declared martial law, and human rights violations became rampant. The health care needs of the masses were relegated to the back burner. It was at this juncture that dedicated medical professionals started the CBHP, whose driving force soon became the training of local health workers.[37] The trainings were run by NGOs with links to the Roman Catholic Church and Protestant social action programs. Alongside the instruction they received in health-related matters, CHWs were also trained to organize and mobilize communities for health work. Most of those trained had very little education, but they helped to compensate for the absence of state-provided health services. In the process, however, they became targets of suspicion and then of repression. Paranoid about being undermined, the government branded the organizing and mobilizing work of CHWs as Maoist-inspired revolutionary activity. Doctors who volunteered as community trainers during the 1970s recall walking for days to reach remote villages, conducting training sessions in rustic huts, and hiding their hypodermic needles from the military during what became routine searches. Needles were construed as weapons, and their mere possession marked one as a subversive.

Decades later, CHWs continue to provide health services to the needy. And as recent events show, they are still looked upon with paranoia by the establishment. CHWs are in the ironic position of being tasked with serving the marginalized while being marginalized themselves. A spokesperson for the army noted that the majority of the forty-three CHWs arrested had minimal education—clear proof, he stated, that they were not health workers but rather misguided rebels. The colonel was hardly unique in insinuating that "those with no education" (read "the poor") are incapable of being trained in the supposedly technical area of health work. At hospitals, where she accompanies patients whom she has referred, Ate Linda has been told by doctors and nurses, often after a glance at her well-worn rubber slippers, "You are *just* a health worker."

CHWs thus work in an arena of acute structural violence.[38] Yet the constraints under which they struggle have taught community health workers to exert agency in novel ways. They respond to the most desperate of needs, finding ways to work around existing regulations. Ate Linda gladly goes about educating mothers about the uses and benefits of the very contraceptives deemed "dangerous and immoral" by the conservatives who shape health policy. To get herself moving, she says, she only has to remember the incidence of maternal mortality in the country (162 per 100,000 live births),[39] mostly caused by easily preventable complications in childbirth, as well as the risks of dying from an unsafe abortion: about 1.4 million pregnancies are unintentional and about a third end in abortion.[40] Maybe, she muses, there is a different heaven for those who do her kind of good work.

Ate Linda recently also became a public official, duly elected as *barangay kagawad* by her constituency.[41] She chairs the local Health Committee and has in many ways become a figure of the community's refusal to accept the marginal status imposed upon them. Remaining primarily a ground-stumping CHW and community organizer, she doesn't care if the nurses in the hospitals sometimes turn up their noses at her. In her community, children run up to her and greet her with, "There's my doctor!" Electing her into public office is her community's way of asserting their resistance to structural violence.

The forty-three remain incarcerated as of this writing, but now they are forty-four. One of the women has given birth.

Beauty Contestant
T. RUANNI F. TUPAS

It is now her turn to answer.[42] This is the final Q & A portion at the 2008 Binibining Pilipinas (Miss Philippines) contest, and thus far she appears to be the ultimate Filipino beauty contestant: young, tall, slender, and very pretty. Then comes the judge's question: What role does she think her family has played in her becoming a candidate for Binibining Pilipinas? She answers haltingly, her English interspersed quite strongly with Tagalog pragmatic particles and defensive laughter:

> Well, my family's role for me is so important, because there was the wa—they're, they was the one who's . . . very . . . haha . . . Oh, I'm so sorry. Umm, my *pamily* . . . my family . . . Oh my God. I'm . . . O.K. I'm so sorry. I . . . I told you that I'm so confident. *Eto*, umm, wait . . . Hahahaha! Umm, sorry guys because this was really my *pirst* pageant ever, because I'm only seventeen years old and . . . haha . . . I, I did not expect that I came from—I came from one of the *tof* ten. Hmmm. So . . . But I said *dat* my *pamily* is the most important persons in my life. Thank you.[43]

The moment of Janina San Miguel's downfall seems enormously bizarre to many. She has just been voted the best in the long gown and swimsuit competitions, almost assuring her of the title, as well as the honor of being a global representative for the Philippines, possibly the world's third-largest English-speaking country. Yet her answer, with its superficial content, indiscriminate use of the phonemes "p" and "f," and lack of agreement between subjects and verbs, is a textual repository of what many Filipinos would call incompetent English. One of the most vilified contemporary public displays of English language use, it falls far short of the Philippine ideal of what it means to be intelligent or educated: not only to speak in English but to speak in an English that approximates the American English ideal set by the schools. At the same time, the Janina moment crystallizes the dominance of English in most Philippine public arenas, where even those who lack proficiency in the language assay it as a conditioned choice.

The crowd erupts in cries and insults hurled against Janina, who has both entertained and shamed them.[44] It does not matter if most of them speak in similar ways; after all, only a very small group of people in this country has ever had a good command of English.[45] Like most postcolonial societies, the Philippines continues to grapple with its colonial past, with language as a persistent point of contention and subversion. The English language came via a free universal education, introduced by the Americans at the turn of the twentieth century as part of the ideological infrastructure for benevolent domination. In sharp contrast with the previous Spanish colonial practice of withholding Castilian from *indios* or "natives," English was—and still is—presented as a language of equality, neutrality, and mobility. But while universal education was indeed free, "quality" education never was. Early mass-based English-medium education in the country was to a large extent industrial or vocational in nature. An elite group of Filipinos took English alongside lessons on social grace and etiquette in exclusive Catholic schools, and an even more privileged group, the *pensionados,* was sent to the United States for further training in the language. This pioneering group would come back and take up leadership positions in the educational system, as well as in business, industry, and policy-making bodies.[46] At the end of the official colonial rule of the United States, the 1939 census revealed that only 26.6 percent of Filipinos were able to speak in English.[47]

English language proficiency remains a requirement for being admired and esteemed in Philippine society. Yet access to English depends on one's access to other social resources such as an urban, middle-class education. English may be the language of dreams for many Filipinos aspiring to go abroad to get decent jobs not available at home, or specifically of young adults hoping to crack into the difficult but still relatively exclusive world of business processing outsourcing (see "Call Center Agent," this chapter). But it is social positioning that largely determines the kind of English most people speak and learn in school in the first place. Speaking in English, in other words, is a choice and a nonchoice at the same time. English is a symbolic language of privilege, and thus almost everyone chooses to speak it; however, the socially stratified nature of Philippine society assures that some Englishes are more powerful than others. Yes, they are all "English," but some are good and some bad, some educated and some uneducated; spoken by the rich, the poor, and the middle class. Some make money, some make "servants of globalization,"[48] and some make Janina.

So while Janina is young, tall, slender, and very pretty indeed, she is "brainless" and "stupid," too. A senior legislator and main proponent of an English-only medium of instruction bill in the Philippine Congress thinks the "sensational failure" was "tormenting to watch."[49] The English language, or rather "educated" Philippine English, the century-old symbolic colonial wedge between the rich and poor, betrays her social background as a daughter of a jeepney driver and a laundrywoman in Manila. Precisely *because* Janina is a beauty contestant, not a world boxing champion like Pacman (Manny Pacquiao, who falls equally short of the idealized standard), the entire country feasts on her English.

As Janina attempts to repair the situation through various strategic cues such as laughter, use of personal narrative, and conversational discourse, the host asks her to shift to Tagalog instead. But she continues to answer in English. Can she hear the voices asking her to use Tagalog as an alternative vehicle of expression? Can she hear her own voice as she continues to struggle with English while the crowd watches in utter disbelief? As she unravels herself through what many refer to as an "epic" display of self-inflicted embarrassment, she participates in the construction of her own marginalization. She chooses to speak in English, a choice she is not privileged to make; and as she attempts to speak in an English reflective of her marginalized social positioning, she reaffirms the power of English to disempower her.

Now she leaves center stage, returns to her earlier place, and then turns around again to face a rowdy crowd and a spellbound nation beginning to comprehend what has just happened. This is the real beauty of this contemporary moment. Janina, the beauty contestant, is a collective recuperation of a nation's language politics, a reminder that in this bewildering world of global transformation, some things do not change.

VIETNAM

Edited by ERIK HARMS

We have seen these figures before. Yet they are all brand new, novel, or as Vietnamese would say it, very modern: *rất hiện đại*. The figures described in this chapter produce a sense of déjà vu: the petty trader, scientist, aspiring foreign student, prostitute, touch-up artist, investor, public/private entrepreneur, the mountain villagers encountering new forms of governance and market practices, and the transnational Vietnamese who goes away and then returns. These figures are new but have appeared before.

This sense of new things we have seen before nicely illustrates the way many Vietnamese experience modernity. These figures embody a temporal condition akin to the way in which Vietnamese, without contradiction, organize their lives according to the cyclical movements of the lunar calendar and zodiac, as well as with the universalizing linearity of the Gregorian calendar. The Year of the Tiger was understood as ever so new in 2010, yet once again the same. Yet none of the figures in these essays would ever confuse 2010 with other Tiger years, such as 1998, 1986 (the year of the *đổi mới* economic reforms), or 1974 (one year before the "Liberation" or "the Fall" of Saigon). Time is both linear and cyclical, progressing and repeating itself at once. The temporality of Vietnamese modernity defies expectations; while often celebrated for boldly moving forward in a direct line toward a pinnacle of achievement or development, Vietnamese modernity also arrives, recedes, turns back, pauses, restarts, and reappears.

The figures in these essays demonstrate this temporality well. Ann Marie Leshkowich shows how the Petty Trader (*tiểu thương*) is understood both as a relic of the past and as a savvy cosmopolitan preparing to send her daughter to business school abroad. Once depicted by the state as alternatively dangerous or backward, the *tiểu thương* has more recently been hailed as an important symbol of progress in Vietnamese economic development. While anxieties associated with capitalism no longer mark representations of female traders, Christophe Robert highlights how the figure of the Prostitute continues to embody male anxieties and fears associated with market activity. Moral panics regarding prostitution stand in for unarticulated concerns about unscrupulous economic practices, practices well illustrated by the figure of the Domestic Investor, who Allison Truitt vividly depicts making land deals in areas of the city the investor herself cannot navigate. Lost in a world she partially owns, the investor bets on the power of government development projects to insure returns on speculative investments, while seeking to evade state regulation. Such links between private entrepreneurs and the socialist state also appear in the figure of the Enterprising Cadre, who, in Ken MacLean's description, parlays his position in a state research institute into a lucrative private consulting firm. Like this entrepreneur, who thrives at the interface of the public and the private, the directionality of history appears blurry and unpredictable. In Christina Schwenkel's essay, the unexpected paths of modernity also mark the fall and subsequent recuperation of the fortunes of the Soviet-Trained Scientist, whose formerly modern but now outdated training in veterinary science marks her as old-fashioned, but whose time studying abroad allowed her to cultivate cultural capital that marks her as cosmopolitan, savvy to the terms of modernity associated with international business. By contrast, the Aspiring Overseas Student I describe hopes to study at a foreign college and has fully embraced a vision of the modern capitalist future, only to find herself faced with a string of impediments; it's not so clear whether the modern world embraces her back.

The trajectory of socialism and capitalism—so often conceived, depending on ideological perspective, as either moving through historical stages or reaching the end of history—is here shown to be much more of a winding road, with switchbacks, scenic routes, and crowded intersections, as well as straight and narrow roadways that other famous figures of modernity such as Baron Haussmann or even Eisenhower would have surely admired. Some of Vietnam's newest roads lead directly to the Vietnamese highlands, where the ambivalent embrace of modernity is expressed in Truong Huyen Chi's portrait of the Cham H'Roi Girl who engages with new modes of production, rides a motorbike for the first time, and actively combines traditional livelihoods with those borrowed from the outside. It is also expressed by the Khu Mu Mountain Village Head, who wants to offer the author Christian C. Lentz a localized vision of modernity but must also negotiate with extra-local power relations and play the role of bureaucrat. In the process, local tradition is deemed incompatible with foreign modernity. But foreign contacts need not undermine all forms of tradition, as in the case of Nina Hien's example of the Photo Retoucher, who is able to mobilize new technologies to recuperate auras that resonate with cultural sentiments. Even more explicitly, Lauren Meeker illustrates how the intersection between traditional culture and global modernity appears in the figure of the *nghệ nhân,* or Cultural Expert, whose state title indexes the global market for cultural forms portrayed as decidedly local. Finally, in Ivan Small's essay, the Vietnamese Transnational represents a figure conditioned by the historical circumstances of the second Indochina conflict, but who nonetheless resonates with long-standing notions that cultivating oneself as Vietnamese can actually come through the process of moving across spatial boundaries. Here the quintessentially Vietnamese concept of "coming home" (*về quê*) is intimately tied into the notion of going away.[1]

Anthropologists have discovered important ways in which the "modernization myth" has been "turned upside down, shaken, and shattered" in the face of unanticipated economic decline or other hardship.[2] This is partially but not wholly the case for Vietnam. While social scientists critique grand narratives, Vietnamese today have embraced modernity with clarion calls to "industrialize and modernize the nation" and with efforts to imbue everything imaginable—from ATM machines to New Urban Zones—with "civilization" (*văn minh*). Anthropologist Philip Taylor notes how Vietnamese notions of civilization reproduce a notion of modernity that consigns significant numbers of Vietnamese citizens to a spatial periphery and temporal past.[3] But the very notion of a linear march to the modern future is complicated by the fact that Vietnamese modernists have made these kinds of claims before, and they make them now after having turned modernity upside down, inside out, and spun it around. For example, the concept of "the new" in Vietnamese has appeared in so many iterations that it is itself, for lack of a better word, old. To cite the most obvious examples, the modernity of the 1920s and 1930s was called *tân thời* or "new times"; in 1946, the (in)famous campaigns to build socialist character in the north were framed around building a "new cultural life" or *đời sống mới;*[4] and the well-known renovation policies of 1986 are called *đổi mới* or "change to the new." In recuperating modernity in a postmodern age, Vietnamese have actually undermined the teleology of modernity not by renouncing it so much as reviving it. We have seen this brand-new, unprecedented situation before.

Writing of the journalist, novelist, and "king of reportage" Vũ Trọng Phụng (1912–1939), Peter Zinoman notes that his work can be understood as quintessentially modern for the way he sought to "mine Vietnamese tradition for a means to domesticate and make sense of the essentially unpredictable and accidental character of modern life."[5] Like Walter Benjamin, Georg Simmel, and others who were writing in that intellectually fruitful yet politically fraught first half of the twentieth century, Vietnamese journalists such as Vũ Trọng Phụng anticipated the idea of *exploring modernity through the depiction of figures*. They were on different sides of the globe, but highly educated Vietnamese were reading the same Baudelaire as Benjamin, and Benjamin himself uses a Vietnamese visitor's impressions of Paris as an epigram. It is Nguyễn Trọng Hiệp's words that open Benjamin's meditation on the flaneur: "One goes for a stroll. The great ladies are out for a stroll."[6] As for Vũ Trọng Phụng, his works are filled with characters—Red-Haired Xuân, Mr. Civilization, Ms. Deputy Customs Officer—who are stylized in a way that "suggests a journalistic representation of a common sociological type as much as a fanciful work of literary imagination."[7] The king of reportage analyzed modernity in ways both modern and critical of modernity, embracing and indeed inventing modern literary conventions that challenge the assumptions of modernity itself.

Modernity is unprecedented once again. If many of the Vietnamese figures of modernity appear almost like a second coming, a return, they also appear, impossibly, as novelties—things that by definition exist only by virtue of having appeared for the first time. In this return of the novelty, we see the return of a particularly Vietnamese engagement with modern ways and traditions. It is not the figure itself so much as the experience the figure expresses that conveys the Vietnamese vision of modernity. Through the figures in these essays, Vietnamese modernity emerges not as a discrete moment in history but as a set of engagements with the extra-local and the Other, a set of engagements with new and transformative modes of production, new relations of mobility and communication, and new ways of presenting oneself as an active subject with a purpose in the world. These figures all have what Truong Huyen Chi, describing the H'Roi Girl from the Central Highlands, calls "a project in life."

Petty Trader (*Tiểu thương*)
ANN MARIE LESHKOWICH

It is November 1996. On a hot afternoon, Dung fans herself while waiting for customers to approach her women's clothing stall in Bến Thành market. A stylish woman pauses to look at shirts. "This black one is from Hong Kong," Dung tells her. "How much?" "60,000 [*đồng*]."[8] The customer looks annoyed. "35,000 is good," she snarls. Dung smiles sweetly, "50,000. It would be the first sale [of the afternoon]. . . . Buy to help me out. It's the right price, guaranteed." By invoking the belief that the first sale sets the tone for those that follow, Dung subtly pressures her customer. Pulling down another shirt, Dung comments, "This one is higher quality . . . perfect for you. . . . It's 110,000." The woman walks away. Turning to me, Dung complains, "I'm caught between two strategies: Say a reasonable price or inflate the price." State a reasonable price and customers might trust Dung, but they also might bargain down below her cost. "Talk nonsense" (*nói xạo*) and she might scare customers away. Dung sighs, "If you don't demand a lot [*nói thách*], you don't get a high price."

Dung is one of more than fourteen hundred *tiểu thương*, or petty traders, who run stalls in Ho Chi Minh City's most famous marketplace.[9] A *tiểu thương* would strike most Vietnamese as an inapt figure of modernity. Embodying timeless qualities of Vietnamese femininity—determination, resourcefulness, sweetness, and self-sacrifice—she plies her wares to support her family, yet her habits of buying cheap, selling dear, and talking nonsense provoke moral ambivalence.[10] Over the past thirty-five years, officials touting first centrally planned socialism (1975–1986) and then market socialism (1986–present) have branded *tiểu thương* backward, uneducated anachronisms to be replaced by modern retailers, with perhaps a few preserved as tourist attractions. Casting the *tiểu thương* as a figure of tradition against which modernity becomes legible, such claims deny the material significance of *tiểu thương* to actually existing socialism and market socialism.

For twenty-five years, Dung has navigated the symbolic and material contradictions of being *tiểu thương*. Born in the 1950s to a revolutionary family, Dung secured a secretarial job with a state-run company after liberation (1975). Over the next decade, the government sought to build socialism by redistributing large businesses, including those owned by ethnic Chinese. Gendered stereotypes of *tiểu thương* as subsistence workers protected them from being labeled "capitalist." When officials finally announced in 1984 that Bến Thành market would become a cooperative, Dung contributed 20 *chi* (2.4 troy ounces) of gold to join. She quickly learned that alongside its official state commerce, Bến Thành was a center for black market trade. Scholars of socialism elsewhere argue that the informal economy, by delivering goods that centrally imposed scarcity denied consumers, simultaneously undermined and prolonged actually existing socialism.[11] While other citizens might recall the late 1980s "subsidy period" as a time of long lines and deprivation,[12] Dung claimed that Bến Thành's *tiểu thương* and the cadres with whom they shared their profits "lived very well."

Đổi mới officially began in 1986, but it again took time for the new measures to affect *tiểu thương*. Then, one day in 1989, officials simply declared that the stalls now belonged to individual traders. Profits were high at first. Dung, her mother, and her sisters soon acquired four stalls, making them one of Bến Thành's "big families" (*đại gia đình*), a term that can also mean both extended family and great or illustrious family. By the late 1990s, however, the allure of entrepreneurship led to increased competition and lower profit margins. Capital markets favored the politically connected, leaving the supposedly lowly, untrustworthy *tiểu thương* with no option besides usurious "hot loans." Newspapers reported on plans to redevelop Bến Thành as an international trade center. Meanwhile, anxiety about growing inequality fueled scapegoating of *tiểu thương* as unscrupulous cheats antithetical to a modern economy. Banners strung from the market's rafters exhorted *tiểu thương* to conduct business in a "civilized" manner worthy of the city bearing Hồ Chí Minh's name. The implication was clear: Left to their own devices, traders were liable to behave otherwise.

In lengthy conversations with me during the late 1990s, Dung contested these stereotypes. Although she did not garner the riches that the public imagined, neither was her business an unscrupulous, petty, and backward affair. She fueled the development of "market socialism" by shaping fashion trends, employing struggling relatives, creatively juggling her cash flow, and investing profits in her husband's tourism business. At the same time, Dung's success rested on "strategic essentialism."[13] By sweetly bargaining with a customer, lying that a shirt produced in Vietnam was made in Hong Kong, or deferring taxes by appealing to the collector's sympathies, Dung garnered temporary material advantage through conforming to the traditional *tiểu thương* stereotypes that otherwise vexed and marginalized her.

More recently, Dung has benefited from increasing political and social acceptance of private entrepreneurs. The 1997 financial crisis halted Bến Thành's ambitious redevelopment plans. Foreign tourism has grown, and journalists have begun to praise the acumen of "marketplace" businesspeople (*doanh nhân "chợ"*) whose attractive, multilingual salesclerks charm foreigners into buying T-shirts and pottery at prices above those in "modern" department stores.[14] By 2008, Dung had acquired stalls near the market's entrance and in the newly opened night market outside. She now caters to tourists with designer knockoffs and embroidered handbags.[15] Almost sixty, Dung increasingly delegates selling to young employees who chat up customers in English, French, Japanese, and Korean. The gold and jade jewelry adorning her fingers, wrists, neck, and ears testifies to her prosperity. Her English-speaking daughter sometimes helps with the stalls, but Dung is saving money to send her to business school abroad. Although Dung tells me that marketplace trade no longer poses "problems like in the past," she is adamant that her daughter never become a *tiểu thương*. Once again, achieving modern prosperity requires the *tiểu thương*'s profits but consigns her symbolically to the past.

Prostitute (*Gái*)
CHRISTOPHE ROBERT

On an early evening in June 2008, I ride my motorbike down dusty streets near Peace Park, a few paces from An Đông Market in western Saigon. I am reacquainting myself with the neighborhood after a long absence. I realize I gave off the wrong signal by looking left and right while slowly riding down the boulevard. A woman suddenly appears in my field of vision. She rides alongside me and whispers a tentative "You, hello." I ignore her and keep riding, watching her from the corner of my eye. We remain silent. At the traffic light, she idles next to me for a short while and then moves on to the next potential client.

The mobile sex workers who cruise nightly down this dusty boulevard are older and homelier than the prostitutes who crowd Vietnamese newspapers and television shows. Their clothes are outdated. Like their scooters—older models from the mid-1990s—they seem stuck in an earlier stage of the new Vietnamese market economy. Their activities mirror the small trades of street sellers in the neighborhood. They charge low prices and service their clients in parks or cheap hourly rooms.

Prostitutes are common in Vietnamese cities today. In bars and cafés, nightclubs, karaoke lounges, massage parlors, street corners, and parks, their presence is discreet and yet insistent, alternatively invisible and visible. The practices of mobile prostitutes such as the one who hailed me are far removed from the lurid clichés and mass-mediated representations of prostitution. Foreigners do not patronize these women, although in official discourses in the 1990s prostitution was consistently associated with foreign tourists and the decadence fostered on Vietnamese youth by new criminal groups and consumer society alike.

In *The Philosophy of Money*, Georg Simmel makes an apparently startling claim. For him, "We experience in the nature of money itself something of the essence of prostitution."[16] Commodified sexual relations—"sex work," bought and sold as labor or service—can be understood as extreme manifestations of impersonal financial transactions in capitalist economies. This insight into exchange and commodified personal relations helps us better understand images and representations of prostitution in Vietnam.

At three key moments in recent Vietnamese history—1990s, 1960s, 1930s—the figure of the prostitute became prominent in the public sphere.

Each time, the relevance of debates on prostitution stemmed less from what they actually said about sex work than from the political and social commentaries they triggered about rapid economic and social change. The proliferation of mass-mediated discourses about prostitution in Vietnam since the 1990s is not a new phenomenon. It echoes political struggles against American intervention in South Vietnam in the 1960s and 1970s. For Hanoi leaders and progressive intellectuals in Saigon, the prostitute was then a figure of abjection and national humiliation, both metaphor and metonymy for the violence of American neocolonialism and capitalist exploitation. These representations built upon analyses of writers such as Vũ Trọng Phụng, who in the 1930s castigated French colonizers for abusing Vietnamese "concubines." In all three cases—1990s, 1960s, 1930s—male anxieties surrounding foreign presence, threats of cultural disintegration, and contamination of the national body are paramount. Male fears of social and cultural disintegration are cast in moral terms: Political threats are represented as sexual threats undermining patriarchal authority.[17]

In these representations, the prostitute has consistently been a figure of rootless mobility. Urban Vietnamese today imagine young prostitutes as rural, uneducated, greedy, and connected with "black society" networks, a murky criminal underworld of pimps, drug dealers, heroin addicts, gamblers, swindlers, and corrupt cops. These networks are imagined to exist alongside legitimate businesses, but in ways that are not fully knowable.

Like the criminal networks with which they are associated in popular imagination, prostitutes derive much of their power to fascinate from their ability to appear and disappear at will, while being very real in their local presence and influence. The association of prostitution with AIDS in the 1990s increased the hysterical mystery surrounding this montage of symptoms and anxieties. AIDS was associated with foreignness; urban legends flourished about its origins, etiology, and spread. This reinforced popular notions that contamination from the realm of "social evils" happens by simple contact with criminal social types.[18] A moral narrative of reprehensible decadence emerged quickly and durably in the 1990s. It fit well the agendas of both anxious parents and manipulative government officials and censors.

Debates about prostitution in Vietnam since the 1990s stem from widespread anxieties in the wake of market-oriented economic reforms and the rapid reemergence of a consumer society. What is striking about these debates is how little they really are *about* prostitution. Instead, as Simmel suggested in a different context, they enable Vietnamese to debate shifting political and ideological landscapes on a broader tapestry of social relations, including the visible presence of commodified women functioning symbolically as commodified images.[19]

These debates have to do with moral panics and anguished and ambivalent reactions to the new, exemplified by adult anxieties about youth. Similar anxieties have recurred with every new generation since the 1900s, with youth cast as an uncontrollable and threatening segment of society associated with newness and emergence. Beyond simply moral panic, deeper concerns are at play. The return in the 1990s of specters of the American War and French colonialism—in media representations of greedy, immoral bar girls cavorting with Western men—hide more fundamental worries about the future. While most Vietnamese were better off in the 1990s than in the difficult postwar period before economic reforms, they also began contending with increasing socioeconomic inequalities.

Local affinities and engagements must now be reconciled with the reappearance of the foreign and reinvigorated market economy principles that threaten the precarious political and economic stability Vietnamese had begun achieving in the postwar period. The appeal to morality and the shaming of women at the forefront of the new commodification of economic and personal relations can be understood as a disavowal of new desires—for money, power, and sex, but also perhaps for liberation from social norms and patriarchal gender roles.[20]

Domestic Investor (*Người đầu tư trong nước*)
ALLISON TRUITT

Early one morning in December 2001, I accompanied Thúy and Yến to District Two. We took a ferry across the Saigon River, a short trip but one that made the district seem all the more remote, despite the fact it lay across the Saigon River from Ho Chi Minh City's glamorous shopping and financial center. The two women had recently pooled their money to purchase a small plot of land. On that day, however, their destination was the district courthouse. There they hoped to resolve the issue of the land-rights document [*sổ đỏ*]. Thúy and Yến had agreed with the seller to purchase the land for 400 million dong earlier that summer. The two women paid a deposit of 300 million dong and received the document in return. Speculative activity in District Two had since driven up prices, and Thúy estimated the plot to be worth almost 800 million dong. The seller now refused to transfer the document into Thúy's name, and without the document, Thúy and Yến could not resell the land at a profit.

The courthouse was a nondescript building located down a small alleyway. A few people waited inside. An official shuffling stacks of paper looked up to ask Thúy why she had come. She explained the situation. When she learned that the case had been postponed, she rushed outside and immediately called an inspector to arrange a meeting near her house in District One. Later that afternoon she showed the inspector the document, a sheet of paper that noted the dimensions of the lot, the district, and a small map of the area. "What street leads to this plot?" the inspector asked. Neither woman knew. "How will you use the land?" he pressed. They were silent. The inspector laughed, as he had exposed how their interest in the land was in its potential profit, not its actual location.

Investors, once shunned as "speculators" and "profiteers," have recently been rehabilitated as part of the country's larger process of reforming the economy. Many foreign investors remained wary of the country's extensive yet unruly market for land titles, leaving an opening for domestic investors whose transactions forged new relationships to land.[21] By wresting land from a social matrix that tied the householder to the land, these investors generated value through the circulation and exchange of land-title documents.[22] It was in this economy organized around *documents* that a new moral economy around the value of land emerged.

District Two was particularly appealing for these domestic investors. Although it lay just across the Saigon River from the heart of Ho Chi Minh City, much of the land was still designated as agricultural or farmland. Yet these investors already anticipated its appropriation as a planned urban center for the city's growing middle class. Rumors were rampant of a Japanese-government investment project to build a tunnel under the river, thereby providing quick and convenient access to the city's center and the East-West Highway. Like countless others, Thúy's interest in District Two was motivated by cashing in on the city's changing landscape. She intended to purchase land in hopes of quickly reselling it to developers.

Thúy, like other domestic investors, bet on the municipal government's capacity to transform the city into a developed and modernized metropolitan area. Yet these same agencies were ill equipped to handle the surge of interest in buying and selling land. Small investors like Thúy compensated for the lack of a regulatory apparatus governing land transfers by relying on the bonds of personal dependency. In so doing, they confounded claims that the expansion of markets would create objective dependency relations among individuals who related to each other only through market prices and money.[23] People exchanged titles, often authentic documents, through processes that were not quite legal. Such transfers relied on people's personal relations and their uncanny knack for converting those relations into duly signed and stamped documents that had passed through the hands of court clerks and inspectors.

Thúy's own dream of making a fortune was overshadowed by larger processes overtaking Ho Chi Minh City. The speculative activity drove prices upwards in 2002, drawing sharp criticism from municipal authorities. Moreover, the frenzy over purchasing land transformed District Two into an area plagued by illegal land transfers.[24] City officials claimed such transfers destabilized the city's economic growth, although more than U.S. $2 billion reportedly changed hands in the illegal trading of three thousand hectares of land.[25] The government declared the speculative bids a "fiction" that was undermining the orderly development of District Two.[26] By that summer, the city government brought an abrupt halt to buying and selling land, leaving would-be investors such as Thúy holding the land-rights document but not the right to sell it.

Eventually, I came to doubt Thúy's status as investor. As I followed her on several more excursions to District Two, I saw her role instead as a broker (*cò*) who worked the edges of these land transfers, often in the name of her "husband," whom she claimed owned the land. On our excursions, she could barely contain her glee at the thought of so much undeveloped land. In her eyes, the gold on the arms of women was proof of the lucrative world of real estate. But whenever we were accompanied by potential buyers of her "land," she could not remember where the plot was located, relying instead on local motorbike drivers who drove her around in circles.

Thúy leveraged her connections, dropping names of high-ranking officials and making appeals to divine or supernatural intervention to pull off her increasingly ill-fated transactions. After the unsuccessful visit to the District Two courthouse, Thúy sought out the advice of a fortune-teller, who ultimately rejected her interpretation that she was a victim of "misfortune" (*xui*). Thúy stormed out of the woman's house. Both the District Two courthouse and the fortune-teller stood as unwilling and unsympathetic participants in her efforts to capitalize on the city's rapid transformation.

Enterprising Cadre (*Cán bộ dám làm*)
KEN MACLEAN

Hưng is a member of the "transition" generation. He, like millions of others, came of age after the Second Indochina War (1959–1975) when—contrary to official promises and popular expectations—living conditions worsened rather than improved. The centrally planned economy, although not the sole cause of the poverty, hunger, and "entrenched thinking" that characterized postwar life, nonetheless came to symbolize the inability of actually existing socialism to satisfy basic needs, much less realize its stated ideals.

By the mid-1990s, living conditions had improved dramatically, largely due to a series of reforms that transformed some previously illicit forms of economic activity into licit ones. Further administrative reforms followed, and these eventually made it possible for civil servants—provided they had the right combination of knowledge, skills, and connections—to fashion interesting and sometimes lucrative careers that relied upon yet strategically blurred the boundary imagined to distinguish the public sector from the private one.[27] These cadres, as several of my informants noted, were "brave enough to do" (*cán bộ dám làm*)—that is, to become entrepreneurs at this "public-private" (*công-tư*) interface.

Hưng was at the forefront of this trend, now widespread at all levels of government nationwide. Originally from Hanoi, he founded a private consulting firm *inside* a state research institute based in Ho Chi Minh City in 2000, more than a year before the Communist Party officially endorsed the socialist-oriented market economy as the new development "model" for the country as a whole at its Ninth National Congress. The director—who was eager to develop a "private" revenue stream not subject to "public" oversight—permitted Hưng and his team to work *outside* the institute on a nearly full-time basis on one condition: They had to redistribute a portion of their revenues to the institute to help reduce the budgetary shortfall that a steady decline in state subsidies had created.

Hưng's firm, despite the additional burden of this unofficial tax, quickly became a success, in part because of his technical expertise, enthusiasm, and natural charm, all of which were plainly evident at a workshop on rural land use planning in Hanoi, where I first met him. But the firm's growing list of clients, which included other state agencies in addition to international nongovernmental organizations and multilateral development banks, also sought out Hưng because of his demonstrated ability to deliver on his contractual promises. In short, Hưng got things done, on time, and close to budget despite the bureaucratic resistance he often encountered from cadres who had "not yet turned towards the new" (*chưa đổi mới*), as one of his colleagues put it, referring to officials slow to embrace the changes wrought by the reform process of the same name.

Hưng was well liked by his colleagues, as well. They affectionately called him Ông Địa, the tutelary spirit of wealth. Initially I assumed the unusual nickname to be a play on words, as *hưng* means "prosperity." Visually, the name fit as well. Hưng, while he lacked the requisite mustache and goatee, did possess the ample belly, moon-shaped face, and beatific smile found on statues of Ông Địa. One day during lunch, I asked several of Hưng's junior colleagues whether my guess was correct. They said it was, but for the wrong reasons. The nickname, Quang explained, had nothing to do with their shared physical attributes; instead, they used it because Hưng, like Ông Địa, had the power to give them what they wanted provided they kept him "well fed." Quang's answer mystified me, until he reminded me that many southerners regard Ông Địa to be a manifestation of the Kitchen God, the guardian spirit of the hearth, whose unusual place in Vietnamese culture provides insights into how the tactics used "to buy over" (*đút lót*) others, including state officials, both have and have not changed since the reform era began.[28]

Since food is almost always prepared and consumed in the company of others, the Kitchen God also monitors everyone's behavior, a duty that is publicly acknowledged on the twenty-third day of the final month of the lunar year. On this day, families throughout Vietnam "bribe" the Kitchen God with lavish offerings—gold votive paper, new clothing, culinary delicacies, and ample amounts of alcohol—before he makes his annual journey to Heaven on the back of a magical carp. Once there, the Kitchen God reports to the Jade Emperor, providing a detailed account of each family's conduct over the previous year. Since a favorable report is widely believed to help ensure happiness and good fortune in the coming year, many people take an added precaution: They smear the Kitchen God's mouth with sugar, honey, or sweet sticky rice in the hope that he will speak highly of them or at least cast their misdeeds in a somewhat more favorable light.

When all the above is taken into account, Hưng's unusual sobriquet seems somewhat less playful than I first assumed. Endearments, while sweet, can convey more than affection; moreover, they often carry a significant cost for those who give them—a requirement that becomes abundantly clear just prior to the lunar New Year celebrations, when many civil servants give their superiors imported liquor, luxury goods, and/or cash in the hope of securing future returns. Fortunately, Hưng's staff did not have to provide such "gifts" to obtain raises, promotions, or other professional opportunities, which made him quite different from other public civil servant/private entrepreneurs. Nor were they required to forge receipts or manipulate field data to generate additional revenue, as was also commonplace. Instead, the staff kept Hưng "well fed" by meeting his exacting professional standards, which I knew from personal experience required long hours both in the field and in the office preparing reports, typically without additional compensation. While these differences matter, the similarities also indicate that the "transition" from a centrally planned economy to a market-driven one has reconfigured rather than reformed the attitudes, values, and practices that shape how Vietnamese mitigate risk and accumulate favors in their sprawling public-private bureaucracy.[29]

Soviet-Trained Scientist
CHRISTINA SCHWENKEL

In 2006 I attended a small gathering in Hải Phòng organized by Hoa for her daughter's fifth birthday. While eating cake and spring rolls, I inquired about the increasingly popular practice of celebrating birthdays in a country that had traditionally observed death anniversaries. Hoa explained that birthday parties were a "foreign" cultural practice still unfamiliar to many families. Hoa's husband and another couple at the table agreed. "Did you celebrate your birthdays when you were young?" I asked them. None had, but three of the adults, Hoa included, had grown familiar with the custom when they were university students in Eastern Bloc countries. "My Russian friends would throw us birthday parties and invite us to their homes to eat. Everyone was so kind and interested in us," Hoa reminisced.

These adults represent a particular figure of modernity in Vietnamese society whose once-significant role in socialist nation-building unexpectedly shifted with the collapse of the Soviet Union. Sent abroad as Vietnam's best and brightest, who would embody and implement the progressive ideals of scientific socialism, these highly trained engineers and scientists returned to occupy an uncertain and ambiguous position in Vietnamese society. As their specialized knowledge, tastes, and experiences quickly became "outdated" and rendered incompatible with a global market economy, these specialists had to retool their skills and cultural capital to fit with the new demands, desires, and needs of a capitalist-oriented modernity.

Hoa's experience is representative of the many stories I heard from Vietnamese "socialist moderns" trained in the Soviet system in the 1980s.[30] A model student excited by the prospect of studying overseas, Hoa took an entrance exam in medicine during her senior year and requested placement in an East German university. She scored high and was subsequently assigned to study veterinarian sciences in Russia, where she conducted her graduate work from 1981 to 1987. For Hoa and her colleagues, the opportunity to pursue an advanced degree in a more prosperous country was also a means to escape endemic poverty. Decreasing agricultural productivity and a shortage of food and commodities made life extremely difficult in the postwar subsidy period.[31] To go overseas, where "living conditions were better," was a means to reduce the burden on poverty-stricken families.

Studying abroad could raise a family's social status, as well as its standard of living. Because monthly stipends provided by the Russian government were considered insufficient, Hoa and her Vietnamese friends participated in the informal economy to make extra money. Hoa started small—sewing clothes in her free time to sell to Russians on the black market. After expanding her social networks, she and fellow students participated in the global trade in blue jeans, a highly desired commodity purchased in Thailand and shipped to Russia via Vietnam. "We had so many creative ideas to make money. And we were better at business," Hoa boasted, while describing how students purchased goods to send home to their families, who sold them for cash on the black market to supplement their meager salaries.[32]

Hoa trained in veterinarian sciences for a specific purpose—that of preventing poultry diseases in cooperative farming. Prior to market reforms in 1986, Vietnam's centrally planned economy required a precise mapping of future anticipated needs, including how many scientists were necessary in which particular fields.[33] Yet this domain-specific training proved problematic with the collapse of the Soviet Union. When Hoa returned in late 1987, economic reforms had been introduced and agricultural cooperatives were being dismantled. The state no longer had a job for Hoa nor a need for her expertise, as control of land and livestock returned to individual families. Hoa's scientific knowledge and skills for building a modern and prosperous socialist society had no place in a market-driven economy that valued her cultural capital quite differently.

Scholars of postsocialism have pointed to the difficulties people faced in translating and applying their socialist cultural capital to a global capitalist system.[34] This has also been the case in Vietnam. After their return, Soviet-trained specialists rarely worked in their fields of expertise. With few exceptions, these men and women had to reevaluate their skills and reinvent themselves for a vastly different knowledge economy. Tuyến, who holds a degree in chemical engineering from East Germany, has been able to use her language proficiency to work as a translator for German companies and government agencies. Others have remade themselves into entrepreneurs, drawing upon market skills acquired from years of informal trading. And still others have found secure, low-paid positions in government departments and ministries. Hoa seemed less fortunate, with no political connections or funds to start a business. In an economic milieu that considers English to be the language of capitalist prosperity, her Russian fluency positioned her squarely in relation to an "obsolete" socialist history. Hoa subsequently returned to school to study English and, like many other Soviet-trained professionals, took advantage of new employment opportunities that followed the expansion of overseas development assistance programs. Recognized as an educated woman with international experience, Hoa has since found employment with multiple foreign aid projects, earning up to five times the average government salary. Few people know that Hoa is a scientist with a graduate degree from a foreign university; she is aware that it does not carry the same status as newly minted degrees from the West. Yet these devalued and oft unspoken histories are anything but irrelevant, as they influence the formation of new modern and flexible subjectivities, and they also reveal the diverse ways, such as the birthday party, that knowledge and experiences gleaned from the socialist era continue to linger and shape contemporary encounters with modernity.

Aspiring Overseas Student (*Sinh viên du học*)
ERIK HARMS

Hương, who recently turned twenty-one, goes by "Kat" when speaking English to friends. She likes to be called "Kitty," and signs her e-mails, personal blog, and Facebook posts with the name, "Kat, aka Kitty."[35] Her e-mail address—hellokittysmile1988@yeehaw.com—is a name, a birthdate, and a philosophy-of-being in itself. She wears bright clothes with cartoon motifs, sports a colorful backpack, and always puts her fingers in a "V," cocks her head, hugs her companions, and grins from cheek to cheek in the many pictures she posts to her blog. She cultivates international friends, prefers speaking English whenever possible, browses the Internet at the World Bank reading room, and frequents public events at Hanoi's numerous international cultural venues—the Goethe-Institut, L'Espace, and the American Chamber of Commerce.

Currently enrolled in a top Vietnamese university in Hanoi, Hương-Kat-Kitty-hellokittysmile wants to go to college—a *foreign* college. She is an aspiring *sinh viên du học* (overseas Vietnamese student), sharing similar dreams as the approximately fifteen thousand Vietnamese who study outside of the country each year.[36] But unlike many of the other students—and despite her optimistic attempts to craft an idealized image of herself as a modern, cosmopolitan member of Vietnam's rising cohort of globally educated youth—she comes from an impoverished background. Multiple failed applications to foreign universities reveal that there remain distinct material limits to her ability to fully transform herself from Hương into hellokittysmile. She has been applying to universities around the world for three years now and, despite her strong English skills and extensive extracurricular activities, she hasn't left Hanoi. In 2008 she was admitted to one mid-level British college. But without financial aid, she could not attend.

Kat-Kitty's smile conceals a fractured home life. The attempt to transcend her circumstances, the difficulty of doing so, and her optimism in the face of adversity all epitomize modern Vietnamese aspirations. Her life also highlights how often such hopes are dashed by material limits. While she received a scholarship to attend and graduated with high marks from Hanoi's most prestigious high school, Hương grew up and still lives with her mother in

Hanoi's Nguyễn Công Trứ housing block, a crumbling socialist-era complex built between 1961 and 1963.[37] One afternoon in 2008, while leading a group of American students on a tour of Hanoi, a local scholar brought the group to a crowded tenement directly in the center of her block, which had been divided and subdivided several times over and housed several thousand more residents than originally intended. Pointing to the clogged sewers, impeded air shafts, overcrowded alleyways, makeshift market stalls, pell-mell disorder, and unhygienic conditions, the scholar pronounced this the worst housing in the entire city, a symbol of the city government's failure to secure safe liveli-hoods for the most vulnerable. Returning from their visit, several of Hương's American friends described their shock at seeing such living conditions. Hương listened silently. Later, in a quiet moment, she took me aside and con-fided, "That's my home." Hương lives in poverty, her father has a violent streak, and her mother survives by selling drinks to passersby in the street. But in her outwardly displayed international presentation of self, Kat-Kitty-hellokittysmile inhabits a virtual dreamworld of international possibility. Her cyberself often blurs with the self of her origins, but her origins always prove a dramatic challenge to the dreams she hopes to achieve.

Through the Internet—visiting college Web sites, e-mailing friends around the world, instant messaging, and posting on Facebook—hellokittysmile connects virtually with the world she hopes to inhabit for real. After scouting out the best colleges and universities in the world, she focused her sights on Oxbridge. Sponsored by a Hong Kong-based foundation that provides scholar-ships for Asia-based students to attend selected universities in the UK, Hương even flew to Malaysia for a prestigious university interview, making it to the final round. But the final results were, in the words of her rejection letter, "unfavourable." Her second choices included top-caliber American universi-ties and small liberal arts colleges, chosen according to the financial aid they offer to international students. In an e-mail to me, she described part of the inherently bilingual and eminently modern process: "Em dang fill common application va viet essays, sau do se la financial aids forms" (I'm filling out the common application and writing the essays, after that will be the financial aid forms). In e-mails like this, her language slips joyfully between English and Vietnamese, which is written, like many of her blog and Facebook posts, without diacritics. These e-mails are ebullient and full of life. But behind this playful code-switching lie the limits of language. The formal English of an application process can be as inhospitable as colloquial English may seem welcoming; slight errors reveal it as a shibboleth, a subtle marker of her in-ability to fully pass as the sophisticated international Other she hopes to be. Admissions officers, when receiving her e-mails, must surely wonder about the sophistication of an applicant with an e-mail like hellokittysmile1988. As a virtual avatar, hellokittysmile may have gained electronic entry into the world of university applications, admissions essays, and even secured fee waivers and scholarships to cover the costs for an interview in Malaysia, but this name also marks her as an outsider. Furthermore, Hương, the girl who lives in Nguyễn Công Trứ housing complex, can't afford the printing, the envelopes, and most certainly not the postage for her overseas applications. Despite fee waivers, she never managed to send the applications to the American universities. Postage simply cost too much.

Cham H'Roi Girl
TRUONG HUYEN CHI

H'Lien was thirteen when she first drove a motorcycle on her own in 2008.[38] She drove two heavy sacks of red beans to a bulk-buying tent at a local factory. The third child and first daughter in her family, Lien lives with her parents, four siblings, and a grandmother in a H'Roi hamlet in the foothills of the Central Highlands, half a day by bus from Tuy Hòa (Phú Yên Province). She dropped out of the village school after three tearful years trying to learn to read and write in Vietnamese. Now fourteen, Lien is a major working hand in her family. A kidney problem saved her eldest brother from military conscription, yet he is fit enough to join the family working on their fields of rice, sugarcane, and other crops. Lien and her mother share usual household chores, while their ailing grandmother looks after Lien's otherwise healthy "ghost-stricken" sister.

Both of Lien's parents brought a sizable area of land to their marriage, making her family among the well-to-do in the community. The recent sale of sugarcane to a nearby foreign-owned factory has secured daily consumption and occasional medical costs. Not all of Lien's friends in the hamlet, however, enjoy this new stability. Lack of access to resources, exclusion from the workforce, bad health, and misfortune keep their households in chronic poverty; half of Vietnam's ethnic minority population, or 13 percent of the country's eighty million, are in this category.[39]

More than twenty years since the Renovation (1986) and despite poverty reduction efforts, the gap in the standard of living between the Kinh majority and ethnic groups persists. While the Kinh prosper economically, the H'Roi and their ethnic minority counterparts are left behind in lagging regions. In 2006, the poverty rate for ethnic minorities was five times higher than for the Kinh and Chinese.[40] For better or for worse, Lien's hamlet continues to be listed as one of some three thousand villages qualifying for special government aid.

Despite the salient place devoted to the improvement of the material and cultural life of ethnic groups in the national discourse, the H'Roi are not an officially recognized minority.[41] There is some discontent among the elderly in Lien's community about their being grouped into the Cham. Having little in common with the coastal Hindu- or Islam-influenced Cham, the H'Roi identify themselves in the same social space with indigenous Central Highlanders. Youths of Lien's age feel the most immediate effects of the state classification. The irony is that while their hamlet is poor enough to qualify for government aid to turn old wooden houses into brick ones, the H'Roi as a local group are too small in number to justify a language program in schools. Lien and many of her peers never completed primary school, mostly due to their frustrated efforts in learning the national language. Without a high school diploma, H'Roi youths are excluded from local factory and administrative jobs; yet the prospect of having H'Roi as a language of instruction or a subject in the curriculum remains distant. In these ambivalent encounters with modernity, with state agendas shifting from socialist reconstruction to postsocialist restructuring, young people from those ethnic groups with a proportionately small population and without full state recognition like the H'Roi seem to be the most disadvantaged.

Lien experienced citizenship firsthand when her parents filed for a birth certificate to enroll her in primary school, or through the fact that conscription was recently waived for her brother. Lien's grandmother conjured up a more distant version of nationhood through recalling her evacuations from the battlefields between Việt Cộng (Communist) and Quốc Gia (Nationalist) almost forty years ago.[42] Their H'Roi country was devastated and divided by the war, much like that of the Montagnards.[43] Suffering from hunger and uncertainty continued to haunt their life through the 1980s, when the government was trying to turn a population it deemed backward into "new socialist men."[44] Nevertheless, instead of socialist modernity, more and more Central Highlanders have chosen evangelical modernity in the past two decades. The fact that they explicitly embrace alternative identities, just like their ethnic minority counterparts in the northern mountains and elsewhere, upsets the postsocialist construction of the Other: It is no longer the supposed backwardness of these populations that poses a threat to the advancement of the nation but instead transnationalism and a constant dynamism toward an ever-evolving and self-questioning sense of modernity.

Lien and her family have not joined the house church in their neighborhood. They remain ambiguous about both rituals and health and adopt a wide range of strategies. When Lien has a fever, a sacrificial ritual is performed to restore her spirit. Since her sister had a couple of seizures, a series of elaborate rituals was held to cure her from being possessed by unfavorable forces.[45] Nevertheless, Lien's mother frequently takes free medicines from the commune's health post. At other times, the family would not hesitate to try modern medicine. The grandmother was sent to Ho Chi Minh City for diagnosis of a tumor, while the son's kidney problem was thoroughly tested. A copy of their medical portfolios, including large X-ray negatives, is among the most impressive displays of modernity in Lien's house.

One evening when Lien, some of her friends, and I were strolling along the village road, a girl giggled and commented that they only needed to read well enough to sing karaoke. A year later, the same group of girls met me in a much more somber mood. They were sad about the news of the construction of a dam upstream that would flood the cultivation land of many villagers. Lien's family was among them. "My father said we would not take the compensation cash, whatever the rate," Lien said. "Without land what would we do?" Her eyes resembled the look of her grandmother recalling the despair of the war-torn life. Grievances and protests of land enclosure in the wake of development across the country are something the government is trying to contain. "What would you do then?" I press. "The factory only recruits the Kinh with diplomas. . . . I'll be a tailor; I'll make pretty clothes for my friends and relatives." The same eyes now reflected the joy and purposefulness of having a project in life, agency of intention,[46] and a refusal to be a victim of modernization.

Mountain Village Head (*Trưởng bản*)
CHRISTIAN C. LENTZ

Although almost everyone else was reaping rice in their hillside fields that October afternoon, the mountain village head (*trưởng bản*) stalked the roadside forest with a homemade crossbow. When I found Mr. K there, he appeared distracted by something weightier than small game. At his house, the normally hospitable host skipped the pleasantries of tea. He asked whether I had permission to visit, requested my papers, and recorded the details. He insisted we go report my arrival immediately.

On the road to Mường Phăng's commune offices, we met his intended interlocutor—the provincial policeman. They spoke in the region's lingua franca, the Black Thái language. Then, in terse Vietnamese, the policeman demanded my papers. He asked about what I did; who I worked with; my interest in the village. "It's like this," he grunted: "You are allowed to work in this village but you cannot sleep here. You are a foreigner and the conditions do not fit you. The food is inappropriate and your safety is not guaranteed. Therefore you must go to a hotel, sleep there, and return in the morning."

Back at his house, Mr. K paced around, complaining how "boring" and "exhausting" such procedures were. "If you want to eat here, you should get a letter of permission," he said. "This letter should state that eating here is acceptable." Was he serious, I wondered? Or was he satirizing the myriad forms of permission my visit required? His wife divulged that two commune officials had visited earlier and ordered her not to feed me. "If he eats with you, he will get sick to his stomach," they told her. No tea, indeed. Like her husband, she was upset.

I left distressed by my role in bringing them insult. Their home, his office too, had been ruled unsafe to host me overnight, their food unfit for me to eat. The officials had declared the village head and his wife too poor and dirty to host a foreigner.

My relationship with Mr. K had begun on different terms. When I first visited in August, accompanied by district and commune minders, he welcomed us warmly and with dignity. His wife brought us tea, which he poured into ceramic cups. He withdrew a notebook from the rafters and, without prompting, began to tell about village affairs. He identified the village as Khu Mu, which like all others in this region is organized around internal ethnic homogeneity. He read figures on agricultural area, crop type, and livestock. Because corn and rice suffered from pests, people in his village experienced hunger at least once and sometimes twice annually. The electricity and telephone service available in neighboring Black Thái villages stopped short of his.

Many village heads just rehearse such data in a ritualized state performance, but Mr. K distinguished himself through knowledge and concern. He knew residents not as abstract statistics but as living, breathing entities. Responsible for affairs of life and death, of economic production and social reproduction, the village head plays a leading role in communal life. As such, he also mediates relations at a scale larger than his own bailiwick. Concretely, ties of trade and kinship bind villages together. Abstractly, ethnicity is bound up in nation. Relationships of communal belonging are expressed through spatial metaphor as either "inside" or "outside." Yet the boundaries of one relationship alternately converge or diverge in relation to others. Khu Mu villages dot the borderland landscape noncontiguously; kinship and trade relations connect them across administrative boundaries of commune, district, province, and state. Being Khu Mu places one inside an ethnicity, but should one live nearby in Laos, one is outside the nation. Maintaining a communal relationship, therefore, may involve crossing a heavily policed boundary. Characteristic of modernity, the village head embodies a multiply fractured, sometimes contradictory orientation: an official split between administrative units and a communal leader straddling inside and outside social relations.

Just as acting communally and performing bureaucratically orient the village head in different directions, holding this position in the mountains around Điện Biên Phủ situates him in historically constructed relations of power. Tai speakers long ago settled this region and organized their villages into *muang*—spatial units of political organization and settlement, land, and labor management.[47] The Khu Mu served as bonded labor to Tai peoples, and later, French scholars described them as "primitive" and like "savages."[48] During and after the anticolonial war, many *muang,* like Mường Phăng, became modern Vietnamese districts or communes, their hereditary Thái leadership recognized as state officials.[49] Through the 1960s and 1970s, the ranks of local government were supplemented or supplanted by Communist Party loyalists from "downstream," many of whom resettled from the Red River Delta to these "sparsely populated" mountains.[50] The legacies of these migrations can now be seen in who holds what office. Many of Điện Biên's district and province officials are Kinh, while many in Mường Phăng's commune are Thái. "Because Khu Mu people do not have a king," said Mr. K, "we must listen to everything, listen to the Thái language and learn it as well." Although explaining his fluency in Black Thái, he also indicated how Khu Mu people have figured in and adapted to relations of spatialized, ethnicized domination.

Indeed, our autumn encounter points to the mountain village head as a figure central to the making of this frontier land's modern boundaries. He mediates between the official bureaucracy of modern Vietnam and the communal life of family, friends, and neighbors. Spatial lines demarcating where his village ends and another begins also signal forms of socially recognized difference that, over time, have become the basis for and justification of inclusions or exclusions. Acting as village head and being Khu Mu require negotiating these boundaries; transgressing them poses real hazards. As a foreign researcher, I complicated these boundaries, destabilizing categories of ethnicity and nation, state and space—all of which were otherwise so familiar to him. My presence not only prevented Mr. K from catching anything on that October hunt—it also ensnared him in a net beyond his own making.

Photo Retoucher
NINA HIEN

> *Turning the impossible into the possible*
> —Charm slogan, HAI BÀ TRƯNG STREET, HỒ CHÍ MINH CITY

One day at the Charm studio in the year 2000, a poor woman entered with her daughter to have a photograph taken. "Charm," a quality and object that promises beneficent and bewitching results, was a suitable name for a shop specializing in beautifying surfaces—especially one in which the alchemization of old photographs into efficacious amulets (specifically altar portraits for spiritual ancestor worship rituals) was being performed by photographers and digital photo technicians. These workshops were places where little and big material deceptions, as well as small acts of recovering what had been lost, were occurring many times every day.

The woman's face was terribly scarred, and Anh K, the main photographer and photo technician, speculated that she had been the victim of a fit of passion involving acid thrown in her face. Understandably shy because of her visual spectacle, she had entered only with a desire for a portrait with her daughter. But after the shot was taken, Anh K offered to fix her skin (retouch the image). His motivation was not for more money but to help her. A devout Catholic family man in his mid-forties, he had been an electrical engineer and had stumbled into the business in 1999 around the time that the country was going digital. At that point, billionaire Bill Gates was the top idol in a newspaper poll of Vietnamese youth (surpassing Hồ Chí Minh, to the horror of the state), computers were being considered the key to good fortune and fortunes, and Photoshop software was being integrated into vernacular photographic practices in *magical* ways.

These digital recoveries extended long-standing notions about the providential qualities that photographic images were thought to carry. Many people considered the photograph not only as an index of the subject but also as a live connection to it, following a popular Vietnamese saying, "Fixing the image [could] fix the fate." A future could also be destroyed by defacing a photograph, as another saying went, "to make it stink." It was dangerous if the wrong image were to fall into the wrong hands—but not if the right photograph fell into the right hands.

Technicians such as Anh K were the experts enacting the lucky touch. They were the equivalent of the specialists who made animate and efficacious icons of Buddha in dotting-of-the-eye ceremonies. With their digital handwork, they would "retouch to make beautiful" the images—the main service ordered by customers. Vague as these requests might have been, they seemed to know exactly what to do. They clearly had a common understanding of Vietnamese aesthetics and were entrusted as its interpreters, revivers of auras, and keepers and reproducers of authenticity. They mediated and negotiated the links between "traditional" customs and modern technologies, the realms of the material and the spiritual, the qualities of surface and depth, and the assertions of realism and idealism. At times perceived as experts, artists, magicians, and physiognomists, they often did not really know (or abide by) any timeworn customs. They would often invent customs as they went along.

Initially, Anh K had been skeptical about the process, which seemed overly superstitious to him (especially in a political climate where the state dogmatically denounced "superstitious" practices). He had just been looking to build a good business. In the process, however, his views changed. "I have found out a lot about mysterious things. Suppose photography can change a life?" Following what he considered a general logic of "Oriental philosophy from India," he observed, "The bodhisattva, who lives on a mountain, can change his 'aura' and bring a good effect to every creature. . . . Eight months ago I began working with photographs. When I [was] doing it, I always [thought] about goodness, although it does depend a lot on the technique. Eight months is not long enough to get a clear response. But many people *do* bring me baskets of fruit."

Not surprisingly, photography's arrival into Vietnam has been located in spiritualizing practices. When the first photo studio opened in the country in Hanoi in 1869, its name was The Road to Filial Piety, and it advertised the regeneration of the spirits of loved ones. Photographs eventually replaced name character tablets on altars because they were thought more effective at insuring that the correct souls visited the correct homes. Painted altar portraits have a long history, but only the wealthy could afford them. For painted portraits, the physiognomically accurate face had been essential. However, when photographic and then digital processes took hold, painted portraits dwindled and an accurate face was no longer the focus—likely because the photographs by their nature were thought to contain the genuine person already. Additionally, what probably bolstered the status of these practitioners as well (and the industry, too) was the historical detail that the great leader Hồ Chí Minh—under another pseudonym—had supported himself in Paris as a photo retoucher. (The museum at the Photographic Association of HCMC displays his business card, and apparently he once advised a photographer about the difficulty of erasing unlucky moles.[51])

Back at Charm, the finished product revealed that beyond erasing her scars, Anh K (by his own initiative influenced by the memory of a Vietnamese lullaby) had added a background of moonlight and bamboo to convey motherly love. He also lightened the skin tone of the daughter, which had appeared darker in contrast. And he straightened out the tiny smirk of her mouth. All this was intended to make the pair more "harmonious."

When the woman arrived to retrieve the final portrait, she exclaimed that she had "won the lottery!" Pronouncing the photo "a gift from heaven!" it was of no matter that the picture looked nothing like reality. More important was that this new image conveyed a sense of posterity. It could traverse time, fixing the past as well as redefining the future both materially and spiritually for them. And surely, Anh K received a huge fruit basket for that deed.

Cultural Expert (*Nghệ nhân*)
LAUREN MEEKER

As my friend and I rounded a corner in the nearly deserted streets of Lim Town, Bắc Ninh Province, at lunchtime during the 2005 Lim Festival, we heard the amplified strains of a *quan họ* folksong echoing nearby. In a small auto parts shop, we encountered a group of young and middle-aged men sitting down to eat lunch and sing. We excused ourselves for interrupting and stopped to ask a few questions: I asked if they were *nghệ nhân,* and they responded that no, they were simply ordinary laborers who loved *quan họ.* Today, they said, they were just "festival singing" and relaxing with friends from another village because they enjoyed singing *quan họ.* They explained that they had learned to sing and preserve *quan họ* from *nghệ nhân* in their village but were not themselves *nghệ nhân.*

Nghệ nhân is defined as amateur artisans or folk performers who have reached a high level of expertise in a craft or folk performance genre and who are also actively involved in passing on this skill to subsequent generations. While the term has long been used to designate skilled folk practitioners, in recent years it affords official recognition to certain people.[52] Use of the term conveys a deliberate attempt to maintain Vietnamese cultural specificity, but it also implicitly references an international context of cultural exchange. According to ethnomusicologist Tô Ngọc Thanh, while UNESCO calls them "Living Human Treasures," the Vietnamese "are already accustomed to calling these people *nghệ nhân.*"[53] As Vietnam works to increase the visibility of its cultural heritage in international venues, the term *nghệ nhân* has taken on added layers of meaning that directly reference that international context.

Why is the ordinary laborer who is also a singer trained by *nghệ nhân* not a *nghệ nhân* him or herself? What could be more culturally authentic in the socialist nationalism of the Vietnamese state than the laborer who embodies a traditional folk form? If the men above are not *nghệ nhân,* then who are the *nghệ nhân?* The "most typical *nghệ nhân*" include named individuals: Nguyễn Văn Thị, Ngô Thị Nhi, Nguyễn Thị Kước, Nguyễn Thị Bé, Vũ Thị Chịch, Nguyễn Thị Nguyên.[54] These men and women are all *quan họ* singers from Bắc Ninh. The list of names at once references the abundance of the Vietnamese cultural heritage and asserts an equivalency of names that enables them to be collectively representative as *nghệ nhân.* Unlike the men at Lim, these "most typical *nghệ nhân*" have been *officially* recognized as living embodiments of traditional *quan họ* practice and essential agents of transmission of that practice.

For the state, the *nghệ nhân* represent cultural, political, and economic interests of the nation. The figure of the *nghệ nhân* makes a fleeting appearance in the 2001 Law on Cultural Heritage. In Chapter 3, Article 26, the government declares its policy to value *nghệ nhân* and their importance to the preservation and popularization of traditional arts. *Nghệ nhân* now appear in law because "the treasury of intangible cultural heritage is held in the memories of the *nghệ nhân.*"[55] *Nghệ nhân* quite literally embody the intangible cultural heritage of Vietnam.

Perhaps the hesitation on the part of the men in Lim to self-identify as *nghệ nhân* stemmed from an unspoken understanding that *nghệ nhân* is title, not practice. The Lim singers, like the *nghệ nhân,* are the practice of *quan họ,* the everyday singers who sing for love of the song. What they *do* is what makes the designation of *nghệ nhân* possible in the heritage nation. Yet they fall outside the title itself. Those who are not designated *nghệ nhân* or who do not self-identify with the term are left in an ambiguous place. Regardless of what they actually do, they remain outside the authenticity net cast by cultural workers. In today's Vietnam, *nghệ nhân* is less a state of being than a title designating a publicly appointed person who is a repository of valuable cultural knowledge.

To qualify as title, the *nghệ nhân* must meet an age requirement: they must be at least seventy years old (in 2005), a calculation based on age at the time of the August 1945 Revolution.[56] In other words, *nghệ nhân* were physically present, fully trained, and singing in the prerevolutionary past. In order to be representative of the cultural heritage, the *nghệ nhân* must quite literally be rooted in social traditions of the past. The younger men at Lim, therefore, do not qualify for the title, despite similarities in social practice. Such practices are the heart of the concept of cultural heritage but are now representative only when originating in the memories of the aged *nghệ nhân.*

The *nghệ nhân* represent a tension between representing culture and embodying culture that intensifies in concert with Vietnamese institutional efforts to codify and "brand" cultural heritage through international organizations such as UNESCO.[57] The *nghệ nhân* are intimately bound up in (and perhaps by) the global market for culture. In that market, *nghệ nhân* are cultural resources that help drive up the value of Vietnamese traditional culture.[58] The *nghệ nhân* is also a political mask or "front" that is institutionalized in the context of the global market for culture and that "tends to take on meaning and stability apart from the specific tasks which happen at the time to be performed in its name."[59] The body of the *nghệ nhân* is designated as the medium through which culture is transformed into capital in a world hungry for heritage. In this process, the figure of the *nghệ nhân* is the mediating body that allows two seemingly incompatible realms—the culture market and lived culture—to appear to coexist.

Vietnamese Transnational(s)
IVAN SMALL

It is 8 a.m. but already sweltering in the coastal town of Quy Nhơn, where I am sipping coffee at a café with Hải and his friend Vinh. Vinh has just returned from San Jose, California, now staying for a month in his old home.[60] I ask him how he feels about returning to Vietnam from America, sparking a conversation comparing the two countries. "The U.S. is a good place to make money, but life in Vietnam is happier." Scowling at the isolation and hard work of Vietnamese life in America, Hải explains, "I have a green card, I can go back and forth. I stay there six months with my daughter, but my life is here. My daughter, her life is in San Jose. There are more opportunities because she is young. But we can live in both places and be a family."

Hải, Vinh, and Hải's daughter—Vietnamese who maintain footings in both Vietnam and the United States—represent a growing body of Vietnamese "transnationals" able to take advantage of improved economic, legal, and travel opportunities to establish multiple lives and identities in and across geographical worlds and generations. Over repeated visits to Quy Nhơn in 2008 and 2009, I would regularly visit Hải, listening to his stories about life in California and Texas. Yet in the end he was always content to return to Vietnam and his modest house by the ocean. Hải often said that America made Vietnamese into better Vietnamese—the "environment," in his view, provided opportunities and resources that facilitated character development. He was quick to add, however, that one must retain links to the homeland (*quê hương*)—to "stay Vietnamese."

Quy Nhơn is typical of many south-central coast towns in that there was large-scale participation in the boat refugee exodus of the 1970s and 1980s, leaving an indelible impact on local kinship networks: over half the people have relatives abroad and many of the current residents have their own memories of attempted escape by sea. The ocean horizon invites one to imagine the hypotheticals of a life on the other side of it, and there is a strong correlation between overseas networks, family remittances, and personal migratory desires. Hải's ability to negotiate between different Vietnamese lifeworlds in the United States and Vietnam offers insight into the allure of mobility and the perceived possibilities of collective social transformation through transnational living.

The Vietnamese transnational has been structurally facilitated by significant policy changes in the United States and Vietnam in the last decade and a half. First, the reestablishment of diplomatic and trade relations allowed for increased return migration and economic opportunities as Vietnam

sought greater integration with the global economy.[61] Overseas Vietnamese—
especially in the United States, where three-quarters of the diaspora reside—
provided important social and economic capital, linguistic capabilities,
and political and business connections to help facilitate this. Secondly, the
Vietnamese government has moved to embrace the overseas (Việt Kiều)
population. Politburo Resolution 36 (2004) declared overseas Vietnamese to
be an "integral part of the nation" and was followed by policy measures to
stimulate and facilitate transnational movement.[62] In the past decade, return
visits from overseas Vietnamese have expanded significantly: half a million
individuals such as Vinh now return annually to visit their homeland.[63] The
reestablishment of kinship and social networks has likewise facilitated family reunifications and transnational marriages, whereby overseas Vietnamese
sponsor relations in Vietnam for emigration, such as Hải, and forge new con-
jugal bonds with friends and confidants, as was the case with Hải's daughter.

For many Vietnamese participants and spectators of international mobility, transnational life offers an ideal identity, free of the structural social and
economic barriers often blamed on a corrupt, failed socialist government, as
well as the racism and isolation acknowledged as endemic to the experiences
of Vietnamese overseas who have neither the time nor resources to return
to the "homeland."[64] The opportunities for Hải's family to move back and
forth—to take elements of different worlds and combine them into a single
transnational life—not only gives Hải personal satisfaction but offers a chance
for his children to "become better Vietnamese" beyond Vietnam while retaining connections within it.

Hải's migratory passage from the familiar to the radically unknown highlights a form of modern diasporic agency more "routed" than "rooted" in
practice.[65] The modern individual, as Immanuel Kant might have it, is one
whose life is not patterned by past circumstances. Kant departs from earlier
philosophical inquiries by asserting the ability of the modern subject to think
for oneself "without the aid of experience."[66] The "modern," as such, lives
actively and transcendentally at the cusp of existence, with no blueprint from
the past to guide him. The future is unknown, because one asserts the agency
to make it so rather than falling back on past patterns of cognition, experience,
and expectations. Kant's emphasis on the individual agency of the modern,
however, understates the intersubjective condition of its emergence. The modern is also spectral. Benedict Anderson argues that with technologies of communication and long-distance travel come heightened regimes of ontological
comparison. The once distant Other becomes recognizable and inhabitable,
even more so with the proliferation of familiar diasporic bodies overseas.[67]

Hải's transnational social aspirations are not singular. Rather, they reside within a networked identity in which his daughter's future life is vicariously and imaginatively apprehended. Hải crossed the migratory bridge to America through connections like Vinh: friends and family who went previously and subsequently sponsored his emigration. Hải extended that bridge to his daughter by arranging her marriage to a Vietnamese American. Hải actively forges a transnational and transgenerational identity characterized by global mobility, capital, agency, and heterogeneous belonging in which collective and comparative familial transformation across generations and communities is a gauge of aspiration and success.[68] The social evolution of such transnational figures beyond and between the horizons is followed with keen interest by a new generation of Vietnamese, who gaze, like Hải, across the ocean and into the future to construct and imagine lives beyond their experiential grasp.

CAMBODIA

Edited by JONATHAN PADWE

For much of the past century, Cambodian political life has alternated between authoritarian regimes and periods of instability when competing factions struggled to obtain control of state power. The most recent such period of political struggle emerg ed in the years following the national election of 1993. Organized by the United Nations Transitional Authority in Cambodia, the 1993 election was intended to put the country on a course for greater autonomy after more than a decade of rule by the Vietnamese-backed People's Republic of Kampuchea (PRK).[1] As it turned out, the decade that began with Cambodia's first relatively free election since 1951 saw the unfolding of a winner-takes-all competition for political power that was analogous in some ways to the immediate postcolonial period—a precarious moment when the future shape of rule was yet to be determined. By the beginning of the new millennium, however, that competition had run its course: deftly and often ruthlessly outmaneuvering political rivals, Prime Minister Hun Sen and his close-knit group of political allies and financial backers were able to take firm control of the levers of state power. "This decisive melding of bureaucratic, military and economic power," writes historian Steve Heder, "is rooted in a sea change of socioeconomic transformation driven by this . . . predatory entrepreneurial elite."[2] The figures of Cambodian modernity presented in this chapter inhabit a terrain shaped by the political struggles of the 1990s and by the consolidation of power that followed them.

It is a terrain marked by expropriation and dislocation, disenfranchisement, and the abuse of human rights. In the early 1990s, Cambodia seemed poised to participate in a global phenomenon of democratization set in motion by the collapse of the Soviet Union and the end of the Cold War. The hopes of the international community for such an outcome translated into an outpouring of donor funding for the war-torn country and contributed to the emergence of Cambodia's burgeoning nongovernmental "sector." Indeed, the offices of NGOs and internationally sponsored humanitarian projects became a prominent feature of the country's cultural landscape, serving as symbols of the possibility of national and personal advancement, inculcating behaviors among Cambodia's numerically insubstantial middle class and, in the process, helping to define a contemporary understanding of what Cambodian modernity is all about. Yet for all their determination to strengthen civil society in Cambodia, the combined efforts of foreign governments, multilateral institutions, NGOs, and a smattering of local social movements have made little headway against a rising tide of patronage and crony capitalism.

With the increasing consolidation of power and wealth that has followed the end of armed struggle in the country, inequality has also increased dramatically, a fact that underscores the incongruity of what has become an annual political ritual in Cambodia: each year, donor countries hold a consultative meeting to pledge new aid to the government (the 2010 pledge was a record U.S. $1 billion), and each year the UN Office of the High Commissioner for Human Rights releases a new report providing damning evidence of abuses such as land grabbing and expropriation, the suppression of free speech, corruption, and political impunity. The 2007 report noted that "deliberate and systemic violations of human rights have become central to the government's hold over power."[3] How has it come to this? Here the prime minister, his opponents, and his critics agree on at least one explanation for the current state of affairs: the Khmer Rouge revolution played an important role in bringing the country to this point. The legacy of Democratic Kampuchea—the regime responsible for the deaths of up to two million people—continues to play an important role in social and political life today, and memory of the period remains a powerful cultural force.

For Walter Benjamin, to experience the unfolding ruin of the European bourgeoisie in the twentieth century was to inhabit a dream that was dreamt in the Paris Arcades in the nineteenth, and he quotes Michelet to the effect that "every époque dreams the one that follows."[4] Such an insight might help to account for a troubling observation that joins the experience of all of the figures of Cambodian modernity assembled in this chapter: their ability to understand and act within the present moment is conditioned disproportionately by events that took place over thirty years ago. If we can imagine, with Giorgio Agamben, that "the birth of the camp in our time appears as an event that decisively signals the political space of modernity itself," then perhaps we can also imagine that Cambodia was, for a time, the capital of the twentieth century, and that the world of postconflict authoritarianism and postsocialist development that these figures inhabit was dreamt during the cataclysm that continues to hold sway over their lives.[5]

Given the centrality of Democratic Kampuchea to explanations of what ails Cambodia's path to "development" today, it is important to recognize that the Khmer Rouge regime represented one possible outcome of the modern project.[6] The regime's attitudes toward centralized planning, productivity, and the utility of human life reveal high-modernist aspirations that could never accommodate social reality, just as the Khmer Rouge rice field, cut into 100 x 100-meter grids, could never accommodate the realities of hydrology and topography.[7] And yet today, the Khmer Rouge regime is imagined as an effort to reject or turn away from modernity, rather than as a culmination of its possibilities. So it is without irony that the prime minister uses the word "anarchy" (*anathipitey*) to refer to the Khmer Rouge, whose regime was more fixated than most on the centralized control not only of people's labor and time but also of the most intimate aspects of human existence.[8] In his oratory, "anarchy" serves as a sort of a code word: the prime minister frequently asserts that his party's rule and his government's muscular use of power is justified by the need to overcome anarchical forces that would return the country to war.

This combination of a rapidly shifting political economy coupled with a postwar that seems never to come to a close is one of the defining characteristics of the contemporary Cambodian moment. It is a problem that fosters the emergence of new forms of governmental and cultural practice, and in the process it brings into existence new figures of modernity. The figures presented in this chapter are all articulated in relation to these projects and are positioned among these and a series of concurrent cultural forces. The World Musician, Kong Ney, is dislocated for a second time after being evicted from the building where he'd taken up residence as a squatter; at the same time, a world tour under the auspices of Peter Gabriel's international musical juggernaut places him directly in the current of the mid-90s moment of global opportunity and reconfigures the relevance of his music for young Khmers (Mamula). The Government Official, Dr. Dara, occupies a newly open space in the bureaucracy, a space from which she is called upon to translate an emerging international discourse of medical ethics for a national research apparatus that is only now taking shape after years of dysfunction (Grant). The Cham Modernizer, Abupaka, leads a program of cultural preservation that contends not only with the legacy of ethnic and religious persecution under the Khmer Rouge but also with the emerging challenges posed by international Islamic orthodoxy (Pérez-Pereiro). For these and the other figures assembled here, the past provides important material from which individuals construct their present, even as the challenges posed by living in the present inform the ways they understand the past.

Cham Modernizer (*Neak sakammniyum Cham*)
ALBERTO PÉREZ-PEREIRO

Arriving at the village, I was greeted by Abupaka and his band of students—nine boys and girls. Armed with notebooks, pens, pencils, rulers, and a large piece of construction paper, they gathered around a low table, anxiously waiting for the elder to arrive with the texts. One of the girls explained that they were going to copy a document onto paper so they could study it without damaging the fragile original. A man in his sixties emerged from his house with a bundle of documents. These were texts that he had handwritten himself and hidden during the Khmer Rouge period. As the document was produced, the students, under the direction of Abupaka, carved out a grid pattern on the paper, with each student taking responsibility for copying a section. Most of the text was written in Cham characters, with titles of sections written in Arabic. Although the students knew the Cham writing system, they worked slowly, sounding out each syllable until the sound in their head matched a word that they knew. There are few opportunities for reading and writing in Cham, so while they understood the script, they had not fully internalized it. Their difficulties notwithstanding, it is remarkable to find people in this age bracket with any degree of Cham literacy, much less nine at a time.

To be sure, these students did not simply come together on their own. They represent an attempt by Abupaka to cultivate a generation of young Cham devoted to the protection of their language and culture. Abupaka and his students are members of the community of Imam San, a subdivision of the Muslim Cham minority in Cambodia. Unlike other Muslims, however, they maintain a strong sense of attachment to their history as an independent people living along the littoral of the South China Sea in what is today central Vietnam. As a result, the community has been loath to abandon practices that are believed to originate in their former homeland. Some of these are seen as aberrations by the rest of the Muslim community, such as the custom of praying once a week instead of five times daily. Others are regarded as fundamentally un-Islamic. Most prominent among these is a spirit possession ceremony in which members of the community are visited by the souls of the royal family of Champa and their court.

The Cham modernizer, as represented by Abupaka, has emerged as an agent for making the traditions of this minority group relevant in a context where they are under severe pressure from foreign Muslims to purge their practices of any non-Islamic elements. In recent years, the number of Muslims coming from abroad to proselytize and the number of Cambodian Muslims traveling abroad to study religion have both dramatically increased. Cambodia's Muslims are often regarded as being on the periphery of the Islamic world, without proper access to religious teaching. The community of Imam San, with its unorthodox prayer practices and communion with spirits, is portrayed as everything that is wrong with this state of ignorance. As a result, well-funded missionaries from the Middle East, Pakistan, and Malaysia have enjoyed considerable success in convincing Muslims to abandon older practices and embrace a view of Islam as a pure, unitary religion without local variation. There is no place in the new community for those who refuse these fundamentalist interpretations. The community of Imam San is excluded from charity projects, and its members are scorned for their obstinacy in refusing religious teachings from the Middle East—the source of the faith.

Unwilling to abandon their traditions and their connections to historic Champa, Cham modernizers have resolved to protect their heritage by adopting the practices, techniques, and habits of modern people as exhibited by the Khmer state and foreign non-Muslims. Trips to the National Museum in Phnom Penh have inspired them to undertake their own heritage protection projects, such as preserving manuscripts and other cultural artifacts. This is done not only as a way of maintaining a connection to an ideal past but also as a way of showing both parity with the Khmer in whose state they are living and superiority to those "cultureless" Muslims who slavishly follow the dictates of foreigners while discarding their own Cham identity.

Abupaka has spent the past several years gathering sympathetic students and instructing them on the importance of presenting themselves as modern people who are able to speak English and possess documentation of formal education and even business cards (whether they have ever been employed or not). Abupaka has also been able to provide material support to these students, as his job at a local NGO has made it possible for him to subsidize the university education of eleven students. These students are seen both to bring technical expertise into the community and to act as advocates for the interests of their people—a task that their grandfathers, for all their knowledge of Cham tradition, could never hope to perform without the requisite linguistic and social skills.

As the students copy the manuscript, the old man thanks me for attending, because they would need the help of foreigners to fend off the missionaries. Abupaka chimes in, explaining how many foreigners, sympathetic to the plight of the community of Imam San, have helped not so much with money, although some have, but rather with knowledge. "The young people are protecting our language and culture," the old man says. "They will learn many new things at school and in the city and they will use it to protect the community."

World Musician (*Neak pleng antarachiet*)
STEPHEN MAMULA

As a charismatic performer both prior to and following the Khmer Rouge regime in Cambodia and as a musician who commands increasing attention on the "world music" stage, Kong Ney is a difficult man to get ahold of. But finally, after repeated interview attempts in July of 2009, I found myself waiting for him in the damp heat of a Phnom Penh NGO where he teaches, performs, and lives with his family. He emerges from a rehearsal room door at Cambodia Living Arts, a tiny but illuminating figure attired in graceful white silk, aided by an assistant and smiling generously. It is to his stunning presence that I extend my hand, which he carefully clasps and examines tactilely, scrutinizing my character, it seems, via sensoria refined by decades of blindness. In his embrace I feel physical frailty and ponder the experiences of his life: civil war, revolution, genocide, his displacement and existence as a squatter for years, and political instability stretching to the present day.

Facing me, only paces away, Kong erupts in song, his extraordinary tone instantly recognizable: wailing, soaring, serpentine, and in this intimate context, unmediated by amplification. In addition to his astonishing voice and the *chapai,* a two-stringed guitar he plays, Kong communicates kinesically, *grooving* bodily to the musical pulsations that he generates and that appear to generate song and story in him. Experiencing Kong's performance sparks memories of the great Chicago bluesmen, West African Griots, or Sufi praise singers. Their sounds and meanings are similarly oriented: tangibly corporeal and inextricably tied to both the suffering and triumphs of the human (or divine) spirit. All are steeped in distinct, deeply rooted expressive traditions that nonetheless breach boundaries of cultural context, intimating a universal communication.

Kong Ney's significance is multilayered: artistic, social, political, and cross-cultural. Within today's Cambodian modernity, his importance is as a mediator between poles of popular and traditional musical style, urban and rural geography, stable and dislocated residential experience, and age and youth. Not insignificantly, Kong's musical repertory, style, and instrumental technique, which might easily be consigned to the category of highly traditional folk and classical forms, today serve as flexible templates, adapted by a new generation of musicians and syncretically integrated with components of popular music—electric instruments, modern harmonies, Western song forms, and pop dance rhythms. Along with a handful of surviving artists who are often taken as representatives of an earlier era, the music of Kong Ney reverberates in altered form, in translation, on dance floors of Phnom Penh nightclubs and in the diasporic music of North American bands such as Dengue Fever, Prach Lee, and the Khmer Fusion Project. These are performers who merge traditional form with alternative rock, hip-hop, and experimental jazz styles, respectively. On the flipside, this syncretism (and the mass media through which it flows) functions as a backdoor intro to classical Khmer styles for Cambodian youth. It is one source for the enthusiasm and ease with which Cambodian teenage girls will enact a semblance of *apsara* dance among friends or indeed at the request of a Western researcher.

Kong's artistic import is thus twofold. He is, on the one hand, an icon for the revivalists and an anchor of traditionalism in a Cambodia where such movements respond at an emotional level to recent history. On the other hand, he is also a catalyst for new and emerging creative forms that respond to similar cues by moving in the opposite direction. Moreover, and importantly, his musical sensibility transcends the purely aesthetic, engaging symbolic domains of suffering, dislocation, and survival. His vast repertory of songs educates his listeners musically, politically, and historically:

> For three years we suffered unforgettable hardship;
> Everything was destroyed.
>
> Blood was spilled and children orphaned;
> Cambodia became a place of killing.
>
> They forced the people to dig and plow . . .
> Exhausted they fell . . . to the ground, bodies
> swollen, tired and hopeless.

To place Kong in historical context is to foreground the links that connect him to a line of performance masters extending back to the age of Angkor. Only 10 percent of Cambodia's musicians, singers, and dancers are estimated to have survived the Khmer Rouge. Following their defeat in 1979, Kong reemerged publicly within the context of the squatter complex where he lived in Phnom Penh. The Bassac complex, built in 1966 and popularly known as "the Building," was designed by Van Molyvann, an icon of postindependence Cambodia's highly stylized period of modernist architecture. The complex included the National Theater, in addition to a series of apartment buildings where

Kong lived and that would, in recent years, become renowned for housing among its multitude of squatters dozens of highly skilled performers—some survivors and some born in the aftermath of war. The Building was partially destroyed in 2008 and 2009 to make room for the city's growing hotel and leisure industry—an industry that now has displaced those same musicians it employs, forcing them to the outskirts of the city.

Prior to the Building's destruction, Kong was ascribed "living master" status by Cambodia Living Arts. He gained considerable attention in 2006 when legendary rock artist and world-music producer Peter Gabriel arranged for Kong and his pupil Ouch Save to make a three-week performance tour through twelve UK cities and recorded him on his internationally distributed Real World label.

Listening to Kong play, such a short distance from me, it is easy to become lost in the musical sounds themselves, even as those sounds have powerful roots within the social politics of Cambodian modernity. His placement within today's Cambodia is remarkable for the dual dislocations that frame it, the first engendered by a surfeit of violence during the war and the second by a surfeit of development after it. And yet, displacements of this sort are the norm in Cambodia, and it is displacement that most clearly links what is unique and iconic about Kong Ney with what is representative. For in many ways, Kong's experience reflects that of many Khmers. His life has been intricately caught up in the disruptions of the past, yet his current livelihood is tied not only to the intrusions of global commerce but also to the opportunities it affords. His life is impossible in the absence of an intimate association with the formations of modern governance—he lives, after all, in an NGO. He relies on the tourists who buy his recordings, even as their hotels have displaced his house. His music is traditional, yet it is a traditionalism mediated by "global" aesthetics and attached, for Cambodians, to a series of contemporary narratives about the meaning of the past. Kong Ney's experiences at once reveal the fragility of expressive culture and the multiple forces operating to restore it in what continues to be a highly precarious *now* in Cambodian history.

Village Police Chief (*Me pos polis nouv knong phum*)
EVE ZUCKER

Village Police Chief Phal and his partners, Nhim and Por, were engaged in banter at the small three-sided palm-leaf shelter that constituted the village police post. They were having their evening meal, which today was sautéed snake with boiled rice. The repartee, however, was interrupted when a small group of men and a woman with sacks slung over their shoulders wandered in from the wilderness to the west. Phal called one of the men over and began questioning him: "What's your name? Where are you from? Where are you going? What are you carrying?" The man, initially nervous, seemed to relax a little as the questioning eased into mild joking. He was then dismissed, but not without a passing final remark: "Carrying personal belongings . . . yeah, right . . . carrying weapons!" The exercise of power was clear, even if this time it was without the typical extraction of a small fee or bribe for passage.

Working for the state was nothing new to Phal. He had served in the government armed forces before becoming a policeman, and prior to that he lived under the Khmer Rouge. In fact, even his wedding was part of a state plan. During Democratic Kampuchea, the Khmer Rouge had selected a wife for Phal and married them in a group wedding ceremony. This form of marriage was considered a modern replacement for traditional marriages, and it shifted the focus from the union of individuals and families to a union with the state.

Phal, now in his late forties, remains married to the same woman and they have three children. He is a practicing Buddhist and a respected member of his village community, located just outside the provincial capital. In the remote village that is Phal's post (and my field site), Phal takes his police work very seriously. He made this clear to me one evening when taking out his police badge, explaining that it empowered him to enforce the law. It is his job, he elaborated, to ensure that those in the vicinity of his post act in accordance with the law and it is his job to report (and possibly arrest) them if they do not. In another conversation, Phal told me he is an outsider to the local population, a position that is partly expressed in his living quarters, which consist of a small temporary shack shared with other policemen. Here he keeps his uniform, his gun, and little else. His family remains back at his large, comfortable home near the provincial capital.

In his home village, Phal is viewed as an upstanding citizen, despite the fact that much of his earnings have been derived from bribes. In Cambodia the police extract bribes at checkpoints and other sites of engagement with the local citizenry. The system is pervasive, since state workers' salaries are too low to support an individual and his or her family, and people therefore seek to subsidize their earnings by other—often illegal—means.

Through his activities as a policeman, Phal sees himself as a representative of the modern Cambodian state. But Phal signifies Cambodian modernity in other ways, too. He is extremely good at adapting to shifting ideologies, trends, and circumstances—a skill he developed to survive in radically changing political and social circumstances.[9] Like many Cambodians of his age who have lived through unimaginable upheaval, Phal expects change and understands that survival means remaining flexible and adapting to new conditions.

It is perhaps this tolerance of change that allows Phal to be accepting of his teenage son's concerns and lifestyle, which at least on the surface radically conflict with his own. This son, at least on occasion, is a *kathoey,* the Khmer term for a transgender individual.[10] In Phal's home, his son's fashion sketches were on display, as were photographs of him appearing as both a male and a female. Phal told me that his son has enjoyed dressing in female attire since he was a child. At the annual harvest festival in Phal's village, his son and his companions enjoyed creating a spectacle by cross-dressing for the occasion. Phal, with some amusement, introduced his son and the "queen" of the group to his guests at the festival. Such openness adds layers to Phal's identity as a former soldier and a policeman. It also makes him more "modern," at least according to what today is considered modern in Cambodia. Cross-dressing, as Phal explained to me, is considered today to be an act of freedom that can only be achieved in peacetime. And so, Phal not only accepts his son's cross-dressing as an expression of modern Cambodia, he also sees it as a means for him and his son to perform their modernity.

Expressions of Khmer modernity are anchored in Cambodia's history, which has demanded that people craft their identities to suit changing regimes and sociopolitical cultures. In the postconflict environment of his police post, Phal sees himself—and others see him—as a representative of the state. But people also recognize him as an individual who sometimes uses that power for illicit personal gain. In Phal's home village, meanwhile, he is a modern father celebrating the freedom of peace vis-à-vis his gender-shifting son while retaining respect within his community for his knowledge of tradition. Like his son, Phal shifts identities with changing circumstances. For Phal, such shifts are intrinsic to being modern in Cambodia.

Broken Woman (*Srey kouc*)
ANNUSKA DERKS

Mao sat on the floor of a brothel in a slum in the center of Phnom Penh, with her friends Li, Rha, and Mom, contemplating their lives as sex workers. They were well aware how society judges "broken women" (*srey kouc*), or "women who sell their bodies," depicting them as "shameless," "extremely bad," "cheap," and "lower than the sole of a shoe." Mao described a scene in which an elderly woman walked by a group of sex workers and spat on the floor to show her contempt. She thinks a lot about the difficulties she faces and is afraid she may die soon. But, as Li remarked, since they were all *kouc haey* (broken or spoiled already), they can just as well continue earning money and make the best of it. After all, they agreed, compared to the villages where they came from, now they at least experience some excitement. They can have fun, go out with their boyfriends, eat new kinds of food, sleep in concrete houses under a fan, and dress up every day.

After being banned during the Khmer Rouge era, prostitution reemerged before booming during the United Nations Transitional Authority in Cambodia (UNTAC) period and the economic liberalization of the 1990s. The sex worker has thus become a prominent figure in contemporary Cambodia. Her appearance dominates certain corners and times of Phnom Penh's street scene. Her existence has given rise to a whole industry of related professions, from running brothels to running shelters. She is said to attract thousands of tourists to the country. She is the main character in numerous reports written by concerned NGOs. She is the focus of attention of various health programs and experiments. Municipal decrees and national laws are devoted exclusively to her. And she stirs discussions about the moral future of a nation that is striving to leave behind its recent history of war and destruction and to enter a new era of prosperity, development, and modernity.

Sex work in Cambodia takes many forms, occurs in diverse places, and involves various arrangements. The women (and to a lesser extent men) involved are underaged as well as adults, from rural as well as urban backgrounds, illiterate as well as educated, Cambodian as well as Vietnamese, full-time workers as well as occasionally taking up a client. Most engage in what consists of a large gray area of commercial sex practices, where blurred lines distinguish between what is called direct sex work, offered in brothels and in public parks, and indirect forms of sex work, such as those found in coin-rubbing places, massage parlors, karaoke shops, bars, beer gardens, or under the guise of beer promotion work in restaurants.

This diversity of venues and forms has emerged in part because of the complex politics of prostitution, in which the state's recurrent repression of the practice is intimately tied up with state officials' involvement in it as patrons and clients of the sex trade, as a source of economic gain and masculine status. The periodic crackdown has not contributed to the extinction of sex work; it has merely led to a dispersal of the practice and a constant renewal of its form. This diversity makes it extremely difficult to actually typify a sex worker—indeed, *the* sex worker does not exist. Yet, as a figure she does reveal the tension within contemporary Cambodia between the quest for economic gain, power, and modernity and the fear of decay, immorality, and foreign influences.

The sex worker has become intimately linked with this new era but is considered to have lost what is critical to being Khmer: namely to be proper men and women.[11] Women like Mao are regarded as "broken" (*kouc*): physically because of their loss of virginity and socially because of their improper behavior, as they speak in ways, are active at times, occupy spaces, and take liberties that are not open to "virtuous" women.[12] Hence, to many Cambodians the sex worker is associated with the dangers and negative consequences of becoming "too modern" (*toansamay peek*). This tension is felt at the personal level, where women like Mao struggle in their daily lives. Her parents died years ago, and as the oldest daughter she was responsible to support her younger brother, now staying with an aunt who "comes to get money every day" and threatens to leave the boy in the brothel with Mao when she stops providing money. Thus by invoking her obligations as a dutiful daughter, Mao validates her career as a "broken woman."

A year after the discussion that opened this essay, I met Mao again in the park near the Independence Monument. It was around 8 o'clock in the evening and still early for finding clients. The atmosphere was joyful, with groups of young women with whitened faces, red lips, and tight T-shirts chatting, joking, and frolicking with the young men who served as pimps. Mao was not dressed up for work, though. The brothel where she had worked the year before had been burned down by the government authorities, and she had been forced to move. She told me that her boyfriend gave her money the nights she did not work and that, instead of taking clients herself, she had started putting up sex worker friends with customers in order to earn money. Doing sex work had become increasingly difficult, not only because of her age (at twenty-three, she was considered "old") and her dwindling energy but also because of the daily struggles with police and clients. Yet it was exactly because of her years of experience and her ability to vocalize the growing difficulties in sex work that Mao was able to take up a new role—namely as the *praothien srey,* or peer leader, in an NGO effort to empower and increase HIV/AIDS awareness among sex workers—a position she hoped that would eventually allow her to travel abroad to present the plight of Cambodian sex workers at an international conference. It is thus the challenge of being a sex worker that informs the way she dreams of a future self beyond a reputation of being "broken" or "too modern."

(Buddhist) Ascetic Who Remembers Past Lives (*Lok tapos cham chiet*)
ERIK DAVIS

Tong Voddhu sits cross-legged on a low table in his white robes, blessing bottles of water and tiger balm by blowing into them. His breath captured in the bottles and jars, Voddhu hands them back to the small cluster of visitors sitting on the floor around him. All of us have come to see the prodigy who claims to be the rebirth of the most important Cambodian Buddhist of the twentieth century. The air just outside the small sanctuary vibrates with the noise of the temple's construction.

The temple already towers over rice fields in a place that was one of the last areas held by the Khmer Rouge in the late 1990s, and it promises to get even larger. Like Voddhu himself, the temple's size and ambition promise a sort of outsized redemption: a Buddha image over thirty meters tall sits in the center of the complex, and an even taller sanctuary faces this image.

Voddhu is the cult leader at the center of this temple, which is independent from and somewhat at odds with the national Buddhist hierarchy. His powerful political connections allow him to continue his construction efforts and unorthodox practices, but the Ministry of Religion and Cults monitors him, and he now wears the white robes of a lay ascetic rather than the saffron of the Buddhist monk. He doesn't live at the temple but arrives in the morning in a chauffeured Landcruiser; he does not shave his head but sports a thick coiffure of shiny black hair above his square face. He encourages visitors to address him as Grandfather, though at thirty-three he is younger than most of us.

Voddhu and his temple attract visitors because of the way they frame Cambodian history in a familiar narrative of death and rebirth. Voddhu's outsized construction ambitions connect his work to the glories of the Angkorean Empire, while proclaiming the permanence of his future-oriented vision of the world.[13] His past-life memories, however, connect him to the glorious period of Cambodian independence and the rise of Khmer Buddhist modernism. He remembers his last 1,001 lives, but only that of Venerable Buddhist Patriarch Chuon Nath is truly important. Chuon Nath embodied Cambodian national aspirations as a powerful force for Cambodian independence and Buddhist modernism.[14] As Buddhist Patriarch, he translated Buddhist scriptures into Khmer for the first time and published these in codex form; he composed the national anthem and authored the first Khmer-language dictionary. Chuon Nath died in 1969, as the country began its free fall into civil war.

Voddhu remembers his past life as Chuon Nath and retains his vast knowledge and spiritual powers, both of which lend weight to his moral pronouncements. Voddhu was born just before the Khmer Rouge took over his part of the countryside and does not recall a period in this life prior to their reign. At the age of three, he escaped his Khmer Rouge village and ran away to the depths of a cave deep in the mountains, where a sage who had lived hidden inside the mountain's depths for thousands of years adopted him. Voddhu studied ancient scriptures and magic and subsisted entirely on a diet of fish from underground streams while living with this ancient sage in the heart of the mountain. When he finally emerged, he came face-to-face with his family, fleeing the liberating armies of the Vietnamese. Between these two lives, Voddhu recalls a period in heaven, where he met the future Buddha Maitreya. Maitreya will come at the end of this world cycle to renew true religion and proper social order; according to Voddhu, that period is now, and Maitreya has already been born somewhere in Cambodia.

Voddhu's claim to continuity with Chuon Nath exemplifies a widespread Khmer longing for a renewed moral nation of wealth and promise—a connection to a lost national history. His explicitly millenarian aspects, on the other hand, connect to an older image of authority and national longing. He builds his temple on a monumental scale and includes such millenarian objects as the "gong of victory," which will magically sound when the future and final Buddha Maitreya reveals himself and institutes a new world of justice and truth. The statues of Preah Ko Preah Keo—the holy cow and boy of Khmer mythology—are also millenarian objects believed to have been taken captive by the Siamese during the Khmer Middle Period and that will hopefully one day return to Cambodia, bringing their glory, wisdom, and power with them.

Voddhu's story is extravagant in its ambition but common in its themes: the recovery of a moral compass and unity for the Khmer nation, the healing of past traumas, and the continuity of national identity and moral leadership are symbolized and synthesized in the matter of Voddhu's memory, which reaches back to an era before the horrors of the 1970s. Voddhu claims this memory, the power to bless people and objects, and he claims authoritative knowledge of the imminent arrival of the Buddha Maitreya. Such claims may prove a significant attraction for those who share a sense of dismay at Khmer history and their own place in it—as victims, perpetrators, bystanders, or all three—by promising a new moral unity for a fractured nation.

When the blessing of water bottles, tiger balm, and postcards depicting Voddhu standing in front of his temple monuments is finished, I walk outside with a group of Khmer spiritual tourists from Battambang. They're unconvinced by Voddhu's claims to the memories of Chuon Nath, but they seem to accept most of the content of his predictions at face value; like Voddhu himself, they imagine their future in terms of different, chosen continuities with the past. By connecting Chuon Nath and Maitreya in his own person, Voddhu places himself at the center of this imagination of national moral restoration.

Government Official (*Montrei reachga*)
JENNA GRANT

I last saw Dr. Dara at the beginning of New Year, when I went to her office on Kim Il Sung Boulevard in the northwest part of Phnom Penh. Monivong and Russian Boulevards were jammed with motos (motorcycles), shiny but exhaust-spewing SUVs, and overloaded taxi vans, so my motorcycle taxi followed the stream of others along sidewalks. I was anxious I might not catch Dr. Dara before she left for lunch and then the holiday. I needed to pick up my renewal letter, a letter that would state officially, on blue Ministry of Health letterhead, that my research protocol had been approved for a second year.

Dr. Dara is a government official, a medical doctor, and a researcher in her own right. She is part of the secretariat for the National Ethics Committee for Health Research (NEC) established by the Ministry of Health in 2002 in order to review all health-related research proposals in Cambodia. My previous visit to the NEC office had been similar in tenor to other dealings with other government bureaucracies in the capital, where one is uncertain what the rules are and how they will be applied. Dr. Dara had paged through my application, back and forth, and had finally removed her large glasses and shook her head. Further changes were required. Dr. Dara's decision may have seemed arbitrary to me that day, but this is what the ethics official does: translates standardized rules for conducting medical research in Cambodia to particular circumstances of researchers, studies, and populations. It is a second level of translation; the first level was adapting international guidelines for biomedical research to conditions in Cambodia.

The secretariat of the NEC is representative of a whole class of bureaucrats that formed over the decade of Vietnamese-backed socialist governance in the abrupt twilight of the Cold War, followed by the brief period of neoliberal democracy promotion under UNTAC (1992–1993). In contemporary urban Cambodia, the government bureaucrat is an intermediary between forces of power consolidation and resource disbursement, where sociopolitical structures of authority under the Cambodian People's Party meet the need to address cultures of accountability imposed by international donors.

Dr. Dara's day-to-day job is mired in the bureaucratic mundane, but the NEC helps to govern the knowledge and value that may be produced from Cambodian minds, bodies, behaviors, and fluids. The practical and symbolic work that she performs could only be possible in the present moment: when biomedical research is increasingly transnational; when the diseases that burden Cambodians—HIV/AIDS, malaria, TB—are of interest to international researchers and donors; when a now stable Cambodia possesses the government and health structures to collaborate with international researchers; when human rights and health are merged into a discourse of moral force; and when local ethics committees are seen as a solution to the problem of how to protect "human subjects" from risks associated with biomedical research.

Though Dr. Dara and her committee evaluate whether researchers have designed their research to minimize harms (and whether they have the correct documentation to prove it), the ethics of transnational medical research are not merely the domain of health professionals and bureaucrats. The global proliferation of human rights discourse and the link between health and human rights, particularly in the case of HIV prevention and treatment trials, means research ethics may be contested by a broad public.[15] In postwar Cambodia, human rights discourse was written into the 1991 Paris Peace Agreements in order to prevent abuses like those committed by the Khmer Rouge regime. Human rights were promoted during the period of UN administration and are now debated vigorously by the multitude of local and international NGOs, the press, and the government.[16] A recent controversy surrounding the clinical trial in Cambodia of tenofovir, a drug that may prevent HIV infection, illustrates how activists and even the prime minister utilized the language of health and human rights to critique biomedical research.[17]

But what does it mean to conduct ethical research on or with Cambodians? How will they access the benefits—be it knowledge, medicine, profit—generated through their participation? The figure of the ethics bureaucrat in Cambodia emerges along with these questions, which are debated globally by academic and industry researchers, activists, and bioethicists. Poverty, lack of adequate health care, and limited social and political rights present challenges to mechanisms used to ensure ethical research in more affluent settings, such as informed consent. Dr. Dara connects ethical problems with solutions acceptable within the biomedical model. Depending on your point of view, the ethics committee may increase dialogue on ethics and help ensure ethical practice, or it may be a legal-bureaucratic formality that enables research—and its attendant flow of resources, jobs, and services—to continue.

For me, at the moment when I was rushing to my meeting with Dr. Dara, it was largely a matter of expedience: without approval, my own research in Cambodia would be impossible. When I finally arrived at the NEC office, I was relieved to find Dr. Dara still there, seated at a far table, her petite frame bent over an embroidery project. She smiled warmly at me and had her assistant fetch my renewal letter. She asked what I was doing for New Year, and then she told me to be sure to write a good final report.

LAOS

Edited by JEROME WHITINGTON

Golden City Boten, established on a unique land concession in northern Laos, is a luxury residential city for Chinese elite built on some 1,600 hectares with a thirty-year lease renewable for three periods.[1] Established ex nihilo as a special economic zone by Chinese investors, the city demonstrates the extent of extraterritorial sovereignty involved in the contemporary globalization of Laos. This kind of sovereign configuration is an effect not only of the size or duration of the concession but, as Pal Nyíri explains, it is also an effect of the use of the yuan as the sole currency, the authorization of a privatized police force, the moving of accused criminals and bodies of murder victims into China for legal procedures, and the extant labor policies that use mostly Chinese labor and require fluency in Chinese among the few Lao employees. "Sure it's China," remarked one local observer. "China rented it!"

Yet Golden City Boten might be an apt geopolitical rendering of Laos' predicament of modernity. While on the surface the only thing "Lao" about the space is the soil and the legal arrangements, it reveals as much about Laos as it does China's foreign development strategies. Concessionary spaces in Laos, if one uses the term loosely, are territorially extensive, numerous, and flexible in their arrangements. To use Ong's notion of graduated sovereignty,[2] foreign investment in Laos bears on the extensiveness of foreign cultural and social involvement, carefully managed by what amounts to a highly decentralized, distinctly Lao political structure. For whatever one wants to say about foreign exploitation of Lao economic factors, it must be understood as a deliberate strategy on the part of that complex thing too easily called the Lao state.

It can hardly be said that the prerogatives of Lao people are simply displaced by foreign objectives. The resulting assemblage amounts to a dynamic intersection of the foreign and the Lao.

If the contributions that follow are any indication, Lao modernity revolves around an experience of ambiguity. In Lao as in Thai, *tan samai* means "of the age," and it implies more a sense of a fashionable changing contemporary rather than modernity as such.[3] In the essays that follow, the contributors address different sites for such ambiguous passages: Buddhist monks who cannot live without their cell phones, foreign experts who grapple with the structural limits of Laos's rural economy, Miss Beer Lao as the rotating icon of the gendered nation, village chiefs trapped between party objectives and local exigencies, and finally, countercultural hippies of the American period, now reformed, who reflect on the socialist cultural project and current transformations under high-growth capitalism.

The fact that Lao people themselves think in terms of "modernity" and "tradition" helps us understand that the concept of modernity provides a popular analytic of what are inevitably complex power relations, generative technical possibilities, social kinships, and transnational commitments. The Mobile Phone Monk described by Patrice Ladwig is one site for such anxieties for the passing of tradition, but it is likewise an emergent exploration for new potentials. For Ladwig, the ethical dynamic of Buddhism may be revitalized by the challenge technology presents to religious practice. In that case, technology enables dynamic ethical work. Inevitably, the question of technology in Laos leads to the central importance of development as a frame for both capitalist expansion and the country's particular kind of paternal state developmentalism. These two aspects of development receive very different emphasis in Laos, the one marked by the Lao term *chaloen* and the other by the term *phatthana*. Both may be translated as development, but *chaloen* means something more like prosperity, while *phatthana* refers to the temporal growth of an organism or society. The common explanation is that prosperity is the end result of the process of growth. But the words come from different sources and are used in very different spheres of life. "Prosperity" routinely appears in the names of temples and businesses, whereas "growth" almost never does, and the former seems to have its roots in Khmer political expansiveness, while the latter received its current usage in the American political project of the 1950s and '60s.

The expansive prosperity of the country's newfound economic growth is aptly demonstrated by Holly High. She describes the sexually charged but primordially innocent figure of Miss Beer Lao, whose ever-changing faces are called upon to signify the unification of a political-consumer market for a prestigious symbol of national prosperity. Even so, the company is 50 percent foreign owned. Miss Beer Lao circulates through patronage networks on the polished gift form of the calendar. This highlights the ways gendered national symbols flirt with commodification but are thoroughly integrated into remarkably durable noncommercial relationships. During my fieldwork on hydropower, I once got wrapped up in a lighthearted debate about whether Beer Lao or the Theun-Hinboun Power Company (THPC) was Laos' most successful business. It was a humorous conversation that left my (male) Lao interlocutors and I feeling quite fond of each other, the very kind of relation Miss Beer Lao is meant to inspire. But High's analysis might also suggest the gendered prestige of national paper products. The THPC dam has the distinction of adorning the 20,000 kip banknote—the largest at the time—so it is highly appropriate that Beer Lao can lay claim to the nation's most popular wall calendar.

The pathos of state development planning has a completely different emphasis than the positive, affirmative values of mobile phones, beer, or electricity—"development" as *phatthana* rather than *chaloen*. Michael Dwyer's figuration of the Mitigation Expert nicely captures this pathos of modern knowledge. Called upon to ensure that big development projects are only minimally harmful to the marginalized people whose lives they affect, expatriate mitigation planners have hopeful expectations that "their" projects really might this time achieve impressive development objectives. But they are routinely frustrated by the financial managers of transnational highway projects and large hydropower dams who do not care all that much about the effects of those monumental political projects. The method of following the expert in his work establishes in clear outline the ethical limits of the development enterprise. It is also striking the frequency with which foreign experts (hopeful, frustrated) play this role in Laos.

In my figure, the Beleaguered Village Leader, I trace a different site of social development, incidentally also a mitigation project, in which the village chief, as a government official, is called upon to perform a political role that puts him under extreme and very intimate duress. Obviously most chiefs do not experience this, but it is an exceptional office to the extent that holding political power can be intensely and structurally unfavorable. The forms of power at stake are wrapped up in the party apparatus, conventions of Lao masculinity, and a new ecological modernity produced by the incredible volume of resource and infrastructure development in Laos today.

Nick Enfield's Hippie, Interrupted raises the historical question of American involvement during the 1960s and '70s—a question lurking in the background of several other figures. The American cultural influence was an artifact of deliberate political destablization and a cynical brand of "development" in which pouring corrupt cash on an economy proved to be the quickest way to destroy it. Current cultural politics, and the anxieties that accompany new social problems, evoke the socialist response following the revolution but are also remarkable for their differences. Moreover, I would suggest that Dwyer's Mitigation Expert or the predicament of the Beleaguered Village Chief cannot be understood without adequate understanding of this painful period. It is a question ultimately of the achieved legitimacy of the Lao state, which rests quite squarely on *chaloen,* economic prosperity, and the country's continually negotiated political autonomy in a globalized world. Contrast Enfield's description with the social control of the Burmese junta or the Khmer Rouge to understand why Lao political modernity is worth paying attention to. The subtlety of its ability to build close connections with Thailand and China, without simply being swamped by their vastly larger and more aggressive economies, is a skilled politics of balance and ingenuity.

The country represents on a different scale the historical problem of "Southeast Asia" and its anthropology, that it is defined spatially by being between other places and achieves its coherence on the basis of its cultural pluralism. The historical problem is no small issue for the anthropology of Laos, which occasionally seems to be waiting for a lost unity or suffering from a sense of not measuring up to its neighbors. For instance, in a widely read book, anthropologist Grant Evans has argued that Laos was already underdeveloped in 1641—an observation that cannot fail to stifle creative, relevant social science just as it positions Laos as perpetually undeveloped and less-than-modern.[4] Instead, theoretical work based on actual practices may be in order. Lao studies could benefit from the theoretical ambition that has always characterized Southeast Asian studies, and the "figures" approach lends itself to this.

Laos is changing extremely rapidly, and anthropologists working there struggle with inherent epistemic uncertainty. Understanding Laos' contemporary uncertainties, subjections, and strategies through an analysis of key social figures emphasizes personal moments of contact situated in historical processes and transnational relations. In every figure of Lao modernity here addressed, what is "Lao" is put into question socially and practically by the events at hand, for anthropologists but especially for the people they study (who may not be "in" Laos and who may not "be" Lao). If one takes Golden City Boten as an extreme case, then understanding discrete figures each on their own terms may prove a provocative method not for differentiating an authentic "Laos" from the rest of the world but for understanding that Laos is authentically enmeshed in contemporary global processes.

Miss Beer Lao (*Phou Saw Bia Lao*)
HOLLY HIGH

If you have been to Laos, you must have seen her. She hangs in noodle soup restaurants, beer cafés, market stalls, government offices, and private homes. She has traveled the length and breadth of this small nation and can now be found smiling in chilly Udomsay, coyly glancing back in cosmopolitan Vientiane, and throwing sultry eyes over Attapu. She is Miss Beer Lao. Her annual starring role is to appear in the Beer Lao calendar, a four-page full-color publication issued each December by Laos' most celebrated company, Beer Lao. Each year there is a beauty competition held to determine which four entrants will appear in the coveted calendar. So, the faces change. And so, too, do the themes: how she is dressed, decorated, set, and posed. But Miss Beer Lao as a concept transcends these changing faces and themes. As a figure, she encapsulates the fantasies and fears of postsocialist transition in Laos.

The competition has been running for over a decade. Strict stipulations require that entrants be women aged between eighteen and twenty-three (minimum height of 158 cm, or 5 foot 2 inches) and look "innocent." The entrant should not have any professional modeling experience. It is not enough to be simply beautiful: the winners must be quintessentially "Lao," not only in their features but also in their virtues: short-listed candidates are asked to respond to unashamedly nationalistic questions. Despite this, local non-Lao ethnicities are encouraged to apply. For instance, in 2006 a Hmong girl was given a special prize apparently on the basis that she was the only representative of Laos' minorities to make it to the penultimate short list.

Beer Lao is one of the most well known and emotionally elaborated commodities currently produced in Laos. Jingoistic television advertisements explicitly link the product to nationalist sentiments by featuring images of symbols of Lao-ness such as That Luang (a large and striking stupa in Vientiane, widely considered a national symbol) and a wrist-tying ceremony. Indeed, Beer Lao can be observed playing an important role in rural rituals such as weddings, Buddhist festivals, and New Year celebrations. Beer Lao is undeniably embedded in heartland Laos. The company, however, has recently been partially sold to foreign interests: Carlsberg now owns 50 percent, while the government of Laos retains 50 percent. The sentiments that surround Beer Lao, then, must be understood in terms of a nationalism that is taking shape within the context of globalization.

Consistently high growth rates (6.4 percent in 2009) have continued in Laos despite the 2008 financial crisis. Incomes have increased for many, but there is also a growing gap between rich and poor. New identities have emerged, such as the young women that now labor in Vientiane's garment industry or the youth who earn significant wages as seasonal agricultural laborers in Thailand and spend the remaining months unemployed in Laos. TV satellite dishes, motorcycles, and mobile phones have transformed the scenery of rural Laos. New beauty products such as fashion clothing, cosmetics, and jewelry affirm that this burgeoning consumerism is steadfastly an expression of valued personal transformation. While sought after, these transformations have also been interpreted as evidence of a decline: public concerns about "human trafficking," corruption, the loss of Lao culture, prostitution, and shadowy landgrabs by foreigners reveal that globalization has been received ambivalently in Laos: on the one hand, personal transformations, cosmopolitanism, and wealth are eagerly sought, while on the other, fears about contamination and invasion by foreign bodies abound.

It is worth noting that beer is associated with prostitution (or at least sexual availability) in Laos. For instance, beer cafés (not brothels) are the main venue for selling sex. It is small wonder, then, that Miss Beer Lao is such a sexually charged figure. In a final twist, however, a Beer Lao executive explained that there is the expectation that winners will not get married in the year that they serve as Miss Beer Lao. A woman must appear "innocent" in order to win the competition and must remain so for the year that her picture adorns the calendar. If she were to marry, he said, "people who are *son jai* [interested, often indicating amorous interest] might hear," presumably puncturing the fantasy. The point, it seems, is to maintain the image of Miss Beer Lao as attractive but untouched—sexualized but not sexually experienced, enticing but not yet consumed—an image of the possible pleasures of consumption but also the virtuousness of remaining aloof. The figure of Miss Beer Lao, then, can be understood as an effort to tame the perceived threats of globalization (foreign ownership, commodification, and sexual exploitation among them) by domesticating them into a "Lao" form, although the precise nature of what a truly Lao form is remains an object of debate and improvisation.

The calendar is designed explicitly to communicate a message about Lao identity. For instance, the "concepts" of the calendar are chosen by the government: previous concepts have been handicrafts (2006) and electricity (2005). Paradoxically, this message about Lao identity is communicated through the medium of a Gregorian calendar (not the lunar calendar more commonly used in rural Laos) and by means of a beauty contest that is patterned along recognizably international lines. The product is highly appealing. One newspaper reported that it is "the most sought after calendar in Laos." It alone among the myriad of calendars produced each year is almost impossible to purchase in the market. Calendars are distributed by the company as gifts to government offices, businesses, clients, embassies, and Lao missions abroad. The calendars can be found displayed throughout Laos, a sign of the depth and breadth of these networks. Miss Beer Lao, then, provides one of the few threads of unity stretching across the otherwise diverse settings of rural and urban Laos, highland and lowland, privileged and marginalized, ethnic Lao and otherwise, home and abroad. Miss Beer Lao sits in these diverse settings as an image of the fantasy of national unity. This fantasy perhaps gains some of its appeal from the countervailing fears of fracture, foreign domination, and decay that have accompanied the postsocialist era.

Mobile Phone Monk
PATRICE LADWIG

"Do you believe in that stuff?" an elderly owner of a photocopy shop asked me in Vientiane in 2005. I had brought him an old book on Buddhist magic printed before the communist revolution in 1975. "I think that monks in the past could really do incredible things like perhaps described in your book here. But today? They all have mobile phones and chat continuously. I think the era of magical monks is over. Monks can do a lot of things today, but other things have been lost." His words had a sort of melancholic undertone, and our conversation continued to circle around discourses of loss and change in Lao Buddhism. When I ordained myself in the same year, all sixty monks and novices in the monastery had mobile phones, and not having one would have been a sign either of extreme poverty and backwardness or of holiness through voluntary austerity. Not one of us belonged to the category of austere renouncers refusing to use mobiles.

In Laos, mobile phones—among monks themselves and Buddhist laypeople—have become accepted as a completely normal part of everyday life and one of the advantages of modernity. Western romantic and orientalist notions of Buddhist monks as reclusive renouncers often represent the link between new technologies and asceticism as problematic. However, for most Lao monks with fancy mobile phones, high tech is a part of everyday life. Nevertheless, the obvious acceptance of new communication technologies in a community of believers cannot only be measured by the number of mobile users. While most Lao see the obvious need of monks having mobile phones, the remarks of the photocopy shop owner and other laypeople are also quite telling. The simple question is: Who is using the mobile for what purposes and what kinds of relationships are maintained through it?[5] Temporarily ordained novices, or adults joining the order of monks (*sangha*) for a week because of the death of a relative, are not really expected to lead an austere life and can happily chat along. However, for monks with longer *sangha* careers, or more so for monks dedicated to meditation and other ascetic practices, the mobile phone might be an "object" to be controlled and used with care due to its moral implications. Indeed, the mobile phone can show that "objects" have moral implications beyond the intention of their users. Thevenot remarks that "the autonomous intentional individual is usually regarded as a perquisite for moral agency. But it achieves such moral agency only with the support of other elements—the functional agency of objects."[6]

This reflects one of the dilemmas of world-renouncing religions such as Buddhism and points to the inherent tension between worldliness and ascesis. Renunciation is based on discipline, rules, purity, and difference from the life of the householder.[7] Silence, control of gestures, and abstinence from worldly pleasures are ideally the characteristics of the monk, and a certain distance from the world is the precondition for developing the proper lifestyle of a monk. In contrast to that, the mobile phone stands for openness toward the world, constant accessibility to interaction, for modernity, and the new pace of life that has entered Laos since the economic reform process. The figure of the mobile phone monk plays on the contradictions between what Max Weber has labeled "otherworldly asceticism"[8] and the rise of new communication technologies. Moreover, mobile phone monks—and indeed the use of modern communication technologies by renouncers in general—dramatize the interplay of ostensibly timeless tradition and transient modernity.

The introduction of social and technological change often poses radical questions linked to the inherently conservative nature of renouncer traditions—and not only in Laos. However, the comparatively rapid influx of modern forms of communication into Laos in the late 1990s provoked extensive discussions on what Theravada monks are and are not allowed to do. The rules of conduct for monks—meticulously laid down approximately 2,500 years ago in the *Vinaya Pitaka* (*vinayapitaka,* or "basket of discipline") and compressed into 227 rules for the lives of monks called *patimokkha*—obviously do not feature mobile phones, laptops, or social networking sites. New technological and social developments therefore constantly have to be renegotiated in the light of these rules of conduct that are over two thousand years old. However, simply contrasting rules of conduct against social practice can be misleading. Instead we should ask the question posed by James Laidlaw as to "how values and ideals, which are in themselves unrealizable, can nevertheless inform a life which answers also to other, conflicting values."[9]

Theravada Buddhism, moreover, promotes a "balanced" tradition of renunciation that rejects some of Hinduism's very strict asceticism by giving monks a choice between varying grades of ascetic practices. In practice, monks have always had a certain degree of involvement with their communities, and most of them are in constant interaction with them due to their community obligations and their dependency on a ritual economy.[10] However, very austere monks belonging to the forest tradition, sometimes said to develop special powers due to their meditation practice, often have a much more restricted use of mobiles. During my research in one of the few forest and meditation monasteries of Laos, I discovered that they tended to be switched off most of the time, which was necessary to keep up with the demands of meditation exercise. Laypeople also expected these monks to be less reachable and less connected to society so that they would be able to maintain their purity. At one end of the ascetic spectrum, discourses of loss might be legitimized, as the very movement into worldliness through modern communication technologies might cause a loss of reputation. Dumont succinctly captures this dilemma: "Situated outside the world but linked to it, the renouncer is impotent against it; if he ventures in that direction his ideas become ephemeral."[11]

The mobile phone monk has now become a standard figure of Laos' modernity and will soon be replaced by other monk figures attached to other technological innovations. In neighboring Thailand, blessings and donations are sometimes already performed via mobile phones. In some cases, discourses of loss will be associated with mobile phone monks, but it might also be possible that technologies like mobile phones themselves become enchanted in Laos. Nevertheless, the dilemmas and contradictory symbolic nature of the figure will emerge again and again with every technological innovation that changes the lives and communication forms of monks.

Mitigation Expert
MICHAEL DWYER

"If you want good governance, you'd better use a map." Peter was explaining to me that the fancy layers of geographic information—the aerial photos, the zoning boundaries, the crop suitability matrices—weren't just the fantasies of some technocrat. Yes, they accomplished key technical tasks, identifying the quantities and locations of rural farmland that could be allocated into state projects like watershed protection areas, biodiversity conservation forests, and industrial tree plantations. But just as important was the political power of the map over the state itself: Peter's ambition, he explained, was to free up land along a new highway corridor by intensifying agricultural production, stabilizing in-migration, and mapping out land use zones for years to come. This would generate not only extra land for state forestry and conservation but also buy-in from "your political people, your management people," a holy grail that could only be attained through long hours in state planning rooms and village meetings. Done right, a zoning exercise could tame not only Laos' upland farmers but its officials as well. At least that was the idea.

Peter is a foreign expert, a mitigation specialist. One way to think of mitigation is as the institutionalized protection of society from the market: an effort to deliberately slow the rate of what Polanyi called societal "improvement" so that "the community [does not] succumb in the process" of industrial development.[12] The mitigation profession sits at the heart of Laos' present-day efforts to pursue capital-intensive national development projects—power plants, roads, plantations, factories, and the like—because it helps recast those classic state building projects into terms that lend themselves to private investment. As engineers and state officials have looked to nature and the private sector for development options, the mitigation expert has emerged as someone whose job it is to render a messy landscape of possibility and unpredictability into "impact" scenarios that are predictable in space and time. The mitigation expert creates plausible calculability.

Peter's highway corridor project highlighted the difficulty that this entailed, both personally and professionally. On the one hand, the road expansion's mandate called for protecting villagers from a possible landgrab, the expected result of collusion between local elites and foreign investors, as land values rose with increasing ease of access. Map-based mitigation was intended to make this feasible by fusing technical with political predictability. On the other hand, the stimulation of state-backed cooperative investment between foreign investors and hinterland farmers was precisely one of the project's raisons d'être. The question, from a mitigation perspective, was the relationship between land rights, land use, and development planning. Where was the line between speculative landgrabbing and proactive development intervention? Was it possible to keep this line from being crossed?

The mitigation expert had an answer, although it bucked the very notion of mitigation. The only way to prevent such a landgrab, he argued, was to assist villagers in their own land *development* efforts. Strengthening their rights to existing patterns of land use would not suffice: the complexity, extensiveness, and unsustainability of upland farming meant that current land uses had to be changed before the formalization of property rights would actually be worth doing. Land development meant intensification—literally plowing capital and labor into the land in order to make less land produce more. This would also generate the spare land needed in order to bring local elites—a hazy mix of business and government officials—into the process. In contrast to a haphazard and corruption-wracked landgrab, Peter's proposal—and his maps—conjured a planned and calculated enclosure, a form of dispossession made palatable by the fact that it would be offset by half a decade of agricultural extension, subsidized land development, and land set-asides for both demographic expansion and increased consumption levels.

The problem, however, was that his proposal began to cross the line between infrastructure mitigation and rural development. Peter's proposal never made it out of the pilot stage. The highway was being funded by a loan from a multilateral development bank, and Peter's plan needed bank staff's approval. In preliminary discussions, the loan designers made it clear that this sort of mitigation work would have crossed a line between the mitigation of negative impacts and the provision of overly expensive subsidies. This would have forced the loan to do work that was seen by the lending industry—and in turn by its customers—as belonging to the private sector, not to the state. A staff member of the bank that was making the loan thus explained that, when faced with questions about how to do mitigation, they had to err on the side of *not doing enough* to protect impacted communities because poor governments didn't like to borrow money with too many strings attached. In walking me through the fact that mitigation provides political coverage for internationally scrutinized lenders, he seemed to be suggesting that by exposing itself to criticism through the underfunding of mitigation work, the bank was actually doing a service to the poor governments of the world by taking political heat while acting in the governments' interests.

This was quite a proposition, but it cut right to the heart of competitive lending, one of the central pillars of privately financed—or neoliberal—development. If the mitigation expert and the loan officer police this often fuzzy line between society and the market, they do so facing in opposite directions. Peter's perspective made him the more tragic figure. He was faced with a contradiction, a structural requirement not to look too closely at the landscapes targeted for national development. Describing decades of mythology and misinformation about upland agriculture, Michael Dove called this requirement "the political economy of ignorance."[13] The mitigation expert, for better and for worse, knows this economy intimately. Pinned between detailed knowledge of the human landscape of development and structurally mandated parsimony, he personifies—and perpetuates—the contradiction of neoliberal development, one project at a time.

Hippie, Interrupted
N. J. ENFIELD

In the spring of 1976, a few months after the Lao People's Democratic Republic had been officially established by victorious revolutionary forces, a young man named Mr. K went out with friends in downtown Vientiane to catch a movie. Little did he know that instead of returning home later that evening, he would be on his way to a remote lake island to begin a decade of detention and reeducation as part of a new government program to remedy the social ills left behind by the recently deposed U.S.–installed regime.

Then in his early twenties, Mr. K had moved to Vientiane from a small rice-farming village in the deep south of Laos a few years before his detention. Like so many young men on the move, his aim had been to find work, perhaps build a family, and take advantage of a growing urban economy to help his parents and extended family back home. But when he arrived in the capital city in the early 1970s, it was a case of no work and all play. For a small town, the place was jumping. A U.S.–backed anticommunist government was host to a community of military and other expatriates. Vientiane remained somewhat of a haven compared to the chaos of the revolutionary-controlled uplands. It was a swinging scene for those young Lao men and women inclined to take part or take advantage. Mr. K made friends with the American and European hippies who were pioneering the shoestring backpacking trail. He took to their hippie ways: long hair, bell-bottoms, sex, drugs, rock '.n' roll.

All this had to change when the communist government took charge in late 1975. Foreigners fled the country, and the new authorities began warning local kids to clean up their act. A first order of business was to rid the lowlands of their social ills, the urban vice that stood out as an emblem of the former regime's faults. Young Mr. K and his hippie friends were ordered: cut your hair, burn your bell-bottoms, quit smoking pot. For Mr. K, it seemed like an empty threat, but on that spring 1976 afternoon, as he stepped out of the movie theater and onto the street, he found a military truck parked on the sidewalk. Soldiers were rounding up those young people who had not paid attention. Mr. K was a sitting duck, with his long hair and bell-bottom trousers an unambiguous sign of his misfit status. Perhaps oblivious to the irony of a hippie being locked up by revolutionaries, the only mildly rebellious Mr. K was detained for his crimes of fashion and taken to a government reeducation facility on an island lake north of the capital. Here he remained a detainee for ten years.

Along with a catalogue of other social undesirables—prostitutes, drug dealers, deadbeats—Mr. K had been removed from Vientiane society to enter the new government's archipelago of reeducation centers. The purpose of these centers was to fix the social and political faults of the old regime. Those who were guilty of petty vice were small fry in the larger scheme of things, and Mr. K's experience was a league apart from those detainees who had served the former regime's aim of thwarting the now-successful revolution. Many never made it out, not because they were executed, but because life was so tough that many detainees fell victim to poor health and disease. In the greater scheme of things, Mr. K and his fellow detainees were luckier than many.

Fifteen years after Mr. K's incarceration, European socialism had collapsed and Laos was coming out of what looked from the outside to have been a very heavy slumber. Mr. K was finally released from his detention and reeducation. He had come to feel that his earlier way of life had been a waste and that he could—and should—make a better contribution to society. While in detention, he had learned the basics of medical care and had taken on new responsibilities by assisting with in-house medical facilities. Recognizing his proven civic responsibility, the authorities eventually released him and gave him a job. Around the fifteenth anniversary of the revolution, in the beginning of the 1990s, while many reeducation centers had emptied, just a few were still operating, housing some of the big fish of the former regime. Mr. K was the success story of a little fish: a good person, once a victim of bad influence, now reeducated and back on the rails.

But as Mr. K applied himself to his straight and narrow life, the reopened society of Laos quickly welcomed those old ills again, thanks to new economic conditions and reactivation of the not-long-previous openness to outside cultural influences. With the good comes the bad, and there would soon no longer be a scarcity of sex, drugs, and rock 'n' roll. Today—now thirty-five years since Mr. K's detention on that Vientiane city sidewalk—vice flourishes in Vientiane and the rest of lowland Laos. Amphetamines and opiates are serious social problems. Drug tourism is vibrant. Prostitution thrives in a range of forms. AIDS is killing people. The current government, an overripened form of the fresh movement that had so avidly locked Mr. K away, still talks the upright talk of antivice, but the approach to controlling it is more random, less avid, less systematic, and far more tolerant, as evidenced by the wafer-thin veneer of vice in today's Vientiane, well fueled by an influx of money from a variety of sources: overseas relatives who fled as refugees back when Mr. K was in reeducation, the lucrative development industry, and the spoils of a local capitalist economy.

With an overview now of the larger context, it is tempting to view the social cleanup that befell Mr. K as a mere blip, a passing aberration. He might be justified in complaining that he was in the wrong place at the wrong time. He paid what might seem a very heavy price for small-time deviance. Now an older man with grownup children, Mr. K looks around to see a new permissive generation committing the same sins as he did, in the same neighborhoods, yet without paying a dime. Does he feel cheated? Hell, no. He's a reformed man.

Beleaguered Village Leader
JEROME WHITINGTON

Chief Buathong was the unhappy representative of a village of some twenty-five households along the Nam Gneuang River. I first visited his village in central Laos in 2004. He had been handpicked for the position on the basis of his good behavior, approved by the villagers and then inducted into the Lao People's Revolutionary Party—against his wishes, he told me, but one suspects he was flattered at the time. Now he spent all his time in meetings and was not even paid enough to cover travel expenses. He had no time, he kept repeating. His visage brightened momentarily. Being in the party wouldn't be so bad, he said—if it weren't for the district's policies. Whatever the case, his anxious predicament was visible in his collapsed posture. We talked for hours into the night, since he hoped I might have some means of interceding: thirteen households in his village had signed a petition rejecting changes in land use rules and the promotion of agricultural intensification. He surely sided with the villagers, but it put him in a tight spot. A good chief is one who is honest, he told me, looking crushed. A good chief is resolute enough to tell district authorities what villagers need and to withstand the hours of meetings in which officials work to undo their resolve.

Buathong's village had been selected for an intensified program of agricultural development and shifting rice stabilization. The farmers I spoke with described in detail the collapsing productivity, an influx of rodents, and increased reliance on forest products sold for meager cash to itinerant traders. Above all, Buathong was expected to be a role model for the other villagers, and if he rejected the development program, the whole village would follow suit. The focal point between villagers and the district, he was the hinge of everyone's expectations. He was *gnoung yak,* he said, an idiom that means busy to the point of being harried, as if a jumble of problems all came together to make it impossible to sort them out. He spoke of the district officials using the words "power" (*amnat*) and "control" (*bangkap*)—heavy, metaphysical terms with intense potency. He worried about his family. If he raised objections to the policy, he would probably be punished—perhaps jail or reeducation seminars in the district capital.

In a country with a largely agrarian economic base and a broadly dispersed and ethnically heterogeneous population, one might expect that political authority would remain decentralized and subject to the vagaries of communication and transportation. This is true in the case of Laos except for the remarkable labor, organized through the Communist Party, involved in cultivating and managing village-level political ties through the ambivalent institution of the village chief. This is all the more acute when agrarian policy and development intervention is at stake. Village chiefs are routinely called upon to do the work of making district policy make sense in light of diverse and often unworkable local circumstances.

One can only think of the classic dilemmas of the *meuang* system, in which low population density worked hand in hand with forms of masculine potency and the limitations of decentralized rule.[14] Yet development techniques involve interventions in livelihood conditions and ecological relations, with all the attendant risk villagers must ultimately bear. Across the rivers of Laos, series of large dams are being built, along with timber and mining fueling nearly all of Laos' foreign exchange. Already in the case of many villages, often fanciful rural development policies are called upon to fill in the gaps left by collapsing fish populations and wholesale hydrological changes. The modernity of this corner of Southeast Asia is an ecological modernity; its nature-intensive capitalism produces new political relations induced by pervasive livelihood uncertainty.

As Tania Murray Li has argued for Indonesia, local compromises of power often leave open ways to avoid the worst impacts of policy precisely because government offices rarely have the means to enforce unpopular projects.[15] Li draws on Michael Herzfeld to show that compromise involves a kind of political intimacy, by which Herzfeld means that the failings of the state have a deep emotional resonance.[16] For Chief Buathong, that intimacy struck at a level of basic anxiety in which he was caught between two very different kinds of expectations. No doubt all political offices require managing contradictions. But the material basis of political investment in development projects introduces a vital risk to villagers' livelihoods and a more durable mechanism of political involvement at the village level. Compromise is simply less possible.

I went to find Buathong a few months after we initially met. His village was easy to find, but then I became disoriented and confused. Eventually it became clear that his house had been disassembled. The plot looked strangely naked, exposed amid the nearby fruit trees. An elderly man told me Buathong left to work on a cousin's rice fields near the Mekong; the lumber from his house had been sold, and he was hoping to sell the land to relocate. I tracked down the vice-chief, a man I had met on the prior visit, and asked about the petition. Looking at me with all seriousness, he told me there had never been a petition. I offered up some details, but to no avail—officially, the petition did not exist. Giving up, I wandered around the village thinking about the heavy wooden planks of Buathong's house. There had been no trees like that around here since American bombing sorties flew overhead, when the area had been vacated and later resettled. How much did Buathong fetch for his house, deconstructed under duress? How far would that get him in an unfamiliar town on the Mekong? Those must have been his questions, too, written in the lines across his brow. The story of Buathong, the besieged leader, seemed to echo only in the vacuum left by my questions.

As I left the village, a woman berated me for fifteen minutes in a dialect I could not really understand about district policy and the failure of their rice crops. I have no idea what she said, but I was reassured by her anger that Buathong's absence did not indicate the final triumph of anxiety as a method of rule.

THAILAND

Edited by JANE M. FERGUSON

Few nations in modern history can compete with Thailand in terms of regime change and political transition. Since the nineteenth century, Siam/Thailand has experienced a score of military coups and has drafted seventeen new charters and constitutions. Political unrest and overt violence boiled over in the streets of Bangkok in 2010, when the United Front for Democracy against Dictatorship (UDD), also known as the "Red Shirts," demanding the dissolution of parliament and new elections, clashed with military troops. Nearly a hundred people were killed and thousands were injured. As news and discontent spread throughout the countryside, crucial existential questions of Thai modernity were once again brought to the fore. While the conceptual triad of "nation-religion-monarchy" forms the basis for Thai aesthetic nationalism, challenges to the political order and military backlash have exacerbated class differences and interrogated the role of the people, the military, and the monarchy in their advocacy and contestation of what has been called "Thai-style democracy." This upheaval stands in stark contrast to the image of Thailand as the peace-loving "land of smiles" and other such pictures of sandy beaches, emerald green rice paddies, and culinary delights profitably exploited by the country's powerful tourism industry.

In Thai, to be modern (*tan samai*) means to be "up-to-date" and "with the times." But within these tumultuous times, how can we begin to comprehend the lives of Thai people who must contend with these challenges and contradictions as part of their everyday experiences? Tracing modernist discourse in Thailand through history means understanding the ways in which material and ideological relationships have been forged between local and far-off power-wielding institutions. But to describe the institutions themselves without studying their participants would not provide the nuance potentiated by ethnography. By offering a window into the lives of nine of Thailand's figures of modernity, this chapter will demonstrate how Thailand's historical particularities are in dialectical relation with broader categories and processes such as ethnicity, gender, class, religion, and globalization.

Unlike every other Southeast Asian country, Thailand has the distinction that it was never formally colonized by a European imperial power. Although Thai nationalist history has chalked this perceived anomaly up to the "cleverness" of Siamese elites, scholars have since become very critical of the ways in which this historical fact has sometimes been treated as an "unqualified blessing."[1] While Thai nationalism was not predicated against a colonial Other per se, the elusive ideology of "Thai-ness" acquires power and salience through political and cultural practices. Bureaucratic categorization of peoples along ethnic lines is considered to be a uniquely modern endeavor, and this can be particularly powerful in the context of a country such as Thailand, where ethnic identity is often collapsed into citizenship. Lest we forget, the name "Thailand" is itself an ethnonym. This conflation is brought into strongest relief in the relations with Thailand's upland minority groups, considered to be "modernity's opposites" in national discourse.[2]

For international anthropologists of Thailand, one of the most influential essays of the twentieth century has been John Embree's "Thailand—A Loosely Structured Social System," which, in comparing Thai society with that of the Japanese, argues that Thais do not have strict discipline in everything from daily comportment and walking to their reciprocal relationships with kin.[3] For some of Thailand's figures as described in this chapter—such as Musikawong's Transnational Farmworker, Tracy Pilar Johnson's Hmong-Thai Schoolgirl, Esara's Bangkok Slum Leader, and Zeamer's Single Woman— the hierarchies and relative privileges of class, ethnicity, and gender are very real and, indeed, "structured." This is not to say that the idea of a "loosely structured social system" is not influential in people's imaginings of Thailand. Similarly, as Mary Beth Mills has noted, often it is cultural constructions of Bangkok's urban modernity that motivate migration from rural areas, but these images are seldom congruent with the lived realities of migrants.[4] The imaginaries can give bearing and sustenance, perhaps even serve as a coping strategy, as they do for the urban Single Woman described by Zeamer or the Thai Airways Flight Attendant in Ferguson's essay, while they confront the realities of gender expectation in Thai (and international) society.

Linguistic research shows that while 97 percent of the population of Thailand speaks the privileged central (standard) Thai language, only about

30 percent speak it as their first language in the home.[5] To take the issue a step further, within linguistic hierarchies in Thailand, speaking central (standard) Thai with the privileged accent is conflated and described as speaking "clearly." But in recent decades, increasing numbers of regional languages have found space on the popular scene and over the radio waves. There have also been efforts to tailor school curricula and pedagogies to "fit" (or perhaps be "appropriate" to) its ethnic minorities, with one example being the "indigenous curriculum," which gives voice, credence, and structure to formerly suppressed languages and cultural traditions such as those of the Hmong. While Thailand's increasing acknowledgment of such pluralism is considered by some observers to be progressive, they can also be criticized for essentializing marginalized groups or giving undue power to some linguistic and cultural gatekeepers, while simultaneously blurring and reticulating broader class issues. For those who must navigate the complexities of what it means to be a Thai citizen but are not necessarily ethnically Thai, such as Ntxawm, the Hmong student in Tracy Pilar Johnson's essay, modernity can sometimes be conflated with "Thai-ness."

While internal "othering" takes place in reference to regional ethnicities and hill tribe discourses, "Thai-ness" is also outwardly oriented, representing itself in the international arena. Angkan, the transnational farmworker described by Musikawong, has been forced to mortgage his farmland in the hope that his farm labor abroad will be converted into enough Thai capital in order to sustain his family. Lacking fluency in international language and laws, Angkan becomes a pawn to global capital, completely drained physically and financially. For the chosen handful of successful Thai boxers, their "elbow grease" is converted into international fame and fortune, such as Kitiarsa's case of Somrak, the Olympic gold medal winner. The bodies (when successful) of these prizefighters become icons of and for an ideal Thai masculinity. Conversely, it is feminine beauty that has come to represent Thai modernity,[6] and in the case of the Thai Airways Flight Attendant, proficiency in international symbolic codes—namely fluency in English—allows the figure to be an appropriate ambassador of Thai-ness. But this emotional work can be equally draining, in spite of its perceived privileged mobility. While we could see each as the embodiment of contrasts—femininity/masculinity and servility/aggression—through their work, ultimately, both male and female figures endure physical hardship in the ongoing construction and performance of Thai gender comportment.

It is important to bear in mind, however, that so-called traditional notions of gender comportment and status need not be regressive for all; for Costa's Mae Somjit, the Grassroots Woman Leader, taking on the appellation Mae, or "mother," would seem to confer a retreat to premodern gender roles. In fact, for Thai social movements, such a move could be interpreted as a hybrid strategy that takes advantage of existing cultural structures for acknowledging certain forms of status and esteem. Furthermore, as Keyes has argued, according to a Thai Buddhist worldview, it is only through becoming a mother that a woman can realize her true "nature."[7] But, as we see from the example of Goi, the Rural DJ in Cassaniti's essay, there is considerable contestation over the proper boundaries of this Buddhist worldview, particularly in relation to tradition, craft, and the ever-encroaching banalities of commodity relations.

While we might consider the Rural DJ to occupy a specific node on a network spanning notions of modernity and tradition or urbanism and traditionalism, Mother Kham, the spirit medium in Andrew Johnson's essay, is positioned at another crossroads: between the living and the dead. In this case, however, ideas about the past are invoked in order to give people bearing and hope for achieving success in very distinctly modern economic terms. Ironically, while the DJ rhetorically resists banal capitalism by invoking traditional values, the spirit medium reaps financial reward by conjuring up the dead at the behest of her clients, who hope for future financial success. Similarly, we can look at the Bangkok Slum Leader as a geographical and social phenomenon specifically created by modernity, which allows for the emergence of unorthodox political leaders such as the example of Khun Hin. As described by Esara, in spite of his own humble background he is able to occupy the structural position as a key conduit of negotiation, perhaps translation, between the people who live in the slum itself and the local authorities.

By tracing the lived realities of Thailand's figures of modernity, we can begin to understand how the complexities of nation, class, gender, technologies, and politics are manifest among the people who experience them, as well as the modes through which these individuals might struggle not only to adapt to the changing realities that surround them but also to effect material and social change. Unlike Thai Airways' slogan, though, this process is seldom "Smooth as Silk."

Grassroots Woman Leader (*Phuunam satrii raagyaa*)
LEERAY COSTA

I was at yet another women's meeting with Mae Somjit, president of the rural community-based organization Project for Tomorrow (PFT, pseudonym). This three-day workshop at Chiang Mai University, organized by the Center for Lanna Women, sought to build networks of grassroots women leaders to solve social problems perpetuated by global economic restructuring and to increase women's participation in Thailand's androcentric political processes. As usual, the relatively older grassroots women like Mae Somjit were dressed in their northern Thai finest—luscious silk blouses and handwoven skirts, accented by traditional silver jewelry. Speaking animatedly in *kam mueang* (Northern Thai language), their conversations moved seamlessly from political gossip and family updates to local development projects and government policies. These women stood in stark contrast to the more youthful professors and NGO staff dressed in contemporary clothing, speaking Central Thai. For months I had been traveling with Mae to NGO and network meetings, women's workshops, and conferences. I was impressed by the respect and deference she garnered from university scholars, civil servants, and NGO representatives alike in what is otherwise a highly stratified, prestige-based society visibly marked in everyday interaction. Notwithstanding her grade school–level education and status as a rural villager and "housewife," Mae had earned an excellent reputation and numerous awards and was frequently invited to speak at events as an example of an "outstanding woman leader."

Historically, women in Thailand have been seen neither as leaders nor as agents in their own right and are notably underrepresented in formal politics.[8] Moreover, fifty years of nationalist projects for development, intimately shaped by global discourses of capitalist progress and modernity, have typically identified rural villagers—and especially women and children—as targets for change. Repeatedly, rural women's bodies have been physically and metaphorically mobilized (e.g., as factory workers, sex workers, and development recipients) by those in power to negotiate varied processes of modernity.

Yet Mae Somjit and other rural women leaders I encountered had found a way both to reinterpret the hegemonic script of development and to challenge habitual urban/rural, educated/uneducated, male/female binaries, thereby charting a geography of modernity specific to their location in the Thai social order. Creating their own community-based organizations largely through volunteerism and constructing themselves as experienced, authoritative experts on social problems in their immediate surroundings, rural women leaders positioned themselves as indispensable partners to the ever-increasing numbers of NGOs and other groups seeking to "develop" the Thai countryside since 1990. For Mae Somjit, this process began by working through her village housewife association to establish a day care center and eventually led to participation in other community groups and her founding of PFT, a volunteer organization focused on girls' education, the elimination of child prostitution, development of employment skills, and women's leadership. In the 1990s, PFT received several significant grants from international NGOs that allowed it to evolve from an entirely volunteer-run organization to a semiprofessional NGO, affirming its place in the local community development scene. This transition made possible sustained contact with more villagers, but it also increased PFT's obligation to foreign funders (practically and morally), exposing the deepening processes of NGO–ization,[9] including donor-driven agendas and a significant "self-help" orientation already present in Thai nationalist discourse. At the same time, however, it expanded Mae Somjit's personal prestige, her celebrity as a grassroots woman leader, and opportunities for empowerment.

Unlike so many rural female youth whose route to modernity has been through urban migration for work in factories and consumption of "up-to-date" products and services,[10] these women forged an alternate path to modernity through community development and women's grassroots activism. Many had only a primary school education and were thrilled (when not scared) to speak to audiences of people with bachelor and graduate degrees, from whom they also sought patronage. The events to which they were invited brought them into the modern, urban spaces of universities, hotels, and resorts otherwise reserved for social elites. Such occasions also allowed them direct access to national and international NGO representatives from whom they could (and often did) ask for money in their efforts to establish or grow their own community organizations—and with it, their personal charisma or prestige (*baramii*). Furthermore, participating in these events provided them with critical information, knowledge and training, and the opportunity to have extended periods of fun with other women while working honorably for the community.

Though occasionally criticized by family and PFT members for her jam-packed meeting schedule that took her away from home and organizational duties and into spaces where she sometimes had to interact with non-kin males, Mae Somjit justified her community development work by linking it to traditional gendered values of motherhood, sacrifice, and Buddhist merit-making. Like many of the grassroots women leaders I met, Mae Somjit identified primarily as a mother and housewife, even at age fifty-six and after eighteen years of intensive community work, an identity reinforced by the honorific "Mae" (mother) used to address her by people of all backgrounds. She spoke of the volunteer community work she did as "sacrifice" (*siasala*) for family, community, and nation and as a form of merit-making, giving it a cultural resonance and legitimacy that made her role as rural leader and empowered woman less threatening to others.

Imagining herself in this way at this particular historical moment reveals the creative ways that Mae Somjit and grassroots women leaders like her have charted a path to and through modernity. They have interpreted the possibilities of community development and women's leadership, not in ways predetermined by government officials, foreign NGOs, or even urban, middle-class feminists, but in a manner that allows them to maintain personally meaningful cultural and gendered values while exploring new ideas of what it means to be women and citizens in postmillennium Thailand.

Bangkok Slum Leader
PILAPA ESARA

Few of the people I knew while working in a Bangkok slum during 2003–2004 would willingly have chosen to live there. Khun Hin—who spent his days at the local nursery school, which doubled as a community center—is among the exceptions. On a typical morning, he would open the center and retire to the TV in the back classroom as parents dropped off their children in the front. At noon, while the preschoolers napped, Khun Hin would gate off the classroom and nap on three children's desks set side-by-side, lulled to sleep by the whir of a fan and the static emanating from the ever-present walkie-talkie by his side. His afternoon tasks included taking out snacks for the children and resuming his usual morning spot. Khun Hin is frugal, sharing his words with few and sharing a smile with even fewer. Despite his habit of spending his days in the nursery school, no one ever mistook him for one of the teachers, and I soon learned not to misjudge his seemingly leisurely routine to mean that he lacked an occupation or purpose. In spite of his casual style of dress and "peasant" appearance, Khun Hin, as an assistant to the community's chairperson, commands considerable authority and is entrusted with the safety of the community at large.

As an elected "community representative," Khun Hin is a middleman between slum residents and district officers. When the slum won an award for community development, Khun Hin was one of the invited guests at the awards ceremony. If the local police receive a tip about gambling or drug use, Khun Hin is alerted on his walkie-talkie and is on hand to guide the police through the slum's meandering narrow walkways. If a recently released convict has returned to the community, Khun Hin stealthily monitors the situation, ready to report repeat offenders. If an unsupervised candle falls burning with merciless intensity, as was the case in a recent tragic fire, now unlike then, the community has firefighting equipment and Khun Hin alone has the keys to their storage unit.

Khun Hin's home is one of twenty-eight official "slum communities" in the local district, and I am told that is it one of the biggest in size and one of a few with a community center. Khun Hin has been a resident and volunteer since the beginning, when resident landowners and squatters-turned-renters organized themselves and applied for government assistance. Now, he and the other representatives provide labor, logistical help, and publicity for government-sponsored events, which far exceed their modest stipends. They also help with other political initiatives such as a local parade declaring the community an antidrug zone and the registration of residents for a new universal health care program that promised medical care for only 30 baht.

The work of slum leaders like Khun Hin is integral to government officials who recognize the linkages between urban poverty in Bangkok, inflows of rural migrants, and the goodwill of provincial voters. Given the increase of slums in Bangkok,[11] these communities are logical targets for politicians who want to reach the disadvantaged despite information that indicates the poor do not always reside there.[12] As a result, Khun Hin is no stranger to government agendas. He and other representatives implemented local poverty registration activities based in his slum as part of a nationwide campaign in fulfillment of former prime minister Thaksin's vow to eradicate poverty in Thailand by 2010.[13] This was in addition to a controversial "war" on drugs and a social order campaign, which scholars Phongpaichit and Baker argue were used to retain public support while Thaksin's administration consolidated state control away from the military and civil society toward big business.[14] None of these campaign promises or political objectives could have been implemented without the on-the-ground efforts of slum leaders.

Occasionally slum leaders will abuse their positions to curry the favor of the powerful, as was the case when representatives were rallied by leaders to attend a religious service for the king but instead found themselves protesting the firing of a government official whom they did not know. Khun Hin's social network in particular, comprised of wealthy politicians and officials—which may have incurred the quiet criticism of some—was nonetheless impressive given the social distance between the capital's elite and the working poor and middle class. I once observed him in the back of a pickup truck, carrying a megaphone in support of a local political candidate, and it surprised me to see a man of such stoic reserve beating the stump. Even more surprising to me was this sight of a man of humble origins asserting a political voice, regardless of whether or not his opinions have been co-opted (as some may argue).

Khun Hin tells me he chooses to remain in the slum to be with his friends, but I see this as a partial truth. Only in a slum can a man like Khun Hin, a former factory worker and overseas contract laborer, take advantage of footholds in Bangkok's "money politics" by making himself a representative of the poor.[15] Ultimately, slum leaders like Khun Hin reflect Thailand's changing political-economic landscape and the ways in which citizens of modest circumstances can carve out a space for political engagement and/or power. While these leaders may wield limited spheres of influence, their participation in the delivery of local social services, urban community development, and city-wide and national political campaigns makes them crucial figures in the social geography of Thai modernity.

Transnational Farmworker
SUDARAT MUSIKAWONG

Angkan sat there on the floor outside with twenty fellow villagers, wives of friends, and some of his friends who were deported back by the company. What did they all have in common? Everyone had lost all their borrowed money paying high contracting fees. Every one of them was an H2A visa agricultural worker who had labored on pineapple and coffee plantations in Hawai'i, peach and apricot orchards in Washington's Yakima Valley, or sowed the seeds of tobacco and onions in Georgia. Accompanied by a researcher, a reporter from New York had come to hear their stories.[16] Were they here to help? Will they prevent my land from being taken by the bank and the recruiter? Only three years ago, Angkan and many others remembered the false promises by the recruiter for a well-known Bangkok labor contractor. She said she could help them get a loan to pay the contracting fee by using their farmland as collateral. Often, migrant labor subcontracting is thought of as a world full of suspicious characters connected to underground economies, while in fact for Angkan it was much simpler. When he needed a loan, his recruiter took him to the Bank of Ayudhya, of which General Electric Capital Global Banking owns the major share of 33 percent.

In the world of finance, many of the major shareholders of Thailand's banks are reputable U.S. companies like General Electric. Signing the right to their lands, Angkan and others paid the contracting fee, which was around 700,000 baht (about U.S. $20,000) for a promise of three years of full-time work in the United States at $8 to $9 an hour. The legal fees amounted to 35,000 baht, but Angkan knew that there was little choice. In his village, there had not been work for the local villagers in the area for over ten years. The ceramics factory employed only Burmese migrant workers. For Angkan, work would help pay for school expenses, repay existing debts, pay for the motorcycle, and fix the house that he inherited from his father.

Angkan went to Bangkok to get "trained" and formally sign the contract, but only after he paid the fees with the loan money. He told me that as he left his village he said, "This will be the last time [that I will leave Thailand for work]." Now in his early thirties, he and his wife appeared aged well beyond their years, and they have three children. He worked abroad while she tended the rice and vegetable fields for subsistence farming. Before spending two years unemployed, he worked in a Korean plastics factory, in construction in Singapore, oil drilling in the Middle East, and on a Kibbutz farm in Israel.

In Bangkok, he signed what seemed like blank papers—contracts that had many pages in English but few pages in Thai. A recruiter scolded them when they asked for a translation. "Do you want to go to America? Because if you do not, you can leave now!" Everyone signed. The training consisted of telling the American Embassy that 35,000 baht was paid for the recruiting fee. Angkan thought to himself, "What can I do?" He and the other recruits went back to the village after signing contracts, medical examinations, and submitting the H2A visa request. All of it was humiliating, but he needed the work. After three months waiting and paying interest on the loan by borrowing from family and other villagers, word was sent by the recruiter that it was time to go to America. For their air travel, they all had to wear the same recruiter logo T-shirt. A very tall man named Bill met them at the Los Angeles airport. Bill said some things in English, and one of the other workers started to explain what he was saying: that Bill would take their passports, because they would probably lose them. Angkan protested: "I did not want him to take my passport, but the other worker who knew more English than I did said if I did not want to get sent back, I needed to be obedient. This is what they said at every farm."

Sometimes the workers were sent to farms to work for a couple of hours. When there was work, it was backbreaking, but there were many weeks without work. Many of the workers talked about how, as their debts increased, the stress and anxiety grew unbearable. They were under constant surveillance by their bosses. Another villager told me,

> After working for three months in Hawai'i, the boss came while we were working in the fields and said to pack up. They drove us to an empty building. We slept there overnight packed on the floor. There were guards with guns around the building. We all knew they were going to send us back. One of my friends tried to go outside to smoke a cigarette. A guard came and slapped him around and he came back crying. We only worked on and off for three months, never full time, and debt piled up. We came back to Thailand with nothing.

Now faced with lawsuits threatening to take their land and homes as collateral for their unpaid debts, many of the villagers sought to fight dispossession by going to the local Ministry of Labor offices and the police. But Angkan said, "What can we do? The recruiter, she is a big thread with many con-nections, but I am only a small string." Out of the thousands of cases of vil-lagers, hundreds are coming forward to work with the U.S. Department of Justice under investigations of labor trafficking. In a new logic of regulated labor migration and late capitalism, free trade means that labor is flexible, so that migrant labor displaces domestic labor and state regulation of migra-tion through temporary "guest worker" visas, making ripe conditions for labor trafficking. The poor are indebted, dispossessed, disposable, and trafficked, yet ultimately, labor contractors and banks turn a profit.

Thai Airways Flight Attendant
JANE M. FERGUSON

This Thursday afternoon finds Nataporn working as the purser on Thai Airways Kunming to Bangkok flight. As the flight is the second leg of a "quick turn," there is no time for the crew to leave the aircraft after unloading passengers in Kunming before taking on another set of passengers bound for Bangkok. The loads are full both ways for this Airbus A300, and Nataporn hasn't had a moment to eat her crew meal. Compounding the problem on this particular aircraft is the fact that a design quirk of the rear jump seats and the door swing of the lavatories means that every time the lav door is opened, the jump seats must be retracted as well. For Nataporn, this means she eats sit-ting down and intermittently stands up as passengers enter and exit the lav. A seventeen-year veteran of Thai Airways, Nataporn is no stranger to this form of dining.

Sarawanee, a fourteen-year-old girl from Bangkok waiting to use the lav, notices Nataporn and in earnest admiration, strikes up a conversation: "I want to be a flight attendant someday! I love Thai Airways, I think your job is so stylish, and I love to travel and see so many different places in the world!"

Putting down her spoon and carefully wiping her mouth with her tissue, Nataporn smiles politely to Sarawanee, briefly thanks her, and returns to her meal. Sarawanee, however, is still interested in talking. "How can I become a flight attendant?"

Flattered by the innocence of Sarawanee's remarks and questions, Nataporn explains: "Well, this job is not just about looking good in a uniform and traveling to exciting places. You need to speak English well, you need to be willing to work with others, you need to be able to tolerate being away from home and family—"

"Phii Puer! There's an *ika* in 10C—after Sumalee told him he appeared intoxicated and refused to serve him more alcohol, he groped her! He keeps ringing the call button," exclaims Hattaya, interrupting Nataporn, yet carefully holding a teapot in one hand and a tray of sugar packets and limes in the other.

Ika, meaning "squid" in Japanese, has become a Thai Airways slang word for a male passenger who drunkenly gropes women. Nataporn, being the purser (as indicated by her Thai-English airline argot appellation, "Phii Puer"), is at the top of the chain of command for the flight attendants working this flight, and returning to "flight attendant mode," she leaves her tray of half-eaten food on the galley counter to go and confront the squid in 10C.

For Nataporn and other Thai Airways flight attendants, they occupy a complex structural role in Thai modernity: the airline itself is symbolic of the nation, as technology and transportation bring ideas about Thailand, its food, and most problematically its service and its women to the international arena and back to Thailand as well. Advertisements for the airline are graced by the smiles of flight attendants in uniform and slogans such as "Smooth as Silk" and "We love you as much as heaven" (*Rak khun tao faa*). The lived reality of this work for Nataporn, as a marketed icon of and for Thai femininity, is that she navigates the complexities of gender, class, and emotional work, miles above sea level in a pressurized aluminum tube. For the much longer transcontinental flights, Nataporn must change uniforms as well; at the beginning of the flight, she dons the "traditional" Thai uniform, replete with sarong and sash, but for serving breakfast, she changes into a Western-style blouse, skirt, and apron.

In Thailand, government interest in aviation has historically preceded military necessity. Although the country's security was ensured by its "buffer state" position between French Indochina to the east and British Burma to the west, in the early twentieth century the military grew formidably. During the First World War, a squadron of Siamese fighter pilots and SPAD aircraft were sent to assist the Allied side in Europe. Aviation technologies throughout the twentieth century have been icons of modernity; during the 1950s, Yangon's Mingaladon Airport was the transit hub for the region, and since then this position has been usurped by Bangkok's Don Muang Airport, and now Suvarnabhumi International Airport. The opening of the latter in 2006 was received with great fanfare, and families even parked cars and had picnics with the glistening new airport in view on the structure's opening day.

The flight crews of Thai Airways are drawn disproportionately from Bangkok's upper middle classes. Invariably they have university degrees, and in today's globalizing world this can cause potential culture clashes in having to serve an increasingly diverse flying public. Migrant workers from Thailand's impoverished northeast traveling as part of international labor recruitment schemes are occasionally treated with resentment or disdain by the educated—otherwise elite—Thai flight crews. On the other hand, the objectification of Thai women and gender inequities from other cultures create difficult situations as well, as exemplified by the "squid" incident above.

After apologizing to the passenger in 10C, Nataporn returns to the aft galley only to find that her half-eaten crew meal has already gotten cold. Looking at her watch and sensing the descent of the aircraft, Nataporn quickly realizes that she must prepare the cabin for landing. Sighing, she tosses her meal in the trash, knowing she has to attend to a number of tasks ahead of her before the two cabin chimes will indicate that she must return to her jump seat for landing.

Kickboxer
PATTANA KITIARSA

Thailand won its first-ever Olympic gold medal when Somrak Khamsing outscored his opponent in the featherweight division boxing competition in 1996. Somrak celebrated his victory by holding and hoisting the image of His Majesty King Bhumibol Adulyadej high above his head, as the loudspeakers played the national anthem and he tearfully sang along. Somrak's celebration of his Olympic victory was immensely powerful in the eyes of Thai people, who witnessed a fellow national from a poor country background winning the most prestigious athletic award on the world stage.

Born and raised in a village near the provincial town of Khon Kaen, northeastern Thailand, Somrak started his Thai-style boxing (Muai Thai) career when he was twelve years old. He first learned his trade from his stepfather and fought in local temple fair venues before entering professional fights in Bangkok and other major cities. Only after Somrak became a famous Muai Thai national champion in his late teens did he turn to the international-style amateur boxing with the Thai national team. It was the 1996 Olympic victory that elevated him to the status of national hero.

Muai Thai is a major culturally embedded ground of cultivating national manhood. Monthien Muang Surin, a Khorat native and ex-Muai Thai champion in the 1970s, told me in an interview that "Muai Thai is our blood. You can prove it easily. When you meet a young boy, three or four years old, press your hand against his forehead and stay a little further away from him. Observe closely how he reacts to your domination. All hundred out of a hundred Thai boys would naturally kick or punch you back in the air."

Conventional views tell us that Muai Thai is an ancient martial art that Thais have inherited from their ancestors. This idea stems from the popularization of "Muai Thai mythology," depicting heroic kings, princes, and warriors as champions and masters of the sport.[17] Muai Thai has two traditional social roles. First, as an art of wartime fighting and self-defense, it was part of Siamese traditional basic military training, in combination with weapons such as knives, swords, and spears. Second, Muai Thai was a folk performance during annual temple festivals, along with other pastimes such as cockfighting, fish fighting, kite flying, or boat racing. It was a venue for young men from different localities to show off their physical prowess and earn prize money. Top fighters were chosen to represent their villages at higher-level venues in the capital cities. Many were later appointed as pages in the royal palace or adopted as guards by nobles.

Muai Thai entered its modern stage as European-style modernity reached Siam in the second half of the nineteenth century. When the Marquess of Queensberry boxing rules were published in London in 1867, Muai Thai was still a bare-handed combat sport with few officially sanctioned rules. Even though boxing attracted a large crowd, fighters did not wear trunks, gloves, or other protective gear other than loincloths and hemp coverings for their fists, and they fought on the bare ground. Under royal patronage by the boxing enthusiast monarchs, Muai Thai became an integral part of military training when the King Chulalongkorn Military Academy was established in 1887. The Ministry of Education formally organized a boxing tournament at the Royal Plaza in 1897 and introduced the sport to school children a decade later, while the Ministry of Finance began to collect a 15 percent tax on the gate fee during Muai Thai competitions around the same period. In the 1920s and 1930s, Muai Thai adopted Western boxing rules (e.g., wearing gloves and trunks and building permanent rings), while it retained its traditional elements such as paying homage to the teacher at the beginning of each bout and playing traditional Thai music during the fight.

Modern Muai Thai is first and foremost a prize-fighting competition. Pairs of men duel for prize money under the referees' supervision. The promoters control the gate and spectators bet on the result. Through a dubious metaphor conceiving boxers as "hunting dogs,"[18] Muai Thai is a way for capable boys and men to earn some monetary rewards. However, money and material gain do not mean everything in the world of Muai Thai; it also imprints in men a sense that boxers are ideal representations of individual and national heroism. Muai Thai fighters' performance is governed by a set of cultural values called honor or dignity (*saksi*) and shame (*khwam na la-ai*). Both of these are culturally loaded constructs conditioned by the cultural practices of face. A Muai Thai fighter has to embrace and uphold such boxing values by strictly following certain sets of professional ethics and moral obligations. Match fixing, for example, is considered the severest form of violation because it is an act of public embarrassment and disgrace.

Muai Thai is a method of modern male inclusion, as well as an expression of masculine honor for young men from different parts of the country. The boxers come from the vast rural peripheries, as Muai Thai presents a passage to Western-style, Bangkok-centered modernity. Indeed, boxers epitomize men at their physical and mental peaks. They are fighters who have spent years training their bodies, turning them into weapons to fight opponents onstage. Fighting under agreed rules and supervision, the ring of Muai Thai and the world surrounding it has become a modern "sacred inclosure" where men's aggression is measured and watched.[19] Muai Thai is a theater for the public to take pleasure in the bouts of human cockfighting and for young men themselves to experience and express human hurt and agony. Their life passage to modernity is inevitably filled with sweat, blood, and pain.

Single Woman
EMILY ZEAMER

Stuck in a Bangkok traffic jam, I passed the time in conversation with the taxi driver, mentioning in passing that I was conducting research in Thailand. Since we were near a neighborhood known for its many brothels, he asked me, with a grin, if I knew why there were so many prostitutes. I confessed I didn't. "Because of Thailand's population problem," he informed me. Had I heard about it? "Too many women, not enough men—the women don't like it, but they have to share!" he roared.

While it turns out (I checked) that the gender balance in Thailand is much the same as the rest of the world, the city seemed rife with evidence of a female population explosion. Single women complained it was difficult to find a man interested in settling down; it seemed that there had never been so many attractive women for them to choose from. The numbers did not quite add up.

But the phenomenon of the urban single woman was also evidence of Thailand's economic transformation. Younger women—especially those who came of age after the first years of the economic boom in the late 1980s—were often referred to as "smarter" than their predecessors. Not only better educated, they were also seen as more willing to stand up for themselves in their relationships with men. Independent incomes provided working women with more flexibility in making domestic arrangements. When younger women spoke of marriage and motherhood, it was often to say that they would rather wait.

"I think 100 percent of married women have problems," Jiem, in her early thirties, told me not long after we met. Men still saw women as possessions, while women were taught to accept whatever a husband delivers. "The man comes home one evening angry or in a bad mood, she has to take it. If he loses interest in her, she has to accept it. Whatever he wants, she has to go along with it."

Jiem seemed to relish her single life. She was enthusiastic about her job selling life insurance and annuities, which she saw as ingenious financial tools that could keep families from falling into the cycle of poverty. While her working days were busy with appointments and meetings, she often spent evenings in her tiny apartment, reading books on her two favorite topics: spirituality and entrepreneurship. Her daily routine seemed far removed from the grief and confusion that she described as typical of married life.

It was several months before I discovered that Jiem was not as single as I assumed she was: she had a husband and a teenage son. She told me that when she had been promoted to work in Bangkok the year before, her husband had elected to stay behind for his work. Their only son was a dormitory student at a selective public high school in the district capital and was already preparing for his college entrance exams. Now that her child was nearly grown, Jiem saw her duty toward her family as nearing an end. She was now free to reimagine herself as a modern single woman, empowered to pursue her own goals.

Jiem's cynical view of marriage resonates with popular Thai views on the incompatibility of masculine and feminine "natures." Thai popular culture is filled with stereotypical tales of fickle and promiscuous men and steadfast yet heartsick women.[20] While women are thought of as innately nurturing, it is also considered the moral responsibility of every good Buddhist woman to care for her family. Marriage and motherhood are thus seen as the ideal fulfillment of both feminine instinct and spiritual duty. At the same time, masculinity is seen as inherently active and virile, and it is widely accepted that sexual release is necessary for a man's health. Given the incompatibility between masculine and feminine desires, Thai women have long been taught that the stability of a marriage depends on the virtue, diligence, and above all the patience of the wife. Thus, a solitary woman—whether divorced or never married—represents the failure of both feminine nature and duty.[21]

Clever, independent, yet also alone, the stereotype of the single woman has more recently been recast as a bellwether of the corrosive effects of capitalism and globalization, destroying the fabric of traditional values. In these conservative discourses, economic development figures as a destructive force, leaving in its wake a wreckage of broken homes and barren, lonely souls.

Yet I have found that even the most self-consciously modern Thai women still strive to live up to traditional standards of feminine success, which are still largely equated with caring for others and fulfilling family duty. Jiem, a

married woman, had just begun experimenting with the freedom and autonomy she associated with single life: the timing of her choices showed clearly
that she saw freedom for a woman as something won not by avoiding family
duty but by conscientiously fulfilling it. The fragmented fantasy of the single
woman reflects a shared sense that the ground is shifting. In a world charged
with new opportunities, it seems that principles of tradition and patterns of the
past provide the best guide, if still an uncertain one.

Rural DJ
JULIA CASSANITI

It has been months after the coup d'état of September 19, 2006, and Goi,
the DJ of a rural northern Thai radio station, still hasn't been able to get on
the air. The Thai government has closed down all local stations ("for fear,"
people whisper, "that some of Thaksin's supporters might stir up dissent").
Goi is getting anxious. Finally, permission is received and she heads out to
the small studio in the shed behind her house, takes her place behind the computer, and links in to the head broadcasting station in Chiang Mai. Her radio
station, cm77.com, can soon be heard throughout the village. What is heard,
however, is not a political commentary on the coup and its aftereffects, nor a
light-hearted Thai pop song, both possible (and likely) broadcasts elsewhere.
Instead, the sound is that of a monk chanting in a soft Pali cadence, and it is
only hours later that Goi or any of her fellow DJs speak, in a clear and calm
Northern Thai language (*kam mueang*). When Goi signs off and reemerges
from her studio, she is happy and smiling.

At first glance, this moment seems to represent the antithesis of modernity: it is clearly traditional, harking back to a Thai imaginary of Pali monks
and Northern Thai culture. Yet there is also something uniquely modern about
it, about Goi, and her rural DJ friends. The traditionalism the rural DJ advocates is a self-conscious and reactionary one, marked by a rejection of what
it sees as other, negative forms of modernity. And in her choice of medium it
is especially contemporary, using technologies not simply to spread this type
of modern traditionalism but also, in doing so, altering the possible landscape
of the traditional. As Charles Hirschkind tells us for the case of new Islamic
forms of modernity, the rural DJ alters the soundscape of other Northern Thai
people by appropriating the means of "modern technologies" (in this case, the
airwaves) to put forward a quintessentially liberal traditionalist agenda, one
to which everyone has access.[22] The rural DJ is in a way utopian: she wants
to return to an imagined Northern Thai past, one without the need or value
for currency, where people were (the image holds) at peace with themselves,

each other, and the environment. Ideologically, however, the imagined past is one that is markedly modern. She lives with her parents as she "ought to," together with her female lover—a relationship seldom publicly condoned; she pays respect to her elders but talks down sternly to an old man found drunk in a temple; she lives in a rural community but was educated in an urban one; she preaches respect for nature but rather than being apprehensive of the wilderness takes everyone at the radio station on a Western-style camping trip complete with tents and guide; she makes merit at the temple but says real merit-making, following a modernist reading of merit, is to be aware of nonself and impermanence internally.[23] The rural DJ rejects negatively perceived outside influences of capitalism through her use of traditional cultural idioms.[24] She does so, however, in a novel and interpretive way.

These cultural idioms are often Buddhist, but they are also a particular kind of Buddhism, one that is partially a product of the more mainstream form of modernity being rejected. Rather than the Buddhism of her village, the Buddhism used by the rural DJ is considered by some locals to be modern, following particular historical trajectories of Buddhist thought inspired in part by the scholar-monk Buddhadhasa Bhikkhu and others like him. The northern DJ challenges modern hegemonic distribution of religious "truth," but unlike premodern radical movements begun by charismatic leaders at the peripheries, the postmodern movements she supports originate and grow from disenchanted young professionals in urban centers.[25] Making use of ideologies crafted at these urban centers (and even more widely casting nets from multiple global discourses) and applying them in localized, rural imaginaries, the ethnoscape of the northern DJ thus appears traditional.[26]

The king's popular sustainability campaign and other like-minded government programs have given legitimacy to scaled-back, environmentally conscious modern citizens, bringing both awareness of and increased allegiance with this figure of modernity. As with modernity elsewhere, the promise of education in Thailand inadequately correlates with career opportunities. Along with the normative Thai practice of returning to one's hometown to care for aging parents, many younger people also bring back certain urban ideologies. Faced with ambivalence about aligning identities with the rural traditionalism of their past on the one hand and disenchanted with what they come to see as an urban rat race on the other, the northern DJ and others like her are reinventing themselves.

A few weeks after the radio station got back on the air, Goi was at a community organization meeting, planning the village's annual *tin jok* cloth festival, the biggest local event of the year. An argument had started up around whether or not to sell the cloths on display at the festival, and Goi was adamantly against it. Idealistically, but with conviction, she spoke up: "Once you make money off something, once your weaving is for sale, you start to weave for the money. Your culture becomes a commodity and you lose touch with your weaving, with your way of life." The others in the room disagreed. Goi left the meeting and returned home, heading to her backyard studio to announce on the radio an upcoming culture night at a local temple she was planning. A week later, the event took place, the children having congregated from hearing her announcements on the radio. They sang and danced in the traditional Northern Thai style Goi taught them, and she was happy with the turnout. Through her work with the radio station and her other more subtle forms of resistance to what she sees as an overwhelming tide of popular capitalism, Goi, the northern DJ, represents a marginalized but growing figure within Thai modernity.

Spirit Medium
ANDREW JOHNSON

Mother Kham leaned back in her blue plastic chair. Kham was in her mid-fifties, her face lined but still lively. She wore a bright yellow polyester tunic and turban, colors she wore when possessed by the "Lord of the Golden Throne" (Jao Pho Thaen Kham Leuang), a fortune-telling spirit of a long-dead warrior king. She reached out her hands and face from under the rented blue and yellow tent and raised them up toward the gray, glowering sky. "Fall, fall, fall!" she called out, squeezing her hands together as if wringing the rain out of the heavy clouds.

At the same time, another spirit medium, similarly dressed in brightly colored polyester tunic and turban, took me by the arm and dragged me past where her peers were dancing under the tent to a brass band. The band's singer smiled, embarrassed, as the medium poked me in the chest, pointed toward the band, and rubbed her index finger against her thumb suggestively. Her spirit, unlike that of Kham, did not speak. After I gave the singer a tip, the medium repeated the action, this time raising one finger, indicating that I should give one hundred baht, or about U.S. $3. She continued until I refused to give any more. It was as I returned to my seat when I noticed the parallel: the medium, like Kham, had recognized a potentiality. While the rain clouds suggested the arrival of the rainy season and the subsequent prosperity toward Chiang Mai's agricultural economy, this medium saw in me a different form of potential, and while Kham drew the rain from the clouds for the farmer's benefit, the other medium drew the cash from my wallet for the singer's benefit.

These mediums, referred to in Northern Thai as a "ridden horse" (*maa khi),* host various kinds of spirits, from guardians of land or neighborhoods to the displaced souls of warriors or witches, and all are conceived of as largely benevolent spirits, having remained on the earth to improve their own karma by aiding humanity. As they are so concerned with furthering the fortunes of their (once) fellow humans, traditional Northern Thai mediums, in contrast to monks, provide advice and services on immediate worldly matters: romance, money, and illness. As Chai, a young Northern Thai spirit devotee put it, "Monks are in the world of monks, spirits are in the world of people." But the power that spirit mediums have over fortune also extends toward misfortune. Chai related a story about how his community in the distant Chiang Mai suburbs held a praise ceremony for the local guardian spirit after a lapse of several years. The spirit descended in a mad rage, accused the town of neglecting him, and claimed responsibility for a rabid dog that had bitten several people the year before.

Mediums, as the arbiters of the inchoate forces of fortune and misfortune, play an increasing role in direct contrast to a Weberian assumption about modernity's disenchanting effects. Walter Irvine noted the rise in spirit mediumship that accompanied Chiang Mai's urbanization,[27] but such a rise stands in direct opposition to the rationalizing forces of the state and organized religion. Pattana Kitiarsa describes the efforts of the Thai state and Buddhist *sangha* in attempting to limit the power of mediums by publicly attacking mediums' claims to spiritual power, yet she concludes that "What Thailand's spirit cults offer to their followers—what significant numbers of people clearly need—is advice, comfort, and a promise of understanding the future in an uncertain world."[28]

Yet mediumship is rapidly changing as Thailand urbanizes: figures such as Chai's medium and Mother Kham—those mediums who center their practice on a certain location or neighborhood—give way to mediums based around a particular spirit's fame or a medium's individual charisma. As an example, "Lord Chiang Mai Gate," the guardian of an urban neighborhood in the central part of the city, lacks a medium, yet the cult of "Lord Hundred-Thousand Coins" flourishes. In the constantly shifting urban realm, cults centered on personal networks rather than auspicious places have more relevance to Chiang Mai's increasingly dislocated residents. Additionally, in an economy based on wage labor, a person's fortunes do not rise and fall as a village (e.g., with cycles of rain and drought), but rather through the seemingly inexplicable forces of an economy that rewards one person and starves another. Spirit mediums, then, as they shift from a neighborhood to an individual focus, reflect that change.

Mediums are themselves not immune from the dislocating forces of the modern economy. Kham was displaced from her home in San Sai, the dwelling place of her inhabiting spirit, when the boom in Chiang Mai's suburban real estate caused prices to soar, and she moved to Mae Taeng, a satellite town to Chiang Mai's north. She travels an hour on the back of her daughter's motorbike, suitcase with her lord's regalia in tow, for the yearly rite of propitiation in late May or early June at her shrine built on friends' property near her former home. Her devotees form a line outside of her shrine, asking for help with college entrance exams, beating the army conscription lottery, or advice on unfaithful husbands, and her rainmaking is simply a demonstration of her kingly power. After she gives them advice or recipes for magical formulae, she offers a brief blessing: "May you be happy, may you be cool, may you be healthy. May you get a thousand [baht], may you get a hundred thousand, may you get a million. May you progress."

Hmong-Thai Schoolgirl
TRACY PILAR JOHNSON

Late in 2002 I sat with a group of Hmong girls in the playground of their school, nestled in the mountain highlands of northern Thailand. The discussion turned to what would happen in the coming months when they would graduate and leave the mountain village of Ban Rongrian to attend school elsewhere. Some would go to Chiang Mai, while others would go even further. These students were both excited and anxious about the prospects of leaving Ban Rongrian. The anxiety they felt centered on their ability to speak Thai and to thus present themselves as Thai. One girl, Ntxawm, was particularly concerned about the words that she relied on when speaking Hmong for which she was unable to find the appropriate translation when speaking in Thai. The example causing the most concern was how to translate the Hmong word '*kuv*,' meaning 'I,' into Thai. The question as it was posed to me was, "How do I say '*kuv*/I' in Thai?" or in other words, how was a young Hmong student to talk about who she was in Thai?

The problematics of enunciation—or the ways in which social actors struggle to articulate themselves across the field of language and of social practices—had become the background for many conversations about education taking place on the mountain. The previous fall, a new indigenous curriculum (*laksut thongthin*) had been introduced into the village school by a local upland nongovernmental community development organization. Based on the premise that each new generation of Hmong youth was losing its culture—most prominently through the inability to speak Hmong correctly—the curriculum had as its goal teaching upland youth about their local culture.

The curriculum, with its desire to return to "authentic" Hmong traditions and values, would combat this loss, thus ensuring that Hmong youth would become modern Thai citizens, with their Hmong cultural identity intact.

The curriculum, although sponsored by the Thai national education department, sat uneasily within the system of education as practiced in the village of Ban Rongrian. The school was exemplary of the tension inherent in the Thai education system for educating its minority peoples. This tension stems from particular Thai understandings of identity that are based on a binary opposition between what is Thai and what is not. Here, Thai-ness signifies a modern national identity that stands in stark contrast to Thai ethnic minority peoples, such as the Hmong, who have been marginalized through an extensive regime of power/knowledge that continuously constructs them as the "other." The school promises to equip Ntxawm with the tools that she needs to express a Thai identity at the same time that it strongly prohibits any play along the borders of this identity. One of the things that guards this border is a political economy of speech in which Thai language ideologies demand that Ntxawm, if she is to be thought of as Thai, must speak Thai clearly, at the same time that a complete lack of pedagogical commitment to truly educating these young Hmong students denies Ntxawm the possibility of ever learning how to speak Thai clearly.

In discussing Ntxawm's question, I contrast competing claims of modernity: those of the Thai state and those of a young Hmong girl. The girl struggles daily to integrate competing notions of self into a multivocal narrative. As Ntxawm imagines continuing her schooling at the junior high and high school (*matayom*) in Chiang Mai and fulfilling her dream of opening up a hairdressing shop, she draws on a particular form of identification with the Hmong word "*kuv.*" When she speaks "*kuv*/I," she can draw on the whole of her history as she projects herself into the future, whereas when she is forced to use one of the more hierarchically based and danger-ridden Thai language forms of address, such as "*nu,*" her past and her future are written for her, and she is simply a Hmong girl who must remain subservient to the majority of Thai people with whom she interacts. Embedded in the problem of finding a word for "*kuv*" in Thai is the problem of how Ntxawm can translate this imagined worldview into the Thai context and of how she can imagine herself as being something more than the Other.

The indigenous curriculum, with its grounding in a nascent Hmong consciousness, also risks failing Ntxawm in that it too tries to posit a "one true" Hmong identity. It makes the same mistakes as the Thai state it struggles against in its return to the past to uncover an ideal of authenticity, and thus it fails to allow any room for the imaginative "*kuv*/I" of Ntxawm's dreams.

Indeed, as Ntxawm and many of her fellow students said to me, the indigenous curriculum is "ancient history" (*samaii boran*). She, along with the majority of her friends and family, worry that the curriculum is pulling her back into a past in which the Hmong stand as the quintessential Other to the Thai. Ntxawm and her community question whether the curriculum can truly assist a girl like Ntxawm in successfully making her way in modern Thai society.

But while the project may be erecting a border similar to that established by the Thai national curriculum, it is possible that the reflexivity allowed with the indigenous curriculum aids Ntxawm in her new imaginings. The indigenous curriculum presents an alternative view of Hmong culture to that presented by the Thai national curriculum. This may be just enough to provide a space for Ntxawm to play with the notion of identity as a series of fluid and constantly shifting identifications, to change the conditions of possibility for her speech as a means to change the conditions of possibility for her future actions. It may be the opening for a true melding of how she sees herself as both Hmong and Thai, providing her with the tools she needs to play, or rather to push, the boundaries of both as she embraces a multivocal and more modern future.

INDONESIA

Edited by JOSHUA BARKER
and JOHAN LINDQUIST

Indonesia is not what it used to be. In early 2010, Julia Perez (aka Yulia Rahmawati), widely known as Jupe and one of the country's most well-known sex symbols and celebrities, announced that she was planning to run for district head in President Susilo Bambang Yudhoyono's home district of Pacitan in central Java. Jupe, who lived in France and the Netherlands for over a decade—and likes to speak in a mix of English, French, and Indonesian—made a name for herself when she returned to Indonesia in 2008 and released a hit *dangdut* album entitled *Kamasutra,* with sexually suggestive songs such as "Opening the Durian" ("Belah Duren").[1] Following in the wake of singers like Inul, who became an overnight sensation for her gyrating dance style, *ngebor* (literally: drilling), Jupe illuminates the changing nature of the Indonesian public sphere after the fall of dictator Suharto in 1998. She has pushed the boundaries of celebrity, both by running for political office and for speaking publicly and explicitly about sex. Not only did her first album include free condoms, but she was also named the country's "condom ambassador" by the Indonesian National AIDS Commission, and later generated widespread debate and moral backlash when she spoke openly about vaginoplasty on the television show *Celebrity Investigation* (*Investigasi Selebriti*).

Jupe's rise to fame has inevitably illuminated the anxieties of the post-authoritarian moment in this deeply heterogeneous archipelago nation where traditional forms of authority have been increasingly undermined, and the blanket of mass media—notably newspapers, television, and the Internet—has spread dramatically. These dual changes have created not only new forms of openness but also a rise in sensationalist journalism and intensifying forms of moral conservatism. Jupe's explicit sexuality, for instance, has led to frequent demonstrations by Muslim groups, who claim that she is a protagonist for "free sex." She has, for instance, been one of eight singers blacklisted by South Sumatra's Indonesian Council of Ulema, or Muslim scholars (a fact that also illustrates the decentralization of religious authority in Indonesia); and Home Affairs minister Gamawan Fauzi suggested amending eligibility criteria for public office, thus making it more difficult for celebrities like Jupe to turn to politics.

Jupe appeared to take it all in stride, claiming that the minister's suggestions were undemocratic and that campaigns claiming that she had falsified her educational certificates were slander. As she put it in one interview, "No one trusted Evita Peron, they all judged her, but she proved she could do it."[2] During her first campaign trip to Pacitan in April of 2010, the branch leader of the People's Conscience Party (Hanura), one out of eight parties backing Jupe, claimed that Pacitan needed Jupe since she spoke four languages—Dutch, French, English, and Indonesian—and was thereby well situated to attract tourists and foreign investors to the southern coast of Java. Jupe herself could only agree, as she happily taught students in an Islamic boarding school to count to ten in both Dutch and French before revealing that she would turn Pacitan into an Indonesian Monaco[3]—all events carefully staged for the media.

Jupe's political campaign, however, ended before it really began when she dropped out in August, months before the December election. Officials in the coalition had been telling reporters that they were increasingly frustrated that she never responded to their text messages. The head of the Pacitan branch of Hanura claimed that the coalition was suffering from Jupe's withdrawal, but they were already negotiating with other celebrity singers who might take over the campaign and help Pacitan realize its full potential.

In many ways, Jupe is an excellent entry point to contemporary Indonesia since she represents the most omnipotent of the figures that we describe in this chapter—namely the *selebriti,* which in its nearly direct translation suggests an opening up to a broader globalizing world. The end of Suharto's repressive New Order regime has been the occasion for the emergence of a new set of figures on the Indonesian scene. The figures on the following pages are thus all unequivocally historical; Jupe's fall, rise, and fall within the political sphere suggests an accelerating process of change and historization. By drawing attention to her and others, we seek to highlight the variegated effects of Indonesia's political opening, its adjustments to the new global economy, and its greater envelopment within webs of mass mediation. Through these figures we aim to provide a glimpse of some of the ways that Indonesians are recasting their cultural and social imaginaries as they mark off an era (*jaman*) as "post-1998," one that has yet to gain the kind of coherence and sense of future direction that many have come to expect.

The contributions to this chapter highlight several important features of the contemporary moment. First, the character and effects of capitalism and commodification are everywhere evident, but they are far from uniform. The *wanita karir,* or Career Woman, who is firmly positioned in Jakarta's landscape of consumption and fantasy (Jones), is a minor everyday version of the *selebriti,* as she deals with many of the same tensions that Jupe illuminates and generates. In some places and in some sectors, old figures of economic importance are either fading in importance or are on the verge of disappearance: the *taikong,* or migrant smuggler, in Lombok (Lindquist) and the Rich Person in Bandung (Barker) are two examples. Both are being replaced by figures that are more cosmopolitan and better schooled in bureaucratic rationality. Elsewhere, as in postconflict Aceh and on Yogyakarta's streets, we see how new figures of capitalist transformation, such as the capital-owning Street Vendor (Gibbings), the small-scale Acehnese capitalist (Grayman), the Overseas Female Labor Migrant (Silvey), and the Career Woman, are being forced to adapt to older cultures in which only certain kinds of economic figures are considered to be socially or politically legitimate. In these examples, one can already begin to discern some of the ways in which the socially disruptive forces of capitalist transformation are being overcoded and constrained by discourses that serve to reinforce older hierarchies and patterns. At the same time, one can also see—in the *rumah Saudi* and in the gaits of women arriving in Jakarta's Airport Terminal 3—how new hierarchies and patterns are starting to reshape the social landscape.

Second, the contemporary moment is characterized by a notable ambivalence in regard to older figures of societal power and political resistance. The Activist (Lee), the Ex-Combatant from the Free Aceh Movement (Grayman), the NGO Worker (Danusiri), and Mr. Hajj (Darmadi) are still very much present on the scene, but they remain only as hollow shells of their former selves. Whereas under the New Order these figures were full of gravity and authenticity, they now seem strangely empty and eerily reproducible. The individuals who for one reason or another have found themselves to be giving flesh to these figures appear as uninspired but not quite ironic. While the discursive and structural grounds for their power have fallen away, they do their best to adjust to the new circumstances while refusing to give up their figures altogether.

A third feature of this contemporary moment is the emergence of new figures who purport to speak with the kind of fullness and conviction that is lacking in the more traditional figures of societal power and political resistance. These figures—including the *pelatih spiritual* or Spiritual Trainer (Rudnyckyj) and the *teledai* or Muslim Television Preacher (Hoesterey)— seek to mediate what they believe to be the new sources of power in Indonesian society today: Islam, technology, and capital. They position themselves not as leaders but as experts, exemplars, and facilitators of a vast enterprise of self-improvement aimed at bringing individuals into line with a notion of what it means to be a good Muslim worker, manager, entrepreneur, and family member. Like the *pakar telematika*—the Telecommunications and Multimedia Expert (Strassler)—these figures claim the capacity to address the sources of anxiety and instability abroad in society. But they, too, always run the risk of being recast as charlatans or hypocrites.

Fourth, the contemporary moment is characterized by the continued importance of people who are primarily produced as empty signifiers through the mass media but who in their individual lives remain structurally invisible to—or are explicitly marginalized by—the current political and economic order. The *orang dengan* HIV/AIDS or Person with HIV/AIDS (Boellstorff), who emerged with the first Indonesian cases in the 1980s, has, as in many other countries, come to inhabit a moralizing public discourse, while a diverse population of infected individuals must deal with both the personal risks of disclosure and the political economy of medication. The *anak jalanan* or Street Kid (Brown), whose conceptual appearance can be dated to the financial crisis of the 1990s, inhabits an equally ambiguous position as an innocent child who has not yet grown up and is in fact not yet recognized as a person, but whose attempt to survive on the street calls forth various forms of state intervention. Finally, the *tenaga kerja wanita* or Overseas Female Labor Migrant, who embodies the contradictions of class and gender mobility, is both a heroic figure of national development and a tragic figure of exploitation and abuse, bound up in a moral economy of debt. Taken together, these three figures illuminate the seemingly unresolvable contradictions that many Indonesians must certainly continue to face today and tomorrow.

Telecommunications and Multimedia Expert
(*Pakar Telematika dan Multimedia*)
KAREN STRASSLER

In March 1999, a tape recording was leaked to the press of a phone conversation between a "voice like that of" President Habibie and a "voice like that of" Attorney General Andi Ghalib. The conversation between Habibie and

Ghalib about the latter's investigation of ex-president Suharto revealed the judiciary's lack of independence and the government's insincerity in responding to popular calls to bring Suharto to justice. When Ghalib denied that the voice was his own, a relatively unknown lecturer at Gadjah Mada University, Roy Suryo, offered his analysis of the recording. Using a digital "spectrum analyzer," the workings of which he explained in detail in interviews with the press, he asserted that the recording was indeed *asli* (authentic). His findings were widely hailed, and Roy Suryo proceeded to position himself as a similarly pivotal figure in a number of ensuing scandals. Shrewdly parlaying his self-proclaimed expertise into celebrity status, he became a regular pundit on the news circuit, writing columns in major newspapers and hosting his own television show (*e-Lifestyle* on Metro TV).

Press reports likened Roy Suryo to a "detective on the film stage," and there was indeed a highly theatrical quality to his performances of technical mastery. Accounts of his activities are peppered with terms that sound to most Indonesian ears like an esoteric, foreign code: "sound processor," "win-amp," "audio compositor," "frekuensi," "metadata," and so forth. As central to his public persona as the incongruous moustache overlaid on his chubby baby face are the ubiquitous *benda pusaka* (spiritually powerful objects) he carries at all times: "three cell phones, a *handy talkie* [a handheld radio transceiver], and a laptop."[4]

Roy Suryo thus carved a niche in the post-Suharto political and media landscape for the *pakar telematika dan multimedia,* who uses sophisticated technology to gauge the authenticity of various kinds of evidence at the heart of a wide range of scandals. Despite the politically sensitive nature of many of the cases to which he lent his expertise, Roy Suryo insisted that his goal was a disinterested one: that he was motivated to seek truth through "pure science."[5] Asserting, in September 2000, that photographs allegedly showing then-president Gus Dur with a mistress were authentic, he disavowed any political motive ("I am moved by feelings of a desire to know").[6] Technology in the right hands might offer unalloyed, impartial truths, but it could also be used to mislead a gullible public. Observing that "manipulation by technical means is now so advanced . . . that people's perceptions are easily confused [read: tricked]," he cast as a public service his analysis of Internet-circulated, cell-phone photographs of two celebrities engaged in intimate acts. He argued that experts "who are truly competent" serve "as expert witnesses who can give an assessment that is more objective rather than just an emotional opinion."[7] Although no one else has achieved his household-name status, a quick scan of news reports reveals a number of such experts who are routinely tapped to weigh in on various technology-related scandals.[8]

The *pakar telematika dan multimedia* is symptomatic of Indonesia's post-authoritarian political imaginary, which is haunted by questions of authority, legitimacy, and authenticity. Skepticism about the truth claims of "evidence" is not new; scholars have long noted that conspiracy theorizing pervades Indonesian political discourse and practice. Documents of uncertain authenticity and origin—what Nils Bubandt has recently called "hard copy rumors"—have often played a role in political crises.[9] The ubiquity of the *aspal* (*asli palsu*)—the authentic but false document—attests, moreover, to the endemic corruption that generates widespread distrust of documentary evidence.[10] These long-standing anxieties and doubts were exacerbated in the post-Suharto era, as the evacuation of the authoritarian center yielded a search for sources of authority and anchors for truth divorced from political power. As "reform" became hitched to the promise of "transparency," a new sense of urgency and possibility impelled the search for "authentic evidence" that would adequately ground truth claims, even as the more polyphonic public sphere multiplied political agencies and narratives, making "transparency" all the more elusive.

The crisis of credibility that gives rise to the *pakar telematika dan multimedia* is also clearly tied to the proliferation of media outlets that followed the post-Suharto relaxation of press controls. Highly competitive news media with an insatiable appetite for scandal—political or otherwise—provide the *pakar* with an audience, blurring the lines between politics and celebrity. Meanwhile, the explosion of decentralized, consumer-oriented media technologies— personal computers, the Internet, VCDs, digital photography, cell phones— contributes to a climate of confusion and suspicion about what constitutes a credible account and how truth claims are to be verified. The *pakar telematika dan multimedia* reveals the simultaneously competitive and symbiotic relationship between the conventional mass media and these new media forms; he operates from within the mainstream electronic and print media to comment on, assess, and regulate the new media. (Roy Suryo participated in the formation of the Department of Telematics, which replaced the New Order's Department of Information,[11] and he helped draft an Internet pornography law that passed in March 2008.) Ultimately he works to shore up the "traditional" authority of the electronic and print media—and the state—as arbiters of truth against the dangerous rumors that circulate via alternative media circuits.

In post-Suharto Indonesia, a more diversified and unregulated media ecology combines with political freedoms to generate a public sphere plagued by persistent doubts about the authority and credibility of various kinds of truth claims and concerns about how to control information flows that escape conventional forms of regulation. The *pakar telematika dan multimedia* emerges as a new figure of authority in this environment. Yet his authority has not gone uncontested. In the Indonesian blogosphere, Roy Suryo is widely reviled and ridiculed as sensation hunting,[12] a "charlatan" ignorant of the very technical matters over which he claims mastery.[13] A video posted on YouTube in July 2008, titled "Boy Suryo: Pakar Multimedia dan Telematika," features a spoof in which a Roy Suryo look-alike—complete with fake moustache— describes his methods to an earnest television talk-show host.[14] Boy Suryo dramatically explains absurdly basic things about the computer, such as how to "click" and the way to identify how recently a file has been modified, concluding improbably with the assertion that photos of a parliamentarian in compromising poses with a singer are "1,000 percent *asli.*" Poking fun at the *pakar* and the televisual spectacle that surrounds him, the video—a false recording that nevertheless reveals a certain truth—not only challenges the authority of the old media but mocks the very search for authenticity upon which the *pakar telematika* feeds.

Muslim Television Preacher (*Tele-Dai*)
JAMES HOESTEREY

Abdullah Gymnastiar, the charismatic television preacher known popularly as "Aa Gym," captured the hearts of Indonesians with his humorous sermons and self-help message of Manajemen Qolbu (MQ, "Heart Management"). Between 2002 and 2006, millions of viewers watched his television shows, stadium crowds gathered for his sermons, and hundreds of thousands made pilgrimages to his Islamic school and Manajemen Qolbu training complex, Daarut Tauhiid. One particular morning, MQ trainees and "spiritual tourists" gathered in the courtyard behind Gymnastiar's house, where he and his wife Ninih sat on an elevated stage, flanked on all sides by a huge backdrop displaying the logos of his twenty-three companies, along with motivational banners, a kiosk selling his books and sermons, a promotional sign for his television drama *The Smiling Family,* and a framed portrait of Gymnastiar, Ninih, and their seven smiling children. Together, trainees, tourists, and Gymnastiar and his wife watched Gymnastiar's video autobiography—what he calls his *qolbugrafi.* During the Q&A session that followed, someone asked, "What's the secret to your success?" Gymnastiar replied, "The three M's: *Mulai* [begin] with yourself; *mulai* with small things; *mulai* right now. Success in business requires courage." Then, gazing deep into his wife's eyes, Gymnastiar continued, "And success at home requires love, compassion, and two-way communication." A group of women began to clamor, and one chimed in loudly, "Are you men listening? Love and compassion!"

"This is not real Islam. It's about the economy, stupid," one Indonesian intellectual remarked when I asked his opinion about Aa Gym and Manajemen Qolbu. I admired the witty turn of phrase and understand when academics chuckle at the smoke and mirrors of Islamic television and the self-help slogans of Aa Gym; yet our amusement alone does nothing to explain why Indonesians are watching *tele-dai* programs, buying their books, and paying for their text messages. Dorothea Schulz, writing about the celebrity preacher Cherif Haidara of Mali, urges scholars to explore "the ways in which material objects, consumption practices, and certain forms of media engagements are constitutive of religious experience, authority, and legitimacy."[15] In this essay, I consider how the preacher-disciple relationship is configured within the marketplace of Islamic modernity.

Muslim television preachers worldwide are popular in their respective countries and occasionally across national borders (for example, Amr Khaled of Egypt broadcasts on pan-Arab television, and his books are translated into Indonesian). In contemporary Indonesia, *tele-dai* are among the most iconic figures of public piety. The word *dai* ("one who invites people to Islamic life") has entered the everyday lexicon, due in part to the popularity of *tele-dai* contests modeled after "American Idol" and featuring popular *tele-dai* as jurors. In this sense, *tele-dai* have become a "new celebrity type" in Indonesia.[16]

The figure of the popular preacher in Indonesia, however, is not exactly new. Gymnastiar's predecessors include national figures such as Hamka (of *Tasawuf Modern* fame) and Zaenuddin MZ, the "preacher of a million followers" who attained widespread popularity in the 1980s with his Sundanese humor, cassette sermons, and film and television roles, in which he figured as the moral protagonist.[17] The privatization and proliferation of television media in the last decade, along with the increased popularity of Islamic programming, also enabled the figure of *tele-dai* to gain social, economic, and even political traction.

These preachers collectively make up a cast of characters who must be considered individually, for each crafts a particular persona and targets specific markets. As one television executive explained, "Aa Gym's specialty is 'Heart Management' and is popular with women, Arifin does *dzikir* [remembrance of God] recitation, and Yusuf does *sedekah* [alms-giving]." Arifin Ilham leads "Dzikir Nasional" recitations in Indonesia's largest mosques (alongside politicians such as Hidayat Nur Wahid), and his followers can subscribe to *Al-Qur'an Seluler* to receive inspirational text messages. Yusuf Mansur rose to fame with his autobiographical story about his struggles in jail, where he found God, repented, and developed seminars about the "Power of Giving." Jefri al-Buchori, aka Ustad Gaul (hip preacher), popular among youth for his self-professed "funky" style of propagation, helped lead the "million Muslim march" in 2006 that demanded the passage of a controversial antipornography bill. Popular *muslimah* figures such as Zaskia Mecca and Inneke Koesherawati have branded themselves as icons of feminine piety.

In addition to considering these historical antecedents and contemporary comparisons, we should note an equally important phenomenon: how *tele-dai* promote themselves within the market niche of the burgeoning self-help industry. Through television shows, newspaper advice columns, and training seminars, *tele-dai* often cast themselves as self-help gurus to whom followers turn for counsel on personal problems; in short, they do not choose to function conventionally as orthodox preachers from whom Muslims seek rulings on Islamic law. One revealing example of this general tendency to adopt a new role was the $250-per-person seminar, "Mars and Venus at Home and in the Workplace," featuring Gymnastiar, American psychologist John Gray, and Indonesian get-rich-quick guru Tung Desem Waringin. Through training seminars and televised sermons, Gymnastiar marketed himself as the embodiment of piety and prosperity, as loving husband, and as successful entrepreneur. He transformed his life story into a brand narrative that cemented affective and economic exchange relationships with his consuming devotees. Gymnastiar promoted this narrative in the marketplace of a psychoreligious modernity.[18]

Those awestruck "spiritual tourists" at Daarut Tauhiid did not have a relationship with Gymnastiar; they had a relationship with the idea—the brand narrative—of Aa Gym as the perfect and financially successful husband of a happy family. When Gymnastiar took a second wife in 2006, the brand narrative collapsed, former admirers were furious, and his business empire crumbled.[19] As the story of the rise and fall of Aa Gym suggests, brand narratives mediate the affective and economic relationships between preacher-producers and consumer-disciples. Within the marketized preacher-disciple relationship, devotees play an important role in shaping the public meanings and economic value of religious brands. The economic viability and religious authority of *tele-dai* depend, in part, on the consumption of (or refusal to consume) these metanarratives about popular preachers who market themselves as the embodiment of "modern" Islam. The phenomenon of *tele-dai* certainly is about the economy, but it is also about a very real, lived Islam.

Spiritual Trainer (*Pelatih Spiritual*)
DAROMIR RUDNYCKYJ

As we sat at a roadside restaurant in Cilegon, Banten, on a pitch-black evening, Haidar expressed increasing frustration that, as he saw it, employees of state-owned companies lacked the motivation to work hard. He had formerly worked for a major multinational corporation in Jakarta and was now a human resources trainer contracted by Krakatau Steel, a massive state-owned enterprise in western Java. Haidar became increasingly agitated when describing the work ethics of employees at state-owned companies. He was annoyed that he had heard employees joking that KS (the acronym for Krakatau Steel by which the company was known across Indonesia) actually stood for *kerja santai,* or "relaxed work." He was likewise unimpressed by the lackadaisical manner of Krakatau Steel employees arriving at work. "They show no embarrassment at showing up ten, fifteen, twenty minutes late! And they do it over and over! They have no shame about it!" Haidar was becoming increasingly convinced that what he saw as a set of moral failings could only be resolved by merging the principles drawn from American business management primers with Islamic history, Qur'anic injunctions, and examples from the life of the prophet Muhammad. Several months later, he became an employee of the Emotional and Spiritual Quotient (ESQ) Leadership Center, a rapidly growing company in contemporary Indonesia that has trademarked a spiritual training program that seeks to enhance both the economic productivity and religious discipline of Indonesian workers by enhancing their Islamic practice.

Haidar was one of a number of spiritual trainers, or *pelatih spiritual,* whom the ESQ Leadership Center had hired to reproduce spiritual training on a mass scale to audiences across Indonesia and beyond. While *pelatih* originally referred to a coach, Indonesians increasingly use the word also to refer to the growing number of business consultants who serve as workplace trainers. These trainers dispense principles drawn from a variety of global sources concerning how people can become effective, productive employees of modern corporations. Spiritual trainers are significant because these figures provide a compelling example of how the nation's legacy of national development has become an existential problem. This is an existential problem inasmuch as the intensification of individual Islamic practice is seen by a new generation of young, well-educated, middle-class Indonesians as the remedy to the ills and excesses that are taken to be symptomatic of Suharto-era developmentalism.[20] Spiritual trainers claim that the New Order was characterized by corruption, cronyism, and patronage, traits succinctly captured in the abbreviation "KKN" (*korupsi, kolusi, dan nepotisme*). They seek to change the course of Indonesian development by enhancing the Islamic ethics of middle-class Indonesians.[21] They see what they have termed "spiritual reform" as a remedy to a political and economic crisis that they have conceived of as a moral crisis.[22] The "crisis" they cite was the tumultuous period that beset the country in the period immediately following the end of the Suharto regime, characterized by a dramatically declining currency, the flight of investment capital, and a period of political instability in which five different presidents held office over a span of six years.

Haidar, the spiritual trainer with whom I became best acquainted, is in some ways unique, but in other ways he is broadly representative of this figure. He is unique insofar as he had spent quite a bit of time overseas. He had studied in Malaysia but also had spent a year abroad in the United States as an exchange student during high school and had obtained a master's degree from a European university. Furthermore, prior to beginning work as a human resources trainer, he had held a job at a prestigious multinational corporation in Jakarta. In other ways, however, he is representative of the cohort hired by the ESQ Leadership Center and other programs in contemporary Indonesia that combine Islamic ethics with management knowledge.[23] These men were in their twenties or early thirties. They were all relatively well educated, with undergraduate and sometimes graduate degrees. Most of them had been educated at universities that sought to merge the tradition of Islamic study with scientific disciplines considered "modern" in Indonesia. They saw enhanced Islamic practice as a means to achieve the high standards of living that they understood as characteristic of developed nations, not as something that was in opposition to the United States or the West. But what I found most striking about these young men was that they were completely convinced by the message of spiritual reform. That is to say, they had absolutely no doubt that Islam held the key to a better life—for themselves, for other citizens, and for the nation at large.[24] It was absolutely inconceivable to them that ESQ did not offer a remedy for Indonesia's crisis. Their confidence was revealed by their refusal to accept the possibility that the principles of ESQ were grounded in anything less than absolute scientific and religious truth.

In their complete conviction, spiritual trainers like Haidar evoke another ideal type—the pious Protestants that Max Weber identified as the progenitors of what he called "the spirit of capitalism."[25] Weber persuasively demonstrated that the only way Calvinists could live with the doctrine of predestination was by convincing themselves of their salvation in spite of the overwhelmingly unlikely odds that any specific individual would, in fact, be admitted to the kingdom of heaven. Self-confidence came to occupy a central place in the pantheon of values that constitutes contemporary capitalism. Thus, Weber provided an insight that has perhaps gone underrecognized in the century of polemics that his work has incited: that faith lies at the core of capitalism as a way of life. And we continue to be told that the resolution to any crisis of confidence is complete faith—in the market, in freedom, and in the invisible hand. Hence, spiritual trainers in Indonesia make visible the centrality of faith in holding together the global economic and political orders in which they and others are enmeshed.

Person with HIV/AIDS (*Orang Dengan* HIV/AIDS)
TOM BOELLSTORFF

The Pathway Foundation is an NGO involved in HIV/AIDS prevention and treatment. It is located in Makassar, the capital of South Sulawesi Province; with about 1.25 million inhabitants, Makassar is the sixth-largest city in Indonesia. I have a long history with the Pathway Foundation; its *gay* founders named it in July 1993 while meeting in the room I was renting at the time (note that the word "*gay*" as used here is the Indonesian term). The Pathway Foundation has since become a respected NGO, with *gay* men, *warias* (male transvestites), and *lesbi* women as staff and clients, while it serves also "normal" society, providing support for people living with AIDS, the Indonesian acronym for which is ODHA.

On March 25, 2007, I was visiting Rizal with Ayu, a *waria* staff member of the Pathway Foundation known as a talented advocate. Like many ODHA who had been injecting drug users,[26] Rizal also had hepatitis C and tuberculosis. When we had visited Rizal a month before, he was already thin and frequently nauseous from his illnesses, despite taking antituberculosis and HIV antiretroviral drugs. Rizal's mother had called Ayu the day before in tears: Rizal had stopped eating but resisted going to the hospital and had weakly slapped his mother in anger at the suggestion.

When Ayu and I arrived, Rizal's mother led us to the room where he lay on a small bed. He was having difficulty breathing; his eyes, yellow from hepatitis, were fixed on the ceiling. Ayu asked Rizal why he did not want to go to the hospital, and he said it would make things hard for his mother. Ayu replied, "Staying in this bedroom, not eating, is also making things hard on her. If you regain your strength, that's what will make your mother happy." Rizal's bone-thin chest started to jerk in and out; tears fell from his yellowed eyes. Ayu asked, "If Tom and I come with you to the hospital, will you go?" Rizal agreed. We told Rizal's mother, and she started making preparations. She brought rice with broth, and Rizal ate some of it with his pills—but after a minute, he vomited it all back up. It was hard to watch someone so thin vomiting away precious nutrition and medication.

Eventually Rizal's insides calmed down; his mother got him dressed, and we eased him into a taxi. Thirty minutes later we were at the only hospital in Makassar with an AIDS ward. Ayu's talents were evident as she chatted up the staff: a check-in procedure that often took three hours was over in fifteen minutes. Rizal was now on a gurney, not yet in the AIDS ward but waiting in the main hall, where gurneys were lined up as far as you could see, filled with patients suffering from many diseases, none knowing Rizal had AIDS. And there was Rizal with an IV feeding nutrition into his body, even as his eyes still searched the ceiling, as if seeking a higher truth.

In discussing Rizal, I have chosen a story of the ODHA as someone who is not a heroic figure of *gay/waria/lesbi* resistance advocating reform of the nation's health care system, but someone who is sick and dependent on others and whose frustrations are shaped by dynamics of disclosure. As elsewhere in the world, for most Indonesians HIV/AIDS is not the ticket to stable employment in a health-advocacy organization, it is a cataclysm of illness and ostracism. The ODHA is a symptomatic figure of Indonesian modernity, "symptomatic" in senses that emically deconstruct frontiers of the metaphorical and literal. "ODHA" stands for *orang dengan HIV/AIDS*, "person with HIV/AIDS," and the first Indonesian to identify openly as such was Suzanna Murni, who in 1995 learned she was infected and worked to support other ODHAs before dying in 2002.

Many persons with HIV/AIDS in Indonesia cannot gain access to testing or treatment, and they die without a definitive diagnosis. But now that antiretroviral drugs are more affordable and accessible, some ODHAs can live nearly asymptomatic lives. Most keep silent: a few disclose their condition to select family and friends, and fewer still live openly as ODHA, working to dispel myths about HIV/AIDS. The ODHA is emerging as a category of Indonesian personhood, but one invisible to much of Indonesian society. The invisibility of most ODHAs means that they are an absent presence, a situation that recalls how unseen persons and "shapeless organizations" have long been considered threats to the nation. Anthropologists such as Leslie Butt and Karen Kroeger have observed a tight association in Indonesian public discourse between HIV/AIDS and conspiracy, which is a kind of illicit recognition of those afflicted.[27] James Siegel has noted how the modernist history by which such recognition became "centered in the Indonesian nation" is "indissociable from the history of 'communication.'"[28] As a "communicable" disease that does not leave an immediate mark on the bearer and is primarily transmitted through stigmatized practices of sex and drug use—themselves seen to be symptomatic of modernity—HIV/AIDS now informs these dynamics of recognition, misrecognition, and nonrecognition. HIV/AIDS remains an "absent presence" for most Indonesians, but this does not mean it has no social impact. By attending both to representations of "the ODHA" and the life experiences of actual ODHAs, we can learn how conceptions of disease and selfhood shape dynamics of belonging in the archipelago.

Just fifteen days before my meeting with Rizal, I spent a day at the Pathway Foundation with Susanti, a *waria* staff member known as a talented educator. Only other staff knew that Susanti was also an ODHA. On this day, a group of *gay* men and *warias* was meeting with Susanti and me to learn about HIV/AIDS. But they had, of course, been "learning" all their lives, so it was not a complete surprise when one young *waria* said, "Well, if I found out I was an ODHA, I'd drink poison." There was nervous laughter from the group; Susanti, in the midst of the laughter, just sat quietly, with a smile somewhere between unease and fear. Then she said, "There could be an ODHA right here with us: how would they feel?" Virtualizing her feeling self into the room, Susanti named the ODHA as a space of potential empathy and recognition. She and Rizal represent differing modalities of the ODHA as absent presence, but their linked struggles compel us toward a politics of inclusion. Since the late 1990s, HIV/AIDS activist discourse has drawn from the vision that called for "access to treatment" a parallel vision concerned with "access to prevention." Given the experiences of ODHAs like Susanti and Rizal, it appears that we may now be seeing the emergence of a debate regarding "access to hope" that seeks to foster national belonging built upon commitments to compassion, recognition, and health.

Activist (*Aktivis*)
DOREEN LEE

An activist and a self-styled "communist," Iwan was the brunt of many a joke. Officially, he belonged to the FPPI (Front Perjuangan Pemuda Indonesia, or Indonesian Youth Struggle Front), a collection of earnest young men and a few women in their late teens to early thirties, many of whom had migrated to the capital city of Jakarta from the provinces. The founding members of the youth organization had attended university in the central Javanese city of Yogyakarta, and several of them hailed from *pesantren*—Islamic boarding schools. Their religious background did not prepare me for the constant stream of their jokes. No subject was deemed taboo. The FPPI defied expectations in yet other ways. Despite their religious education, FPPI activists were secular, populist, and left-leaning, and their conversation reflected this mix. They were as likely to discuss liberal Islamic scholars and religious leaders such as Abdurrahman Wahid, a former president of Indonesia, as they were to talk about the leaders of political parties and Che Guevara. The FPPI was known for leaving a particular graffiti symbol—the encircled initial "R"—everywhere in the wake of their demonstrations; ® stood for *rakyat*—the people. Like many other activist groups in Jakarta embedded within the complex networks of NGOs, international funding agencies, and generational links among university alumni, the FPPI had at its core activists who had been politicized in student movement actions in the late 1990s. When we assembled in the living room of their rented secretariat quarters, the senior members would begin to tell stories of the glory days of 1998, when they had succeeded in toppling the dictator Suharto.

When Iwan arrived, the tone of these gatherings would abruptly change. Iwan's personality provided rich fodder for satire. In Iwan, the tropes that were thought to separate activists from the rest of conventional, mainstream society—youthful idealism, concern for the people, and a utilitarian Marxism—were indeed present, but faulty. Iwan was a Jakarta chapter member who had grown up in the city and prided himself on his original Betawi roots. While the other FPPI members looked stylish with their long hair and tight T-shirts, there was something awkward and sweet about Iwan. With his longish, limp hair and tucked-in shirts, Iwan was hopelessly out of fashion. He lived in a self-cultivated atmosphere of being under constant surveillance. But his bubble was often punctured with a swift jab by his comrades' jokes. One example: as proof of his political radicalism, Iwan kept offering me secret manifestos and transcripts of the most recent (and illegal) Indonesian Communist Party (PKI, or Partai Komunis Indonesia) gathering. The PKI had recently held a congress on an outer island, he said. He claimed to have ties to this shadowy group, a nascent force that would soon make a triumphant return to Indonesian politics. Proud of his secret, Iwan offered it to me, a foreign researcher-at-large. Hearing this offer, his comrade Savic mocked him and laughingly shrieked, "*Alaaaaah!* I've had that document for years! Someone gave me a photocopy." The secret document was never produced, but the mere claim that it had already been copied and disseminated to other activists diminished Iwan's gesture, along with his pretensions to involvement in underground politics and unique access to valuable documentary evidence. In his dismissal, Savic meant to say Iwan was just an ordinary activist. What could he show me, apart from what I had already learned in my dutiful research of the 1998 Student Movement?

Among senior activists like Savic, there was a strong sense of "Before 1998" and "After 1998," a distinction that determined what could be openly said by activists about their past practices. Even though Indonesian society still responded with deep paranoia toward communism and its symbols, the renewed interest in the history of the Indonesian Communist Party on the part of leftist activist and civil-society groups provided a small measure of rehabilitation for leftist terminology and populist ideas. In the era of openness and transparency after 1998, Iwan's utterance of the magically subversive word "communism" was no longer the act of defiance that it would have been in the thickly anticommunist time before 1998. Instead, it had become a pretension of Iwan's that could easily be dismissed by his peers. During my fieldwork in 2003–2005, activists remained committed to the form of politics they excelled at; they continued to demonstrate on the street and professed their ambition to foster alternatives to existing political and economic systems. They tended to talk less about the romantic and dangerous activist realm where resistance politics were being organized in secret and more about their past contributions to radical history.

The place of the *aktivis* in history seems secure, but why should this be so? As a former political media celebrity, the *aktivis* is strangely prominent (as a feature of the Indonesian media's coverage of "new generations" of politicians and in the continued coverage of street demonstrations as well), but their changing demands and social origins remain undertheorized by scholars and journalists alike. National and international media attention has positioned the figure of the activist as a culturally significant yet socially marginal segment of Indonesian political society, a broker of democracy whose experience of state violence legitimizes his or her political identity. Popular notions about *aktivis* suggest that activists enable transformations. In the wake of their efforts, conditions are politicized and politics are righted. Set against the political structures of Suharto's authoritarian New Order, activism in the late 1990s seemed new, a phenomenon that reflected the spread of global capital and resistance to associated forms of exploitation, as Indonesian activists took up the language of workers' rights, human rights, and democracy. But contemporary Indonesian activism is less startling if one considers it as the revival of a historical type and sees the *aktivis* as a descendant of the *pemuda*—the revolutionary male youth who populate nationalist historiography as the agents of change.[29] The revolutionary, then, becomes the prototype of future activists to come, ensuring an unbroken chain of political youth in Indonesian history. Activist youth—primarily university students involved in leftist and populist movements—represented and channeled the politics of the masses as the New Order collapsed to give meaning to a liminal stage in their own lives. As educated but unemployed, socially mobile but cash poor, urban and itinerant individuals with few socioeconomic responsibilities toward home or family, activist youth had greater physical mobility, imagination, and access to technologies of information than did other groups in society. The nationalist language used by post-Suharto activists to represent their relationship to oppressed workers, farmers, and urban poor, and their signature style of dress, worked as powerful references to the iconic *pemuda,* creating a circuit of referentiality where history animated the present.

At present, the space for activism is expanding for other social and political movements in Indonesia, as some of the other writers in this chapter suggest. Yet activism remains most deeply associated with urban male youth, like Iwan, whose defining characteristic is his proximity to the politics of 1998 and the politics of the people. One is dependent on the other.

Ex-Combatant from the Free Aceh Movement
(*Mantan Kombatan GAM*)
JESSE GRAYMAN

In post-tsunami and postconflict Aceh, the competition over reconstruction contract work plays out on an uneven playing field. This became evident to me through Alfi, my twenty-four-year-old part-time research assistant in Banda Aceh, who has recently become increasingly preoccupied with taking over the family business from his father. Alfi runs a well-known print shop in the old market area right behind the city's iconic Baiturrahman Mosque. Dozens of NGOs, government agencies, and especially the Aceh-Nias Rehabilitation and Reconstruction Agency routinely farm out their print jobs for books, banners, and pamphlets in a theoretically transparent tendering process to Alfi's shop and the shops of his competitors, but Alfi has struck upon a formula for winning tenders more often than anyone else in his line of work. Alfi is not just young, he is also short and thin and could pass for a high school student. It would be hard to take him seriously during the backroom negotiations among the *bapak* (older men) power brokers who award the contracts. So Alfi shows up at meetings like these with two men more formidable and much larger than he is, one at each side. They are ex-combatants from GAM (Gerakan Aceh Merdeka, the Free Aceh Movement), the guerrilla organization that fought for Aceh's independence from Indonesia for thirty years before finally signing a peace agreement with the Indonesian government in August 2005. Alfi typically does not need to introduce his business associates as ex–GAM because most people in Aceh recognize the skittish eyes and menacing expression of an ex-combatant. Furthermore, ex–GAM combatants have become the expected and winning participants of most contract bidding processes in Aceh today. Alfi and his family have no formal connections to GAM, but Alfi wins a contract when his tender is packaged with the borrowed prestige and power that GAM offers to his business—for a fee, of course. The military and police forces sent by Jakarta to occupy Aceh during the conflict departed from the region in 2005, and the local security forces now stay largely in their barracks. GAM—whose very existence as a resistance movement was denied by the Indonesian government during the conflict years lest it gain legitimacy—emerged as a legal signatory party of the peace agreement with equal status to the Indonesian government. After demobilization, GAM's command structure first transformed itself into a civilian organization at the beginning of 2006 and then into a local political party (Partai Aceh) that contested provincial and district-level legislative elections in 2009. Once confined to a black-market economy to support itself while the Indonesian armed forces and police dominated both the illegal and legal market economies during the conflict, GAM leaders have come to hold public office (including the governorship and many district headships) and have the opportunity to award lucrative government contracts to their former comrades in the struggle. Other non–GAM leaders and business owners are pressured under implicit threats of violence to do the same, in a cycle of exchange not unlike the patterns of corruption and nepotism that were developed and perfected during the New Order era.

Former GAM members thus now openly claim and enjoy a disproportionate amount of the sudden largesse from Aceh's legal economy. In this context, I like Alfi's story and consider it significant for two reasons. First, Alfi's associates are low-ranking ex-combatants who furnish him with the credentials he needs to win relatively small contracts; they come from a village where Alfi has extended family, and he is doing them a favor almost equal to the benefits they are offering him. This example contrasts with the prevailing public face of postconflict reintegration in Aceh, which largely features the high-ranking GAM commanders entering local politics and big business, leaving a lot of their rank-and-file cohorts behind feeling increasingly disgruntled and disillusioned.[30] The alternative typically chosen by ex-combatants feeling left out is to pursue petty *preman*-ism (thugism or gangsterism), and Alfi's story provides an example of this fairly innocuous new role for the ex-combatant.

The second reason I value Alfi's example is the playful and gutsy bluff that he deploys to beat his competitors. What matters is not specifically who Alfi's business associates from GAM are, nor whether Alfi himself has formal ties to the organization, but simply the projection of the image of GAM as a team of strongmen backing Alfi's business proposal. Alfi is perhaps one of the first businessmen in Aceh's small printing industry not only to recognize the reconfiguration of "big men" since the peace treaty but also to maneuver tactically within the new parameters they have set. As Alfi navigated this flipped political economy, he introduced the strategy of including low-ranking ex-combatants in his proposal, to his own benefit and theirs. He found GAM before GAM's increasingly wide-reaching predatory practices on small businesses found him.

Another young man did not navigate this new terrain as well. Down the southwest coast of Aceh in his hometown of Blang Pidie, Afrizal tried to get in on a housing construction boom that was about to start up following receipt of a new tranche of government funding from Jakarta. His friends at the government office disbursing contracts encouraged Afrizal to submit a proposal, for which he had to include several million rupiah in administration and application "fees." Alas, the construction project was given to the contractor with GAM connections, and Afrizal lost his hefty investment. Since then, he has tried in vain to make the right connections within GAM networks, hoping to participate in their activities, but he is also repelled by their crass corruption, in this case on a scale much more consequential than any of Alfi's business adventures. Afrizal's voice joins a steadily growing chorus of criticism that combines frustration, jealousy, resignation, and even some admiration directed at this emergent ex-combatant class that has come to dominate Aceh's new economic and political landscape. For the moment, GAM's open participation and assimilation into established patterns of political and criminal organization common throughout the archipelago is an ironic and, some say, even durable measure of their veterans' increasingly successful reintegration into Indonesian society.

NGO Worker (*Orang* LSM)
ARYO DANUSIRI

The atmosphere in Geunting Timur, located in the regency of Pidie in Aceh, was tense that morning. The village was one of the project sites of HAGENT (not the real name), an international nongovernmental organization involved in a reconstruction project initiated following the massive tsunami that struck the Acehnese coast in December 2004. Together with the *geuchik* (village chief), HAGENT's team of Indonesian facilitators—Syamsul, Ridha, and Boni—was waiting for a group of supervisors from the main office in Banda Aceh, who were coming to assess the progress of the housing construction. The facilitators were anxious: on their previous visit, *orang* Banda (an indexical term for the expatriate and Indonesian high-level staff from the main office) found numerous constructions that were not "earthquake resistant"—the minimum safety standard determined by multinational donors and humanitarian communities for all post-tsunami building projects in Aceh.

The team of supervisors, consisting of two young British civil engineers and an Indian supervisor from the Pidie office, arrived in two imported SUVs. That morning, the facilitators had intended to keep the supervisors from revisiting an area with low-quality construction, but one of the supervising engineers quickly moved toward one of the housing projects located on the village's main street and proceeded to inspect the columns. He immediately started to complain about the inadequate size and quality of their construction. Syamsul tried to explain the situation: "We have instructed the workers, but they didn't listen because their payment didn't cover the costs. . . ." Before he could finish, one of the supervisors replied, "I am afraid it's going to have to be a carrot and stick approach. You're going to provide encouragement, support, advice, and training, but you can't approve something like this. Once you start rejecting this kind of work, believe me, they will listen." The facilitators' faces were lined with anxiety as they followed the supervisors, who moved on to inspect other houses. Months of hard work would have to be destroyed, and they could not imagine the effort it would take to rebuild the houses.

During the New Order, one of the most salient articulations of the NGO worker, the *orang* LSM (Lembaga Swadaya Masyarakat can literally be translated as "Self-Reliant Community Institution," while *orang* means person), was that of an activist who struggled for democracy and human rights in opposition to the Suharto regime. Despite the fact that many NGOs collaborated intimately with the government, the image of the NGO worker as radical was ubiquitous throughout Indonesia. Even today, a decade after the fall of the New Order, these particular moral connotations often overshadow the dramatic expansion and diversification of NGOs that have accompanied the relaxation of funding controls under the current regime. On a national scale, however, corruption cases involving well-known NGO figures have increasingly challenged these positive images. Furthermore, many local communities' decentralization policies have made the *orang* LSM an increasingly important mediator for development projects funded by foreign donors, a situation that in turn has created employment opportunities for many young urban Indonesians with university degrees. In Aceh, where foreign aid has reached unprecedented levels,[31] this process is especially pronounced, and Syamsul, Ridha, and Boni are just three examples of a professional class of *orang* LSM.

These men responded in different ways to the incident described above. Syamsul, the community facilitator, pointed his finger at the *geuchik* and the laborers from the village, since they had not followed instructions. Boni, the architect, claimed that the "earthquake-resistant house" was a standard that is impossible to implement on the site because the design is too sophisticated for the laborers. Ridha, another community facilitator, defended the village's attempts to save money by hiring poorly trained local laborers and using inexpensive but adequate materials. He concluded rhetorically, "If we cannot serve the community's needs and demands, what does 'community-driven approach' actually mean?"

When the men decided to join HAGENT, they had not expected that working with local communities would be so complex. For instance, Boni, from West Sumatra Province, who had made prototype housing projects the subject of his undergraduate thesis, joined HAGENT hoping to conduct "a real project" and design "a small beautiful house" for Acehnese villagers. Yet unexpected difficulties emerged from the discrepancy between the community's preferences for simple houses and NGO standards. Syamsul, an Acehnese, who graduated from the Islamic State University in Banda Aceh with a major

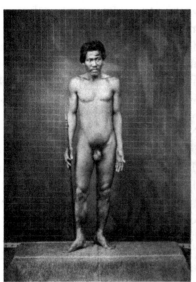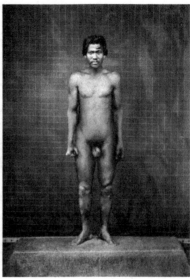

"Study of Lamprey's Malayan Male I & II," by Yee I-Lann (black-and-white digital print on paper, 2009). *Courtesy of Valentine Willie Fine Art and Yee I-Lann.*

Artist's Statement: In Study of Lamprey's Malayan Male I & II, I have appropriated one of John Lamprey's ethnographic photographs from the pair "Front and Profile Views of a Malayan Male, c. 1868–69." I found this image in a book entitled *Photography: A Cultural History,* by Mary Warner Marien. The original carbon prints of John Lamprey's Malayan Male now reside at the Royal Anthropological Institute of Great Britain and Ireland in London.

I was uncertain why I wanted to pursue John Lamprey's image and what exactly I wanted from it. The men "got me," both the subject and photographer, perhaps because of the pathos of the Malayan Male's averted gaze, his figure's demeaning nakedness, and the measured gaze of the photographer. I suspect my motivation for wanting to "relook" this image was to study the relationships within "the gaze," my own included, and to try and reposition this gaze.

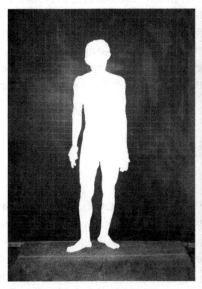

I also wanted to see if this image from a colonized past, about power and an "other," could change its meaning and be empowered in a postcolonial world and how that may reflect in our contemporary surroundings. It was a problematic process, however, as every nuanced change or juxtaposition—every figurative twitch, every prop, every manipulated eye-line—asserted connotations and meaning and chronicled a kind of further violation or inventory of agenda that I was uncomfortable with.

The only "comfortable" solution I found to address John Lamprey's Malayan Male was to cut him out, leaving a memory of his presence and experience in our time—when our society is particularly obsessed with framing, measuring, and indexing identities and subjugating its populace to notions of racial supremacy and "otherness."

in education, found out the hard way that "facilitating" was more complex than teaching students in class. Ridha had been a student activist in Banda Aceh and joined HAGENT with big dreams about working as a grassroots organizer, building democracy from the ground up. But he quickly discovered that his role was not explicitly political and rather required him to ensure that the NGO's agenda would match the preferences of the community. These new NGO workers thus became brokers or middlemen in the spaces of "friction" between the politics of foreign aid and the demands of local communities.[32] These figures thus remind us that Indonesian modernity depends on the capability of its members to transform the intersections of global and local realms in productive ways.

Overseas Female Labor Migrant (TKW or *Tenaga Kerja Wanita*)
RACHEL SILVEY

Immigration officials and airport police have a game they like to play in the airport's arrival terminal that is reserved for processing the overseas labor migrants returning to Jakarta. As they watch the TKW walk into the terminal, they take great pleasure in guessing the country in which each migrant worker was most recently employed. One day, a terminal guard listed the clues he used to make his guesses. He laughed as he pointed his chin in the direction of particular women: "If her cell phone is very fancy [*canggih*], and she walks with a swing in her hips [*berjalan goyang-goyang*], you know for sure she is back from Hong Kong. Usually the ones coming back from Saudi are covered in black and wear sunglasses, and the ones who have been in the UAE wear colorful headscarves with matching handbags. Those ones coming now with their hair dyed orange, you know they have been working in Taiwan. You can always tell from their style [*gaya*]." Then, much more seriously, he added, "It's all very dangerous and chaotic. There are so many problems for these women. We can't control it. Yeah—this is what Indonesia is like [*Indonesia beginilah*]."

Indonesian women's overseas labor migration began on a large scale when the government started promoting such migration as a development strategy in the early 1980s. Since then, "labor export" has grown into a major source of income throughout the country; migrant recruitment has taken on industrial proportions in rural areas; and it seems that now, every family in Java and in many other areas across the country knows at least one TKW or former TKW. Internationally, Indonesia is now second only to the Philippines in the number of women it sends abroad as caregivers and domestic workers. More than two-thirds of the registered migrants are women, and more than 80 percent of the women work as domestic servants.[33] Most TKW come from rural areas and have only elementary-school educations. While abroad, TKW can earn between five and fifteen times the wage levels that would be available to them as domestic workers or factory workers within Indonesia. Their remittances have become a vital source of income for Indonesia; the total of their earnings nationally was predicted by journalists to reach 40 trillion rupiah in 2008, while activists estimate an even higher sum—60 trillion. Given either of these estimates, the revenues from this "industry" would be second only to gas and oil as an overall income generator for the nation.[34] Yet in order to earn money to send home, TKW are required to leave their families behind for two to three years at a stretch, and while abroad they risk extreme overwork, nonpayment of wages, harassment, and rape. They have become iconic subjects of the feminization of global migration,[35] as well as key figures in public debates about national identity, cultural propriety, and the future of economic development in Indonesia.

The debates surrounding the TKW reflect the gendered tensions of modernity. The TKW is a "woman out of place," a figure whose transnational mobility and associated *gaya* both threaten the national order and promise a way forward. Popular representations of the TKW as WTS (*wanita tuna susila,* or women without morals, prostitutes) cast them as dangerous and shameful women who have forsaken their families and their nation in order to satisfy their own selfish, consumeristic desires.[36] Alternatively, the state portrays the TKW as *pahlawan devisa* (heroes of foreign exchange), respectable workers whose income is necessary for the national economy and who provide valuable, self-sacrificing service to their communities and families through the remittances they send home. NGOs focused on migrants' rights emphasize the personal stories from the TKW that portray them as victims of exploitation, abuse, violence, and neglect, problems that activists attribute to greedy middlemen, inhumane employers, and state actors who cannot be bothered (*tidak mau ambil pusing*) to provide protection or support for the women. In contrast, a forthcoming popular film entitled *Hong Kong Rhapsody* celebrates the "success stories" of the TKW in Hong Kong, women who, like "global Cinderellas," earn small fortunes and enjoy almost middle-class lifestyles.[37] The desires and fears that circulate around the subject of the TKW—regarding her consumption patterns, styles of dress, sexuality, obligations, and rights—reflect more general Indonesian hopes and anxieties about how globalization may be tied to transformations in the gendered social order.

One day, a village leader took me and a migrant-rights advocate on a walk around his community in Sukabumi, West Java. He pointed to the houses with shiny new tiled porches and satellite dishes: "That's the Hong Kong style of renovation. That one over there, that's the Korean style. This one here doesn't have a TKW overseas yet, so it hasn't been renovated yet," and he pointed to a bamboo structure with a dirt floor. "Our development depends on the incomes of the TKW. Without them, we have nothing," said the village leader. "But," countered the rights advocate, citing a story of a woman who had been tortured by her former overseas employer, "this kind of development all comes at such a cost. The injuries to the TKW are the injuries to our nation." The TKW is caught somewhere between grinding poverty and potential cash flow, the allure of new styles of consumption and the threat of abuse, rural unemployment and international mobility, and gossip about good mothers and rich whores. She lives in the thick of these extreme possibilities that revolve around her, while she stands as a gendered symbol of the nation's place in the transnational sphere.

Field Agent (*Petugas Lapangan*)
JOHAN LINDQUIST

It is almost *maghrib,* the time for the Muslim evening prayer, as we make our way along the one-lane highway that connects eastern and western Lombok, an island of 3.5 million inhabitants just east of Bali. Ibrahim, the manager of Nusa, a labor recruitment agency that sends migrants to Malaysian palm oil plantations, and Adi, his assistant, are in the front of the SUV smoking clove cigarettes and listening to Jakarta pop music, which expresses their unspoken lament. Both have been sent from the main office in the capital, and neither speaks the local Sasak language. I am in the back seat with Pak Haji Ismael, a local elementary school teacher in religion who moonlights as a *petugas lapangan,* or "field agent,"[38] and handles the actual recruitment of migrants for Nusa and other agencies. We are returning from a meeting held at the house of Pak Haji's son-in-law, a police officer in East Lombok who used his local connections to organize a meeting for twenty potential migrants. At the event, Pak Haji acted as the host and led the opening prayer before introducing the guests from Nusa, who handed out brochures and talked about the company and the various job contracts that they were currently offering in Malaysia. Back in the car, Pak Haji is satisfied—I can tell from the way he strokes his string of beads—and he tells us he plans to visit each of the local men the following week. As we move along slowly behind a line of cattle trucks, he suddenly tells Adi to pull over. It is time to pray. We stop at the side of the road, and the three men get out of the car, leaving me behind to contemplate the day's events.

The *petugas lapangan,* or PL for short, has become a critical figure in

Indonesian transnational labor recruitment in recent years and should most broadly be considered in relation to the historical prevalence of various forms of brokers (*calo*) in Indonesia since the colonial era. As documented labor recruitment has become increasingly decentralized during the last decade as the Suharto-era monopolies have collapsed, PLs like Pak Haji Ismael have become key interstitial brokers in historically specific environments at the boundaries between formal recruitment agencies like Nusa, state bureaucracies, and the villages, where relations of trust, power, and debt that organize village life throughout Indonesia are in play and must be taken into account.[39]

Since the end of the New Order, there has been an increasing formalization of labor migration from Indonesia to Saudi Arabia and Malaysia, in particular, where over a million Indonesians work on palm-oil plantations, construction sites, and as domestic servants. The era of undocumented migration has rapidly been replaced by one in which passports and visas are the norm. A number of political and economic factors have impelled the labor-export trade to become more formal and well documented; these factors include an intensifying revolving-door regime of migrant importation and deportation from Malaysia, the Asian economic crisis of 1997 and the ensuing collapse of the Indonesian rupiah, and the deregulation of the Indonesian labor-recruitment industry. The shift to a documented labor-recruitment industry is particularly obvious on Lombok, which during the 1980s and 1990s was infamous as a source of undocumented male migration to Malaysia. This was the era of the *taikong* (sometimes spelled *tekong*), the smuggler, who beginning in the 1970s transported migrants by boat directly to Malaysia and, in later years, overland through a network of middlemen via the multiple harbors and beaches along the east Sumatran coast and the Riau Archipelago before crossing the Straits of Malacca to Singapore or peninsular Malaysia.

In the last decade, however, the *petugas lapangan* has come to replace the *taikong* as the figure that mediates processes of migration. The PL provides workers not to other informal brokers or directly to the employer abroad but rather to local recruitment companies—most with main offices in Jakarta and other major cities—that on Lombok alone have come to number more than 150. These PJTKI (Perusahan Jasa Tenaga Kerja Indonesia, Indonesian Labor Provider Company) have exploded in number as labor export has become a major and diverse legal industry. PJTKI vary broadly in terms of professionalism, size, and sustainability, but all are dependant on large numbers of PL in the actual recruitment process. PLs have no written contracts and are paid according to each migrant they deliver or according to how much they can extract from each recruit. For a female domestic worker, the going rate is approximately 1 million rupiah, or about U.S. $100, while for a male plantation or construction worker it is approximately 300,000 rupiah, or about U.S. $30—comparable to the monthly salary for a day laborer or even an office worker on Lombok. These high fees and the dramatic increase in PJTKI and transnational migrants—currently over fifty thousand per year from Lombok alone—have led growing numbers of people to become PL. Reminiscent of the bazaar economy Clifford Geertz described more than forty years ago, the migrant labor economy is characterized by ad hoc transactions and a rhizomatic quality, as men in many shapes and sizes roam the island on motorcycles in search of potential migrants.[40]

But while the *taikong* has generally been perceived as a thuggish figure, a kind of *preman,* the PL suggests one who is associated with a *kantor,* an office, and follows procedures. Indeed, this is precisely what people like Pak Haji Ismael spend much of their time doing. He wears button-down shirts and handles all the paperwork that is demanded in the manufacture of legality— including a birth certificate, an identity card, a medical certificate, various government letters, and finally, a passport for the recruit. He understands how much money must be handed out along the way and deals with the process that the migrant cannot navigate on his or her own. But he also knows how to speak to migrants in their language and engage them in an economy of trust. Although there are certainly *taikong* who have become PL, elementary schoolteachers and other low-level bureaucrats such as Pak Haji Ismael are the rule, not the exception, in the contemporary regime of transnational migration. They are poorly paid, well-educated workers who work short hours, are well known to be reliable, and are used to speaking in public and approaching officials. In the current moment, the PL embodies qualities and a character that convince villagers to become migrants. He is, strictly speaking, the right person in the right place at the right time.

Street Vendor (*Pedagang Kaki Lima*)
SHERI GIBBINGS

The Indonesian variant of the street vendor is the *pedagang kaki lima* or PKL: the "five-legged seller." The phrase "five legs" refers to a three-wheeled cart in combination with the seller's two legs. In 2007, during my fieldwork in Yogyakarta, Central Java, I observed a period of escalated tensions among PKL. Vendors were forced to take a side either for or against a government plan to relocate them to a newly renovated marketplace. From the "against" side, flyers were circulated in an attempt to convince vendors that the government's plan was unclear and lacked transparency and that their livelihoods would be destroyed, as they had been in so many other failed relocation projects.

Those opposed to the plan held demonstrations and received frequent news coverage. Organizers of the "for" side were more subtle in their campaign. They met with street vendors individually and often secretly to convince them of the benefits of relocating. The "for" and "against" sides were composed of different kinds of PKL. Those opposed to the relocation plan earned, on average, ten to fifteen times more than those who were in favor of it. While the former were characterized as rich and greedy non-Javanese outsiders who sold new and expensive products and should be grateful that the government was providing them with an alternative location, the latter were characterized as poor Javanese who were struggling to survive while selling mostly second-hand goods.

The differences between the two groups map onto two already existing images of PKL—one old and the other relatively new. What caught the imagination of the public was the new type, the capital-owning PKL masquerading as the *rakyat kecil,* or little people. In the older view, PKL are seen as poor, usually from Java, uneducated, simply dressed, humble, and overly respectful to shop owners and government officials. But starting in the 1980s, the category of PKL moved from being relatively undifferentiated to being more diverse and socioeconomically stratified. It was in this context that the new figure of a capital-owning impostor, who merely masquerades as a PKL of the poor and humble type, became possible. While the differentiating of PKL into these two types is still not widely recognized, discourses circulating about PKL among the public, the government, and the street vendors themselves can be understood more clearly if one is aware of these distinctions. In certain moments, such as during the relocation of street vendors, the difference between the two images becomes quite pronounced. During the relocation I observed, some new capital-owning PKL tried to hide behind the representation of the old PKL, posing as the *rakyat kecil* in order to avoid the negative connotations associated with the new image.

In the early 1960s, as the Indonesian economy crashed, PKL were mainly people from lower classes. Largely ignored by the government, PKL sought protection—or were sought out to be protected—from *preman,* or gangsters. Through the first two decades of the New Order, however, the figure of the PKL slowly changed, as migrants poured into urban areas such as Yogyakarta from villages around Indonesia.[41] In this context, military personnel, police, and government workers also increasingly became PKL in order to supplement their meager pensions or incomes. As the number of PKL increased, the government sought to regulate their mobility and labor. In the late 1990s, another wave of PKL emerged with the Asian economic crisis. Workers from various sectors—such as university-educated youth—became street vendors

because of the greater freedom (fewer taxes) and higher income the job offered, compared with office work. Thus PKL as a group became even more
diverse.

The evolution of the perceived figure of the PKL has coincided with an
ever-increasing desire for modernity and development in Indonesian society
at large. These images of modernity have been projected by urban planners
onto the street through the promotion of fantasies picturing clean and green
pedestrian streets resembling those in Europe. In this process, PKL came to be
regarded—much like the *becak* in Jakarta—as a hindrance to the developer's
vision, in that they were viewed as dirty (*kotor, kumuh*), chaotic (*semrawut*),
unorganized (*tidak diatur*), and likely to cause traffic jams (*kemacetan*).[42]

One of the vendors opposed to the relocation was Pak Agus. But Pak Agus
did not see himself as "dirty" and opposed to the vision of a modern city. In
fact, he saw himself as someone who had willingly climbed on the development bandwagon, since he was working toward economic self-improvement
without requesting help from the government. Responding to the critique of
PKL as "dirty," he exclaimed,

> I realize the sidewalks were created by the government for walking
> and not for selling goods, but I feel that it's the government's fault!
> First, the government can't give jobs to its citizens. Second, if PKL
> start selling on the street, the government should stop them right
> away and not wait until there are too many. Third, dishonest govern-
> ment officials [*oknum pemerintah*] often give permits to street ven-
> dors for money.

Thus, according to Pak Agus, the failure to achieve modernity was the government's fault, a result of government corruption and lack of capacity. But Pak
Agus then shifted to another available interpellation: one that cited the *rakyat
kecil*. He explained to me, "In reality, PKL don't have rights to use the sidewalk because they disturb public interests, but it happens because they have
to feed their families." Thus, Pak Agus adopted the old discourse on PKL and
positioned himself as *rakyat kecil*.

Yet Pak Agus is often categorized by others as representative of the
new type of PKL—perceived typically as capital-owning, well-connected,
educated, non-Javanese vendors who make a living selling the same goods as
those available in stores—because he has multiple selling locations and earns
an income greater than many government officials. Such PKL are generally
viewed as being ungrateful and are frowned upon for claiming the *right* to
occupy the sidewalks without permission. They are said to act as if every

problem could be solved with money. If his purported membership in the fraternity of *rakyat kecil* were challenged, Pak Agus would counter the attack by asserting he is merely trying to feed his family, but in fact he is clearly a successful trader and man of means, relative to the poorer vendors and many other residents of Yogyakarta. Just as the *preman berdasi* (thug in a suit) was a street figure who improperly became a capital owner—a kind of imposter in the ruling class—in this situation, the new PKL figure appears as an imposter of the *rakyat kecil.*[43]

Most of my interactions with Pak Agus had been at his small street location, so when I ran into him selling hundreds of shoes from one of the largest stands at a street market, I was taken aback. I had no idea he had the capacity to sell at this capital-intensive level. Upon seeing me, he appeared embarrassed and began to explain that he needed to sell here because his other locations were doing poorly. He emphasized that he "borrowed" money and simply hoped to support his family and maintain their survival. Finally, he deferred to God: "If Allah permits that there is livelihood, we will find it anywhere. In the end we want to work hard, and to sell in line with Allah, and if we do that we will definitely receive." In his peculiar status navigating between these two tropes of "rich" and "poor" PKL, Pak Agus treads carefully, downplaying his wealth and attributing it to the will of Allah.

Street Kid(s) (*Anak Jalanan*)
CHRIS BROWN

At a busy downtown Surabaya intersection, kids—about eleven boys and seven girls on this day in 2004—wandered up the irregular lines of cars, minibuses, and motorbikes looking for money. Some simply held out their hand, and in certain cases managed to do so while clutching a baby in the other arm. Others ran long feather dusters perfunctorily over the vehicles before asking for payment. A few offered magazines or newspapers for sale to drivers. Older teenagers favored more elaborate schemes, which involved circulating through streetside food stalls with a guitar or set of improvised drums, or maybe a battery-powered portable amplifier and microphone. But most of the time the kids just shook a flattened bottle-cap rattle (*ecek-ecek*) to accompany their droning, barely intelligible song, which ceased the instant coins were produced.

Strictly speaking, *anak jalanan,* or *anjal* for short, make a living not so much "on the margins" as right in the midst of things. The first provision of their survival is agility: theirs is not a predicament of being stuck in out-of-the-way places, it is an art of repeatedly dodging just barely out of the way while remaining close enough to eke out a profit from everyone they brush up against. The increasing speed of traffic—especially as traffic lights are eliminated in a deliberate attempt to eradicate *anjal* by denying them habitat—demands ever-increasing mobility and daring. In their own words, "Our only asset/capital is our audacity" (in Indonesian, *modal kami hanya berani;* in Javanese, *bandha nekad,* shortened to *bonek*).

Present-day Indonesian sources frequently place the genesis of the *anjal* at the watershed of contemporary Indonesian history: the financial crisis and political turmoil that appeared in 1997. According to this story, the "child of the street" materialized precisely at a time when the future of Indonesia suddenly seemed to be unfolding in those same streets. One could argue that young people have roamed the streets since streets were made, but the subject at issue here is less a demographic group than a discursive figure. Rather than attempt to "correct" an apparently ahistorical lapse in the discourse by identifying historical antecedents to or anticipations of *anjal,* I focus on how, for many Indonesian reporters, researchers, and social activists, *anjal* plausibly seem to be "a new social phenomenon popping up like weeds,"[44] described as "parasitic plants spreading wildly through the cultural boulevards of our lives."[45] It is notable, for instance, that even today the very phrase "*anak jalanan*" is often defined in parentheses for the reader when it occurs in news stories and NGO reports.

Back in downtown Surabaya, when a van from the Social Agency pulls up, kids young and old scatter, flitting over the walls and fences of private compounds and then, as if reaching home base in a game of hide-and-seek, turning to watch with open curiosity. (Their very presence on streets is deemed illegal.) One of the agency men cajoles them not to run. He offers a ride to a dedication ceremony for one of the agency's new buildings. He throws in the enticement of a free buffet. The offer is plausible; street kids are routinely sought by event organizers looking to fill out attendance and demonstrate charity at their affairs. A few kids are tempted, but more taunt the civil servants mercilessly and refuse to budge. The officials give up and cruise to another intersection. Eventually, they hit a pocket of kids who have had a hard day. Yielding to persuasion, the children climb aboard the van, boisterous at first, then increasingly taciturn as the vehicle eventually leaves the city behind.

After the kids have been deposited inside an isolated, gated compound, the expedition leader gathers them in a somewhat decrepit building and gets them to start a game that involves passing a soccer ball around a circle and repeating each other's names, an icebreaking and identity exercise. It seems rather bizarre, considering that the only people who don't already know these kids' names are the officials. But from the point of view of the agency, these kids have no identity (specifically, no *identitas*—that is, identity documents), a situation the bureaucrats set about remedying. While the group builds solidarity, one by one the kids are drawn aside by uniformed social agents and "data-ed" (in Indonesian, *didata*), a process that requires each child to provide information for one of the officers to enter into the blanks of a file form. To fill in the space for "place of origin," children are not permitted to answer "Surabaya"; the agents question them until they provide the name of a village—any village. Data-ing concludes with fingerprinting. Finally, the group gets boxes of disappointingly poor food (bad enough that only one of the social agents bothers to consume his portion). But hardly have the kids begun to eat when a uniformed police officer—described as a high-ranking officer—enters and demands attention. Playing the role of Bad Cop as if it were second nature, he informs the kids that, if it were up to him, they would all be tossed in jail. He somehow takes up another half an hour elaborating on his promise that, next time, if they get caught begging again, they won't have any social agency coddling them; instead, they'll be handed over to the police, held in jail, then shipped off directly to their village of origin. Browbeating concluded, he leaves, and the kids are loaded back into the van. Picked up before noon, it will be dark before they are back near the center of town.

At first glance, the significance of the *anak jalanan* appears to be similar to that of the criminal, a figure that many modern social critiques interpret as exposing the essential slavery of bourgeois discipline. Foucault has described how Fourierists celebrated the negation of civilization and discipline by liberty, "the life of a savage, living from day to day and with no tomorrow."[46] The Indonesian word for this savage liberty is *bebas*, "to be free from constraints," and it is a term that comes up repeatedly in talk concerning *anjal*. But it is not just street kids who are said to exemplify this freedom; all young children are described as constitutionally *bebas*. *Anak jalanan* are distinguished from other children only by their refusal to relinquish this attractive liberty; they indefinitely defer the moment of deferring their immediate desires. On Java, the deferral of immediate desires is precisely the move that makes children into people. Children are characteristically described as "not yet people/ Javanese" until they begin to subject themselves to a variety of constraints, first and foremost the registers of formal, respectful Javanese—registers that *anjal* may not even learn and never use.[47] The bureaucratic efforts to confer an identity through the process of data-fication and, if necessary, compulsory return to one's original home essentially constitute an attempt to circumvent the futility of making *anjal* defer their freedom by imposing an apparatus of state personhood (*identitas*) in place of the more proper self-effacement of a Javanese subject.[48]

Thus, the newly salient presence of *anak jalanan* at the end of Indonesia's twentieth century did not represent a novelty just because children took to the streets to try to make a living. Venturing forth to look for one's fortune (*merantau*) is a venerable practice. Nor is it the spurious and fluid criminality of *anjal* that sets them against the grain of the social; on the contrary, Indonesian figures of criminality are commonly imagined to embody positive codes, structures, and disciplines of their own, rather than figuring the absence or rejection of any such structures.[49] Instead, *anjal* exemplify a thriving medium permeating the gaps and holes in social structures, identities, and hierarchies, a medium that does not aim to coalesce or colonize, to occupy or to build its own structures, but merely sustains itself, dodging and weaving, by sheer act of will (that is, *bonek,* the asset of audacity). In urban Java, where criminals threaten to supplant the state and the power of the social, it is the *anjal*'s freedom, their escape, and their refusal to defer that negates such orders. In doing so, street kids also demonstrate the superfluity of giving up freedom in order to make a living. And this, more than cautionary fear, may be what makes them so disconcerting to other Javanese.

Mr. Hajj, Pak Haji
DADI DARMADI

Pak Haji Rosyid, a well-built Sundanese man in his sixties, dressed in a white sweatshirt and trousers, sits alone on a bare floor in a mosque locally known as Masjid Baitul Ikhlas, "the House of Fidelity." On this chilly morning, with his head wrapped in a Saudi-style red and white turban, he has just returned from a jogging session at the nearby Giri Mekar public park in southern Bandung, a state-funded park that he and his contractors had built, transforming a polluted commercial district into an urban oasis. Pak Haji, or Mr. Pilgrim, like many of his Indonesian peers, usually wears the white cap and robes known as *baju haji,* or hajj clothing, in daily life. For Pak Haji Rosyid, they symbolize his Haji status, which he has enjoyed for nearly three decades, a distinguished length of time. Yet he is no longer as exceptionally distinguished by his white cap and robes as he was during the New Order. With the booming hajj industry that has developed in Indonesia during the last decade, increasing numbers of Indonesians have visited Mecca, and hajjis and hajjahs have begun to exert a powerful impact on social customs, halting and reversing Western fashions and habits, and changing the way many Indonesians dress and behave.

Having worked as a successful businessman for many years, Pak Haji Rosyid is a skillful trader and contractor; he is perhaps the most powerful Muslim figure in the area. But success did not come easily. In the late 1950s, the young Rosyid, born to a wealthy Muslim family in Garut, was devastated upon learning that his family wealth had been depleted following a series of attacks by a group of Darul Islam guerrillas who sought to set up a rival government as Indonesia's modern state-building process was just getting underway. Rosyid fled Garut and moved to Bandung to seek his fortune as a street vendor. After years of struggle, he became the owner of a successful motorbike dealership and rental agency. His dealings in modern means of transport brought him in contact with a young and energetic middle-level military officer who offered him his first contractor's job. During the 1960s and 1970s, as the military and its businesses expanded in the wake of anticommunist campaigns, the military built bases and installation units throughout the area. For nearly two decades, Pak Rosyid was a devout government partner, a military loyalist, and, for many local people, a trusted businessman. He lived in a wealthy and close-knit extended family of nearly twenty people spanning three generations. His neighbors did not regard him as a socially aware and active neighbor and citizen. In fact, his quick success led to rumors that he, as a usurer, lent money at 50 percent interest, while his polygamous lifestyle sparked furor from his family.

But Pak Rosyid's spiritual journey to Mecca in 1980 changed everything, as his new hajj title won him broader social recognition. His contacts with fellow hajjis during the pilgrimage—and especially his new association with local *kiyais,* or Islamic leaders—provided social support that came to play a significant role later in his life. Although the hajj ritual emphasizes solidarity and egalitarianism regardless of wealth or status, in Indonesia the title of *haji* is conferred to recognize social standing. Pak Rosyid, of course, was not the first to experience this transformation. Oma Irama, dubbed the "King of Dangdut music," went to Mecca to perform the hajj, and shortly afterward, in 1973, he changed his name to Rhoma Irama and adopted a new nickname, "Bang Haji," that gave him two decades of success in music and films.

In 1988, a year after his second hajj, Pak Haji Rosyid turned the courtyard of his home into an open-air playground, attracting many young children every afternoon. These children later became known as students of Baitul Ikhlas Madrasah, named after the mosque Pak Haji Rosyid had built in honor of his deceased mother. As his personal wealth grew, Pak Haji used it not only to build his own housing complex and to buy luxury cars for his family but also to expand his private *madrasah* to include elementary to high school levels. His schools, funded mostly from his company's profits, offered a place for children who could not afford state schools. Pak Haji Rosyid never gives speeches or teaches pupils in class, but his new religious commitment has brought him closer to religious elites in neighboring villages. In the everyday life of Giri Mekar villagers, participating in Islamic gatherings at Pak Haji Rosyid's mosque has become a means to develop a new kind of personal piety and civic engagement, one that stands in contrast to state-sponsored social activities. At these gatherings, Pak Haji Rosyid speaks often of his strong opposition to both Islamic militancy and communism—a clear indication of his moderate religious and political views. He has applauded the Reformasi but at the same time lamented that the movement has not brought economic recovery to the people when they need it.

Like other Hajis in Indonesian history, such as those who initiated the Banten Revolt in the 1880s or incited other anticolonial movements in various parts of Java and Sumatra, the contemporary Pak Haji is typically a figure able to craft messages with widespread popular appeal, who acts as a force to mobilize supporters and create organizations with a strong social base and coherent strategies for change. Today, Baitul Ikhlas is a vital institution in Giri Mekar not only for its religious activities but also for its social and educational system. It provides an orphanage, housing for the elderly, and collects alms from Muslims in the area. Pak Haji Rosyid describes himself as a Muslim who understands his commitments to be *kaffah*—comprehensive and totalizing. His polygamous marriages remain under wraps, but his renewed faith following the hajj has led him to make serious attempts to ameliorate poverty and economic hardship. His reborn Muslim faith, found and developed during the New Order, has also led him to question the democratization process and to advocate for a strong system of government like that which prevailed under Suharto's authoritarian regime.

Pak Haji Rosyid's status as Haji provides him with a public image of piety, economic power, and authority. As a "cultural broker," Pak Haji Rosyid functions as an intermediary between national politics and local politics, a position that has benefited him and his organization.[50] By adjusting to changing circumstances, he has played a critical role in conceptualizing and responding to moments of uncertainty in modern Indonesia. His efforts to elevate poverty reduction to the top of his operational priorities and to provide alternative forms of education to groups unable to attend state schools have made him an important local figure. Pak Haji Rosyid and others like him play an increasingly vital role in local understandings of what it means to lead a virtuous Muslim life in Indonesia.

Rich Person (*Orang Kaya*)
JOSHUA BARKER

Yanto is a man in motion. Sometimes he hopscotches around the archipelago, from Bandung to Jakarta to Bali to Surabaya to Aceh, all in one week; at other times, he circulates in Jakarta, going from golf course to upscale restaurant to government office to five-star hotel lobby, all in one day. Born into poverty in central Java, he moved to the city of Bandung in his twenties and worked his way up from being an office boy at a state-owned industry to being the president director of a company that sells and rents in-house telecommunications systems for banks, oil companies, and government departments, many of which have locations spread out across the Indonesian archipelago. Now in his mid-forties, he lives with his wife and two sons in a one-story mansion in a middle-class neighborhood in Bandung. His wife is Sundanese and comes from a family that was once quite well off but has been in decline for many years. In 1995, Yanto was one of only perhaps a half dozen people in Bandung who owned a coveted Mercedes ("Baby") Benz. Now he owns four Mercedes and two other cars, as well as numerous properties around Bandung. His business outgrew the second-tier city some years ago, so he makes a weekly toll-road commute to his new office and a second house in Jakarta.

Among relatives, friends, neighbors, and employees in Bandung, Yanto and his family are known as "rich people" (*orang kaya*).[51] The figure of the rich person is a peculiar one in Bandung, for it simultaneously evokes a sense of distance and a sense of intimacy. The sense of intimacy is lacking in other figures used to describe the capital-owning classes, such as *konglomerat,* which applies to those who have attained celebrity status by virtue of their extreme wealth, or Chinese, which has sometimes been used to situate capitalists on the other side of an ethnic divide. The nondescript *orang kaya* stands in contrast to these figures, since he or she is a figure who is still within reach and in many cases is quite local. Indeed, the locality of the *orang kaya* is one of the things that has sometimes made urban Indonesia seem quite unusual: the fact that *orang kaya* and their opposites—the heavily stigmatized *orang miskin* (the poor) and the less stigmatized *orang biasa* (ordinary people)— live in such close proximity to one another, often under the very same roof.

Early incarnations of Bandung's *orang kaya* figure overlapped with a more negative connotation of the Pak Haji (described in the previous essay) as a landowner rich enough to go on the hajj but despised by his poorer neighbors for his greed and bad behavior. In the 1950s and 1960s, the figure of Pak Haji-the-rich-person was joined by a new kind of *orang kaya:* the local self-made urban entrepreneur (*pengusaha*). Because Bandung was mainly a government and university town and had only a limited manufacturing industry, these new *orang kaya* very often made their money in construction—building the houses, streets, and institutional buildings of the rapidly growing city. Both Pak Haji and the urban entrepreneur used their wealth to acquire land, but whereas the Pak Haji was thoroughly rooted among his neighbors and used the trappings of religion as a means to bring his social status in line with his class, urban entrepreneurs circulated within the city and the province and had close ties to government, relationships that sometimes gave them a quasi-aristocratic (*menak*) aura. Urban entrepreneurs had ties to the lower classes mainly through their employees, who might include tradespeople and day laborers as well as domestic servants. Many of these workers—especially the domestic ones—would be brought to the city from the entrepreneur's home village and would stay with him for decades. Thus, although Pak Haji and the urban entrepreneur both played the intimate role of patron to many poor families, Pak Haji did so locally, while the urban entrepreneur did so through his company and through relations stretching back to the village. People who exemplify these figures still exist in Bandung today, but more often than not they are referred to as "*orang kaya* of the old days" (*orang kaya dulu*), and the stories that circulate about them focus mainly on their decline at the hands of their immoral children and, for the lucky ones, on their reputation for generosity.

Yanto represents an innovation on the old entrepreneur type, but one that is already beginning to seem somewhat outdated. He is the head of a household that is in most respects the idealized product of Suharto's New Order era: a two-child *pribumi* (non-Chinese) family based on an alliance between old status and new money.[52] His wealth comes from riding the economic wave of a massive investment in national and corporate infrastructure, led first by the government and later by the private sector. His business activities have taken him all over Indonesia, rather than being confined to Bandung. Yet he is not cosmopolitan. Even though his business has been deeply affected by globalization, he has remained resolutely uninterested in—and perhaps somewhat fearful of—spending time abroad or learning English. This resistance does not mean he embraces everything Indonesian. Over the past decade, he has increasingly sought to cocoon himself and his family apart from contacts with ordinary people. He has long lived in a lightly gated housing complex, and five years ago he moved his family to a new house behind high walls. As he has few ties to his neighbors, it is mostly through relatives and domestic employees—his servants, his driver, and his nanny—that he and his wife are connected to the world of the lower classes. In this connection, communication is almost entirely one way: very intimate gossip and stories about the *orang kaya* get relayed into the slum and the village, but very little information flows the other way.[53]

Economic forces tighten the cocoon. Yanto complains that it is becoming more and more difficult to find domestic workers, since many villagers now choose factory work or higher paying domestic jobs abroad in Saudi Arabia or Malaysia. In his household, only the driver has worked there for many years; the others come and go on a regular basis. Domestic labor is becoming more formalized and more flexible. With urban real estate values climbing upward, homes in newly built housing developments are retaining less and less space for domestic workers.

In Victorian England, the decline of live-in domestic work marked a watershed in relations between the classes. In the big cities, spatial segregation along class lines replaced the "upstairs/downstairs" culture of the old country manor. The figure of the local *orang kaya* in Bandung, sandwiched between an emerging middle class on the one hand and an increasingly cosmopolitan capital-owning class on the other, is only just beginning to look anachronistic. While comparable figures will undoubtedly remain in smaller towns and in more rural areas, in Bandung it is probably only a matter of time before this figure disappears. If and when it does, it too will mark a watershed in class relations.

Career Woman, *Wanita Karir*
CARLA JONES

Over Frappucinos in a central Jakarta Starbucks, Santi and I talked about the misunderstandings her family and female superiors at work have about women like her, a young professional woman. Santi is thirty-three, a divorced mother of a seven-year-old son, and she loves her work at a well-known women's magazine. Yet she is constantly aware of carrying a powerful label, *wanita karir,* or career woman. As a figure whose priorities are questionable, a *wanita karir* is a problematic individual, a woman whose visibility, mobility, and desires are seen as linking improper femininity to social decay.

Santi's description of the tensions in her life is emblematic of the category career woman. Although the stereotypical *wanita karir* is a young woman who has not married, the fact that Santi is divorced can be blamed on her enjoyment of her career, while her devotion to her son ameliorates blame and guilt about that enjoyment. Even her female superiors, women who themselves have achieved career success, perceive her generation of professional women to have misaligned moral compasses, as they seem to prefer work over family and personal consumption over domestic frugality. Santi explained that she had become a more pious Muslim—relying on Allah for emotional support of her life choices, choosing to wear a sheer headscarf, and attending *pengajian*

(Islamic study groups) more frequently—in part to assuage the pain of being criticized as a *wanita karir.*

Images of Indonesian women who work in white-collar employment, service industries, and other office settings associated with recent economic progress in the country circulate differently than do representations of other kinds of female laborers. Although related discourses elaborate the social costs of different types of feminine work, such as migrant domestic labor, factory production, and sex work,[54] each of which has also contributed to Indonesian economic change, the figure of the *wanita karir* has a particular valence, in part because of her greater visibility. As office workers commute in and out of central Jakarta on public transportation, small groups of attractive women garbed in professional dress, carrying (often knockoff) designer accessories and texting or calling on their hand phones, become a human sign of the broader pride and worry that the city evokes. A *wanita karir* is thus a figure whose social space absorbs the thrills and ills of a society experiencing change. Studying representations of public intimacy in the late New Order, Suzanne Brenner has argued that middle-class women appeared to have choices about family and work that, when made, are not merely individual but that "have a bearing on the very future of Indonesian society."[55] The same can be said for post–New Order *wanita karir.*

Santi's impressions of the criticism she senses all around her touch on the many ills that the *wanita karir* are seen to embody. As a figure of desire who cannot control her own desires—consumer and sexual—the *wanita karir* becomes both the subject and the object of social anxiety. As such, individual *wanita karir* are not only signs of social anxiety but reflect consciously on it. First, just as individual women office workers tend to be mobile, the social type of the *wanita karir* circulates widely. Articles and television shows refer to and comment on the *wanita karir* with ease. She is positioned as the opposite of a competing stereotype—the housewife, or *ibu rumah tangga*— who is self-sacrificing, domestic, static, middle-aged, and often dowdy. The *wanita karir* lives alone, or with other young women, in an apartment with little social surveillance, a situation that allows her not only to go to work but potentially to move on to evening engagements with mixed-sex mingling or even alcohol and drugs. As an antidote to the suspicions raised by this stereotypical portrait, Santi informs her colleagues—and especially her superiors— of her evening commitments, including her regular attendance at *pengajian.*

Second, income earned from office work appears simultaneously substantial yet unconnected to family. Because of the gleaming settings where white-collar work is carried out in Jakarta—skyscrapers set among five-star hotels and world-class malls—the productive labor of the *wanita karir* is closely linked to the temptations of consumption. Images of consumer modernity regularly use the bodies of beautiful, active women as brokers of desire, turning illusion into exchange. As Santi described it, she is hard-pressed to get financial support for her son from her ex-husband and his family because they imagine her job to be well paying and perceive her requests for support as proof that she uses her salary selfishly for individual consumption.

Third, when the *wanita karir* figure represents the inability to channel desire properly, this informs general anxieties about the feminization of consumption and the pathologically disorienting effect of production and consumption on sexual desire. In addition to commodities, *wanita karir* are imagined to spend their salaries on perversions of love. This aspect of the stereotypical figure emerges in two related, fantasized characteristics of the *wanita karir:* her propensity to homosexuality and her ability to buy male companionship. Media reports frequently attribute a perceived increase in lesbian identity in contemporary Indonesia to the long periods of time *wanita karir* spend in the company of female coworkers, whose friendship can be perverted into a sexual relationship. The Pria Idaman Lain (PIL, literally "New Dream Man")—the kept male lover secretly supported through a woman's salary—is a related character that similarly emerges as an example of social degeneration, a commercial form that appears to allow women to avoid domestic duty in exchange for the unentangled pleasures of commodified sex. Perhaps no example better captures the risks of desire gone awry than the case of a *gay* male serial killer whose discovery became a sensation in July and August of 2008. In his confessions to Jakarta police, Ryan described how his uncontrollable desire for luxury goods (hand phones, a motorcycle, and a water dispenser) led him into sexual liaisons with other men, whom he then murdered and robbed. Extreme consumer desire is thus both feminizing and criminalizing.[56]

Santi thoroughly enjoys her job, yet she struggles to define herself in an environment that has already determined what it means to be a *wanita karir.* As a woman who earns, yet whose earnings are not clearly tied to domestic reproduction, who visibly navigates city streets while wearing and using commodities, the *wanita karir* captures anxieties about the relationship between capitalism and social relations in contemporary Indonesia. While these anxieties are never resolved, they temporarily alight on the bodies of women who are associated with office work and consumption.

MALAYSIA

Edited by YEOH SENG GUAN

Malaysia's entanglement with Western modernity has a long, agonistic, and ambivalent history. During the age of empires, the region now known as Malaysia became more closely linked to Europe through sea trade. From the standpoint of postcolonial nationalist history, however, the "golden era" of entrepot commerce is traced back to the fifteenth-century Malacca Sultanate before it fell to a succession of European powers beginning in the early sixteenth century. The Portuguese and Dutch rulers concentrated their colonial possessions on the ports of the Malay Peninsula. But from the late eighteenth century onward, the British progressively expanded their hold into the hinterland, crafting their rule in order to relay wealth extracted from cash crop plantations and mineral resources back to the metropolitan center of the British Empire. For this capitalist enterprise, they instituted liberal migration and land policies to attract a diverse influx of peoples from around the region as cheap and passive labor. To mitigate the religious uprisings faced in other parts of the British Empire, the British publicly accorded a special status to Islam and the sultans, while creating a new class of modernist English-speaking locals through Western education to fill up both the colonial and commercial bureaucracies. By the time of political independence in 1957, the combination of laissez-faire economics and racial divide-and-rule administrative policies coupled with the entrepreneurial drive of migrants had produced a culturally variegated but politically segregated ethnoscape. Foreign companies and local Chinese capitalists exerted strong commercial control, while the majority of Malays, Chinese, Indians, and other minority ethnic groups were largely mired in comparative poverty. In short, imperialist and colonialist projects have produced shifting "structures of feelings,"¹ which in turn have created (and elided) new modernist figures and social types over time.

In the postcolonial milieu, Malaysia's dalliance with Western modernity has continued with a different ensemble of social actors. Arguably, under the long premiership of Mahathir Mohamad (1981–2003), the very concept of modernity became significantly more comprehensive, far reaching, and vernacularized. Building on the gains and patronage networks cultivated through the epochal New Economic Policy (NEP, 1971–1990), when the economy witnessed an impressive average yearly growth rate of 8 percent,² Mahathir radically oriented the country's economy toward manufacturing, construction, and finance. These economic gains legitimized more comprehensive attempts to guide and control the social meanings of modernity as well. For example, in 1991 Mahathir promulgated the grand narrative and catchphrase of Wawasan 2020 ("Vision 2020"), a social, political, and economic agenda that prescribes aspirational changes to the social body of Malaysia in order to become "developed" by the year 2020. Its futuristic, neoliberal, and entrepreneurial themes particularly resonated with the elites, the politically well connected, and the aspirations of a sizeable middle class of the two largest ethnic groups in the country, the Malays and the Chinese.

Malaysia's polychromatic and largely harmonious ethnoreligious populace, often touted as a multicultural exemplar for other countries, has nevertheless attracted close surveillance and tight management by the government. As an antidote to the pathological problems of "race" and "religion" undermining social cohesion and wealth generation, the Mahathir administration constructed the transethnic figure of Bangsa Malaysia ("Malaysian Race"), supposedly to supersede the ethnosegregationist ethos stemming from the colonial period. Paradoxically, this project also envisaged the Malay component of the composite Bangsa Malaysia transfiguring into a Melayu Baru ("New Malay"). The Melayu Baru was both an individual and a class, revolutionized through the social and cultural capital of cutting-edge skills, abilities, and—most important of all—a can-do mindset approximating those of the entrepreneurial Malaysian Chinese commercial and educated class.

The Malaysian government resists overt "class analysis," which remains stigmatized due to its association with the robust (but eventually failed) communist insurgency that unfolded in the aftermath of World War II. Before the collapse of the USSR, the ghostly figures of the "Marxist" or the "Communist" were thus viewed as radical threats to national security, to be vigilantly weeded out. In October 1987, while facing political opposition and mounting public criticism, Mahathir infamously invoked the Internal Security Act to detain a total of 107 individuals without recourse to trial. Many of the victims had been critical of Mahathir's brand of authoritarian leadership and the kind of economic trajectory being crafted, while groups expressing Malay-Muslim supremacist sentiments were not reined in for fear of political backlash. Referring to centuries in which Malaysia's population of various religious and ethnic ancestries have lived in peaceful coexistence, observers note that deepening intraethnic class divisions are a consequence of the intense resource competition created by Mahathir's neoliberal economic and privatization policies but inflected through a racialized grammar.

Another cornerstone of the great leap forward lay in recalibrating the relationship between the secular and the sacred for Malay-Muslim citizens. In addition to punitive actions against "deviant" Islamic sects, a key amendment to Article 121 (1A) of the Federal Constitution removed the jurisdiction of the civil courts over Islamic affairs and in effect created two spheres of jurisdiction between the civil and the Shariah criminal courts.[3] For critics, it signaled a hollowing out of the secular state (guaranteed by the Federal Constitution) on the one hand and a "nationalization of Islam" on the other.[4]

Even after his official retirement as premier in 2003, the imprints and ethos of Mahathir's distinctive pugnacious and visionary authoritarianism remain palpable. At the ocular level, the many iconic structures in Kuala Lumpur (the hypermodern KLCC Twin Towers in particular) and megaconstruction projects around the country launched during his administration stand out as emblems of an explicit engagement with a globalizing modernity. More subliminally, the specter of "Mahathirism" pervades the collective psyche of Malaysian politics, whether as an ethos of governance to be emulated or to be mitigated by future premiers. His chosen successor, Abdullah Badawi, lost Mahathir's favor after stopping or stalling some of his pet megaprojects and was replaced by Najib Abdul Razak. Keenly exploiting new media and modern communication technologies, Premier Najib has once again reasserted the motifs of modernity that have long framed Malaysian political discourse. While the slogans of Wawasan 2020 and Bangsa Malaysia have not vanished from the landscape, the strong visuals and populist discourse of "1Malaysia" have come more forcefully to the foreground. The rationale for all this aspirational activity is explained, in typical fashion, as enabling all Malaysians of finally grasping the prized holy grail of development and modernity.

If entangling with changing forms of modernity is the long thread running through Malaysian history, the figures in this section explore and clarify Malaysia's own vernacularized version of modernity and its corresponding proponents and critics. Schottmann's piece provides a convenient starting point, offering insights into the imaginary of an irrepressible National Leader largely responsible for shifting much of Malaysian ground realities in recent times. Against this shift, or perhaps because of it, Hoffstaedter's portrait of the Reactionary gives us a close-up view of a vociferous segment of the Malay-Muslim population that has viewed their privileged position as under attack with the emergent policies of the ruling government and opposition front. The persona of another kind of critic in the mold of a "public intellectual" is sketched by Syed Muhd Khairudin Aljunied: in this case, the Scholar-Musician is a well-known Malaysian anthropologist and a musician.

Other renditions of how Malaysian identity cultural politics are contested in this particular historical moment can be gleaned in the cluster of pieces by Khoo Gaik-Cheng (the Political Satirist), Rusaslina Idrus (Hang Tuah, Revisited), and Julian Lee (the Supra-Ethnic Malaysian). In all of them, we see the utility of satire, humor, and fictional (and quasi-fictional) figures in the rhizomatic medium of cyberspace in reworking foundational identity or truth claims. Hang Tuah, Revisited clues us into creative speculations as to the true ethnic origins of the legendary seventeenth-century warriors, Hang Tuah and Hang Jebat, long held up as role models for modern Malay politics. Whereas the singularity and authenticity of ethnic origins is the bone of contention in Rusaslina's piece, the Mak Bedah theatrical figure sidesteps these concerns (Julian Lee). Played by various women of different ethnic origins (albeit with identical signature dressing) during the campaign period of the 2008 general elections, her youthful appeal lay in the cosmopolitan and culturally hybrid sentiments of Internet-savvy urbanites based in the capital city. On a similar key, but perhaps much more damaging to the status quo, is Khoo's discussion of online satire and parody mocking the hypocrisy of Malaysian politics. As elsewhere, the power of laughter has invited threats by the current government to legislate and enforce cyber laws despite assurances by the Mahathir administration several years ago that Internet censorship will be abhorred.

The last cluster presents figures that narrate the intersections between urbanism, modernism, and local-level entrepreneurialism. The Squatter (Yeoh Seng Guan) tells of the radical transformation of modes of housing in Kuala Lumpur set in motion during the Mahathir administration and the attempts by those afflicted to preserve more familiar ways of living. Although the Returning Urbanite (Matthew Amster) is situated in the isolated highlands of Sarawak, it is evident that the pervasive imaginary of "curricular urbanism" has wrought its magic, motivating its young residents to migrate to the urban centers for work and more.[5] In this particular instance, we read of a rare reversal and the unsettling disjunctions experienced in returning to his homeland. Finally, the Timber Entrepreneur (Michael Eilenberg), focusing on an individual who has seemingly mastered the art of border crossings for economic gain, is perhaps an apt metaphor for this collection. In attending to the myriad governmentalities of a globalizing world, the many figures who inhabit the space of the postcolonial moderns have to learn to be conversant with cultural complexity or else cease to exist in the same ethos as during Western colonial rule, when emergent "structures of feelings" beckoned new modern figures into being even as older ones were ruled out of favor.

National Leader
SVEN ALEXANDER SCHOTTMANN

"I have always been convinced by the teachings of Islam, but I have also always been very critical of how Muslims interpreted them," Malaysia's former prime minister Dr. Mahathir Mohamad told me when I first interviewed him in his study at the Perdana Leadership Foundation in Putrajaya in 2008. The ornate Qur'anic calligraphy (Ayat al-Kursi) and the leather-bound tomes (*Encyclopaedia Britannica*) on the wall behind his desk served as visual cues to the particular type of modernity that he had sought to encourage among Malaysians. "I asked myself: *Why do Muslims fail?*" Mahathir continued. "Wherever Muslims are, they lag behind others. . . . People around me said that this is because this world is not for us, but I never accepted that sort of escapism."

Along with Singapore's former prime minister Lee Kuan Yew and Indonesia's longtime ruler Suharto, Mahathir is one of Southeast Asia's most important late-twentieth-century statesmen.[6] The political biographies of these leaders amalgamate into one of the most iconic figures of Southeast Asian modernity: the postcolonial nation builder. Himself a product of the social change that had taken place over the previous fifty years, the national leader tended to be driven by visions of social transformation through economic growth. The frequently authoritarian national leader sought to accelerate his country's economic modernization while maintaining its cultural distinctiveness, with the underlying belief that modernity was attainable through conscious borrowing from East and West even as the "redeemable" aspects of local cultures and traditions could be retained.

Mahathir sought to lay out the path by which Malaysians could *menjadi moden,* or "become modern." He held that religion could help the Malay majority population (all of whom are assumed and asserted to be Sunni Muslims) discern those aspects of the modern world that could profitably be adopted from those that should be rejected.[7] All national leaders had to grapple with the need for reconciling tradition with political, social, and economic modernity, but Mahathir (who actually had little formal religious education) went further than others in making the point that religion could provide an inspiration for Southeast Asian modernities, and that it could provide a shield from the ravages of the modern age.

In Mahathir's view, there was nothing in Islam itself that would have prevented the eventual emergence of "modernity" among Muslims. At times, he even appeared to hint at the possibility of "multiple modernities," arguing for instance that the particular mode and trajectory of modernity as experienced by Western Europe after the seventeenth and eighteenth centuries was not universal.[8] Modernity in the Muslim world, Mahathir hypothesized, might well turn out to be of a very different nature altogether.[9]

The two-pronged objective of Mahathir's engagement with Islam (demonstrating that what he invariably referred to as "correctly understood Islam" remained within the Sunni orthodoxy *and* that there was indeed such a thing as a "modern Muslim") marks him as someone seeking to find a synthesis between Islam and the Western-articulated status quo. He was an enthusiastic advocate of modernization, at least in its economic and scientific-technological guises, but he also appeared to be genuinely convinced that the wholesale adoption of the Western model of modernity was unlikely to be successful in the newly independent countries of Asia and Africa more generally and in the Muslim world in particular.[10]

Mahathir argued that Islam would help modulate modernity in predominantly Muslim countries such as Malaysia—in much the same way Islam had acted as a conduit for new ideas, art forms, and technologies in previous centuries. Like other modernist-oriented Muslims before him, Mahathir argued that all the faithful had to do was to return to the pristine understanding of their religion and cleanse their beliefs and practices of the superstitions, heterodoxy, fatalism, and irrationality that had led to the current intellectual, economic, and cultural impasses. Mahathir argued that a return to "correctly understood Islam"—and there was no doubt whose interpretation of Islam was correct—would help resolve what he increasingly saw as the "Muslim dilemma" of poverty and political subjugation.[11]

Mahathir stands emblematically for the embrace of economic but not cultural modernity that seems characteristic of the generation of leaders that came to power after the 1960s. His engagement with Islam and his attempt to articulate a "proper understanding" of the religion's teachings certainly reflect this line of thought, which also underlay the "Asian values" debate of the early 1990s. Mahathir and other socially conservative but economically liberal-oriented leaders argued that "Asian" values such as consensus-mindedness or communitarian thinking had played a major role in bringing about the economic transformations of East Asia.

Like his counterparts in Singapore or Jakarta, Mahathir's vision of modernity can be simplified as the enthusiastic embrace of skyscrapers, motorways, and shopping malls and the resolute rejection of hedonism, individualism, and permissiveness. As prime minister, he repeatedly made the point that Malaysians and Muslims "were not ready" for what he saw as the excessive social freedoms he linked with the Western model of modernity.[12] After retiring in 2003, Mahathir continued his engagement with the questions of Malaysian modernity—multiculturalism, democracy, progress—through his distinctly modern medium of choice, the blog.[13]

The specific path that Mahathir charted for Malaysia's modernization—and in particular his answers to questions as to the compatibility of Islam and modernity—set him apart from Southeast Asian's other modernizer-statesmen, a handful of late-twentieth-century leaders who have been given great leeway in reshaping entire societies. Parallels with Lee Kuan Yew or Suharto's attempts to identify "authentic" trajectories toward modernity are reminders of the usefulness of approaching Southeast Asian modernity in terms of figures. At the same time, each national leader himself is of course the uniquely configured composite of many other figures of Southeast Asian modernity. In the case of Malaysia's former prime minister Mahathir, these might be the colonial subaltern, the Muslim modernist, the nationalist, or even the blogger. The multiple temporalities and sometimes contradictory qualities inhering in these figures underscore the eclecticism and complexity of the vision of modernity articulated by one of Southeast Asia's best-known national leaders.

Reactionary
GERHARD HOFFSTAEDTER

I met Taib at a PAS (Parti Islam Se-Malaysia, or Pan-Malaysian Islamic Party) fundraiser in Klang in Selangor. PAS is an Islamist party that draws its support mainly from Malay Muslims, making it the key opponent of the ruling UMNO (United Malays National Organisation). Nik Aziz, the spiritual leader of PAS, spoke at the event about how to further Islamize the Malaysian state and society. Taib and I were seated at the same table, and a conversation around Islam and its role in politics and everyday life ensued. He informed me that he was not a PAS member but was interested in their views and that he was setting up an NGO himself, tentatively called "Brothers in Islam." The name (wrongly) suggested an affinity with Sisters in Islam, a prominent progressive women's rights organization. We agreed to meet later in the week to discuss his plans.

Reactionaries in Malaysia are difficult to define as a group. What are they reacting against? To what status do they want society and the state to revert? These make for difficult questions. One thing is clear, though: reactionary forces are on the rise and, despite their small numbers, are exerting disproportionate influence on the country's future. They have managed to define a series of battlegrounds against the progressives and have made their stand vociferously enough to be noticed. Thus, the federal government is meeting many of their demands. The main battle lines are around Islam and Malayness, traditionally sacrosanct identifiers for the majority of Malaysians, which remain at the heart of Malaysia's continuing racialized politics.

Taib is Malay but has a Chinese mother who converted to Islam for marriage. Thus his heritage exemplifies the ethnic fluidity and hybridity of maritime Southeast Asia. However, Taib's life experience and political-cum-social outlook locate him within the current simmering tension of identity politics. He sees himself as someone straddling the border between competing identities, a position that has led him to even more fervently affirm one identity over the other. His zealousness should at least in part be understood as a response to this ambivalence, as his social position is by no means "natural," "organic" or "given." Taib's Malay and Muslim identity thus demands constant clarification and performance.

Taib, recently retired from a management role with a major multinational company, devoted his spare time to studying the Qur'an. With an early retirement age in Malaysia, many middle- and upper-class retirees devote some time to study groups, lectures, and private study. His wife is a sharifa, a putative descendant of the prophet Muhammad. While Taib argued that she had previously neglected her religious bloodline, she was now also retired and attending classes on Islam. Her mother's side descended from a cadet branch of Perak's royal family, and marrying into her family offered Taib a dual gateway into Malayness and Islamic identity.

Taib recounted that his wife takes being Muslim for granted, whereas he was "fortunate" to be a Muslim and described it as a "treasure that has been given to him." Thus he sees it as his duty to protect this treasure and make others aware of their duties as beneficiaries of the gift of religious truth and certainty. On another occasion, he described faith as a gift (*hidaya*) bestowed on the believer that brings with it the responsibility to protect it. This conceptualization is shared among many reactionaries who claim that Muslims have neglected their religious duties and adopted Western ways.

Like other reactionaries before him, Taib blamed the government for a string of failures to protect and promote Islam properly, provide Malays with adequate help, and institute Islamic law. Taib's emphasis on current failures best illustrates the reactionaries' project of restoration: their wish to return to an often imagined past where Malay rulers were sovereign and people were subject to *adat* (customary, especially religious, laws) rather than a secular constitution. The restoration thus differs from previous modernist and reformist movements such as the *kaum muda* (young generation) in the early 1900s that sought to reform Islam in the face of tradition and contained an emphasis on equality. Taib and his organization are part of an elite that feels ignored. Thus, he sees it as his role to push the government into his way of seeing things. The purity of Islam and the defense of Islam as the supreme religion of the land feature strongly in his vision of what his organization stands for. This makes apostasy/conversion a key battleground to maintain a numerical supremacy of Muslim followers. Taib turned out to have been a pivotal figure in filing the police report against the church that christened Lina Joy, or Azlina Jailani as she was previously known. This case of a Malay converting to Christianity shook the nation through 2006, with the High Court ruling that it had no jurisdiction over Muslims—making apostasy from Islam legally impossible in Malaysia. Malayness is featured too, as Malays enjoy special rights as enshrined in the constitution and economically through the NEP (New Economic Policy) and its successor programs. Malayness is thus a potent identity marker of difference against non-Muslims on the one hand and other ethnic groups on the other.

In the end, the organization Taib founded was called Muslim Brothers (which recalls the Muslim Brotherhood of Egypt), and it is a prime example of how Islam and Malay rights intertwine and have become almost synonymous in contemporary Malaysian identity politics. Reactionaries are potent because they can stir unrest among Malays over issues such as the special position for Malays, staging protests, and demanding that UMNO politicians agree to their demands. Reactionaries aim to maintain the racial privileges the postcolonial nation-state gave them, while seeking to forget the plural past and silence the multicultural present as alternative visions. Perkasa, for instance, a nongovernmental organization that has hit the headlines recently as protector of the Malays and their political as well as economic rights, remains couched in a thoroughly Islamic imagery and symbols.

Having melded Islam to Malayness in this way makes any debate around issues of affirmative action for Malays, the role of Islam in politics, or the place of Islamic law nearly impossible. That is precisely what the reactionaries, defending an unstable status quo, want. The Malaysian body politic thus remains rooted in silences about its past, present, and future, with reactionaries fiercely guarding Malay and Islamic supremacy as both become ever more challenged and untenable.

Scholar-Musician
SYED MUHD KHAIRUDIN ALJUNIED

Wan Zawawi is no ordinary professor of social anthropology. Charming, cheerful, outgoing, with his radical side symbolized by his longish hair, he is known to many as a scholar who has written influential works about peasants, indigenous peoples, and subalterns at the periphery of Malaysia's development.[14] What is less well known is that he is a man of culture with refined literary tastes. A poet and a musician, his poetry reflects the anxieties of daily life in modern Malaysia, while his passion for music stems from his belief that he was endowed with musical talent at an early age. But it was life in the villages of eastern Malaysia and the many years of study in suburban Australia that instilled in him a conception of life as both a journey and a struggle to alter the conditions of his society. Today he often performs in concerts and gigs, not for the money but because he believes that he can reform society through his music. "There is no social space or physical space to perform these days," he says. "Music performances get raided every time by the authorities. But we need these spaces for the young people to perform, to express themselves, because music cuts through the races. It is a multicultural fox. Just like the independent film scene. You see Malays, Chinese, and Indians performing together, and this is good for Malaysia."

These words tell us much about the tensions in Zawawi's mind and in the minds of many Malaysians like him in the face of what is now commonly termed "Malaysian modernity," a concept that involves the fusion of Malay communalism and the Islamic ethos with selected aspects of Western developmentalism.[15] The effects of this hybridized version of modernity have been felt most strongly by those active in the creative arts scene, because the cosmopolitan ideals that inform the arts are curbed and stifled by an ethno-Islamicized bureaucracy determined to steer Malays toward political predominance at the expense of Malaysians of other races. The bureaucracy sees musical performances as crucial influences in the lives of young Malay-Muslim-Malaysians—influences that must be controlled and prevented from being tainted by the "Western" and "liberal" music promoted by Zawawi.[16]

Impediments put in place by the state breed resistance by the citizenry. Zawawi pulls no punches in his criticism of all agencies that oppose his beliefs. Little wonder then that, like most organic intellectuals, he has never stayed for long in any Malaysian university. When the *Malaysian Idol* winner Jacelyn Victor was accused in 2005 of being "morally decadent" and turning youths away from "Asian values," Zawawi responded by using the same discursive tools used by the majority Malay-Muslim populace. A singing competition, according to him, serves "as a powerful tool to promote the *muhibbah* [good-will] spirit among Malaysians. *Malaysian Idol* is an example of pop culture which has created social spaces for youngsters of different ethnic groups to come together."[17]

And yet for all his criticism of the limiting of space for the arts, Zawawi remains committed to other prevailing imaginings of what "Malaysia" is. This deeper tension arises partly from his own background as a child of Malaysian modernity and a "Malay" whose roots can be traced to the coast of Trengganu, which plays out in Zawawi's writings and in his music. He accepts the cat-egorization of "Malays," "Chinese," "Indians," and "Orang Asli" to describe the Malaysian ethnoscape. Fully aware that these reified identities were born out of the colonial experience, Zawawi's approach to dealing with what has been invented is not to reinvent but to level off and syncretize differences between differing groups and between the haves and the have-nots through pop culture, an approach that is reminiscent of his musical idols—Bob Dylan and Leonard Cohen.[18]

Nor does Zawawi deny the reality of Malaysia as a geobody. In fact, his energies are directed toward affirming that the nation-state and its borders hold true and must always be remembered. Here, Zawawi agrees with many nationalists who share the same thematic concerns and premises of the colo-nialists, despite the problems inherent in these premises. While opposed to the rule of difference and the capitalist economy imposed by the Europeans, Malaysian scholars and artists embrace the notions of progress and territorial borders that are essential to the colonial and postcolonial projects alike.[19]

But we must not take this argument so far as to lose sight of the nu-ances in Zawawi's appropriations of the colonial inheritance. For Zawawi, it is futile to romanticize about the glories of the Malay past and downright ir-responsible for any Malaysian to forget the array of changes, transformations, and problems that colonialism has wrought upon the contemporary moment. Postcoloniality is here to stay, and the task of a scholar and a man of the arts is to make known these subjectivities and chart the possible pathways for the future by deriving lessons from the past. He sees anthropology as a discipline that can capture the lived experiences and voices of peoples consigned to the margins of the nation, and he sees his music and poetry as the means to popularize his aspirations and his feelings about the world and its forgotten spaces and locations. In his words, "I've always regarded my music as a way of anthropologizing and as a way to get away from the formalized language of academe—where I can use adjectives and express emotions—although to some extent my postmodernist anthropology gives me the space to let my informants speak."

Although Zawawi makes no claims to success, he is convinced that being a scholar-musician in Malaysia with a heart for the people is a perilous passage worth taking.

Hang Tuah, Revisited
RUSASLINA IDRUS

For several years now, an e-mail titled "The Truth Revealed" has been circulating in the Malaysian cybersphere. As the title implies, the e-mail tells of a conspiracy, a government cover-up concealing the "true" identity of Malaysia's most famous folk hero, Hang Tuah. There are several versions circulating, but the story pretty much goes like this: In 1998, the Malaysian government commissioned an international team of scientists to analyze the graves of Hang Tuah and his compatriots. DNA analysis conducted by a "team of scientists, archaeologists, historians, and other technical staff from the United States, United Kingdom, Germany, Canada, Yemen and Russia" revealed that the much-revered fifteenth-century Malay warrior was actually . . . Chinese! The e-mail claims that the Malaysian government concealed this shocking revelation and since then has erased Hang Tuah from history textbooks. The author of the e-mail further explains that Hang Tuah and his compatriots were Muslim Chinese who had been sent by the emperor of China to Malacca to protect "the ungrateful Malay Sultanate" from the Kingdom of Siam. In one version, to further bolster the "scientific" authority of the alleged research, a reference is made to the "Federal Association of Arc and Research of Michigan, USA."[20]

Hang Tuah is the quintessential Malay warrior. First mentioned in the seventeenth-century court document *Sulalat al-Salatin*,[21] Hang Tuah is also the central figure in *Hikayat Hang Tuah*, a literary work believed to have been written about the same time.[22] The mythical legend of Hang Tuah has had an everlasting appeal, told and retold in many forms, from theater productions to children's comic books to box-office movies. As the legend goes, Hang Tuah was a warrior who not only had great strength and mystical powers but displayed unwavering and unquestioning loyalty to the sultan. In a Malay feudal society, Hang Tuah epitomizes the perfect subject.

Hang Tuah's famous statement, *"Takkan Melayu hilang di dunia"* (Never shall the Malays cease to be), is the rallying cry for the Malay nationalist party, UMNO.[23] Hang Tuah had been written into the narrative of Malay special rights by *keris*-wielding,[24] ultra-Malay nationalists, who reinterpret his staunch defense of the Malay Sultanate as a defense for the special position of the Malays as the "sons of the soil" (*bumiputera*) versus the non-*bumiputera* (namely, the Chinese and Indians). Designed to ease the deep tensions made so clear in the racial riots of 1969, the special position of the Malays was asserted through acts like the New Economic Policy instituted in 1971. Originally intended to operate like an affirmative action policy meant to balance economic disparity among the racial groups, this policy has over time been misused to argue for innate special privileges for the Malays, causing tension among the different groups.

The lore that Hang Tuah is really Chinese is actually not new. I heard this as a child growing up in Malaysia, and it has also been referred to in popular culture, as in Yasmin Ahmad's 2004 movie, *Sepet.* As many have pointed out, the name "Hang Too Ah" sounds uncannily Chinese and suggests that he might have been related to Hang Li Po, the famous Chinese princess who was sent to Malacca to marry the sultan. Working with Orang Asli (non-Malay indigenous groups) communities for my dissertation research, I also became aware of a different Hang Tuah origin story, in which he came from the Orang Laut clan that was instrumental in helping Parameswara build the Malaccan Empire.[25]

In this cyberlegend, Hang Tuah, the accidental spokesperson for Malay rights, is appropriated as the hero of the non-Malay Other. While open discussion challenging Malay rights is illegal in Malaysia, the e-mail, facilitated by the anonymity of e-mail monikers and the "safe" space of the Internet, has generated heated debates wherever it has been posted on online forums. In one online forum, 599 comments have been made since 2007, and the thread remains active three years later. The comments range from explosively racist remarks to ones that try to inject reason into the conversation.

While this can be dismissed as yet another viral e-mail, its persistent circulation and the heated discussions it solicits suggest a more important story being told here. As folklorist Alan Dundes argues, "Myth may constitute the highest form of truth, albeit in metaphorical guise."[26] This cyberlegend or myth, like other urban legends and folklore, reflects the "hopes, fears and anxieties" of the society it circulates in.[27] The debate over the ethnic origins of Hang Tuah reflects the deep sense of frustration and anxiety among non-Malay Malaysians responding to the rise of ultra-Malay nationalists in recent years. It also can be read as an ongoing act of rewriting history by politically marginalized communities whose pivotal contributions to nation building have been increasingly sidelined. In textbooks, the Malay-centric history (that starts with the glory days of the Malaccan Empire, of which Hang Tuah is part) has become the official national history, silencing the role of the diverse community in making Malaysia what it is today.

Another fascinating twist to this legend is not only the reinterpretation of a traditional symbol of Malayness but the use of science in making the argument. The evocation of "scientific evidence" and the authority of international scientists tap into a modern Malaysia where science is highly valued. In a transnational world where American technoscience television dramas like *CSI* and *Bones* have entered Malaysian popular culture, the lingo of DNA analysis is no longer foreign.[28] The same people watching these shows tune in to alternative political news on their laptops. This techno-savvy generation of young Malaysians grew up knowing Malaysia as their only homeland and is invested in making their sense of belonging known. The legend of the ethnically ambiguous Tuah reveals the struggles of non-Malay Malaysians in asserting their place in a country they call home. Hang Tuah, the traditional Malay icon, the loyal, unquestioning subject, ironically becomes a space to challenge the hegemonic narrative of the state—a vessel for assertion of belonging and citizenry rights.

Supra-Ethnic Malaysian
JULIAN C. H. LEE

Six of us were piled cheek-by-jowl in a grey Hyundai, zooming through the night along the back streets of Kuala Lumpur, chasing a moving target. That target was a well-known female politician on the campaign trail during the 2008 general elections. Of the six people in the car, only two of us were male. The other four were women—the same woman: Aunty Bedah.

When a stream of honking and cheering motorbikes and cars went by in the other direction, the Aunty Bedah who was driving did a hasty U-turn and followed the red taillights of the candidate's entourage. We arrived at last in the heart of Little India. Aunty Bedah parked the Hyundai illegally and out tumbled four women, each in a loose purple head covering that is frequently, though not exclusively, worn by Muslim women, and each with a T-shirt sporting the slogan "Shopping for a Real Candidate." While each woman was a women's rights activist with her own identity, when she was attired this way and sporting banners calling for women to be better represented in politics, each was also Aunty Bedah. Two male supporters followed Aunty Bedah: her videographer and me, generic provider of moral support.

Aunty Bedah was the creation of members of the Women's Candidacy Initiative (WCI) in 2008. WCI is a loose organization of women's rights activists who seek to increase the proportion of women in Malaysia's parliament and who are willing to pursue women's rights and not be distracted by Malaysia's overbearing ethnopolitics. WCI principally regards its work as rendering practical help in the campaigns of independent female candidates.

However, just a few days before the beginning of the 2008 election campaign period, WCI's candidate, Zaitun "Toni" Kasim, withdrew her candidacy owing to health problems. Failing to find a replacement at short notice, WCI members developed a voter education campaign revolving around the character of Aunty Bedah.

According to the campaign story, Aunty Bedah entered the political scene because Zaitun's withdrawal compelled her to speak up for women's rights and to improve women's participation in Malaysia's parliament (which has hovered around the 10 percent mark for the last ten years). Aunty Bedah was crafted as an "average Malaysian woman" who spoke in *rojak,* a term that means "salad" but also refers to a kind of speech that blends any number of the languages in common use in Malaysia.

Although constructed as a single character, Aunty Bedah was played at any given time by a multiethnic mix of female WCI members. Importantly, the composition of these members served to make her public appearances a theatrical event and to turn Aunty Bedah into an ethnically hybridized Malaysian woman. The ethnically, religiously, and linguistically ambiguous character of Aunty Bedah was a product of urban Kuala Lumpur, where practices that traverse identity markers are relatively common and where political concerns that go beyond ethnic politics may more easily congeal.

The Malaysian public became aware of Aunty Bedah through numerous newspaper articles and front-page features bearing her image. YouTube videos featured Aunty Bedah singing spoofs of various pop hits such as "Bedahlicious" (from "Bootylicious"), "Bring Democracy Back" (from "Bringing Sexy Back"), and "Dontcha Wish Your MP Was Good Like Me" (from "Dontcha Wish Your Girlfriend Was Hot Like Me"). These videos were seen as important ways to engage with younger and otherwise depoliticized Malaysians and as a way of attracting media attention to the views of WCI.

Aunty Bedah's principal activity, however, was to approach candidates while they were campaigning and publicly seek their views on issues relating to sexism in Parliament, women's rights, and political representation. She presented herself as ostensibly "shopping" for an appropriate candidate on whom to "spend" her vote. Aunty Bedah (and her male supporters) would then make candidates' answers a matter of public record by describing them on her blog or uploading videos onto YouTube so other voters could make their own judgments.

On some occasions, Aunty Bedah and her multiple avatars received very positive reactions from candidates. On other occasions she was gruffly ignored or delivered beguiling sophisms and rhetorical spin by practiced politicians.

She was also shouted at and jostled, and in one instance hostile supporters of a candidate well known for making sexist remarks snatched away and broke a political placard she was carrying. On the night that we spilled out of the grey Hyundai in Little India, we were not sure what reaction Aunty Bedah would receive. Would the five-hundred-strong crowd have patience for a few women's rights activists?

As it happened, things went well. Probably mistaking us for part of the candidate's entourage, the crowd parted to give Aunty Bedah an easy path to the stage. Once there, one of the Aunty Bedahs spoke with the candidate while other politicians addressed the crowd. Aunty Bedah's report of the discussion indicated that the candidate seemed genuinely surprised by some of Aunty Bedah's revelations. Whether it was owing to this encounter or not, this candidate's party later instituted a policy ensuring that at least 30 percent of decision-making positions in the party would be reserved for women.

Although Aunty Bedah is a fictional creation uniquely associated with the 2008 WCI political campaign, her persona manifests the stereotype of an urban, ethnically hybridized Malaysian. Indeed, her fictionality probably realizes this stereotype better than any real person could. Aunty Bedah appears to come from every major ethnic group in Malaysia, while belonging to none. While Malaysian politics have historically been strongly marked by ethnoreligious concerns, recent scholarship in Malaysia suggests that ethnic identities are losing some of their strength in defining urban political agendas. The electoral advances of two avowedly ethnically unaligned parties in the 2008 general election appear to support this contention. So too does an informal campaign (on Facebook and elsewhere) encouraging Malaysians of all ethnic groups to use the word *macha,* which approximately means "mate" and is otherwise confined to minority Tamil-speaking Malaysians. The phenomenon of Aunty Bedah, a supra-ethnic Malaysian whose activism prioritizes women's rights over any identifiable ethnic agenda, is one more symptom of this shifting political ground.

Political Satirist (*Lawak Educated or Lawak Pakai Tie*)
KHOO GAIK CHENG

On February 19, 2009, satirist blogger Hassan Skodeng quietly posted his first hilarious article, "Perak MB [Chief Minister] tussle to be decided in shootout" on a Web page that had a picture of a long-nosed Pinocchio with the caption, "The truth is out there (Not in here)." It featured pictures of real politicians who were battling over who had the political legitimacy to lead the Perak state government and was written like a news article, not unlike mock features in the American satirical "newspaper," *The Onion.* Its humorous exaggeration plays on the farcical reality that is Malaysian culture, qualifying Hassan Skodeng as part of a new breed of *lawak educated* to have emerged since the twelfth general elections in March 2008, when the Opposition made its first substantial political gains against the UMNO, which had controlled politics since 1969.

Despite the presence of individual satirists like Hassan Skodeng and political cartoonist Zunar, *lawak educated* is not the sole monopoly of individual satirists but is deployed by various cultural actors and commentators when necessary. Coined by blogger Tokjeng to describe the satirical online news program *That Effing Show, lawak educated* means "educated humor/buffoon" or "humor for tie-wearers," as the alternative term *lawak pakai tie* suggests. Established by a group of twenty-something liberal Malaysian men in early 2010, the ultra-hip show is based on cutting humor and sober observations about the weekly news in politics, culture, and entertainment. A casual low-budget program carried out in a small studio conducted mostly in English with a smattering of other Malaysian languages, the show speaks to urban, Internet-savvy young Malaysians who are cosmopolitan, cynical, and looking for creative and entertaining ways to discuss local affairs. *Lawak educated* connotes a mature audience able to divine the line between fact and creative license and to understand fine nuances of irony often lacking in the mainstream discourse of Malaysian politics. More importantly, it works on the assumption that its audience consists of critical-minded, rational individuals able to see through the morally vacuous pronouncements by politicians in the mainstream media. *That Effing Show* reflects the changing face of Malaysia and a renewed sense of democratization.

But *lawak educated* is not a new phenomenon, nor is the *lawak pakai tie* a twenty-first-century Malaysian figure. The political satirist is a modern Malaysian figure who emerged first from a secular British colonial education system and who continues to be open to the influences of cultural globalization. The specifically Malaysian *lawak educated* is a hybrid creature premised on bilingualism (English and Malay) and multiculturalism.

Historically speaking, as early as the 1930s Malay language newspapers such as *Utusan Melayu* and *Lembaga Melayu* published cartoons that satirized the economic and political conditions under British colonial rule.[29] After independence, political cartooning reached its height of popularity in the late 1980s during intense political and economic times.[30] The 1987 crackdown on dissent under Operation Lalang,[31] failed government projects, and government-linked corporate fraud provided fodder for more satire on stage.

Operation Lalang inspired Kee Thuan Chye's play *The Big Purge* (1988) and gave birth to Instant Café Theatre (ICT), a company of multiethnic performers and theater activists who "used clowning and singing as a means of questioning key issues of cultural identity and trauma."[32] ICT lampooned the politics of the day throughout the 1990s, particularly the megaprojects and corruption scandals that accompanied Mahathir's nationalist ambitions. Additionally, the political satire sparked by the Reformasi in 1998 and the numerous controversies leading up to the 2008 elections prove that the genre thrives under sociopolitical circumstances perceived as unjust and repressive.

Compared to the heavily controlled mainstream media channels and numerous layers of bureaucracy and policies that limit dissent,[33] the rise of Internet technology and the promise of a censorship-free democratic space under Mahathir's Multimedia Super Corridor facilitated the migration of the *lawak educated* from small Kuala Lumpur theaters onto the Internet, where it commands a larger and newer audience. Thus the Internet becomes the space for asking searching questions and a place where information can supposedly freely flow from peer to peer instead of top-down or bottom-up. Although satire takes the form of cartoons, theater productions, stand-up comedy, literature, and art, the introduction of do-it-yourself digital technology has given rise to new forms of online satire. For example, there are satirical blogs or political culture jamming, such as doctored film posters and the twice-parodied film clip of *Downfall* on YouTube.

Online satire and parody is exempt from censorship under the Communications and Multimedia Forum of Malaysia content code (Article 7.3). But this does not prevent the government from arresting and threatening to prosecute satirical bloggers and cartoonists under the Official Secrets Act, Sedition Act, Penal Code, or even the above Multimedia Act.[34] Indeed, Hassan Skodeng was charged for posting misinformation with malicious intent for his 2010 April Fool's Day prank, "TNB to sue WWF [World Wildlife Fund] over earth hour."[35]

The Malaysian satirist is unlikely to disappear. Current politics have become farcical, making it difficult to distinguish between serious fact and the stuff of fiction, as the National Alliance government sacrifices long-term national goals for short-term irrational policies that address form but are devoid of content and potentially destructive. Despite the disclaimers on their Web sites, the *lawak educated* and their audience recognize the power of satire to speak truth to power and to draw humorous attention to state hypocrisy and political absurdities. This speaks well of the intellectual maturity of the Malaysian audience, which, while still limited to the urban middle class, may well be expanding.

Squatter (*Penduduk Setinggan*)
YEOH SENG GUAN

Since the middle of 2009, Subramaniam has been sending me mobile phone text messages, sometimes on a daily basis over a short duration of time. Usually they are aphorisms and prayerful statements on counting one's daily blessings. Occasionally, they are updates on the status of his urban *kampung* (village, sometimes spelled *kampong*) earmarked for demolition by Kuala Lumpur City Hall.

His *kampung* was situated within a former railway township now undergoing rapid redevelopment and gentrification. Thousands of modest railway workers' quarters built several decades earlier—some at the beginning of the twentieth century—have been progressively demolished over the last few years. After the residents had been displaced, the vacated land was reappropriated to build high-rise luxury condominiums and carve out landscaped parks. The reason for the redevelopment of the locality was not hard to fathom—its strategic location near the city center and the quickly dwindling stock of "undeveloped" land within the Kuala Lumpur city limits made it a prime tract of real estate.

I had read about the plight of his *kampung* in the daily newspaper one weekend morning. It was not difficult to locate the small and nondescript *kampung* tucked largely behind a Catholic missionary school and a large monsoon drain. The other villagers had quickly led me to Subramaniam's home and acknowledged him as their representative voice. I explained to him that I have a research interest in the few remaining "squatter *kampung*s" that are still found within the Kuala Lumpur city administrative boundaries, and that I had also briefly resided in the locality nearly two decades earlier as an undergraduate student. Subramaniam was intrigued with my narrative, and not long afterward he had included me in his presumably selective communicative network of mobile phone text recipients.

Subramaniam's persona, in many respects, was not typical of other "grassroots" local leaders whom I had encountered in my fieldwork with urban "squatters" in Kuala Lumpur over the years. In his late forties, he was well mannered, articulate in English (besides Malay, Tamil, and a smattering of vernacular Chinese dialects), and a government employee. More strikingly, he had created a dossier meticulously archiving a range of fragmentary documents (such as bills and newspaper clippings of visiting dignitaries) together with oral histories charting the genesis of his *kampung* in order to substantiate the longevity and legality of the settlement. Besides making them available to journalists, Subramanian deployed these documents to garner sympathetic support from any politician or legislator who might care to listen to stories about their plight. Subramaniam explained that he had specifically appealed for the help of key politicians of the Malaysian Indian Congress, a member of the ethnic-based ruling coalition party (Barisan Nasional, or National Front), as well as the current local member of Parliament who hails from the official opposition front, Pakatan Rakyat, or People's Coalition.

Subramaniam was alert to shifts or trends in political rhetoric and emphasis. He highlighted to me that the harmonious multicultural mix of Indian and Chinese families residing in the *kampung* was squarely in tune with Prime Minister Najib Abdul Razak's trope of "1Malaysia," launched early in his premiership after a nearly disastrous general elections outing for the ruling coalition the year before (the "political tsunami" of March 2008). Although I was skeptical, he believed that his letter to Najib outlining all the laudable aspects of his *kampung* would be appreciated and that there would be a miraculous intervention by the powers-that-be. Against all odds, at the time of finalizing this essay (December 2010), the *kampung* as a physical entity is still intact. But many of Subramaniam's neighbors, seeing the writing on the wall (literally sprayed on their front porches by City Hall and metaphorically viewed as a lost cause), have already opted to move out to other places of accommodation elsewhere. Sadly, the *kampung*'s demise as a living community seems inevitable.

The fate of this particular *kampung* vis-à-vis the mutating Kuala Lumpur cityscape is not unique. Indeed, one could plot the generic fortune of the squatter to changing notions of progress, development, and national security. During British colonial rule, new definitions of land tenure displaced indigenous usufruct land practices in the push to "open up" land to facilitate a host of capitalist enterprises—cash-crop plantations, resource extraction, new urban centers, and so forth. The figure of the squatter stood out as an antithesis to this logic. While this justified a battery of legal and moral actions against the squatter when deemed expedient, there were also historical instances (such as in the aftermath of the Second World War) when they were judged as necessary aberrations because of the state's inability to provide humanitarian alternatives.

Official surveys conducted in the late 1960s and early 1970s lamented that up to a third of the city's resident population was comprised of "squatters." In the late 1970s and 1980s, the Prime Minister's Department and City Hall lobbied for and incrementally devised a more explicit "squatter policy." Certainly, within the context of neoliberal developmental models promoted during the long premiership of Mahathir Mohamad (1981–2003) and subsequent administrations, the squatter began to take on a more menacing anti-utopian and antidevelopment persona. Besides being a lawbreaker, the squatter became increasingly judged as a serious impediment to the nation's collective progress and to aspirations to carve a hypermodern "world-class city" out of Kuala Lumpur. The recurring discourse of a "squatter-free" city has normalized this imagery not only to other city administrations in the country but also in the popular imagination.

Throughout the 1980s and 1990s, there was thus a dramatic categorical transformation of the squatter. The debilitating effects of the Asian financial crisis of the late 1990s slowed down this onslaught for several years before its resumption in more recent times. While many squatters chose to flee outside the city limits to escape punitive action, several thousands of those without financial means were also reconstituted vertically into blocks of high-rise, low-cost flats that were usually substandard in design and construction, had poor maintenance facilities, and suffered from high rates of vandalism. To detractors, many of these monoliths have approximated the material and psychological attributes of slums. Indeed, one can argue that while the legal category of *penduduk setinggan* may be a dying vernacular breed within the Kuala Lumpur city limits, it is now replaced by another less familiar kind of socio-spatial existence. Like so many others before him, Subramaniam does not relish the prospect of living in a high-rise, low-cost flat when his *kampung* is eventually demolished. In providing legal security of tenure, these modernist structures have also taken away much more in exchange.

Returning Urbanite
MATTHEW AMSTER

Christian is not a typical returning urban-rural migrant. Unlike most men who come back to the Kelabit Highlands after living in town, he did not return having struggled to make a decent living, nor did he return expecting to get married and start a family. Christian had already done both, leaving behind a good job and returning with his wife and children. What he did not anticipate is how out of place and misunderstood he would be once back home.

I first learned about Christian's return to the remote Kelabit Highlands of Malaysian Borneo in 2002. He had e-mailed me from the newly opened Internet kiosk near the airstrip at Bario—the unofficial center of the Kelabit rural community—asking if I knew anything about growing asparagus and whether I thought it was a good prospect as a new idea for a cash crop. The next year, when I came to do research about the Internet, I saw firsthand both Christian's ambitions and his difficulties as a return migrant.[36] In the 1990s, during my dissertation fieldwork, I knew Christian as a sophisticated town dweller. As is typical of his generation of Kelabit, he first moved to town to complete his schooling and remained there to work. Among those few who do return to the rural homelands, almost all are young unmarried men who have found it difficult to achieve success in town. For these men, returning home is also linked to the opportunity to marry women from related indigenous communities across the adjacent international border in Indonesia.[37] Such men are categorized locally as "Form Five failures," indicating their low level of educational achievement,[38] while their cross-border wives are known for their industriousness as rice farmers, work that few Kelabit women today will readily do. From the perspective of urban Kelabit, marriages between these marginalized young men and their economically poorer Indonesian wives are instrumental in keeping rural communities in the Kelabit Highlands alive.[39]

So, what motivated Christian to move back? By all appearances he was doing well in town, working as an electrician in the oil and natural gas industry. He was happily married to a woman from a related indigenous group, and they had four children. When I had last visited the family in 1999, I was struck by Christian's entrepreneurial spirit and his seemingly stable and well-adjusted middle-class life. He owned a modest house, a car (the ubiquitous Malaysian-made Proton Saga), and maintained a small plot of land outside town with gardens and fishponds—potential small-business ventures. The decision to return to the highlands took me by surprise. As Christian commented, "Most people talk about going back, but nobody actually does it." He explained that his primary motivation to return was a strong desire to provide his children with a similar experience to that of his own childhood, which he looked back on nostalgically.

When he returned in 2000, he chose not to focus on growing rice, which he considered economically unviable—estimating that rice farmers earn only about fifty cents a day. Instead, he began planting elaborate gardens, growing asparagus, papayas, and bananas, and trying, unsuccessfully, to raise ducks. He still has plans to build fishponds for commercial fish production. All these endeavors have yet to pay off. Undaunted, Christian claims to have progressive ideas about how one can make a living in the highlands by being efficient and choosing the right high-yield crops. In the meantime, he spends most of his time doing paid construction work to maintain a basic income.

Sadly, Christian has struggled to be accepted by other men in the village, as he does not fit the common pattern of male migrants who return home to maintain the family farm. Nor, on the other hand, does he serve as a mediator to wider structures outside the village, a "model and a guide," as Geertz once described urban-oriented elites in rural Java.[40] Christian's presence simply seemed anomalous, caught in a marginalized space between highland and lowland, the village and town. While the rural Kelabit people certainly rely on urban-based relatives to help mediate between the village and nation and to articulate and defend local interests, such urbanites are effective allies in part because they do not live in the village. Thus, urban-based Kelabit often act as important regional and global cultural brokers, spearheading projects like bringing the Internet and telephone service to the Kelabit Highlands and mediating between the local community and outsiders, such as tourists, researchers, and government officials.

One day I saw Christian coming back to the village on his motorbike, the engine straining under the weight of rice sacks. Watching as he weaved precariously to avoid potholes and muddy patches on the road, I realized that there was something odd about the scene; I had never seen sacks of rice moving *in this direction* along the road, since nearly everyone in the community grows their own rice. That night I asked Christian why he needed to buy rice outside the community. He explained that after three years he was still not accepted and nobody was comfortable selling him rice, not even close relatives. He believed, correctly, that people found his ideas too progressive and his way of expressing himself too direct. Rather than being embraced for his urban orientation, "a man able to comprehend both the village and the city,"[41] he was shunned for trying to do things in new ways.

"It was not that easy to resign my job and come back here," Christian lamented, adding, in a somewhat patronizing way, that "people in the *kampung* (village) are not able to fully develop themselves, as they are too busy with everyday tasks." Meanwhile, Christian keeps a meticulous journal of his agricultural experiments, recording intricate details with the hope of increasing his yields. He acknowledges his awkward position in the village and hopes it improves, yet he is also pleased that his children can experience growing up immersed in Kelabit rural life. In the meantime, he continues to travel outside the village to buy his own rice.

Timber Entrepreneur (*Cukong Kayu*)
MICHAEL EILENBERG

One late afternoon in 2003, I was sitting with a few loggers at one of the small ramshackle coffee shops in Indonesian Borneo, along a gravel road near the border crossing to Malaysia. The degraded forest in the background and the hastily erected wooden houses and bustling sawmills that lined the road (all covered in a thick layer of dust stirred up by the continuous flow of logging trucks) created a certain frontier atmosphere. However, the scene abruptly changed when a brand new Toyota Land Cruiser with Malaysian license plates stopped at the coffee shop. My companions assumed an air of respect and obedience when the three passengers settled at the side table. Their gaze turned especially toward the most senior passenger, a Malaysian Chinese man named Tung Pheng. Pheng politely greeted my companions in the local ethnic dialect, then turned toward me and whispered with a smile, "Are you a government spy or a timber buyer?" These were apparently the only rational reasons why a westerner might be hanging about in the lawless borderland.

The loggers later told me that Pheng was among the most renowned Malaysian *cukong kayu,* or timber entrepreneurs, operating in the Indonesian border region.[42] According to Indonesian police, Pheng was the "brain behind illegal logging" (*otak pembalakan liar*) in the border area and consequently the most wanted criminal throughout the Indonesian province of West Kalimantan.[43] In late 2000, the first reports on Malaysian *cukong* engaging in cross-border timber extraction began to appear in the Indonesian media. These entrepreneurs were vividly depicted as tough "gangsters" who worked in tandem with corrupt officials and terrorized local communities.[44] When I returned years later, locals told me that the *cukong* had carefully monitored my movements during my previous stay.

At the time of fieldwork, Pheng, a former member of the Royal Malaysian Marines, was in his late forties and married to an Indonesian woman. He is the youngest of three brothers running a business empire based in the Sarawak town of Sibu, where his family clan has been engaged in the lucrative timber business since the British colonial era and, more recently, plantation development. Pheng is regionally known as a man of prowess, whose expertise as a financial broker and entrepreneur within the Sarawak (and Indonesian) timber and plantation sector is highly esteemed, particularly among his employees, business partners, and local communities. His main area of expertise is logging old-growth forests in frontier regions, especially in remote and demanding border regions outside the formal control of the central state. He obtained his experience during the heyday of the Sarawak timber industry from the 1970s until the 1990s, when he worked closely with forest communities along large rivers in the Sarawak interior. However, his reach extended beyond the boundaries of Borneo into other forest-rich regions of Indonesia and Southeast Asia such as West Papua, Vietnam, Cambodia, and Thailand. He even worked as a timber contractor in Cameroon and the Congo. State borders do not seem to limit Pheng's reach. He is a real cosmopolitan.

The ethnic Chinese communities in Sarawak, especially in the Sibu area, have a long tradition of close political, economic, and social relationships with upland forest communities. The ethnic Chinese communities in the Sibu area arrived in Sarawak from southern China during the reign of the British colonialist Charles Brooke in the nineteenth century, when some entrepreneurial *cukong* created small business empires based on trade with inland communities.[45] Their personalized leadership rests foremost on their long-rooted history as economic mediators for upland communities, their patron-client loyalties, and their renowned ability to perform in extremely difficult situations. The term *cukong* itself has recently gained a more negative connotation, as these men are depicted as working between legality and illegality.

In the 1990s, Sarawak had largely exhausted its own forest resources and was therefore pressed to expand its large timber-based industry across the border. The political turmoil after Indonesian president Suharto's resignation from power in 1998 created new opportunities for the *cukong* to expand their business across the border to Indonesia. The Indonesian news media described Pheng as a small king (*raja kecil*) of the border area. There was some truth to this depiction. He was the leading employer and economic investor during the timber boom that lasted until 2005, when the Indonesian government initiated a large crackdown on logging in the province. Originally invited by Indonesian district governments and local communities who encouraged the logging of local forests, Pheng felt secure operating in the area. He did not attempt to hide or conceal his operations, despite having several Indonesian arrest warrants hanging over his head.

While the media portrayed him as a mere gangster, Pheng enjoyed wide popularity among the rural population where he conducted his business. His great successes depended partly on his combined ability as a patron to get things done and provide needed services where governments had failed.[46] Besides creating local jobs in his sawmills and timber camps, he maintained local networks of roads and more generally sustained a booming economy. Many locals often referred to him as a "brave (*berani*) and generous man (*bermurah hati*)," a "rescuer (*penyelamat*)" of the local economy who had made the area prosper in a way that state-owned companies and the government had failed to do.

While extremely generous toward loyal clients, he was ruthless toward competitors and those who broke the bonds of trust. As a small "king," he increased his prowess through the rules of reciprocity, stewarding flows of wealth, favors, and support. The enduring popularity of the *cukong* working at the intersection between legality and illegality along the margins of the state cannot be underestimated; they are seen by many as local benefactors and wealthy patrons in these out-of-the-way places, where national development programs are lacking and formal state laws often collide with local livelihood practices.

SINGAPORE

Edited by SYED MUHD
KHAIRUDIN ALJUNIED

The Malay Gangster, Bangladeshi Worker, Woman Activist, Peri-Urban Tenant, The People's Filmmaker, Schoolteacher, and Social Entrepreneur—these figures are familiar to anyone who has lived in modern Singapore. We encounter them in the common thoroughfares and pathways of daily life. We hear about them in the chatter of gossip and rumors. We read about their lives and destinies in the headlines of newspapers and the leads of television newscasts. Yet, while these figures appear strange and remote to the uninitiated "foreigner," what most often impresses if not overwhelms the visitor to Singapore most—and, in fact, captivates most local elites as well—is the unparalleled orderliness of the largely urban landscape and a generally high standard of efficiency. There are "citizens" and "peoples," but from the point of view of those who perceive the island as a "world dominated by its phantasmagoria,"[1] these subjects feature little in the overall "identity" of Singapore. Singapore, in such a formulation, is a country without Singaporeans, an island without permanent inhabitants—a runaway world.[2] It is unsurprising then that when the prominent cultural critic Ziauddin Sardar visited Singapore briefly in early 2001, he wrote that everything he saw was beautiful, commendable, and glorious, yet intrinsically artificial, transient, inhuman, and unabashedly capitalist. As he provocatively put it, "When you globalize everything what you get is Singapore."[3] The Dutch architectural theorist Rem Koolhaas made a similar observation when he argued that practically everything in Singapore has undergone some sort of refurbishment and change. "Even its nature is entirely remade. It is pure intention: If there is chaos, it is authored chaos; if it is ugly, it is designed ugliness; if it is absurd, it is willed absurdity."[4]

While these observations and impressions are valid, in some measure they mask the problematics of modernity in Singapore as they are understood and experienced by the common folk. For, if anything, the extensive transformations that are still in motion have made Singapore an intriguing site for the examination of how global modernity takes on local forms, of how personal struggles can be traced to public issues, and how ordinary people of different genders, social backgrounds, political affiliations, and class positions have appropriated, coped with, and contained one of the most methodical projects of social control and disciplinary practices the world over. The seven figures examined in the following pages are illustrative of the contradictory nature, effects, and responses to modernity in Singapore. They are but a few among the many "modern strangers" in the Singaporean social landscape who offer us examples of how men and women have sought to subvert or transform the entrenched institutions, laws, and policies put in place by a high-modernist state.[5] I use the term "modern strangers" in the sense Bauman does: to refer to "the waste of the state's ordering zeal." They are the figures who strive to remain at the edges of ideological conformity and reified social identities, and in so doing they interfere with and create uncertainties for a prevailing vision of humanity.[6]

The uncertainties that these modern strangers introduce and the conceptions of the self they reproduce, whether overtly or by implication, remind us that we must not underestimate the creative agency of the subalterns in utilizing, subverting, and even challenging modernity as defined by those in positions of authority and by the forces of globalization. In illuminating this creative agency through the lives and experiences of seven key figures, the line of argument that binds the following essays is that any attempt by the state to impose its power on the people and to regulate the lives of its citizenry will be met with resistance, evasion, withdrawal, disobedience, and, at times, self-immolation. It is these variegated forms of social practices that operate within different logics than what has been defined and imposed by a long-reigning regime that make Singaporean modernity a fascinating field of study.

In the case of the Malay Gangster, Kamaludeen Mohamed Nasir shows that one way to operate within a highly regulated modern society is to situate oneself at the interstices of laws and cultural politics. This is done through engaging in criminal activities while negotiating with policing agencies, as well as mastering the language of the dominant Chinese populace to gain status and autonomy in the world of youth gangs. Deviance, selective fraternization, and linguistic dexterity are thus used simultaneously as levers and modalities to ensure redistributive justice within an inequitable social order.

Disinclined toward treading the pathways taken by the Malay gangsters but resolute in exploiting the material benefits to be gained from a first-world country, the Bangladeshi Worker (Md Mizanul Rahman) in Singapore capitalizes on self-help bodies. The trials and tribulations faced by the Bangladeshi Worker to ensure his lengthy stay amidst various restrictions placed upon him and his inability to return to a place where poverty dominates make apparent one of the central impacts of Singaporean modernity upon migrant labor from developing countries: the sense of in-betweenness that emerges from knowing that one does not really belong to the "developed nation," and yet at the same time not wanting to leave it and return to his impoverished homeland. For most low-skilled foreign workers in Singapore, the alienation from the Singaporean society becomes all the more chronic because they are often treated differentially by ordinary citizens who perceive them as being prone to crime.

This sense of in-betweenness and alienation is not only felt by figures who hail from outside the ambit of the nation; it is shared by a broad spectrum of the local citizenry. In the Woman Activist, Yu-Mei Balasingamchow focuses on Braema Mathi, a prominent social activist who confronts the gender bias inherent in Singapore's modernizing project by advocating for women's basic rights in the face of the largely male-driven modernization programs. Although Braema's brief term in parliamentary politics and her leadership in several civic organizations seldom met with the success she hoped for, it did bring public attention to the dilemmas of Singaporean women. An example of the type of woman who has been championed by Braema Mathi is well illustrated by Loh Kah Seng in his essay on the Peri-Urban Tenant, who, although a staunch believer in the need to be "modern," has now become one of its casualties. Living a frugal lifestyle in rented housing and cut off from the various opportunities for informal income she could draw upon during the colonial period, the Peri-Urban Tenant internalizes her condition by accepting modernity as fate—as something so irreversible and relentless that nobody can challenge it in its manifest totality.

Despite the irreversibility of Singaporean modernity, Liew Kai Khiun shows how Jack Neo, The People's Filmmaker, has kept this ubiquitous process in check by displaying its problems on screen. Neo has done this through several highly successful films, one of which highlights the negative consequences of elitism and economically determined educational programs. But Jack Neo's importance goes far beyond critique and deconstruction. His films have inadvertently created a "community of sentiment" that imagines and shares common concerns about the problems embedded within Singapore's grueling educational system.[7] Adeline Koh's Schoolteacher explores the struggles and discourses of one member of this community of sentiment. The Schoolteacher sees modernity as leading to deculturation among the youths in Singapore—a concern shared by the Social Entrepreneur described in Erik Holmberg's essay. While the Schoolteacher inculcates independent thinking in his students within the constraints of the national educational system, the Social Entrepreneur has carved out his own cultural space by opening a privately owned café and organizing cultural events to promote Middle-Eastern elements within Singaporean modernity.

What these short yet perceptive essays have done is to provoke us to rethink the ways in which modernity in Singapore can be more critically interrogated and approached. By tilting the scales of observation from the eventful to the ordinary, as Veena Das has aptly put it, and by placing agency and structure, the global and the local, the public and private in constant tension, these essays have elicited voices from below and thereby made visible the vitality of everyday forms of individual appropriations and activisms.[8] Indeed, there have been attempts by different figures within Singaporean society (or "modern strangers," if you like) to devise and subtly propagate distinctive forms of modernities that are in line with their respective cultural, political, social, economic, religious, and ideological visions. These alternative modernities expressed through films, political activism, criminal acts, and social interactions call for a new way of analyzing modernity in Singapore—one that will interweave ethnography and theory, the political and the personal, the lived experiences and discourses of men and women, the oppressors and the oppressed, the victors and the vanquished.

Malay Gangster
KAMALUDEEN MOHAMED NASIR

Ajat is a former member of one of the most notorious yet popular triad gangs in Singapore—the Sa La Kau (Hokkien for "369"). He now identifies himself with the Omega gang. "Omega" is an acronym for Orang Melayu Enter Gangster Area (Malays Entering the Gangster Area). The gang members are distinguished by the tattoos on their arms, usually of the Greek letter omega (Ω). They refer to each other as *jam tangan* ("wristwatch" in Malay). Having agreed to meet Ajat for lunch one day, I was surprised to receive a text message from him the day before asking me to meet him immediately if I wanted to interview him. The deal was for me to come alone. Upon reaching the rendezvous point, I saw Ajat on his motorcycle, frantically urging me to put on a helmet and hop on behind him. He told me that he was taking me to meet some of the other gang members. I was caught off guard. "You look at what is written on this helmet," he said. "Does it mean anything to you? Now read it backwards. That's the name of the gang." But the strategy of inducting me into his gang failed drastically. One gang member, Danni, kept alerting the group about the possibility that I might be a police officer from the Secret Societies Branch.

"Your face looks familiar," were four words Danni repeated a number of times throughout our brief meeting. I could sense that, while I was talking to the members, Danni was busy sending text messages to the other members of the group. "You cannot blame us if we think that you are an SSB [Secret Societies Branch] police officer," Danni continued. "You want to do this kind of thing; you got to be prepared for the consequences that things can happen to you. You are around us and things happen. Usually people doing research will do it in a proper manner. Like go through the police or the Ministry. The people there will give you access to the files of gang members," he said. Ajat reassured the rest that I was "OK," since I had been introduced to him by a trusted friend. But I could sense that he was getting increasingly uncomfortable, and so was I. I soon found myself trying to convince the gang members of my sincerity by giving them a minipresentation on the merits of participant observation as a fieldwork methodology.

Much has been written over the past few decades with regard to the "Malay Problem," a topic that has been a feature of Singapore politics ever since the city-state became independent. In fact, the "Malay Problem" discourse has been dominated and sustained by the elites to promote a statist version of Singaporean modernity, one that emphasizes hard work, loyalty, obedience, and the will to progress.[9] In 2007, Malay leaders in Singapore expressed concerns about the growing trend of gang activity among Muslim youths. One recent report revealed that 34 percent of juvenile rioters were Malays, and this was cast as a moral panic given that the Malays make up only 15 percent of the Singaporean population. More Malays reportedly joined youth gangs in comparison to other ethnic groups, such as members of the Chinese majority and the Indian minority.[10]

Youth gangs in Singapore are usually called "secret societies." The irony behind this term is that these secret societies have been contributing overtly to the making of modern Singapore for more than a century. They trace their origins to Chinese triads that delved into prostitution, gambling, loan-sharking, and other activities that provided a major source of revenue for the British colonial government. The symbiotic relationship forged between the Chinese triads and the police has continued till today.[11] To deal with the problems of policing, headmen of the Chinese gangs are "registered" with the Criminal Investigation Department and made to abide by the "rules" imposed by the police. It can be concluded then that the postcolonial state has taken on the same pragmatic approach practiced by its colonial predecessor in the management of the criminal underworld.

Because access to resources in both the legitimate and illegitimate markets is held by the dominant Chinese majority, be it by triads or business conglomerates, Malay gang members find themselves in a double bind. New Malay gangs such as the Omega have been suppressed by the state and practically blocked from engaging in illegal activities controlled by Chinese gangs. Such "status frustration" is expressed by Ajat as he recounts his experience of being in a Chinese gang. "When I actually think about the hierarchy of the gang, it is actually a lot like the Singapore government. The top leaders are all Chinese. This is the problem."

To overcome or negotiate such constraints, Malay youths in Chinese gangs seek to embrace the foreign yet powerful Chinese culture. This is demonstrated in the gangspeak and the tattoos of these Malay youth. It is common to see "Chinese" motifs and inscriptions, such as dragons and Chinese poetry, tattooed on the gang members' bodies. As one gang member explained, "The Chinese tattoos describe my rage, my personality." Most gang members are also conversant in Chinese dialects, such as Hokkien and Cantonese, and they often use them as cultural capital to enhance their status in the gang hierarchy.

What is worthy of note is that in a modern country like Singapore where the path toward becoming modern demands that each and every citizen subscribes to the ideals set by the ruling regime, the manipulation of self-identities has become a means by which Malay gang members ensure their survival. Ajat, as a case in point, sees himself as a Malay gangster. But he is only able to do so within the ambit of his social circle. Placed within the pecking order of the Sa La Kau, of his workplace and his neighborhood, he is a modern Singaporean who understands the language of the majority and who uses the resources of those in positions of authority against them for his own purposes.

Bangladeshi Worker
MD MIZANUR RAHMAN

> We spent several thousand dollars to come to Singapore to work, usually on a two-year contract. I left my family back in Bangladesh and if I don't succeed in Singapore, it is not only me who is going to suffer but also my family and close relatives who offered financial assistance with a promise of repayment from remittances.

These were the words of Habibul, one of the many Bangladeshi workers I had spent time with at Serangoon Road, Singapore's Indian District. Tall, lean, handsome, and no more than thirty years of age, Habibul was among a dozen of his friends who had just lost their jobs and were staying on special immigration passes that bar them from regular paid work. They sought help from some migrant NGOs who were providing them with free food and accommodation. While some of these workers will soon leave Singapore with shattered dreams and broken hearts, this is not a widespread phenomenon. Most of them are happy to remain in Singapore, by any means necessary.

There may be as many as seventy thousand Bangladeshi migrants in Singapore, working mainly in the construction and shipbuilding industries. Many of them have chosen to come to Singapore because of transparent immigration policies, higher wages, and a comfortable living and working environment. The Singapore government now allows migrant workers to stay for up to fifteen years, and this has been a hallmark to consider migration as a career. More and more low-skilled migrants now tend to take up temporary migration as a career, which is further facilitated by family-friendly migration policies such as annual leave for family visits. As Habibul puts it,

I like this place a lot for many reasons—higher wages, cheap mobile calls, close to home, annual leave, the possibility of an extended stay and the presence of friends and relatives. The daytime temperature is also not very hot here; my friends in the Middle East work in hot temperatures. They are not even allowed to enter shopping malls on Fridays and Saturdays. Here, unlike in the Middle East, nobody stops me from visiting malls: I enjoy a lot of freedom!

This almost ironic sense of freedom felt by Bangladeshis working in a country known for its strict laws and harsh punishments has made Singapore a popular destination for other foreign professionals and low-skilled workers such as Habibul. In fact, a large part of Singapore's success is anchored on the immigrant mentality of wanting to succeed in a globalizing economy. Singapore's liberal attitude toward immigration and foreign human resources can be better understood in the light of its economic success and demographic change. The high growth rate policy has resulted in its demand for labor exceeding the supply available from the local workforce. The country's total fertility rate has remained around 1.25 in recent years, far below the replacement level. As a result, immigration and the recruitment of foreign manpower remains a key strategy to sustain the economy and tackle the population problem.

In Singapore in 2008 there were 1.2 million nonresidents, 3.2 million citizens, and nearly half a million permanent residents.[12] Most noncitizens hailed from neighboring countries such as Malaysia, Bangladesh, India, Indonesia, the Philippines, Thailand, and China. In addition to Asian countries, numerous professionals have also arrived from Western countries and put down roots in

Singapore. Domestic workers represent one of the largest groups of foreign workers in Singapore, numbering approximately 150,000, or 30 percent of all work-permit holders.[13] Approximately one in every seven Singaporean households employs a "live-in" migrant domestic worker.

Singapore, as well as most other labor-importing countries in Asia, follows the demand-driven system. This involves hiring foreign workers of all skill levels to fulfill short-term manpower needs. One of the benefits of this demand-driven system is that it serves the migrants and their home countries through a remittance economy that contributes to the redistribution of wealth and the enhancement of welfare among populations in the developing countries in the region. Every month, Bangladeshi workers such as Habibul send an average of 700 Singapore dollars back home.[14] "My family will use the money to buy food and clothes, pay school fees for children and medical bills for parents, and lend money to some relatives who are needy. I also save a fixed amount for the future."

Working in Singapore is also tied to other benefits and costs, as Habibul explains:

> Everyone from my village knows that I am working in Singapore; it
> is prestigious for me and my family to have access to the Singapore
> labor market. Many villagers now take pride in mixing with my
> family members and building new relations with us. I can now
> marry off my sister to a better bridegroom. But I must say that I do
> miss my family a lot. I mean Singapore is a nice place, but it is not
> my real home. I would like to go back, but I cannot do that now. Not
> with the state that my family is in right now.

The policy on low-skilled workers is comparatively restrictive and has remained committed to ensuring that "low-skilled foreign manpower is managed as a temporary and controlled phenomenon."[15] This is why in the event of an economic downturn, it is the low-skilled migrant workers who will be the first to be laid off. Still, as already noted, Singapore has developed a fairly impressive policy that allows migrant workers to work on the island for an extended period. Although dictated by capitalist needs and political conservatism, Singapore's foreign worker policy provides these low-skilled migrant workers a place to stay, helps them acquire skills for an extended contract, and offers help from governmental and nongovernmental agencies when they are faced with difficulties. This life-cycle approach to the management of foreign workers has proven to be economically beneficial for the development of Singapore and the source countries of these workers.

Woman Activist

YU-MEI BALASINGAMCHOW

She might be petite in size and dulcet in demeanor, but whenever woman activist Braema Mathiaparanam (more commonly known as Braema Mathi) rises to speak—be it in the hushed halls of Singapore's Parliament chambers where she was a nominated member of Parliament from 2001 to 2004, amidst the multilingual chatter of an event for migrant workers, or as an audience member at a forum on social issues—she clearly means business. For almost a decade she has been the face of social activism in Singapore, leading a variety of nongovernmental organizations at different times, one of which was the Association of Women for Advocacy and Research (AWARE, Singapore's only feminist organization).

Mathi's de facto constituents, before and after her stint as a parliamentarian, are the disabled, the elderly poor, single parents, migrant workers, and victims of child or spousal abuse or human trafficking—in other words, those who dwell on the social margins of rapidly modernizing Singapore. Her appeals to the state hinge on the need to provide protection and dignity to other human beings, in striking resistance to the statist ideology that commodifies human labor as "digits." At recent events to highlight the problem of human trafficking in Southeast Asia, Mathi appears to be every inch the confident, educated, modern "Singapore woman." But she has also been labeled as "outspoken" for speaking warmly, passionately, and noisily about her issues of concern—the state's responsibilities to those who have not thrived in the procapitalist society of its making.

To be an activist in Singapore is to inhabit a space of indeterminate and shifting size, autonomy, and influence. Those whose persons or agendas find favor with the single-party dominant state may be inducted into the halls of power, but as Mathi's experience shows, that favor can also be withheld: after 2004 she was not nominated to Parliament again. Chng Nai Rui has observed that the dominant if cynical view is, "If civil society can be said to exist in Singapore, then its extent depends largely on what the state permits."[16] Terence Lee has described it as a framework of "gestural politics," where citizens are encouraged by the state to be active and *civic*-conscious, so long as they do not cross the political out-of-bounds markers and other state-defined parameters.[17] Activists are thus caught between their nongovernmental social agenda and the state, whose apparatus governs their legal existence (the Societies Act, which applies to all voluntary organizations including NGOs, proscribes overt participation in politics). Moreover, as signifiers of idealism and social change, activists are culturally isolated from Singapore's economic prerogatives—Singapore is "a whole society subjugated to the needs of capital," as C. J. Wan-Ling Wee has pithily put it—and they are historically cut off from earlier traditions of social activism that were suppressed or systematically deflated by the state after 1965.[18]

To be an activist in Singapore, therefore, is to occupy a space that may be as marginalized and liminal as the issues one represents, regardless of the actual social change that is achieved. To be a woman activist is to step into that space with an added layer of gendered tensions, whether or not one represents women's issues. On the surface, women's education and income levels, legal rights, and economic participation rates seem to indicate that they enjoy all the benefits of capitalist modernity. But the Singapore state is still deeply patriarchal in its orientation and ideology. State policies and discourse recognize men alone as heads of households and firmly situate women in the domestic sphere as wives and nurturers. Nirmala PuruShotam has described this as a "normal family ideology" that "imposes a calendar of life [on women] . . . that flows from childhood, courtship, marriage, wifehood and motherhood."[19] At no point is there room for maturing as a citizen and becoming capable of political consciousness and activity.

A woman activist like Braema Mathi is thus doubly transgressive, as a nonstate actor and as a woman who veers from the prescribed life trajectory. Her position is all the more problematized if she is affiliated with a feminist organization and/or feminist ideas or modes of thinking, because state and public discourses pinpoint feminism as being from "the West"—that is, non-Asian and antithetical, even antagonistic to Singapore's presumed Asianness. While individual woman activists may adhere to different feminisms, in public discourse the term "feminism" invokes the specter of bra-burning extremists (or worse: lesbians). Woman activists are caricatured as outré and unorthodox, and leaders of AWARE, including Mathi, have been spotlighted in the media for exhibiting "masculine" qualities, such as being aggressive, confrontational, strident, "loud," and misandrist. The reality is, however, to the contrary. In point of fact, during a recent interview, Mathi herself stressed that "there are feminist men today" and that "they should be equal partners in the feminist movement."

Singapore today is transiting from the imperatives of an industrial modernity to a globalized one, and the work of woman activists is taking on new dimensions. From initiating the Working Committee to help migrant workers in Singapore, Mathi has gone on to engage ASEAN governments on the broader subject of human rights. Her issues of concern are now more explicitly transnational, although all the more marked as "Western" and privileged, making them easier to marginalize or even ignore. Separately, younger woman activists have emerged as savvy advocates for local issues with globalized relevance, such as urban poverty, environmentalism and sustainability, and migrant workers.

Although woman activists at large do not provoke the status quo in Singapore, they embody at once both the state's hopes and fears—hopes for an active citizenry and fears of unruly challenges to its (patriarchal) authority. In an interview given at the beginning of her term as a nominated member of Parliament, Mathi said, "I want to see how much further I can go in raising awareness and hopefully bringing about small changes." It sounds like a humble proposition, but by invoking self-determination and responsibility to society, Mathi and other activists like her present Singapore's state-directed modernity with a potent challenge indeed.

The Peri-Urban Tenant
LOH KAH SENG

Madam Tay, born in 1943, desired the promises of modernity and social autonomy ever since she was young. With her parents, she lived in unauthorized wooden houses in *kampung*s (villages) at the margins of the municipal area in Singapore after World War II. These dwellings were popular as rentals, housing a quarter of the urban population. As a child, Tay sorted through coffee beans in a local warehouse after school. Earning a dollar a day as an underpaid child worker, she was loosely integrated into Singapore's substantial informal economy. "People went to sort coffee beans when they were very young," she explained. "We started work at 7–8 a.m. and finished at 8–9 p.m." She also helped her parents rear their free-ranging pigs and poultry outside their house, a common way to supplement the peri-urban household's income.[20]

Six decades later, the *kampung*s are long gone, replaced by high-rise public housing estates built by the Housing and Development Board (HDB), in which four-fifths of Singaporeans currently reside and which most of them own. Tay is now a staunch supporter of the developmental state. Personally, she has lived at its economic margins, working at the National Archives of Singapore as a tea lady since 1970. But when I interviewed her in 2006 in her HDB flat that her family had purchased, Tay was adamant that "if Singapore did not have Lee Kuan Yew, our lives would have been very hard." Lee, Singapore's long-serving prime minister (from 1959 to 1990), has been synonymous with the republic's success story and was until 2011 minister mentor in the ruling People's Action Party (PAP) government.

The housing change in postwar Singapore transformed semiautonomous peri-urban tenants like Tay into "citizens" integrated into the formal structures of the state. There was initially strong social resistance against the eviction and relocation undertaken by the late colonial state and expanded by the PAP government. The tenants firmly opposed demolition teams, sometimes assisted by gangsters in secret societies residing in the *kampung*s. Often the resistance was spontaneous, although from the mid-1950s the tenants were also aided by left-wing rural associations affiliated with the PAP that contested the resettlement program. By the early 1960s, however, the resistance had collapsed, as the PAP, elected to power in 1959, robustly integrated semiautonomous communities into the fabric of the state. The secret societies were crushed and rural associations banned, with their members arrested and detained without trial. Major fires from the early 1950s devastated several large *kampung*s, with the British and later the PAP experimenting to speedily build emergency public housing on the fire sites and prevent the wooden houses from reappearing.[21]

The greatest of the fires occurred on May 25, 1961, and rendered nearly sixteen thousand people homeless. Among them was Tay's family. Left alone at home, Tay was so panic-stricken as the flames approached that, in fleeing, she grabbed not her family's belongings or private papers but a few ducks they reared. "I was so shocked that I did not think clearly." The aftermath highlighted the powerful tension between planned modernity and social autonomy for the tenants-turned-fire-victims. Contrasting against Tay's support for the public housing state in the present day, her family had moved into a wooden house nearby after the fire, because "we still wanted to rear pigs." Here was the family's clear choice of preserving autonomy against accepting modernity, despite Lee Kuan Yew's pledge that all of the fire victims would be housed in an HDB flat within nine months.

Over the next four years, high-rise blocks of one- to three-room units of emergency flats appeared on the fire site. By 1967, Bukit Ho Swee Estate boasted over 12,000 flats for 75,000 people. More than four-fifths of the fire victims were rehoused in these flats, but the majority of the residents were not victims of the 1961 inferno but other peri-urban tenants, both young and elderly, relocated from nearby settlements. As the HDB's chief architect intimated privately, the fire was a "God-sent opportunity" to accelerate an entire project of urban redevelopment and social mobilization at the margins of the city.[22] In 1965, Tay's family, facing this expanding transformation, finally moved into a three-room flat in Bukit Ho Swee Estate. Here, residents were forbidden from making unauthorized alterations to their apartments, while supplementing their livelihood with meat and eggs from their livestock became impossible in high-rise housing. Having to regularly pay their rents to the HDB meant economically active adults had to leave the informal economy to take up full-time occupations for regular wages.

The resolution of the tension between planned modernity and social autonomy in the 1960s has produced an ambivalent attitude toward the pursuit of progress among ex–peri-urban tenants. Many of them are long reconciled to contemporary modern living. But a mounting sense of loss of their social autonomy has pervaded their minds; as Tay remembered her move to public housing, "We had no choice." There is growing nostalgia for the *kampung* days, when doors were left open and neighbors were helpful, unlike the social distance in HDB living. Age has also become a salient factor in the cultural imaginary of the generation of postwar baby boomers who became model citizens of modern Singapore. The young people born after the 1960s, they believe, have been fortunate in being delivered into this state of modernity. As Tay said pointedly to me, "Our lives a few decades back were so pitiful. Those who are thirty plus to forty, it was not so difficult." Tay was making an accusation against a younger Singaporean born after the era of the *kampung*s, but she was also lamenting the price that she, a former semiautonomous tenant, paid in the making of modern Singapore.

The People's Filmmaker
LIEW KAI KHIUN

Singapore's Chinese-language entertainer-cum-filmmaker Jack Neo Chee Keong associates himself unashamedly with the people, the common folk. Starting as a performer in the Singapore Armed Forces Music and Drama Company during his military service stint, Neo has been closely involved in the entertainment programs of the state-run Chinese-language television stations in the republic. Although required to use the official language of Mandarin rather than the popularly spoken Chinese dialects in his programs, Neo has nevertheless managed to charm audiences with his humor and parodies.

His significant moment came in 1998 in his debut feature film, *Money No Enough.* It was not only a milestone that rejuvenated the commercial film industry in the republic for the first time since its heyday in the 1950s and 1960s, before media regulations were tightened by the state. More importantly, his production also brought the narrative and the language of the vernacular masses officially onto the big screen. This is noteworthy because Singapore's mainstream television channels have long banned the Chinese dialects in favor of Mandarin, which is one of Singapore's four official languages, along with Malay, Tamil, and English. But, in *Money No Enough,* the local expressions of Hokkien—the main Chinese dialect spoken in Singapore—could be heard in the cinema, even though its usage was not allowed to extend beyond half the length of the film. Underlying Neo's use of vernacular languages is his emphasis on cultivating and mainstreaming a sense of local identity and belonging. Critiquing the state's discouragement of the creolization of the English language in Singapore into a local pidgin patois called "Singlish," Neo stresses that "People say we should ban Singlish. And I say that there is no way you can do it. Now you cannot stop our children from learning those so-called very cool languages from the Americans, from Taiwan, from China. If you cannot stop them from learning that, then we should let our children learn our own Singlish. At least this is our culture, it represents us." In this respect, Neo's films have often portrayed the cosmopolitan pretensions and frivolity of Anglophile Singaporeans as symptomatic of their detachment, not only from the local society but from their own Asian heritage as well. Singlish, for him, becomes a means for the working class to resist the attempts to be scripted by the dominant discourses.[23]

From 1998 to 2010, Neo directed fifteen films, along with their music soundtracks. While all his productions may be classified as comedies, Neo has made use of his films as broader critiques both of government policies specifically and of the hegemony of English-educated Singaporeans in general. These themes are perhaps part of Neo's attempts to connect with his audiences. As he puts it, "Everything in my movies is real." Thus, underlying his portraitures are thinly veiled ridicules and satires of the pressures of the educational system and the cost of living, as well as laments over the apparent peripheralization of Chinese culture and language. The popularity of Jack Neo's films has not been confined to Singapore—many of them have also been popularly received in Southeast and East Asia, particularly *I Not Stupid* (2002); this film's focus on the struggle to excel in a ruthless education system also resonates in many other Asian societies. Speaking as a father himself of the discriminatory process of streaming children according to their ability as early as the age of eight, Neo feels that it is already difficult to bring a child into the world. And consequently, no parent would want to have his or her child arbitrarily classified as a failure. To Neo, this is an anxiety and a sentiment that planners have been unable to factor into consideration.[24]

Nonetheless, even though his productions have occasionally received less enthusiastic comments from both the English-language media and government ministers, Neo does not seem to be at the social and cultural fringes. Apart from the rather explicit commercial endorsements and support for his films from abalone companies and banks, Neo's efforts have also been publicly and formally acknowledged and commended by the state. Increasingly, his films have been less reverently regarded as overtly commercialized and clichéd. More critically, even as he highlights the narrative of the common people, his treatment has been considered not just ethnocentrically biased toward the ethnic Chinese majority but also as serving to reinforce negative social stereotypes. Therefore, instead of trying to project a more autonomous narrative for his protagonists, Neo in some ways has participated ironically in their continued infantilization and peripheralization.[25]

Even with these critiques, the strength of Neo's work lies in his emphasis on the "happy ending" myth of the working class—the struggle from rags to riches. This stands in contrast with the more tragic, pathologized, and aestheticized treatment of the working classes by other filmmakers, such as Eric Khoo, Kelvin Tong, and Royston Tan. While the productions of Khoo, Tong, and Tan are cinematographically and thematically more sophisticated, they have not been able to match the ticket sales of Neo's productions. Here, the persistent appeal of the comedian-director lies in his ability to tap into a critical audience that is derived from the viewers of the Chinese-language television stations for whom Neo is a household name.

Without Jack Neo, the heartlanders of Singapore would have less courage to negotiate through the "globalized" (English-speaking), "cosmopolitan" landscapes of the shopping malls-cum-cinemas in the republic. In other words, the quality of his productions aside, for the past two decades Neo has been bringing entertainment to the homes of ordinary Singaporeans and in the process has also brought them out into the public more visibly. "I think a lot of Singaporeans are speechless," he says. "They don't really say much or vocalize their feelings. Then they see *I Not Stupid* and they're like, 'Hey, man, I'm seeing myself on the big screen.'"[26]

Schoolteacher
ADELINE KOH

I arranged to meet Mark over coffee at a Starbucks café in Holland Village, a trendy, bohemian part of Singapore. Dressed in a crisp white linen shirt and carrying an elegant leather bag, Mark is a typical figure in Singapore's efficient education system: young, upwardly mobile, and tertiary educated. As a relatively young teacher, Mark has experienced the impact of Singapore's education policy, both by going through the system himself and now in his role as an educator.

Educators make up a sizable part of Singapore's expanding workforce. The island's government spends a significant portion of its national budget to train and upgrade these educators; in 2009, this amounted to 12 percent of the total budget for the workforce and totaled U.S. $5.2 billion for the year.[27] The country's education system is, accordingly, enviable: 99 percent of each cohort receives ten years of schooling, and the *World Competitiveness Yearbook* ranked Singapore first for having an education system that meets the needs of a competitive economy.[28]

In our conversation, Mark and I spoke about how education has been used as a tool for social policy. "I'm not sure . . . how I feel about the government using education for social engineering," said Mark after taking a sip of his cappuccino. He continued,

> As teachers we are told that through the early differentiation of talent within childhood education, we are "catering to a diverse array of learning abilities." However, I think by weeding out children based upon a complex system of examinations from such an early age is more akin to a form of ideological programming. From a relatively young age, we are imbibing in students their future roles in Singapore society—whether they are going to be leaders, or whether they are going to be worker bees, or drones.

Mark's skepticism toward the punishing nature of the education system became increasingly apparent throughout our conversation.

> When I was little, students took a national exam at the end of primary school—the age of twelve—from which they were "streamed," or separated, into different tracks depending on how well they performed in this exam. Right now, students get streamed even earlier: at the age of ten. The process of streaming has grown all the more intense at younger and younger ages. When I grew up, there was still some chance that if you were streamed into a poorer stream you could still catch up later on; now, measures have been put into place at earlier and earlier points so that once you are streamed into the "worker bee" category, it is unlikely that you will ever rise to the point of becoming part of the national elite.

What Mark sees to be aspects of social Darwinism within the national education system has been also analyzed by commentators to be a form of social control. Christopher Tremewan has observed that education in Singapore has served to "repress, divert or co-opt many forms of political opposition or social conflict," thus making education "the premier institution" for instilling people with a sense of their "social places."[29] This politicization of the nature of education in Singapore extends to the strategic introduction of subjects such as "Religious Knowledge," which, according to Jason Tan, was "a means of socializing students into accepting [the government's] own political agenda."[30] "Ultimately, how can you tell—at the age of ten or twelve—what a person is going to become?" Mark muses. "By *telling* them from such a young age what they are *going to be*—by telling them that they are smart or that they are stupid—this is how you shape the social roles for young people to assume later on in their lives."

Accordingly, to meet the growing demands of Singapore's education system, educators have become increasingly specialized and highly educated. While the bulk of teachers in 1965 possessed only grade school qualifications, the majority of teachers—particularly at secondary school level or higher—now possess bachelor's degrees, and a sizeable portion of them have professional degrees and graduate qualifications such as PhDs.

As he took the last sip of his cappuccino, Mark looked off into the distance and explained how he has tried to counteract the ills of the educational system by encouraging his students to question everything that is taught to them, especially by their teachers. To him, this has been the least he could do to ensure that they are able to cope with life after schooling by developing the skills to think independently regardless of the mistakes they may make. Toward the end of our conversation, he ruminated:

> I would say that schoolteachers are an important part of Singapore's national architecture. We are the primary force that shapes what happens to our country's future, and the government is well aware of that. However, I hesitate to say that I have any real personal control over what happens. These policies are larger than I am, as an individual. I guess you could see me, finally, as an important cog in the expanse of the state's machinery. An important cog, but, at the end of the day, only a cog.

Social Entrepreneur
ERIK HOLMBERG

I met Dr. Ameen Ali Talib at his restaurant, Café Le Caire @ Al Majlis, in Singapore's Arab Street, where he gave me his account of Arab Street's recent transformation. His narrative places him in the center of a remarkable facet of Singapore's development as a modern and cosmopolitan city-state. His personal story helps illuminate the broader picture of recent developments in the Arab Singaporean community.

According to Ameen, Singapore's Arab Street underwent a remarkable transformation in the first decade of the twenty-first century, becoming a Middle Eastern–themed nightspot area while still retaining its historic buildings and its links to the local Arab Singaporean community. By day, Arab Street is still a center for its traditional business activities, carried out in the same shops by the same families that have been there for generations. By night, crowds of young people—both local and foreign—converge on the southern end of Arab Street (between Beach Road and Baghdad Street) to socialize in a Middle Eastern setting that seems exotic in the context of an island city-state where most of the people are ethnic Chinese.

Arab Street provides a case study of economic revitalization on a local level that was achieved through private-sector initiative without sacrificing local heritage. The significance of Arab Street can be appreciated by placing it within the context of developments in Singapore during the second half of the twentieth century. Singapore experienced an extraordinary makeover after the People's Action Party government came to power in 1959, as state policies brought about a drastic transformation in the country's physical landscape. An unfortunate by-product of Singapore's rise from the third world to the first world is that many of the island's natural areas, farms, beaches, historic buildings, and neighborhoods have vanished, having been replaced by modern high-rise buildings. Some of the remaining historic buildings have been renovated and converted into new uses that distance them from their heritage.

By contrast, Ameen explains that Arab Street evolved into a youth-oriented nightspot area from the ground up through private-sector initiative, without sacrificing either its historic architecture or its traditional family businesses—for example, shops that sell textiles and clothing, such as batik and *baju kurong*. What's more, its new nocturnal identity has maintained the street's links with its Arab character, although Ameen describes the theme of its nightlife as contemporary, cosmopolitan, and Middle Eastern rather than specifically Arab or traditional. According to Ameen, "It all began when I opened Café Le Caire on 23 July 2001. At that time, there was no nightlife at all in Arab Street—all of the shops closed by 7 p.m. and the street was dead at night and on Sundays. Soon, other businesses in Arab Street started to stay open in the evenings, and the first of several Middle Eastern carpet shops appeared in the street."

The revitalization of the locality was accelerated in 2004, when Ameen initiated an Arab Heritage Week event there that attracted more than sixty thousand visitors over a ten-day period. Today there are several Middle Eastern restaurants in Arab Street, as well as other shops selling Middle Eastern products. Café Le Caire celebrated its ninth anniversary on the night of July 24, 2010, with belly dancers performing in the street for a large crowd of appreciative spectators.

Ameen explains that he opened Café Le Caire (which he calls an "Arabic cultural hub") to increase the awareness and visibility of the local Arab minority community in the consciousness of the wider Singaporean population by reviving and institutionalizing Singapore's traditional Arab quarter and promoting Arab music and cuisine there. He wanted to foster a sense of cultural pride among young Arab Singaporeans and create a center of "alternative nightlife" where Singaporeans could socialize without drinking alcoholic beverages.

Ameen's ideas about how to revitalize the local Arab community and Arab Street were shaped by his formative years, educational background, and work experience. He was born in Hadhramaut, Yemen, in 1962, grew up in Aden, Singapore, and Cairo, and became a Singapore citizen in 1995. Ameen grew up speaking Arabic and English, and he was educated in the accounting field, with a bachelor's degree from Ain Shams University in Cairo, a master's degree from the London School of Economics, and a PhD from the University of Warwick. He worked in the accounting field with Klynveld Peat Marwick Goerdeler in London and Ernst & Young in Singapore, and he taught finance and accounting at the National University of Singapore, where he was an assistant professor.

When he joined Ernst & Young in 1990, he was deeply impressed by the friendliness of senior members of the firm who knew his family. Ameen's family has been connected with Singapore since the early twentieth century, and his grandfather, Sheikh Salim bin Mohamed bin Talib, was possibly the richest inhabitant of Singapore in the 1930s.[31] Sheikh Salim owned hundreds of shop houses in Singapore, including the current home of Café Le Caire. Ameen recalls that the feeling of being adopted into the community of his family's friends in Singapore made him feel responsible for doing what he could to help the community. Having experienced what he regarded as an individualistic society during his years in London, he realized that he could not take his membership in the Arab Singaporean community for granted. He treasures this community as a precious resource of social capital that needs to be actively nurtured and enhanced.

As a community activist, Ameen believes that he has succeeded in his mission to institutionalize Singapore's Arab quarter and make Middle Eastern heritage and culture popular and visible in this modern city-state. On August 20, 2006, Prime Minister Lee Hsien Loong mentioned Arab Street as an example of Singapore's cosmopolitan society in his National Day Rally English Speech. Ameen takes pride in Café Le Caire's success as the catalyst in bringing about the evolution of Arab Street into a popular nightspot area from the ground up.

123456789

BURMA

Edited by NICHOLAS FARRELLY

The military government of the Union of Myanmar long trumpeted its vision of modern Burma with an incessant disregard for alternative perspectives.[1] In newspapers and on television and at countless formal events and occasions, Burma's rulers were in the habit of ostentatiously invoking developmental and nationalistic themes. Their official version of modernity refashioned threads of precolonial, colonial, and postcolonial experience to justify the preeminence of a small cohort of senior military officers and their civilian allies. They pointed out that ever since the social and political crises that accompanied British efforts to rule Burma (1824–1948), the country was wracked by civil and political conflict. A brief period of post–World War II parliamentary rule ended in 1962 when a coup brought the military and its strongmen into the heart of the political process. Since then, they refused to relinquish power, and even the 2011 transition to a quasi-civilian system sees former and current military officers in the most important positions. Political transition, let alone democratization, will take time. These men are preoccupied with regime survival, ethnic cohesion, and the fulfillment of what they consider national destiny. National enemies—often stigmatized as "internal and external destructive elements"— are publicly proclaimed targets for elimination. Building a prosperous, united, and modern society is the goal.

What is ignored in this vigilantly censored and almost constantly reinforced vision of "peace" and "development," "democracy" and "order" are the multitude of ways that sixty million ordinary and not so ordinary Burmese seek out their own expressions of politics and culture. Such expressions so defy neat categorizations that they inevitably confront the dictatorial dichotomies and arbitrary distinctions that have become fused to the machinery of Burma's government. During the many years it was unprepared to allow most political freedoms, the government condemned the foreign, the aberrant, and the critical. For more than two decades, pro-democracy icon Aung San Suu Kyi was regularly singled out for her contrarian views on political participation; of course, she was just one figure among the countless Burmese who hoped for political change. With the April 2012 by-elections seeing Aung San Suu Kyi and others from the National League for Democracy elevated to parliament, that change may now have arrived. The excitement and uncertainty of this transition is palpable. However, even today, the government's distinctions and delineations fail to adequately recognize histories of belonging and exclusion for a country that has always nestled at the intersection of East, South, and Southeast Asian social forms. Appreciation of the flows and interactions that are ordained by this geography have been largely ignored in the official version of Burmese modernity.

To partly compensate for the inadequacy of Burma's officially sanctioned modernity, this chapter seeks to introduce a range of ethnographic figures that stamp their own authorities—and subversive potentials—on personal circumstances that cannot be divorced from Burma's official politics and culture. In each of the following essays, it is their individual aspirations and experiences that together serve not only to undermine the government's story about modernity but to more profoundly challenge our expectations about life in Burma (or beyond it) today. Each essay's author shares a preoccupation with examining modernity in Burma using methods that collectively stretch official narratives about what it means to be Burmese.

The variety of personalities that we meet testifies to the vibrant shape of emerging knowledge about this country. Through nine short profile essays, we are introduced to the Urban *Dumsa* (animist priest) of northern Burma, who contends with the pressures of religious conversion and ethnic pride (Sadan); the idealistic Journalist, *Thadin Htauk,* of Burma's newspapers and magazines (Kean); the former Political Prisoner, who fights for freedom and democracy (Mathieson); the Exile, stoked by activist passions in New Zealand (Gilbert and Cho); the Sex Worker in Thailand, struggling with the nightmarish conditions of low-pay sexual servitude (Okamoto); the Tatmadaw Officer, who hopes for a change of regime (Menager); the Korean Soap Opera Junkie (Aung Si); the Entrepreneur, balancing collaboration with curiosity (Farrelly); and the Yangon (Rangoon) Indie Musician, who embraces an idiosyncratic revolutionary style (Aung Naing Thu). These figures blur together to contextualize, discombobulate, and reinforce the challenges of deeply contested, sometimes transgressive modernity in a country where easy answers to decades-long social, political, and economic conundrums have proven ineffective in the face of histories, cultures, and resentments that cannot be easily wished away. In Burma, political repression and censorship are met by open resistance but also by more subtle efforts to nudge society and politics in new directions. For ordinary Burmese, the paths around modernity sketched here are never straight. Some choose to stay in Burma and survive, fail, or prosper, while others opt to flee their predicaments in the hope of better futures elsewhere. Sadly, new lives in Thailand—or somewhere else around the world—can become their own kind of modern nightmare for transnational Burmese.

Even though Burma retains a distinguished place in anthropological theory, studying these paths through today's modernity is a persistent challenge. Not only is the country diverse in terms of languages and cultures, its range of landscapes, economic systems, and historical interactions ensures that there are countless ways for ethnographers (or other observers) to *know* Burma. Over the past century, ethnographers of varying professional and social origins have sought to explain changes in the societies of Burma. We all benefit from their efforts. In early generations they were more likely to be colonial officials, military officers, or missionaries than they were to have any "disinterested" social scientific inclinations. And while there have been times when foreign researchers have been able to work relatively freely inside the country—particularly from the 1930s to the early 1960s[2]—there has remained a reliance on other types of field workers. It is for this reason that the authors of these essays on figures of Burmese modernity are not "mere academics." In all cases, they have practical involvements that stretch beyond any of their scholarly interests. Among their number are development practitioners, journalists, bloggers, and human rights advocates. Indeed, the blurring of the boundaries between these various roles is one part of the explanation for the vibrancy of their ethnographic insights.

Clearly, a limitation that social scientists studying modern Burma face is that some types of source materials are relatively scarce and access to particular areas has been tightly controlled. This explains why research on modern Burma tends to focus on a set of researchable issues in certain parts of the country or its borderlands. The area that receives the most consistent academic scrutiny is along the border with Thailand, and the majority of authors in this chapter have field experience in that area. After a short drive from the Thai cities of Bangkok or Chiang Mai, foreign researchers can roam border districts where peoples from Burma—whether newly arrived migrants or long-term residents of Thailand—are immediately accessible. Often, such research can be undertaken without undue interference from Thai or Burmese authorities. Thailand's hospitality means that part of Burma's story of modernity is filtered through the experience of its brash and more convenient neighbor. Some researchers also cross into rebel-held areas of eastern Burma, such as those slices of terrain controlled by the Karen National Liberation Army or the Shan State Army (South), where they can learn about modern resistance, rebellion, and political struggle. In this chapter, the somewhat overlapping essays on the Political Prisoner, the Exile, and the Sex Worker are all partly captured by border politics and the impacts that dislocation can have on transnational livelihoods and opportunities.

Inside Burma, there have been comparatively fewer opportunities for long-term, ethnographically styled research. In recent decades, few ethnographers have undertaken concerted stints of research in Burma, except for those who declare interests in the small range of religious or cultural topics that have not been considered threatening by the military authorities. Scholars compensate in a number of ways. There are a lucky few who can work long term inside Burma, often with a nonscholarly day-to-day occupation. Some, as noted, undertake their research from the Thai side of the border or from Yunnan in China. Others are inclined to travel to Burma for shorter trips than social scientists would usually consider in other Southeast Asian countries. Monthlong research trips are standard for many. This can mean that the exposure of anthropologists and others to the languages and cultures of the country may be less. There are, however, ways that any perceived inadequacies can be avoided. Some scholars have focused their attention on parts of Burma where language skills from China or Thailand can be redeployed. In other cases, efforts are made to focus on groups where romanized missionary scripts provide more immediate linguistic accessibility.

In these different senses, the essays presented here are all part of a social scientific terrain that cannot be divorced from the machinery of government—and repression—that has operated for so long in Burma. In these essays, we learn that there were until recently still over 2,200 political prisoners in the country. We showcase only one of them, but he represents many others who were similarly motivated to directly challenge military rule. We also highlight the attitude and experiences of a serving officer in the armed forces. He is just one man among the hundreds of thousands who wear a Tatmadaw uniform. But his cautious anticipation that political change can come through internal military reform speaks to a wider set of issues. Elections, parliaments, and "democracy" are, at least for the moment, part of a new vocabulary for official politics in Burma. But with so much uncertainty about these concepts, it is hardly surprising that all of the figures introduced in this chapter struggle to find their place in the swirling currents of Burma's contested and ambiguous modernity. The challenges of facing daily life in contexts where the dominance of authoritarian government has been almost constantly questioned should give hope to those who are fighting for different futures. It is in the voices and stories of these figures that we may see the best prospects for change.

Urban *Dumsa* (Animist Priest)
MANDY SADAN

For the first time since I met him, La Nga Zau La looked tired.[3] Usually this elderly Kachin gentleman was brimming over with life and had a natural exuberance that enthralled everyone who came into his orbit. Yet now, in the mid-afternoon heat, he looked every minute of his nearly eighty years and seemed simply to want to rest. He looked at me and said, "I had a dream recently that I met a woman wearing a white dress and she told me that I would become a Christian." It has become commonplace to say that more than 90 percent of the Kachin people residing in Burma are Christians of varying denominations; this in a country that is 90 percent (mostly Theravada) Buddhist. La Nga Zau La was not one of them. He was in fact head of the Nat Jaw Hpung ("Animist" Committee), which had six members—even by the most favorable reckoning, an infinitesimal drop in the social ocean of Myitkyina, the capital city of Kachin State in the north of the country. The Nat Jaw Hpung had a compound outside the main town center with a billboard that listed how much it would cost to have a dedication made to a particular spirit. The six members acted as *dumsa,* performing ritual recitations, or *hkinjawng,* ritual butchers and builders of the bamboo and wood structures that were used in such rites.

Myitkyina is composed of numerous small communities that have aggregated in this space since the colonial period, with most Kachin people coming to live here after independence and forming their own township enclaves. These townships form tight-knit worlds in which people know each other's business intimately. The right to practice their Christian faith has for many Kachin in these urban enclaves become an important tool in the explanation of conflict against the central government, which overwhelmed this region from 1962 onward. Yet these hegemonic religious claims downplay the significance of some significant fractures within Kachin society; the main Christian churches of the region are frequently contested by breakaway groups, evangelical and house churches, and by the simple abstention from conversion as found with the few remaining *dumsa,* whether urban or not.[4] Despite their social nonconformity, the Nat Jaw Hpung seemed to be kept well occupied. The compound was full to overflowing with ritual structures indicating that offerings were being made regularly. Clearly, a solid body of Kachin Christians in Myitkyina secretly asked for these rituals to be conducted on their behalf when life's challenges may have warranted asking for a little bit more help from the supernatural than a prayer meeting alone might provide.

Despite the overt condemnation of his beliefs by many, La Nga Zau La was also a respected figure in the local community and was frequently called upon to act as an advisor on cultural issues. The ceasefires of the 1990s had opened up a degree of cultural space in this urban center, and the ongoing claims that were being made for redistributive justice frequently used the symbolism of distinct cultural traditions. However, few now possessed both the experience and the authority to mediate this knowledge between notions of "tradition" and the sometimes uncomfortable claims of Kachin modernity in relation to the past, which such symbolic representations attempted to integrate discursively. Clearly the wider Christian Kachin society needed figures such as La Nga Zau La at this time, even though some might have tried to deny that need.

Today a thin network of ardent indigenous spirit practitioners still performs these rituals, often in the face of widespread community opposition. These urban (and nonurban) *dumsa* comprise a particularly strong-minded minority, and as a "type" they all seem to want their practices to reflect a questioning of the normative model of Kachin modernity. Their contemporary cultural presence suggests longer trajectories in which the issues of conversion and the relationship of religion to claims for political and social space within the Burmese state should be considered.

Nonetheless, I was shocked that a dream might end a lifetime's commitment to non-Christian beliefs. "Do you think you will convert?" I asked. We then had a long conversation about La Nga Zau La's family, his two wives and thirteen children, and the fact that he alone among them remained an adherent of traditional Jinghpaw spirit practices. His eldest son had deferred the act of conversion, but it was mainly so that someone would be alive after his father's death to ensure that the spirit could be sent away to the correct place. The probability was high that his son, too, would convert to Christianity after this.

For the first time, I got a sense of some of the insecurities that must have troubled La Nga Zau La, this ebullient, strong-minded, strident "animist" in this overwhelmingly Christian environment. When La Nga Zau La told me of his dream, it added a new dimension to my understanding of the social and personal struggle that he had obviously endured to maintain his position as a "traditional" cultural practitioner in a hostile social environment. Not least, I recalled the moving moment when previously he had shown me a degraded photograph of a young man. This was his seventeen-year-old son who had died as a soldier in the Kachin Independence Army more than a decade previously. His son became one of his family's ancestor spirits, as was often the case with a spirit who died a violent death. For La Nga Zau La, conversion would have involved a poignant emotional break both with the past as defined by the genealogical traditions he followed—but also with a longstanding contemplation on futures destroyed by conflict that came about with the death of his son. In this respect, the figure of the urban *dumsa* represents a greater meditation on the complexities of Kachin modernity than might at first appear from the numerically small community they constitute, where they are remarkable in their insistence on having a public space for this contest in the face of such pressures against them. They continue to vocalize and perform a critical stance toward the simplifying rhetoric of modernity and religion in contemporary Kachin nationalist movements.

Journalist (*Thadin Htauk*)
THOMAS KEAN

It was about the tenth job interview I'd presided over in two days. The young woman answering the questions, a member of an ethnic minority group that lives mostly in southern Shan State, appeared nervous. "I want to report on social issues," she said quietly. "I want to tell people what is really happening in our society." In some respects, she had good reason to be nervous. Myanmar is a country where journalists work under censorship, and the media "is prohibited from accomplishing the primary journalistic responsibility of offering reliable, factual information to the public."[5] Censored publications and the journalists who work for them also lack legitimacy in the eyes of political activists and some urban elites. Equally, the *thadin htauk* (literally "news investigator") is permitted but never entirely accepted by the government because he or she is viewed as a threat to national stability.

In this context, opportunities to publish articles on social issues appear limited. So it might seem surprising then that during a recent round of job interviews I conducted as editor of the English-language weekly, the *Myanmar Times,* this woman's response—an inherently political one, as most social problems are directly or indirectly the product of military misrule—was the most common reason interviewees cited for wanting to enter the media. All aged under thirty, they are representative of a new generation of journalists for whom, somewhat paradoxically, the print media offers freedom and opportunities.

As the late journalist U Thaung noted, Burmese newspapers were born free.[6] This continued under parliamentary rule; despite "frequent disagreements" with the government, the press "enjoyed the fullest freedom in the first decade of independence."[7] Restrictive rules were introduced in 1963 following the military coup, and subsequently most publications were shut down or nationalized. Private publishing returned to Myanmar after the fall of the Ne Win regime, and there are now several hundred licensed magazines and journals. But in spite of a global trend toward greater press freedom,[8] journalists in Myanmar are denied the liberty they possessed five decades ago. The government continues to ignore exhortations from the international community to loosen its control over published material.

Accordingly, the "quality and image" of journalism has been slow to recover from the socialist era.[9] Thousands of young people have entered the industry over the past decade, but the majority appear to have done so with little concept of the role media plays in a democratic society. The relatively high salary, career opportunities, and creative aspects of the job are the main attractions. However, as the responses from these interviewees indicated, a gradual shift is taking place. The rise of private journals has mirrored the growth in civil society, and despite not fitting into the traditional definition of civil society, those in the media consider themselves part of a movement that has seen hundreds of political, educational, health, and environmental community-based organizations established in the space of a few years. Just as these groups use the space afforded to improve their communities, journalists of the new generation feel they are working within the law to promote democracy and accountability, One respected journalist and editor who worked under both the socialist and current State Peace and Development Council systems pinpoints the September 2007 antigovernment protests as a turning point that encouraged more young people to take up journalism and also politicized those already in the industry.[10]

A subtle but significant change has occurred in the publishing industry with the advent of digital production. Previously, all material had to be submitted after publication but before distribution. Subsequently, words would be inked over, pages torn out, and in some cases, whole works banned. The financial consequences forced writers to self-censor.[11] Digital production methods allow content rejected by the censorship board to be replaced before publication, encouraging writers to adopt a more aggressive approach.

The manner in which news is gathered has also changed dramatically since the end of socialism, a time when journalists were "no more than propagandists of the socialist principles. . . . Their duty was to agitate and organize the people to support the socialist cause."[12] In contrast, they now operate with a large degree of freedom until the censorship process, and they are not, for example, prohibited from interviewing and meeting opposition political leaders.[13] The chasm between the military government and the private sector media grows ever wider, with one attempting to stage-manage press conferences and the other, with greater exposure to international media norms, yearning for press freedom.[14]

This has led to several recent successes that have confirmed the belief held by many journalists that the space for reporting and debate is widening, particularly on health, education, environmental, and economic issues. The most high profile of these occurred in November 2009, shortly after a young woman died at a well-known private medical clinic in Yangon after apparently being misdiagnosed. The death was widely reported, and in response to the public outrage this coverage generated, the Myanmar Medical Council banned the surgeon from medical practice for five years.[15] Shortly after, the journal that broke the story printed an article about a teenage girl who committed suicide after being bullied by a teacher, encouraging debate on Myanmar's under-resourced education system. Kyaw Thu, a politics and energy reporter, also cites coverage of government earnings from natural gas as among the most important stories in recent years. While not explicitly exposing government corruption, "readers came to question government expenditure and where the gas money was going."[16] Similarly, political journalists saw themselves as providing an opportunity for opposition political groups contesting the 2010 election to raise their public profile. Veteran journalist and political commentator Ludu Sein Win says these examples have made journalism an increasingly attractive profession for young people who "strive to find fairness for the public."[17]

While a lack of formal training hampers their work, it is censorship that most overshadows what journalists do. One described the censorship process as similar to being handcuffed; many who quit the industry cite the lack of press freedom as a major factor. For the young woman from Shan State, the first few months working as a journalist under censorship were difficult to reconcile with the ambitions she expressed in her interview; a series of excellent pieces following the release of Daw Aung San Suu Kyi were rejected. Her response, perhaps fittingly, was to write a feature on the need to strengthen civil society—a topic that, just a few years ago, a journalist in Myanmar was unlikely to consider tackling.

Political Prisoner
DAVID SCOTT MATHIESON

In the several months between prison sentences in the 1990s, Bo Kyi received an offer of work from Burma's Special Branch police. The offer was apparently straightforward: become an informer for us within the opposition underground, and things will go better for you. Bo Kyi agreed, but with one condition. He told them that if all political prisoners were released, including Aung San Suu Kyi, he would work with the government. This insolence led to his second term in Burma's harsh prison system, a stretch with years of solitary confinement and new rounds of torture. But he was at least among friends for some of the time. Burma's prisons were swollen with his dissident friends.

When he was released five years later, in 1998, Bo Kyi fled to the Thailand-Burma border and exile, with a quiet determination to help his hundreds of friends still locked up. He helped to found the Assistance Association for Political Prisoners—Burma, a collective of former prisoners who all fled after their terms. Their ranks are regularly replenished by dissidents who are released. The work of the association is painstakingly complicated: they need to keep track of prison transfers, health conditions, and acts of torture, while managing the secret funds transferred to assist the families of prisoners for food, schooling, medicine, and sometimes escape. Their resistance requires a network of underground activists and informers—an intelligence system that almost rivals the government's surveillance apparatus.

Until 2011 there were more than 2,200 political prisoners on the association's books. They included a broad cross-section of Burma's civil society and opposition community: long-term student protest leaders such as Min Ko Naing and Nilar Thein, labor activists, Buddhist monks and nuns, bloggers, political party members from the National League for Democracy, comedians, writers, and all the middle-ranking messengers and clerks necessary for a functioning underground.[18] They posed a significant challenge to the military's thread of legitimacy; otherwise they would have been released before the November 2010 elections. These dissidents are part of an eclectic opposition complex that has existed in many forms for decades, even as military rule has endured and adapted with its crude formula of selective repression and social neglect.[19] The government does not eradicate this opposition, it permits the overt resistance it can co-opt, monitor, imprison, or exile.

So dissidents experience a bizarre semblance of a legal process: charges, defense advocates (lawyers), prosecution, judges, evidence, and sentence all to prove that there are no political prisoners in Burma—only common criminals. Authoritarian systems often use rule by law instead of rule of law, capturing the legal system as a necessary tool of repression.[20] The process is to stamp dissidents with the force of law. It is often not enough to simply throw someone into a cell; the government prefers that they be clearly defined as outside the law and society. This is because political prisoners are not just threats to military rule; they serve as harsh examples to the broader Burmese community that overt resistance is punished. Being involved in any capacity with opposition activities is an invitation to be imprisoned. Being stamped as outside the law suits many dissidents, as their activism is predicated on proving the illegitimacy of the military system.

With his efforts to assist prisoners, Bo Kyi was the progenitor of a new form of political mobilization in Burma: the merging of domestic activism and documentation with international advocacy and awareness raising.[21] This has led Bo Kyi from his cell in Yangon's Insein Prison to Geneva, New York, Oslo, London, and beyond, advocating on behalf of all those still incarcerated. Despite the limitations of this resistance paradigm—and the fact that publicizing repression in Burma does not always lead to a reduction of human rights violations—the plight of political prisoners is now a prominent policy issue used by the United Nations and foreign governments to press for democratic reform.

Political prisoners from Burma have a strange aura around them. In my travels with Bo Kyi, I have met dozens of his former cell mates now in exile: a sushi chef in Chicago, a former boxing champion in Tokyo, a monk in Zurich. In Thailand there are more than I can remember, but Bo Kyi knows them all. There are the ones who laugh at doing only a twelve-year stretch and those who sheepishly say only five. And then when a particularly bad prison is mentioned, the jokes get grim. There is also the ambiguous hint of regret—that the safety of exile, no matter the urgency of the work that the association does, takes them away from their distant colleagues still underground and in prison. This feeling of safety drives Bo Kyi to continue his work, when he knows his close friends are continuing to sacrifice their freedom to fuel the idea of a Burma without military rule.[22]

Many Burmese have mixed feelings about meeting former political prisoners—a combination of awe and astonishment. You can see it when the 88 Generation Students as a group walk into a crowded room, or when they address a small crowd at a busy intersection and give a lightning speech about resistance. People are thinking, "These guys did fourteen years inside." And, since 2007, they have all been back in prison again, some for sixty-five years this time, and they effectively asked for it by continuing to protest openly. It is the ephemeral quality that it takes to openly challenge the authorities that many Burmese do not understand but simply respect.

Bo Kyi is still waiting for another offer to work with the authorities; he wants to work with the military to change Burma. He comes from a military family, a fact that his interrogators would bring up as they were mistreating him and yelling "traitor." There is no hatred, no vengeance, just patience—patience with the promise that one day, the military will have to constructively deal with all the people they have sought to destroy.

Exile

DAVID GILBERT AND VIOLET CHO

It is late autumn 2009. Burma is in the media again, as Aung San Suu Kyi faces a trial after an American citizen swam to her house. In the union courtyard of Auckland University, about sixty people have gathered for a candlelight vigil. Local speakers demand sanctions and try to build some momentum for a Burma movement in a city without obvious links to the regime. Naing Ko Ko is at the side of the stage, overseeing proceedings. He also takes questions from local media. Naing Ko Ko is a Burmese exile. Like many others of his generation, he was imprisoned for his political activities. Now he is in New Zealand as a refugee, distant from his former life in Burma. He sustains himself through political activism.

Naing Ko Ko wants to be seen as a politician and intellectual, but he is unable to escape his traumatic past. Questions of his prison experience come up again and again in media interviews:

> People want to know my personal story more than the general situation in Burma. I get asked how many days I went without food, how I was tortured, and very specific questions about what I went through in prison. I feel ashamed to talk about it because what happened to me was inhumane and it makes me relive the shame. I don't want to talk about it, but I don't have a choice because deep down I want to let other people know what's happening in Burma.

For Naing Ko Ko and many other Burmese exiles, suffering is part of identity and, in spite of the pain, it is strategically deployed in advocacy and campaigns. Despite the presence of a small community of Burmese exiles, Naing Ko Ko tells us that he often feels lonely, depressed, and angry. "I sleep six hours per day. The rest of the time I think about Burma."

The cultural and political landscape of exile that Naing Ko Ko lives in is sustained through a constant flow of reports of atrocities through Burmese opposition news media and campaign groups, coupled with transnational networks on social media sites like Facebook and Twitter. Naing Ko Ko is on instant messenger most of the time, waiting for news from home and trying to help with anything he can.

Burma's mass exodus began in 1988, when the isolationist and socialist regime stepped down amidst waves of nationwide protest. The military took power that September after gunning down protesters on the street and detaining dissidents. That was the beginning of the current period of dictatorship, this time without a strong ideological position beyond amorphous concepts of "unity" and "development." An unknown number of activists fled to the border areas to engage in armed struggle and political campaigns against military rule. Naing Ko Ko was a sixteen-year-old student at the time. He actively joined the protests and became involved in the underground student movement. In 1992 he was arrested in Yangon and sentenced to seven years hard labor in the colonial-era Insein Prison. Upon his release, he left for Thailand and began his exile.

Traumatic experiences in Burma and the guilt of having fled drive many activists like Naing Ko Ko into entrenched political positions. The political movement thrives on heroes and sacrifice, but little research has been done on the personal psychological toll of this. One 1996 study of trauma among young Burmese activists in Thailand found that over 40 percent had symptoms of severe depression and that their health perceptions of themselves were comparable to Cambodian refugees who had fled the Pol Pot regime to Thai border camps: "Their traumatic experiences began at the perils of a revolutionary student movement, shifted to the hardships of a jungle escape, and now have been transformed into conditions of violence and insecurity that are characteristic of the lives of illegal immigrants. It appears that this cumulative trauma has had an appreciable impact on the exiles' mental health." Some 75 percent of respondents cited engagement in the pro-democracy movement as a primary coping mechanism for life in exile.[23]

While the exile is usually associated with romantic notions of political dissidence that involves sacrifice for a supposedly noble cause, in relation to Burma the political exile is a minority within the total diasporic population. In Thailand alone, there are an estimated two million migrant workers.[24] In addition, there are substantial numbers in Malaysia and Singapore. In New Zealand, Naing Ko Ko is possibly the only Burmese exile dedicated to full-time activism for political change. This leaves him a solitary figure.

A few months after the vigil, Naing Ko Ko told us over Google Chat that his father had passed away:

NAING: so young to pass away
at 59
I have not met him for nearly two decade
GILBERT: what did he die of?
NAING: I don't know
I am trying to give a call to my network to help me to call home
GILBERT: Haven't you been able to call yet?
NAING: No way

> I just heard from my younger bro
> who sent me an email
> I am crying
> for my poor life

Naing Ko Ko has not seen his parents since he left Burma and has avoided communication. "I feel guilty that I've never had a chance to work and repay the debt to my parents by sending money, so I feel bad to call them and talk to them. I'm very upset about it and of course I miss them, but since I can't help them, I don't want to give trouble to them and I don't feel close to my mother anymore." Isolation from family is one of the most difficult features of diasporic life.

Exiles are a tragic, enduring feature of Burma's political melodrama. Naing Ko Ko has paid a huge personal price for his part in the democracy movement and continues to plan and wait for a time when he can return to his homeland. In the meantime, he finds temporary relief from his anger and frustration through political action.

Sex Worker in Thailand
IKUKO OKAMOTO

In a small dark room behind a health clinic, twenty-one-year-old Ma Aye Aye (not her real name) sits gloomily with us.[25] We met her in September 2009. "I was born in Yangon," she explained, as she started to calmly talk about her life. Her parents divorced when she was only two years old and she grew up with her mother. Her mother earned only a modest income selling vegetables, but she did her best so that her daughters could receive a decent education. Ma Aye Aye completed her schooling up to the seventh standard (or grade), while her sister completed the tenth; this was a good achievement for girls growing up in a single-parent household. Yet she was now in Ranong, Thailand, spending her days as a sex worker in a shabby guesthouse where most of the clients were Myanmar fishermen.

Ranong is a small border town in southern Thailand, located just opposite Kawthaung, at the very southern edge of Myanmar. The Kura Buri River runs between the two towns, and it takes about thirty minutes by long-tail boat to cross it. Every day, a continuous flow of Myanmar people cross the river. All are seeking a better income, if not a better life, in Thailand. Some cross legally, but a majority makes the journey without any official endorsements. Despite all the official rules and procedures for crossing borders, it is not difficult if you are prepared to offer some extra cash.

These days the population of Myanmar migrants in Ranong, estimated to be around two hundred thousand, has come to exceed the number of Thais. Only some portions of these are "registered" migrants, and the rest are deemed to be nonregistered or illegal. Myanmar migrants take jobs that Thais, even those from the poor northeast, are not willing to take any longer. They work on fishing boats that may stay at sea for many months, at processing factories that require standing for long hours in a cold room, or on rubber plantations demanding that workers tap the trees in the early hours of the morning. Myanmar migrants take these jobs even for wages well below the official pay rates, since they will still earn much more than they would back home. It has long been the case that Ranong's economy cannot function without Myanmar migrant labor.[26]

Prostitution is no exception. Myanmar sex workers have now come to almost completely replace Thai and Lao girls in Ranong.[27] As we can easily imagine, these sex workers do not necessarily cross the border to sell sex from the outset. Their stories parallel what we see in Ma Aye Aye's life story: they just wished for a slightly better life, believed what they were told, and ended up cheated, abused, and distressed.

Ma Aye Aye left home at the age of nineteen to work in a beer hall in Mawlamyaine, Mon State, in Myanmar. She married a man working in the same beer hall and returned to Yangon to live with him. Around that time, her husband's violent explosions began. After enduring his temper for eight months, she was approached by a woman living nearby who told her that good jobs were available in Ranong. "I desperately wanted to escape the beatings from my husband." Ma Aye Aye decided to accompany the woman. She traveled by train, car, and boat to reach Kawthaung, just across the river from Thailand. When she arrived in Ranong from Kawthaung, all her money was gone, and the traveling cost became her debt. "I was told that I must work as a sex worker if I did not have money to repay the debt." She realized that she did not have a way to escape.

Just after starting as a sex worker in Ranong, she found that she was three months pregnant by her ex-husband. But she had to continue working. She was once arrested by Thai police and kept in custody for two months. Eventually she was freed from prison (supposedly by paying fines, which became an additional debt), but she could not work as her pregnancy was too advanced. Her owner allowed her to stay at his home to wash dishes. She gave birth to a son in Ranong Hospital, for which she was not charged, as she literally did not have enough money. After just a month, she started to work again. Her income was around 2,000–3,000 baht (equivalent to U.S. $60–90 as of September 2009) per month after repaying her debt.

Ma Aye Aye suddenly burst into tears when the story focused on her son. "I thought I would not be able to raise my son with this small amount of money. I felt I did not want my boy to know my job when he grew up." She decided to place him in the care of a Myanmar couple, whom she did not previously know, when he was only seven months old. Ma Aye Aye had not seen him since. "If I could earn 5,000 baht per month, I may have been able to keep him with me." With eyes full of tears, she told us she deeply regretted what she had done.

All this happened within the two years since Ma Aye Aye attempted to escape from her harsh family life in Myanmar. Now she wanted to return, to erase her intolerable life and experience in Ranong. She could not control her life, and no one, either in Thailand or in Myanmar, seemed to offer a helping hand.[28] Her mother did not know what she was doing in Ranong; she did not have the courage to tell her the truth. She wished to go back to Myanmar the following year, but no one knew if this would be possible.

Ma Aye Aye is just one of five to six hundred Myanmar sex workers working in Ranong. As is often the case, young and healthy girls are preferred. New girls are necessary to meet the demand not only of Thais and of less wealthy Myanmar clients,[29] but also to replace those sent home after contracting sexually transmitted diseases, including HIV/AIDS. Thus, the recruitment of fresh girls who can be easily trapped continues in Yangon, the Irrawaddy Delta, and other parts of the country. Lies, arrests, fines, and debt bondage are common tools.

Signboards against human trafficking are easily spotted in the town of Ranong. Thai authorities say they are doing their best to fight against human trafficking. However, with the rapidly changing structure of Thailand's economy, which is supported by economic and social factors within Myanmar and well-organized but invisible networks of those who gain a huge benefit from the trade in both Thailand and Myanmar, there seems to be no end to this tragic flow of girls crossing the border.

Tatmadaw Officer
JACQUELINE MENAGER

On a sweltering Yangon day in a poorly ventilated church, a wedding ceremony is underway. All the traditional trappings of a Christian wedding are proudly displayed, with some Burmese enhancements: a radio crackles and screams the tulle-drenched bride down the aisle, a drunken uncle corners people to not-so-coherently voice his political opinions through betel nut–stained teeth, and an enormous, garish fluorescent cake weighs down the bridal table. At the heart of this scene is Thet (a pseudonym), giving his daughter away in a love marriage. This is Thet's last family gathering before his relocation to Burma's new capital city of Naypyidaw, where he is being sent without his family. The looming separation is not discussed at the wedding. But after a brief reception of strangely packaged foods and artificial cake, Thet moves into more comfortable territory and begins lamenting his country's political situation. The wedding is taking place only days before the country's contentious 2010 elections and the much-anticipated release of Aung San Suu Kyi. While the international media stresses the importance of these events, in reality such politics hardly affect daily life in Burma. For Thet and many others in the military, however, that is changing. Their relocation to lonely Naypyidaw is turning simmering discontent into potentially explosive dissent against their anachronistic leadership.

The government of Burma constructs a picture of modernity for the international community, overtly signposted with the transition to a new capital, the creation of a new flag, and the democratic election of a new government. However, this official presentation of progress is less indicative of a modern country than the growing discontent among the population and the military itself. As a result of the gradual liberalization of Burma beginning in 1988, many people in the country have grown more aware of the functioning of the outside world and the deficiencies of their own government. Accompanying this transition is a growing population of highly educated and progressive public servants and military personnel, both ready for change and actively working toward it. New generations of Burma's military, taking some of their inspiration from deposed former military intelligence chief General Khin Nyunt's progressive tendencies, oppose the military's official ideology.[30] Thet is one such officer.

Thet is a chief petty officer with a young family; his education and his years in the military have made him starkly aware of the failings of his government. On a personal level, Thet feels the pain of low salaries (supporting his family on a meager U.S. $65 monthly salary plus $10 in monthly rations), the inability to resign, and the imminent relocation to Naypyidaw without his family. Thet has tried to resign from the military; however, resignation is only accepted due to illness—namely HIV/AIDS and alcoholism—or with the payment of 1.5 million kyat (in recent years, around U.S. $1,300), an impossible sum. For the moment, Thet must follow his orders, move to Naypyidaw, and await his retirement at age sixty.

The Myanmar Armed Forces are divided into navy, air force, and army. All three services provide military education, but the culture of the navy and the air force is considered more progressive than that of the army. Unfortunately,

Thet explains, the air force and navy's desire to initiate change is curtailed by the less progressive elements in the army that far outnumber them. Top officers are almost all drawn from the army.[31] Of them, Thet says, "They cannot rule a country. They know only fire, kill, send to the jail." In his mind, progressive military officers potentially present the most destabilizing challenge to military rule.

Thet recounts a popular story of Burma's three sons: the monk, the student, and the soldier. In 1988 one son, the student, tried to instigate change. He failed. In 2007 another son, the monk, tried to bring to light the population's suffering. He also failed. It is now time for the third son, the soldier, to stand up and represent his people. Dissent is palpable, with many soldiers reported to have traveled to Yangon for Aung San Suu Kyi's release.[32] Accordingly, Thet asserts that Suu Kyi is a rallying point for the majority of the population and that her backing will be useful in catalyzing any future action. However, she will need to recognize the entrenched position of the military in Burma. Thet and others estimate that approximately 80 percent of the population is in some way connected to the military, either as an officer or as a family supported by an officer.[33] Whether Aung San Suu Kyi is prepared for negotiation with the military is difficult to say, though her past actions indicate an unwillingness to temper her views and demands to win military backing.

The 2010 election and the release of Aung San Suu Kyi indicate a change of government approach. The wider implications of this altered strategy remain to be seen, and any optimism among officers like Thet must be moderated by memories of similarly inspiring historical events, such as Aung San Suu Kyi's previous releases, which have often ended suddenly and violently. In line with such precedents, Thet expressed his skepticism about the elections, denouncing them as "not just" and accusing his superior officers of merely "changing trousers for *longyis*."[34] Reinvention is not a new strategy, with previous superficial changes to the government's leadership and policies all ultimately resulting in the military retaining control of the government. These transformations aim to legitimize Burma among its neighbors, allowing them to maintain trade relations with minimal international condemnation. "Oppose foreign nations interfering in internal affairs of the state" is one of the government's propaganda catchphrases.[35] The reality is that the imminent threat to the government's stability is not the international community but dissatisfied military officers.

Thet and those like him now face stark choices. The November 2010 elections have granted more political power to some ethnic minorities, with many winning seats. Questions about how long Aung San Suu Kyi's freedom will last and what limits will be placed on her movements remain unanswered. The military high command is not known for leaving things to chance, and their plan for Burma's future will no doubt be unveiled slowly. Recent actions are primarily targeted at the international community; they hope to depict Burma as a modern, democratic country. The government's modernity, marked with advanced weaponry and democratic elections, is a different modernity to that present among shadow figures like Thet. The subversive potential of dissatisfied military officers represents a modern transition in the country's consciousness and presents hope for a future founded on a very different vision of modernity than that promoted by the current government.

Korean Soap Opera Junkie
AUNG SI

A fashionable young couple enters a trendy café in downtown Seoul to talk about the issues that have been plaguing their relationship. Unbeknownst to either of them, the café is owned by the boy's mother, who had abandoned him as a baby over two decades ago and whom he has never met. At this very moment, the mother is entering the café from a back entrance, having been dropped off there in her shiny black Mercedes, driven by a uniformed, white-gloved chauffeur. As she walks around her shop, she overhears the young man explaining to his girlfriend the reason why he has been so stressed lately: he has been obsessed with finding his biological mother and suspects that she might still be in Seoul, only now with a new family. Given the acrimonious circumstances in which his parents separated, his father was totally against the idea of helping him locate his mother. Listening to this conversation, the café owner is about to discover, to her horror, that her abandoned son is a customer in her own shop.

Suddenly, in another world, the phone rings in the living room of a small Yangon apartment. Muttering to herself, Daw Mya Yee picks up her receiver. It is her good friend, Daw Tin Nwe, calling to have a casual chat. "Can't talk now," says Daw Mya Yee, "I'm watching the Korean show."

"Oops, sorry!" says Daw Tin Nwe, "It's a no-electricity night for us, and I forgot what time it was. I guess I'll have to ask you later about what happened."

Daw Mya Yee is a real Korean soap opera junkie: she watches every single episode she can, even the "historical dramas," which she admits are not really to her taste. She has long suspected that the young man in tonight's show—her favorite—would be reunited with his mother, although she has little sympathy for a woman who could abandon her own newborn baby. Daw Mya Yee hurries back to join her family huddled around the TV set and to her half-eaten dinner, but predictably, the episode ends just before the much-anticipated denouement.

The Korean TV drama in its many guises has become staple nighttime viewing in practically every Burmese home that owns a television. The two most common genres—historical action drama and contemporary soap opera—are broadcast for an hour nearly every weeknight and for several hours on weekends. The contemporary soaps, in particular, are not only entertaining topics of conversation among friends but also windows into an affluent, westernized, but still highly traditional Asian culture, at once subtly alien and yet tantalizingly familiar. This culture may well prove to be the template on which young urban Burmese model themselves, with hairstyles and fashions the first to be visibly influenced. Korean soaps, therefore, are to Burma what American TV is to the rest of the world.

Korean series with Burmese subtitles started appearing on Burmese TV soon after 2000, gradually replacing Chinese programs. Subtitles are the only means of understanding what is said, and viewers often make casual guesses about the meaning of high-frequency Korean words, such as *sumida* and *oppa*. Korean personal names are transcribed with a distinctly Burmese flavor, and some programs may even be referred to solely by a Burmese name, as in the case of *Lhe Sein Lay* ("Little Green Cart"). Naturally, all programs are viewed through the lens of Burmese sensibilities and customs, and certain recurring themes that stand out because of their "foreignness" are considered indicative of Korean culture in general.

"There are lots of abandoned children in Korea," Daw Mya Yee points out bluntly, her face a mixture of mild shock and amazement. She is dismayed that this is not a consequence of poverty, war, or natural calamity, but of deep-seated social issues. "Husbands must treat their wives very badly!" she says, for why else would a mother leave her own children or commit suicide? Such behavior would be highly stigmatized in Burma. Korean society also has far less gender equality than Burmese society and is also far more obsessed with wealth and social status. The contrast in the attitudes and perceptions of traditional, wealthy, joint families and more modern, middle-class, nuclear families, is also not lost on her.

The high level of respect shown by Korean children for their parents is seen as a positive aspect of Korean culture. For instance, Korean children make it a point to always greet their parents when they arrive home. However, filial piety could be taken to unnecessary extremes—for Daw Mya Yee, Korean sons and daughters are a bit too eager to have their parents' approval regarding their choice of marriage partner. "Why don't they just elope, like we would in Burma?" she suggests, as a possible solution to dealing with obstinate parents.

People like Daw Mya Yee find Korean TV dramas to be excellent din-nertime viewing, providing a healthy daily dose of escapism before the usual images of uniformed generals inaugurating bridges and being nice to ethnic minorities, especially the ones with whom the military is currently engaged in active conflict. It is perhaps for this reason that the DVDs, which contain full seasons of these shows and can be bought for a few hundred kyat (less than U.S. 50 cents), sell in such great numbers. The constant power cuts that are a familiar part of urban Burmese life can be a nuisance, but they give people an excuse to call up friends and ask about missed episodes, another way of deal-ing with unpleasant realities. However, the visions of daily life in a developed Asian country, which the TV dramas bring into people's homes, do subtly remind viewers about how far Burma has been left behind her neighbors in terms of prosperity and standard of living. The feeling of escaping reality may therefore not be as complete as they hope.

"No!" Daw Mya Yee and family groan in unison, realizing that they will have to miss tomorrow's crucial episode—the blackouts seem to have in-creased in frequency and duration since the election ended. "Oh, well, it can't be helped," she muses. "*Oppa,* can I get you any more rice?" she asks her husband teasingly, using her favorite Korean term of endearment.

Entrepreneur
NICHOLAS FARRELLY

As the air-conditioning hummed not so gently in the corner, I swung my chair to examine the novel character of a Burmese entrepreneur's office. Myint Aung, lounging on the leather couch, regaled me with details of the three dif-ferent projects that he was simultaneously completing and launched into a shopping list of his achievements and outcomes. These initiatives, he insisted, "will transform the nation." Ethnically Burmese—but working all over the country with a dizzying schedule of travel, meetings, banquets, karaoke, drink-ing, hotels, phone calls, and deals—his tone suggested a subtle reinforcement of official narratives couched in a slightly critical view of just how much loy-alty was realistic in a system where the ironies of military rule are apparent to anybody who works in the "real economy." "Development," my entrepreneur-ial informant reflected, "was the highest goal of the SPDC [State Peace and Development Council] and all national business leaders, all working together." I failed then and still fail to quantify how much of this statement he believed.

Myint Aung (a pseudonym) is accustomed to finding the right set of words. In English or Burmese he can hold court about his country, its problems, and the perpetual challenges of business in an economy under military rule. He also finds the world outside Burma profoundly enticing. Myint Aung has traveled regularly to Singapore and various cities in southern China, and he has been to Bangkok once, but the rest of the world remains somewhat mysterious. He has some equipment suppliers in northern Europe who have suggested he should make a trip to visit them at the next opportunity. He wonders, aloud and with an almost childish giggle, about snow and churches and the Pope and democratic politics. Comparisons of prices and modes of life and business are endlessly fascinating to him. He is especially keen to hear about the role of entrepreneurs in other political systems. His curiosity about the outside world focuses on money and business. How much? Who? Where? Can I be involved?

So I ask him how entrepreneurs make their money in Burma. He begins by explaining that the government has, over the past two decades, sought to divest itself of direct control of the old socialist economic structure. The old economy is now more open to entrepreneurial ambitions, at the same time as new sectors (such as telecommunications) have become available for commercial exploitation. Trade with countries including Thailand, Singapore, China, and India has increased, at the same time as links to Russia and Israel, among a long list of other countries, have been maintained. As Justin Wintle notes in his biography of Aung San Suu Kyi, "Only a small minority—politically neutral entrepreneurs as well as loyal servants of the regime and its leaders—may expect a reasonable lifestyle, while those at the very top (the generals and their cronies) live in considerable luxury. But these too must survive on their wits and nerve."[36] In covering the same terrain, Myint Aung, speaking with a special emphasis on "wits and nerve," overlooks the fact that some among Burma's entrepreneurial classes have found themselves blacklisted from visiting countries such as the United States, the United Kingdom, and Australia. They are banned.

Myint Aung's discussion gradually touches on these most notorious entrepreneurs: those with intimate links to the senior military leadership. The so-called cronies are often marked by their fast cars, plush mansions, and expensive tastes in clothes and food. In a country where a majority of the population survives on a few dollars per day, their access to resources and political clout sets them apart. For many Burmese, it is particularly galling that the children of military officers have used their social and political connections to generate profit-making opportunities. Everything from modest cafés and bars all the way through to large-scale construction and natural resource extraction projects comprises part of their commercial vision. Young men from these privileged military backgrounds, some still only teenagers, are the most politically controversial face of Burma's entrepreneurial boom. And while their fathers and uncles continue to hold the levers of political and economic power, they are relatively free to accumulate wealth on behalf of their families. The notion that government figures rely on their salaries alone for financial sustenance is now as quaint as it is inaccurate.

Entrepreneurialism is now fused to government power; some assert that "Today ... civilian entrepreneurs operate only with the blessing of the military regime."[37] But not all entrepreneurs can be so readily identified as military lackeys. Myint Aung does not consider himself a government man and actually insists that much business can be undertaken without formal government oversight. And there are many other entrepreneurs, he points out, who have developed ethnic or social statuses that can allow them significant freedom of investment and action in their local areas. Local military commanders often hope to keep them onside. It makes life easier.

Among Burmese who have missed out on sharing any of the country's newfound wealth, resentment against entrepreneurs is not the only emotion or even the most common one. It is commonplace to hear people openly admire the skills and savvy of anyone who can create opportunities in a system where so little appears to change. An entrepreneur's capacity to generate employment and income for a local area can lead to popularity and status. This all happens in a system that cannot be stereotyped in terms of dictatorial politics or economic stagnation alone.

So while Myint Aung is only one voice among Burma's current crop of entrepreneurs, his ambitions for economic development and personal advancement indicate a challenge to any impression that Burma has not changed since its socialist economic system collapsed in 1988. Over those years, engagements with modernity as a "work in progress" have motivated risk taking and profit making among new generations of entrepreneurial figures. Their entrepreneurial exceptions mark them out in a political and economic context where initiative and creativity have been largely absent. It is only natural that conversations with Myint Aung turn to the future and to his ambitions. "Maybe one day Burma will be as rich as Thailand," he reflects, as the overworked air-conditioning still grumbles in the background.

And then, without much of a goodbye, he needs to dash off to an airport, or hotel, or karaoke bar, or meeting: I am never quite sure which.

Indie Musician
AUNG NAING THU

It is 9 p.m., a Friday night in downtown Yangon. The lights have dimmed in a buzzing nightclub in a seedy district of town. Zaw Min snakes past his two bandmates on the cramped stage, plugs his guitar cord into an amp, and approaches the mic.[38] "We're the What's What, and we're here to make you dance! Let's go! One, two, three, four!" After a fiery sixty-minute set of indie punk songs, Zaw Min decompresses in the clammy "VIP room" of the club. Smoking cigarettes, he deconstructs the gig with his bandmates. Kyaw Zeya, the bass player, shouts over the thud of the club music, "Not enough people moved! We need more fans jumping around." A few sighs, here and there, a pensive drag on a cigarette: "Man. Kids in Yangon are just not willing to try out something new."

Zaw Min leads an unconventional life. Every choice he makes is informed by his deep-seated instinct to not conform to the orthodox norms, structures, and conventions of contemporary Myanmar urban culture. Like many of his peers, Zaw Min, aged twenty-eight, has always "resisted." But this "resistance" has a rather pragmatic character. Zaw Min's livelihood choices in themselves are radical. He has chosen to eschew the economic benefits of two degrees he gained in Yangon—mechanical engineering and English—in order to start an indie punk rock band. Kicked out of his house at age seventeen for disobeying his father's wishes that he become an engineer for the Tatmadaw (Myanmar's Armed Forces), Zaw Min now lives with his wife Thidar Phyo, a performance artist, on the eighth floor of an apartment building in Mingalar Taung Nyunt township. An avid reader and curbside philosopher, Zaw Min decided early on that he could not trade his happiness for the status, upward mobility, and secure and steady income that a government job would provide. For Zaw Min and his bandmates, the decision to commit to pursuing their musical dreams was like a "personal revolution." Coming from a lower-class urban family in an extremely impoverished nation, Zaw Min's livelihood choices are indeed unconventional.

In addition to breaking traditional livelihood norms and family customs, as an indie rocker Zaw Min also contravenes established cultural norms. In Myanmar, the state does not dictate public/civic life as much as it permeates the aggregate structures that define public/civic life. Even so, one can still find spaces waiting to be occupied, spaces where one can "resist." Zaw Min is constantly maneuvering these spaces or loopholes. He is constantly negotiating artistic space within the cultural boundaries that are prescribed by state and society. His attitudes, actions, and choices cannot be neatly delineated into defined categories of "the political" and "the practical"; this is a false dichotomy.

For example, censorship infringes on cultural space. The government censors all published cultural materials, including all forms of printed media, CDs, VCDs/DVDs, and billboards. Zaw Min has a range of mechanisms, actions, and tools he can use to negotiate the demands of censorship. One such tool is concerts. It seems that the government has yet to understand the power of live music. While a permit is required to perform in large public spaces, the censors don't seem to place the same restrictions on gigs as they do on cultural products that will be distributed in commercial spaces. That being said, Zaw Min often chooses not to participate in the larger gigs that typically feature ten to fifteen punk or metalcore bands. This is both because he dislikes the musical style of the bands and because those gigs often attract the attention of the authorities, who have incarcerated musicians perceived as being antigovernment. Zaw Min often considers these incidents when he makes the choice to utilize another tool of negotiation—club gigs. Concerts in clubs don't officially require any permit whatsoever.

While Zaw Min has strong words to say about the structures that define his freedom of expression ("censorship is total bullshit"), if he wants to publish music he needs to engage with the censors. Another resistance mechanism he employs involves playing games with the censor board—for example, with oversaturation. For his next album, Zaw Min wants to include about ten songs. So he will overload the censor board with seventeen songs, expecting them to cut a handful. Another tool is bribery. Although he loathes contributing to the culture of corruption, he is willing to pay a bribe to have his music released, an option that is available and fairly standardized. A final tool available to Zaw Min is self-censorship. This is an option that he prefers to avoid as much as possible, for artistic reasons. For him, songwriting is a cathartic process. "Whenever I write songs . . . some words, which come from my subconscious mind, appear on the paper. When I read it, I can see what's inside of me. It's about finding myself personally. Knowing your true self is the most important thing in life."

But for Zaw Min, maneuvering around government censorship is only half the battle in his personal war for the cultural landscape. He sees the wretchedness of censorship as a much less significant obstacle than his bigger enemy: the conformism of Myanmar youth culture. The dominant trends of metal and metalcore have become too mainstreamed. There is no demand for creativity and innovation in music. Gigs often feature ten bands that sound exactly the same. Myanmar's decades of isolation and relatively closed borders have stagnated musical innovation. Limited Internet connectivity, lack of access to foreign music, and crippling poverty have all had an impact on a culture that values individual singers rather than musicians or bands. The singers from Iron Cross, the most celebrated Myanmar rock band, have made their careers based almost exclusively on Burmese-language covers of Western rock radio hits. The same values of emulation and imitation have crossed over into the supposedly counterculture punk movement.

So while young men and women attend gigs in full punk regalia—skinny jeans, metal spikes, Mohawks, Rancid patches—Zaw Min, always critical of the masses, opines that "they might get a thrill out of teenage rebellion and feel at ease in a group of like-minded peers. But they are a bunch of nonconformists conforming to the same trend."

EPILOGUE

BENEDICT ANDERSON

If one wanders across disciplines, one can get the impression that they are in their own way "figures of modernity," with their own silhouettes, gestures, languages, grandeurs, fetishes, soft spots, and curiosities. If one were interested in soft spots, one might lazily say: nostalgia for history, cynicism for political science, optimism for economics, pessimism for philosophy, sentimentality for anthropology, and so on. Luckily, the soft spots are quite different, so that the disciplines actually can help one another. Besides, soft spots often overlap with grandeurs.

The cynicism of my own discipline, political "science," descends from Machiavelli, but it is shaped by its overwhelming interest in the usually deplorable behavior of political elites and ruling classes and its permanent engagement with the contemporary and, thus, "the new." This kind of "new" is typically marked linguistically by ephemeral or epochal neologisms. In the few pages that follow a fine and variegated book on figures of modernity as seen by anthropologists and historians, I would like to consider a few such political markers.

The Liberal and the Fanatical Muslim

Throughout the twentieth century, Indonesian Muslims were usually categorized in two opposing groups: "modernists" and "traditionalists." But these days the modernity of modernists is far from obvious, while traditionalists are often behaving in rather "modern" ways. The linguistic signs to notice are the pairing of *Islam liberal* with *Islam fanatik,* both understood as more political than historical or sociological. It is striking that these signs are also self-markers, so that one can happily and up-to-datedly speak of oneself as a "liberal" or a "fanatik." Indonesians often say that the "fathers" of the new pair are "traditionalists" (Nahdlatul Ulama) and "modernists" (Muhammadijah). But the vocabulary of newly independent Indonesia in the 1950s ranged from Muslim socialists to right-wing extremists. It is difficult to imagine S. M. Kartosuwirjo, leader of the long-lasting armed Darul Islam rebellion, thinking of himself as a fanatic. Behind the figures of the liberal and fanatic Muslim, one can detect the shadows of an age that has passed—the age of the Cold War, of communism and socialism. In the figures themselves, contemporaneity probably trumps modernity. But there are also many other figures in the world of Indonesian Islam that are well worth consideration.

The Facebook Muslim Girl

Take, for example, the fact that 90 percent Muslim Indonesia has one of the largest populations of Facebook users in the world. One could even coin the term *Muslim fesbuk.* Not long ago, I gave a dullish lecture for perhaps two hundred students at Malang's Universitas Negeri. After delivering the lecture and coping with the following Q&A, I was startled by a large group of Muhammadijah girls, all wearing elegant and expensive *djilbabs,* rushing up to ask permission to be photographed with me. Foolishly, I expected the usual twentieth-century "school photo" with a crowd of students around a seated elderly teacher. To my naïve astonishment, the girls insisted that each should have a digital one-on-one with the "professor." The first girl, very pretty and rather heavily made up, posed with her cheek on my shoulder, and with her eyes and lips melodramatically turned up toward my own. What should I do? Stare vacantly ahead or try to return her alluring smile? Later, a faculty member enlightened me. All the students, but especially the girls, want this type of photo for their *fesbuk,* for instant circulation to (hopefully) envious friendsters who failed to come to the lecture and—who knows?—the rest of the world. For a second or two, I felt like eighty-two-year-old Clint Eastwood's doppelgänger.

The Gay and the Lesbian

In the Southeast Asian countries I know best—Indonesia, Thailand/Siam, and the Philippines—the Anglo-American words "gay" and "lesbian" have entered, unaltered, the three national vernaculars, especially from the 1980s onward. All these countries have long histories of homosexual relationships. (In Chau Ju-kua's lengthy account of his visit to Angkor in 1296, he mentions with some amusement that Chinese traders arriving at the city's gates were enthusiastically mobbed by hordes of competing young transvestites.) The words for the male transvestite—*bakla, bantji,* and *krathoey* (an old Khmer word adopted by the Thai)—are "premodern," while the man who slept with him was unmarked. The transvestite was thus a well-known figure in "traditional" society, easily marked by dress, makeup, language, and sexual desires. (Over woman-to-woman sexual relationships, silence generally prevailed.) Hence the arrival of men who looked and acted just like other men but who had sexual relations with men of the same type was a kind of modernist mystery. One could never be sure anymore who was and who was not. The modernity of the gay and the lesbian was underwritten by post-Stonewall public activism all over the "Western world." For a time, understandably, the words were interpreted through the lens of fashion, which by definition is always new. People who were not gay could happily mimic the chic of the prototype. But all this did not happen without continuing and sometimes violent struggles. Parents might resign themselves to a *bantji* son who could never marry, but they were alarmed by a *gay* son who intended never to get married.

The Genius

Djinius, henyo (from the Spanish *genio*), and *phu mi panya leut* (a clumsy neologism meant to ward off "genius") did not exist, as such, in premodern and even colonial Southeast Asia. Following the rules of Romanticism, the "genius" has to be an individual with a name (no one knows exactly who designed the Borobodur and Angkor Wat or who carved their magnificent bas-reliefs). He or she appears unpredictably out of nowhere and has no genius parents or genius children. He or she cannot be the intended "product" of traditional education or of the nation-state's high schools and universities. The genius represents a kind of hypermodernity, the modernity-to-come, or in a different terminology, an explosive avant-garde. The genius can retrospectively be cast as a "national" hero or heroine, yet always exceeding or transgressing nationality, since he or she is understood as a "world figure"—that is, recognized as such around the globe. Both the Philippines and Siam have heaps of "national artists," but their comfortable rotas include no geniuses. Exemplary is the case of Siam's Apichatpong Weerasethakul, an unassuming man of partial Chinese descent, raised in the poverty-stricken northeast, who last year won the Palme d'Or at the Cannes Film Festival, the highest award in the international cinema world. This success was not a lucky shot; he had won other Cannes prizes for two earlier films. You might think that the "educated" classes in Siam would be thrilled by a countryman's spectacular international success. Alas, he is not a "national artist." So his films have been censored, given very limited local circulation, and sometimes denounced as un-Thai. Of course, in his early forties, Apichatpong is the kindly idol of young Thai indie moviemakers. But he appears—Romantically—as a genius. There is no Thai word for "avant-garde"—yet.

The Ironist, the Caricaturist, and the Satirist

Once again, the vernacular words for "irony," "caricature," and "satire" are borrowings or adaptations of Western terms, but by no means very recent. Only when they are anthropomorphized do they give birth to figures of modernity. Anyone non-Filipino who today reads José Rizal's two wonderful pioneering novels (1887 and 1891) will recognize that "the First Filipino" was a master of irony, satire, and social caricature, fully aware of his debt to the great Spanish satirist Mariano José de Larra (who killed himself at the age of twenty-eight). But most Filipinos think of him as a national martyr and defender of his colonized countrymen. Irony and nationalism seldom go comfortably together. Indonesia's Pramoedya Ananta Toer, born sixty-four years after Rizal, was also a master of these "black arts," but he lived in a different era and was jailed for many more years by his countrymen than by the colonialists. With him, the magical figural words appear. His great collection of short stories from the late 1950s, called *Tales from Jakarta* (*Tjerita dari Djakarta*), has the sardonic subtitle, *Caricatures of Circumstances and Their Human Beings.* One of the most famous stories in his earlier collection, *Tales from Blora* (*Tjerita dari Blora*), includes the ironically titled *Dia jang Menjerah,* situated in the bloody turmoil of the Revolution (1945–1949). The title appears to mean "She Who Gave Up," suggesting that the heroine will become the antifigure of the revolutionary activist who naturally will never "give up." But, as the story proceeds, the reader perceives that *menjerah* is used to mean "self-sacrifice." At the same time, "She Who Gave Up" does not disappear. Pramoedya's irony depends on the paradoxical counterpoint between the two.

Pramoedya belonged to the "revolutionary generation," which in old age he mournfully described as a tragic failure. Perhaps for this reason, he represents above all the Ironist. In the post–Cold War era, in the time of postcoloniality, a newer figure emerges. The best example is probably Amir Muhammad, Malaysian director of the scorchingly funny, faux-documentary, *The Big Durian.* Amir is young enough to have calm contempt for the permanent government of United Malays National Organisation and its toadying Chinese and Indian allies. One can find comparable contempt for ruling oligarchies among younger-generation Indonesians and Filipinos. If irony belongs with tragedy, then scorn goes nicely with satire. Yet Amir's brilliant film is interesting not for his scorn but for his original method in representing it. *The Big Durian* appears to the first-time viewer as a string of interviews with a variety of Malaysian citizens about their memories of and reactions to a Malay soldier who ran amok in part of Kuala Lumpur's Chinatown some years earlier. The memory of the (1969) savage government-steered race riots in the capital is part of the film's subtext, and this is casually mentioned in Amir's quiet, humorous voice-over commentary. It takes a second viewing to realize that all the "citizens" are highly trained professional actors and actresses. Maybe it takes a third viewing to see that most of these over-the-top "citizens" are satirized "figures of modernity": the loudmouth Malay street orator; the sly, amused Chinese businessman; the Eurasian human rights activist; the chatty East Malaysian janitor; the young Indian lawyer just back from study in the UK; the goodhearted, naïve female university student; the cynical Malay taxi driver; the chic young Chinese woman who can't understand why anyone could find pork repulsive; and so on. Amir has them all speak in the language that belongs to each figure—Hokkien, English, Malay. What is so enchanting about this satirical film is that Amir the Satirist, a real figure of modernity, gets his effects exactly from parading a world of "fictional" figures of modernity juxtaposed to one another.

The Criminal

Elderly Indonesians will often nostalgically recall the figure of Kusni Kasdut, bank robber par excellence, Houdini-like escaper from jail after jail, and occasional killer. One source of the nostalgia is the legend that Kusni had been an active participant in the Revolution but earned nothing from it, was disappointed with its aftermath, and was enraged by growing social and economic inequality in his country. You could therefore say that he *had a reason to turn to crime.* The second is that he is remembered, rightly or wrongly, as a Robin Hood of sorts, targeting only rich people and rich institutions. He was an outlaw facing the power of the state, and in the end he was executed by it. But as Walter Benjamin famously wrote, "It is now possible to see a new beauty in what is vanishing." Kusni is well remembered because he was the last of his kind.

   In the early 1980s, I received a telephone call from a nice woman lawyer in West Germany asking me to serve as an expert witness for a client of hers, an Indonesian fighting extradition back to his homeland. The man claimed, quite reasonably as it turned out, that he would be executed if he was extradited home. In letters he told me that his father, a high-up in the military police, had warned him to leave the country immediately. Otherwise he would probably be murdered by Petrus, or *penembak misterius* (mysterious killers). Petrus, mainly elite army commandos in civvies, had been killing thousands of small-time gangsters and bullyboys on President Suharto's secret orders. I told the lady that I would gladly testify that the danger was very real, and that he ought to get asylum. But he would have to tell the German judges that he was a small-time gangster, extorting money for his boss from the owners of bars, whorehouses, gambling dens, and so on. The client, however, refused to do this. In a letter to me, written in perfect Indonesian bureaucratese, he said that he had always served the government by doing jobs that the police and the military wished to avoid—a sort of dirty left hand of the state. He insisted that he was absolutely not an outlaw. So I told his lawyer there was nothing I could do for him.

In the early 1980s, such people were officially called *gali-gali,* an acronym for Gabungan Anak Liar or Wild Youth Gangs, which implied antistate teenage lawlessness. In fact, they were mostly petty adult hoodlums who had been employed for a decade by Ali Murtopo, boss of Opsus (Suharto's personal political intelligence organization), primarily to ensure monotonous electoral victories for the regime. But suddenly, in 1980, anti-Chinese riots spread across many towns in Central Java. The visible participation of petty hoodlums in the riots led the president to believe that Murtopo was not to be trusted to use his bullyboys on behalf of the regime. It looks likely that *gali-gali* was invented to mean an uncontrollable menace to public order, as Suharto geared up for Petrus. After the killings ended, *gali-gali* disappeared, to be replaced by *preman.* A corruption of the Dutch word *vrijman* or "freeman," it came to be used in the late colonial and early postrevolutionary period for a policeman or a soldier in mufti. By the late 1980s, it meant a gangster working for the state and usually managed by special police or military units; you could say, a civil servant in mufti. Such people proliferated enormously after 1990 and are integral to the functioning of today's political and economic systems—and still busy with extortion, intimidation, arson, fake mob violence, and, on and off, torture and murder: a peculiar kind of anti-Kusni figure of modernity.

On a smaller scale, one can see, in the arena of sex crimes, another kind of supersession. Some time ago, respectable newspapers and tabloids reported on the mysterious appearance of a serial rapist, colloquially referred to as Kolor Idjau/Idjo, meaning "Green Bikini-Briefs." He was said to enter houses at dead of night wearing only his signal underwear, to magically overcome women's resistance, and to disappear as eerily as he had arrived. The identity of Kolor Idjo was never discovered; his reality became disputed, but his sepia-photograph outlaw allure did not fade. Only his bright, sexy bikini assigned him to modernity. On the other hand, at the same time Indonesia began to discover that it had serial killers (*pembunuh berantai*): the Batak black-magician Ahmad Suradji, who killed forty-two women in North Sumatra during the 1990s; Siswanto, aka Robot Gedek (Woven Bamboo Robot), who in the same period sodomized and then murdered small street boys in Jakarta and Central Java; and later on, Very Idam Henyansah, aka Ryan, the "Butcher of Djombang," who mutilated and slaughtered gays with whom he had had sexual relations. Such people are thought not to have existed in Indonesia until very recently and are probably copycats of notorious serial killers in advanced countries such as the United States, the UK, France, and Russia. Against the silhouette of legendary Kusni, the antistate outlaw who "had his reasons," they loom up as incomprehensible, terrifying, antisociety figures of modernity.

NOTES

PROLOGUE

1. The study is reported in Ulf Hannerz, *Foreign News* (Chicago: University of Chicago Press, 2004).

2. On such matters, see Engseng Ho, *The Graves of Tarim* (Berkeley: University of California Press, 2006), and Eric Tagliacozzo, ed., *Southeast Asia and the Middle East* (Singapore: NUS Press, 2009).

3. The most important propagator of the globalized "plural society" concept was no doubt the British social anthropologist M. G. Smith, Jamaican-born, a fieldworker in the Caribbean and West Africa (but not in Southeast Asia) and for a period academically based in the USA. See Smith, *The Plural Society in the British West Indies* (Berkeley: University of California Press, 1965), and Leo Kuper and M. G. Smith, eds., *Pluralism in Africa* (Berkeley: University of California Press, 1969).

4. For a somewhat retrospective overview of the concept (by a Southeast Asia specialist), see Judith Nagata, "Plural Societies," in *International Encyclopedia of the Social and Behavioral Sciences,* eds. Neil J. Smelser and Paul B. Baltes, vol. 17, 11513–11516 (Oxford: Elsevier, 2001).

5. To allude to an anthropological introduction to mainland Southeast Asia from an earlier period: Robbins Burling, *Hill Farms and Padi Fields* (Englewood Cliffs, NJ: Prentice-Hall, 1965).

6. Mostly on "studying down" and "up," see Laura Nader, "Up the Anthropologist—Perspectives Gained from Studying Up," in *Reinventing Anthropology,* ed. Dell Hymes (New York: Pantheon, 1972); on studying "up," Hugh Gusterson, "Studying Up Revisited," *Political and Legal Anthropology Review* 20, no. 1 (1997): 114–119; on studying "sideways," Ulf Hannerz, "Other Transnationals: Perspectives Gained from Studying

247

Sideways," *Paideuma* 44 (1998): 109–123, and "up" and "sideways," Sherry
Ortner, "Access: Reflections on Studying Up in Hollywood," *Ethnography*
11, no. 2 (2010): 211–233.

7. I have in mind not Leach's classic *Political Systems of Highland Burma,* itself
drawing on field experiences of a very particular kind, but rather books such
as Manning Nash, *Golden Road to Modernity* (New York: Wiley, 1965), or
Melford E. Spiro, *Buddhism and Society* (Berkeley: University of California
Press, 1970).

8. True, there are occasional entrances and new presences as well: After the Cold
War, for example, field research in Russia and Eastern and Central Europe
became increasingly feasible for expatriate ethnographers.

INTRODUCTION

1. Raymond Williams, *Keywords: A Vocabulary of Culture and Society* (Oxford,
UK: Oxford University Press, 1985).

2. For other collaborative projects inspired by *Keywords,* see Tony Bennett,
Lawrence Grossberg, and Meaghan Morris, eds., *New Keywords: A Revised
Vocabulary of Culture and Society* (Oxford, UK: Blackwell, 2005); Bregje
Van Eeckelen, Jennifer Gonzalez, Bettina Stotzer, and Anna Tsing, eds., *Shock
and Awe: The War on Words* (Santa Cruz, CA: New Pacific Press, 2004).

3. Entry for "figure, *n.,*" meaning 2b, in *The Oxford Encyclopedic English
Dictionary,* 2nd ed., eds. Judy Pearsall and Bill Trumble (New York: Oxford
University Press, 1995), 518.

4. We are grateful to Joseph Errington for this observation.

5. For an interesting anthropological illustration of dynamics of the figure/
ground opposition as applied to Brasilia's cityscape, see James Holston, "The
Modernist City and the Death of the Street," in *Theorizing the City: The New
Urban Anthropology Reader,* ed. Setha M. Low (New Brunswick, NJ: Rutgers
University Press, 2002), 245–276.

6. Walter Benjamin, "Paris, Capital of the Nineteenth Century," in *Reflections:
Essays, Aphorisms, Autobiographical Writings,* ed. Peter Demetz (New York:
Schoken Books, 1986).

7. Raymond Williams, *The Long Revolution* (Harmondsworth: Pelican, 1961).

8. Ara Wilson, *The Intimate Economies of Bangkok: Tomboys, Tycoons, and
Avon Ladies in the Global City* (Berkeley: University of California Press,
2004), 191. Wilson's work on "intimate economies" specificically emphasizes how "symbolic figures condense gender, ethnicity, and class, often with
sexual associations," but we argue that this notion can be fruitfully expanded
to include politics, religion, global exchanges, mediascapes, and other key
features of modern life.

9. For a summary of the sociological literature on social types, see Oz Almog,
"The Problem of Social Type: A Review," *Electronic Journal of Sociology* 3,

no. 4 (1998). Available from http://www.sociology.org/ejs-archives, accessed September 15, 2011.

10. Max Weber, *The Protestant Ethic and the Spirit of Capitalism* (New York: Routledge, 2001); Max Weber, "Basic Sociological Terms," in *Economy and Society*, eds. Guenther Roth and Claus Wittich (Berkeley: University of California Press, 1978), 4–6.

11. For instance, in much social science literature on migration the "immigrant" has emerged as a social type in relation to processes of nation-state building. In this process, a social type becomes integrated with a particular political discourse that defines insiders and outsiders. See Andreas Wimmer and Nina Glick Schiller, "Methodological Nationalism and Beyond: Nation-State Building, Migration, and the Social Sciences," *Global Networks* 2, vol. 4 (2002): 301–334.

12. James T. Siegel, *A New Criminal Type in Jakarta: Counter-Revolution Today* (Durham, NC: Duke University Press, 1998).

13. Rosalind Morris, "Discussant Remarks for Panel on Figures of Indonesian Modernity," American Anthropological Association Annual Meetings, San Francisco, November 19–23, 2008.

14. See Richard Baxstrom, "Strangers, Counterfeiters, and Gangsters: Figures of Belonging and the Problem of Belief," in *Houses in Motion: The Experience of Place and the Problem of Belief in Urban Malaysia* (Stanford, CA: Stanford University Press, 2008), in which he ascribes this capacity to figures rather than types per se.

15. We thank Mike McGovern for helping us express this broader point.

16. Benedict Anderson, "Cultural Roots," in *Imagined Communities: Reflections on the Origins and Spread of Nationalism* (New York: Verson, 1991).

17. James T. Siegel, *Fetish, Recognition, Revolution* (Princeton, NJ: Princeton University Press, 1997), 97–114; 161–180.

18. James C. Scott, *Weapons of the Weak: Everyday Forms of Peasant Resistance* (New Haven, CT: Yale University Press, 1985), 23.

19. Rudolf Mrazek, "Indonesian Dandy," in *Engineers of Happy Land: Technology and Nationalism in a Colony* (Princeton, NJ: Princeton University Press, 2002), 129–159.

20. Fenella Cannell, *Power and Intimacy in the Christian Philippines* (Cambridge: Cambridge University Press, 1999), 225.

21. Vicente L. Rafael, "Introduction: Criminality and Its Others," in *Figures of Criminality in Indonesia, the Philippines and Colonial Vietnam*, ed. Vicente L. Rafael (Ithaca, NY: SEAP Publications, 1999).

22. Benedict Anderson, *The Spectre of Comparisons: Nationalism, Southeast Asia and the World* (New York: Verso, 1998), 3–13.

23. In 1950, Indonesia's population was 12.4 percent urban and in 2000 it was 42 percent urban. Over the same period, the urban population grew from 16.5 percent to 31.1 percent in Thailand; from 27.1 percent to 48.1 percent in the

Philippines; and from 11.6 percent to 24.3 percent in Vietnam. Figures are from Gavin W. Jones and Mike Douglass, *Mega-Urban Regions in Pacific Asia: Urban Dynamics in a Global Era* (Singapore: NUS Press, 2008), 3.

24. Norman G. Owen, *The Emergence of Modern Southeast Asia* (Honolulu: University of Hawai'i Press, 2005), 382–385.
25. Aihwa Ong, *Neoliberalism as Exception: Mutations in Citizenship and Sovereignty* (Durham, NC: Duke University Press, 2006), 77.
26. When Cambodia joined ASEAN on April 30, 1999, all the countries of Southeast Asia but East Timor were officially members. In 2011, East Timor formally applied for membership.
27. Paul H. Kratoska, Remco Raben, and Henk Schulte Nordholt, eds., *Locating Southeast Asia: Geographies of Knowledge and Politics of Space,* Research in International Studies, Southeast Asia Series No. 111 (Athens: Ohio University Press, 2005).
28. John Funston, ed., *Government and Politics in Southeast Asia* (London: Zed Books, 2001).
29. David Kelly, "Freedom—a Eurasian Mosaic," in *Asian Freedoms: The Idea of Freedom in East and Southeast Asia,* eds. David Kelly and Anthony Reid (Cambridge: Cambridge University Press, 1998), 5.
30. Richard Robinson and David Goodman, "The New Rich in Asia: Economic Development, Social Status and Political Consciousness," in *The New Rich in Asia: Mobile Phones, McDonald's and Middle-class Revolution,* eds. Richard Robinson and David Goodman (New York: Routledge, 1996), 6.
31. Ong, *Neoliberalism as Exception*; Vedi Hadiz, "The Rise of Neo-Third Worldism? The Indonesian Trajectory and the Consolidation of Illiberal Democracy," *Third World Quarterly* 25, no. 1 (2004): 51–71.
32. Simon Springer, *Cambodia's Neoliberal Order: Violence, Authoritarianism, and the Contestation of Public Space* (New York: Routledge, 2010).
33. Ong, *Neoliberalism as Exception.* For a further argument on the way neoliberalism transforms governance in China, see Aihwa Ong and Li Zhang, *Privatizing China: Socialism from Afar* (Ithaca, NY: Cornell University Press, 2008).
34. In Indonesia, for instance, radical Islamic groups were oppressed and jailed during the Suharto era but became significant political actors with *reformasi* after 1998 and particularly after the first Bali bomb in 2002, which killed over two hundred people.
35. See Aihwa Ong, *Spirits of Resistance and Capitalist Discipline: Factory Women in Malaysia* (Albany: SUNY Press, 1987); Mary Beth Mills, *Thai Women in the Global Labor Force: Consuming Desires, Contested Selves* (New Brunswick, NJ: Rutgers University Press, 1999); and Diane L. Wolf, *Factory Daughters: Gender, Household Dynamics, and Rural Industrialization in Java* (Berkeley: University of California Press, 1994).
36. Robinson and Goodman's *New Rich in Asia* contains chapters on Singapore,

Malaysia, Indonesia, and Thailand. It includes the Philippines as something of an outlier, whose "economic fortunes have commonly been portrayed as the inverse of those in other countries in the region" and more recently "is commonly viewed as the single economic failure in the region." Michael Pinches, "The Philippines' New Rich: Capitalist Transformation amidst Economic Gloom," in Robinson and Goodman, *New Rich in Asia*, 105.

37. Singapore is the only Chinese-majority country in the region and was founded on Chinese migration flows in the nineteenth century.

38. For an extended discussion of those left out of the so-called Asian miracle, see Jonathan Rigg, "Marginal People and Marginal Lives: The 'Excluded,'" in *Southeast Asia: The Human Landscape of Modernization and Development* (London: Routledge, 1997), 69–151.

39. Sandra Dudley, *Materialising Exile: Material Culture and Embodied Experience among the Karenni Refugees in Thailand* (New York: Berghahn Books, 2010); Alexander Horstmann and Reed Wadley, eds., *Centering the Margin: Agency and Narrative in Southeast Asian Borderlands* (New York: Berghahn, 2006).

40. Christine Chin, "'Diversification' and 'Privatisation': Securing Insecurities in the Receiving Country of Malaysia," *Asia Pacific Journal of Anthropology* 9, no. 4 (2008): 285–303.

41. See, for instance, Nana Oishi, *Women in Motion: Globalization, State Policies, and Labor Migration in Asia* (Stanford, CA: Stanford University Press, 2005).

42. On Asian tourism, see Tim Winter, Peggy Teo, and T. C. Chang, eds., *Asia on Tour: Exploring the Rise of Asian Tourism* (London: Routledge, 2008).

43. On Facebook, see www.checkfacebook.com, accessed July 1, 2011; on Twitter, see http://www.greyreview.com/2010/04/20/105779710-million-users-and-new-estimates-of-twitter-users-in-asia/, accessed July 1, 2011.

44. Nikolas Rose, *Powers of Freedom: Reframing Political Thought* (Cambridge: Cambridge University Press, 1999); Nguyễn-võ Thu-hương, *The Ironies of Freedom: Sex, Culture, and Neoliberal Governance in Vietnam* (Seattle: University of Washington Press, 2008); Ong and Zhang, *Privatizing China*, 4. In both China and Vietnam, state rule under market socialism is not disabled but is actually revitalized by many aspects of neoliberalism.

45. Oliver Wolters, *History, Culture, and Region in Southeast Asian Perspective* (Ithaca, NY: Cornell University Southeast Asia Program, 1999), 41–46.

46. Ibid., 151.

47. On "postmodernity," see Jean-François Lyotard, *The Post-Modern Condition* (Minneapolis: University of Minnesota Press, 1985); on "late modernity," see the entry in John Scott and Gordon Marshall, eds., *Oxford Dictionary of Sociology* (Oxford: Oxford University Press, 2005); on "second modernity," see Ulrich Beck and Edgar Grande, "Varieties of Second Modernity: The Cosmopolitan Turn in Social and Political Theory and Research," *British Journal*

of Sociology 61, no. 3 (2010): 409–443; on "high modernity" and "radicalized modernity," see Anthony Giddens, *The Consequences of Modernity* (Stanford, CA: Stanford University Press, 1991), 150, 163; on "the contemporary," see Paul Rabinow, *Marking Time: On the Anthropology of the Contemporary* (Princeton, NJ: Princeton University Press, 2008).

48. Beck and Grande, "Varieties of Second Modernity," 410–412.
49. Giddens, *Consequences of Modernity*, 1.
50. See Ulrich Beck, "The Cosmopolitan Perspective: Sociology of the Second Age of Modernity," *British Journal of* Sociology 51, no. 1 (2000): 79–105; Dilip Gaonkar, *Alternative Modernities* (Durham, NC: Duke University Press, 2001); Shmuel Eisenstadt, *Comparative Civilizations and Multiple Modernities* (Boston: Brill, 2003). See also Robert Weller, *Alternate Civilities: Democracy and Culture in China and Taiwan* (Boulder, CO: Westview, 1999).
51. For a useful ethnography describing eminently modern sensibilities in the most unlikely of places, see Philip Taylor, *Cham Muslims of the Mekong Delta: Place and Mobility in the Cosmopolitan Periphery* (Singapore: NUS Press, 2007).
52. "As such, modernity and tradition are not opposed, but paired." Paul Rabinow, *Marking Time,* 2.
53. Ong and Zhang, *Privatizing China,* 16.
54. Anderson, *Imagined Communities.*
55. Takashi Shiraishi, *An Age in Motion: Popular Radicalism in Java, 1912–1926* (Ithaca, NY: Cornell University Press, 1990).
56. Clifford Geertz, *Negara: The Theatre State in Nineteenth-Century Bali* (Princeton, NJ: Princeton University Press, 1980).
57. Thongchai Winichakul, *Siam Mapped: A History of the Geo-Body of a Nation* (Honolulu: University of Hawai'i Press, 1994).
58. Faisal Devji, *Landscapes of the Jihad: Militancy, Morality, Modernity* (Ithaca, NY: Cornell University Press, 2005).
59. Mary Beth Mills, *Thai Women in the Global Labor Force: Consuming Desires, Contested Selves* (New Brunswick, NJ: Rutgers University Press, 1999), 14.
60. Compare Clifford Geertz, *The Religion of Java* (Chicago: University of Chicago Press, 1976 [1960]), 148–161, with Robert Hefner, "Islam in an Era of Nation-States," in *Islam in an Era of Nation-States: Politics and Religious Renewal in Muslim Southeast Asia*, eds. Robert Hefner and Patricia Horvatich (Honolulu: University of Hawai'i Press, 1997), 3–41.
61. Georg Simmel, "The Stranger," in *Georg Simmel on Individuality and Social Forms*, ed. Donald Levine (Chicago: University of Chicago Press, 1971), 143–149, quote from p. 143. Zygmunt Bauman uses Simmel's essay to explore the bureaucracy of the Holocaust. See his *Modernity and the Holocaust* (Ithaca, NY: Cornell University Press, 1989); Max Weber, "The Sociology of Charismatic Authority," in *From Max Weber: Essays in Sociology*, eds. H. H.

Gerth and C. Wright Mills (New York: Oxford University Press, 1958), 245–252. See also Benedict Anderson's critique of Weber's analysis of charismatic authority: "The Idea of Power in Javanese Culture," in *Culture and Politics in Indonesia*, ed. Claire Holt (Ithaca, NY: Cornell University Press, 1972), 1–69.

62.   James C. Scott, *The Art of Not Being Governed*; Willem van Schendel, "Geographies of Knowing, Geographies of Ignorance: Jumping Scale in Southeast Asia," in Kratoska, Raben, and Nordholt, *Locating Southeast Asia*, 275–307.

1 THE PHILIPPINES

1.   Victor Turner, "Liminality and Communitas," in *The Ritual Process: Structure and Anti-Structure* (Chicago: Aldine Publishing, 1969), 94–113, 125–130.

2.   Benjamin Pimentel, "Noynoy Takes Away the Wangwang," *Philippine Daily Inquirer,* July 4, 2010.

3.   See Michael Pinches, "Modernism and the Quest for Modernity: Architectural Form, Squatter Settlements, and the New Society in Manila," in *Cultural Identity and Urban Change in Southeast Asia,* ed. Marc Askew and William Logan (Geelong, Australia: Deakin University Press, 1994), 13–42.

4.   Dipesh Chakraborty, *Provincializing Europe: Postcolonial Thought and His-torical Difference* (Princeton, NJ: Princeton University Press, 2000).

5.   For an authoritative account of servants in precolonial Philippines, see William Henry Scott, *Barangay: Sixteenth-Century Philippine Culture and Society* (Manila: Ateneo de Manila University Press, 1994), 219, 225–229.

6.   Mary H. Fee, *A Woman's Impressions of the Philippines* (Chicago: A. C. McClurg & Co., 1910), 75.

7.   Ibid., 239.

8.   Amy Chua discusses her aunt's murder at the hands of her chauffer in *World on Fire: How Exporting Free Market Democracy Breeds Ethnic Hatred and Global Instability* (New York: Anchor Books, 2004).

9.   Edgar B. Wickberg, "The Chinese Mestizo in Philippine History," *Journal of Southeast Asian History* 5 (1964): 97.

10.   Ibid, 9.

11.   Aihwa Ong and Donald Nonini, eds., *Ungrounded Empires: The Cultural Politics of Modern Chinese Transnationalism* (New York: Routledge, 1997), 26.

12.   Louis Althusser, "Ideology and Ideological State Apparatuses (Notes towards an Investigation)," in *The Anthropology of the State: A Reader,* eds. Aradhana Sharma and Akhil Gupta (Victoria, Australia: Blackwell, 2006), 86–111.

13.   On the figure of *bagong bayani,* for example, see Vicente Rafael, "Your Grief is Our Gossip: Overseas Filipinos and Other Spectral Presences," in *White Love and Other Events in Filipino History* (Durham, NC: Duke University Press, 2000); Rhacel Salazar Parreñas, *Servants of Globalization: Women,*

Migration, and Domestic Work (Stanford, CA: Stanford University Press, 2001); and Neferti X. Tadiar, *Fantasy-Production: Sexual Economies and Other Philippine Consequences for the New World Order* (Hong Kong: Hong Kong University Press, 2004).

14. Nicole Constable, *Maid in Hong Kong: An Ethnography of Filipina Workers* (Ithaca, NY: Cornell University Press, 1997); Parreñas, *Servants of Globalization*; Tadiar, *Fantasy-Production.*

15. See especially Walden Bello's extensive critiques on neoliberalism in the Philippines and Asia, "free-trade" and economic globalization, and Philippine debts and the Philippines' overreliance on OFW remittances.

16. See also Walden Bello, *Deglobalization: Ideas for a New World Economy,* (London: Zed Books, 2005).

17. For more analysis on the fissures and gaps in dominant Philippine state narratives of Filipino seafaring, as well as the "crosscurrents of masculinities," see Kale Bantigue Fajardo, *Filipino Crosscurrents: Oceanographies of Seafaring, Masculinities, and Globalization* (Minneapolis: University of Minnesota Press, 2011).

18. I dedicate this essay to KSu.

19. Anna Romina Guevarra, *Marketing Dreams, Manufacturing Heroes: The Transnational Labor Brokering of Filipino Workers* (New Brunswick, NJ: Rutgers University Press, 2010).

20. Nikolas Rose, *Powers of Freedom: Reframing Political Thought* (Cambridge: Cambridge University Press, 1999).

21. These are gatherings promoting religiosity as a way to cope with personal struggles.

22. Eric Gutierrez and Saturnino Borras Jr., *The Moro Conflict: Landlessness and Misdirected State Policies,* Policy Studies 8 (Washington, D.C.: East-West Center Washington, 2004).

23. John Sidel, *Capital, Coercion and Crime: Bossism in the Philippines* (Stanford, CA: Stanford University Press, 1999).

24. The use of terms such as "family farm" and "household enterprise" often connote some kind of tacit agreeability between household members, when in fact interactions are often structured by tension and disagreement— particularly between husbands and wives with respect to the investment of remittances. See James Eder, "Gender Relations and Household Economic Planning in the Rural Philippines," *Journal of Southeast Asian Studies* 37 (2006): 397–413.

25. See, for example, Benedict Kerkvliet, *Everyday Politics in the Philippines: Class and Status Relations in a Central Luzon Village* (Berkeley: University of California Press, 1990).

26. More recent work by Deidre McKay is a notable exception. See "Reading Remittances Landscapes: Female Migration and Agricultural Transition in the Philippines," *Geografisk Tidsskrift, Danish Journal of Geography* 105,

no. 1 (2005): 89–99; and also "Cultivating New Local Futures: Remittance Economies and Land-Use Patterns in Ifugao, Philippines," *Journal of Southeast Asian Studies* 34, no. 2 (2003): 285–306.

27.   See, for example, Katherine Gibson, Lisa Law, and Deirdre McKay, "Beyond Heroes and Victims: Filipina Contract Migrants, Economic Activism and Class Transformations," *International Feminist Journal of Politics* 3, no. 3 (2001): 365–386.

28.   Martin Manalansan, *Global Divas: Filipino Gay Men in the Diaspora* (Durham, NC: Duke University Press, 2006).

29.   See the documentaries "Paper Dolls" and the "Amazing Truth about Queen Raquela."

30.   See also Mark Johnson, *Beauty and Power: Transgendering and Cultural Transformation in the Southern Philippines* (New York: Berg, 1997), and Fenella Cannell, *Power and Intimacy in the Christian Philippines* (New York: Cambridge University Press, 1999).

31.   Arlie Hochschild, *The Managed Heart: The Commercialization of Human Feeling* (Berkeley: University of California Press, 1983).

32.   Neil Brenner, Jamie Peck, and Nik Theodore, "After Neoliberalization?" *Globalizations* 7, no. 3 (2010): 327–345.

33.   Ma. Joy V. Abrenica and Gilberto M. Llanto, "Services," in *The Philippine Economy: Development, Policies, and Challenges,* eds. Arsenio Balisacan and Hal Hill (Quezon City: Ateneo de Manila University Press, 2003), 262.

34.   Aneesh Aneesh, *Virtual Migration: The Programming of Globalization* (Durham, NC: Duke University Press, 2006).

35.   Tadiar, *Fantasy-Production.*

36.   *Ate* means "sister" in Tagalog and is commonly used in addressing an older girl or woman.

37.   The program derived inspiration from China's health care system, a system that works from the villages. Those trained were called "barefoot doctors" because many of them had limited formal education.

38.   Paul Farmer, *Pathologies of Power: Health, Human Rights, and the New War on the Poor* (Berkeley: University of California Press, 2005).

39.   S. Singh, A. Moore, A. Bankole, F. Mirembe, D. Wulf, and E. Prada, eds., *Unintended Pregnancy and Induced Abortion in the Philippines Causes and Consequences* (New York: Guttmacher Institute, 2006).

40.   Ibid.

41.   The *barangay* is the smallest unit of government in the Philippines. A *kagawad* is a *barangay* councilor.

42.   Thanks to Bea Lorente for her insightful views on earlier drafts of this essay and Gene Navera for his expert views on beauty pageants in the Philippines.

43.   Readers may wish to view the video of Janina's response. See "Janina San Miguel—Bb. Pilipinas 2008 Q&A," uploaded March 8, 2008: http://www.youtube.com/watch?v=xKwmseoKFCo.

44. R. Constantino, "The Mis-Education of the Filipino," *Journal of Contemporary Asia* 1, no. 1 (1970): 20–36.
45. See J. W. Tollefson, *Planning Language, Planning Inequality: Language Policy in the Community* (New York: Longman, 1991), and B. Sibayan and A. Gonzalez., "Post-Imperial English in the Philippines," in *Post-Imperial English: Status Change in Former British and American Colonies, 1940–1990*, eds. J. A. Fishman, A. W. Condrad, and A. Rubal-Lopez (New York: Mouton de Gruyter, 1996), 139–172.
46. A. Gonzalez, "The Role and Contribution of the Thomasites to Language Education," in *Back to the Future*, eds. C. D. Villareal, T. E. Arambulo, and G. M. Pesigan (Manila: American Studies Association of the Philippines, 2003), 53–62.
47. Ibid.
48. Parreñas, *Servants of Globalization.*
49. "Miss Philippines World's Ear-Splitting English an 'Eye-Opener' for RP—Solon," Broadcast March 10, 2008. http://www.gmanews.tv/story/84929/miss-philippines-worlds-ear-splitting-english-an-eye-opener-for-rp-solon.

2 VIETNAM

1. See Kate Jellema, "Returning Home: Ancestor Veneration and the Nationalism of Đổi Mới Vietnam," in *Modernity and Re-Enchantment: Religion in Post-Revolutionary Vietnam*, ed. Philip Taylor (Lanham, MA: Lexington Books, 2007), 57–89.
2. James Ferguson, *Expectations of Modernity: Myths and Meanings of Urban Life on the Zambian Copperbelt* (Berkeley: University of California Press, 1999), 13.
3. For important discussions of this, see Philip Taylor, *Fragments of the Present: Searching for Modernity in Vietnam's South* (Honolulu: University of Hawaiʻi Press, 2001); Philip Taylor, *Cham Muslims of the Mekong Delta: Place and Mobility in the Cosmopolitan Periphery* (Singapore: NUS Press, 2007); and Taylor, *Modernity and Re-Enchantment*. An especially insightful example can be found in Barley Norton, *Songs for the Spirits: Music and Mediums in Modern Vietnam* (Chicago: University of Illinois Press, 2009). Norton notes that "spirits have retained their relevance in modern Vietnam because of their capacity to speak to diverse issues and concerns." Modernity, Norton indicates, must be understood as a complex, versatile comingling of tradition with notions of what it means to be modern and advanced. In one telling example, the "Second Mandarin," a spirit incarnated in the course of a *hau ta* (thanking ritual) tells Norton to "pray for spiritual gifts and talent" and to "study in a modern, advanced way" (223).
4. Shaun K. Malarney, *Culture, Ritual and Revolution in Vietnam* (New York: RoutledgeCurzon, 2002), 61.

5. Peter Zinoman, "Introduction: Vũ Trọng Phụng's *Dumb Luck* and the Nature of Vietnamese Modernism," in *Dumb Luck* (Ann Arbor: University of Michigan Press, 2002), 4.
6. For a delightful discussion of these lines introducing Benjamin's classic "Paris—Capital of the Nineteenth Century," see Charles Keith, "A Vietnamese in Paris: Nguyen Trong Hiep and the Capital of the Nineteenth Century," Association for Asian Studies Annual Meeting (2010).
7. Zinoman, "Introduction," 7.
8. Approximately U.S. $5.
9. Dung's experiences and the classification of *tiểu thương* are discussed in greater detail in Ann Marie Leshkowich, "Making Class and Gender: (Market) Socialist Enframing of Traders in Ho Chi Minh City," *American Anthropologist* 113, no. 2 (2011): 277–290.
10. See, for example, Helle Rydstrøm and Lisa Drummond, "Introduction," in *Gender Practices in Contemporary Vietnam,* ed. Lisa Drummond and Helle Rydstrøm (Singapore: Singapore University Press, 2004), 1–25; Ashley Pettus, *Between Sacrifice and Desire: National Identity and the Governing of Femininity in Vietnam* (New York: Routledge, 2003).
11. Katherine Verdery, *What Was Socialism, and What Comes Next?* (Princeton, NJ: Princeton University Press, 1996); Susan Gal and Gail Kligman, *The Politics of Gender after Socialism* (Princeton, NJ: Princeton University Press, 2000); Parvathi Raman and Harry G. West, "Introduction: Poetries of the Past in a Socialist World Remade," in *Enduring Socialism: Explorations of Revolution and Transformation, Restoration and Continuation,* ed. Harry G. West and Parvathi Raman (New York: Berghahn Books, 2009), 1–28.
12. Ken MacLean, "The Rehabilitation of an Uncomfortable Past: Everyday Life in Vietnam during the Subsidy Period (1975–1986)," *History and Anthropology* 19, no. 3 (2008): 281–303.
13. Gayatri Chakravorty Spivak, "Subaltern Studies: Deconstructing Historiography," in *The Spivak Reader,* ed. Donna Landry and Gerald MacLean (New York: Routledge, 1996), 203–235.
14. Vũ Bình and Hoài Trang, "Làm ăn ở chợ Bến Thành" [Making a Living in Bến Thành Market], *Tuổi Trẻ,* October 15, 2006.
15. Dung claimed that the goods she sold were "authentic" factory seconds that had failed international inspection and were diverted to the domestic market.
16. Georg Simmel, *The Philosophy of Money* (London: Routledge, 2004), 376.
17. On the representation of a political threat as if it were a sexual threat, see Neil Hertz's "Medusa's Head: Male Hysteria under Political Pressure," in *The End of the Line: Essays on Psychoanalysis and the Sublime* (New York: Columbia University Press, 1985).
18. See James Siegel, *A New Criminal Type in Jakarta: Counter-Revolution Today* (Durham, NC: Duke University Press, 1998), on the manufacture of images of criminal types by the mass media.

19.   See Charles Bernheimer, *Figures of Ill Repute: Representing Prostitution in Nineteenth Century France* (Durham, NC: Duke University Press, 1997), 98 ff., on prostitutes as commodified images in the new capitalist economies of nineteenth-century Europe.

20.   But this has to be repressed. In this context, one ought to examine closely another "public secret" and another figure often associated with prostitution in Vietnam: corrupt government officials who patronize prostitutes. These cadres formulate government and media discourses about the immorality of prostitutes and decadent youth while participating eagerly in the corrupt and opaque economy they themselves have created since the 1990s—including by sharing prostitutes with clients as they distribute or seek favors.

21.   Karl Polanyi coined the phrase "fictitious commodities" in relationship to land, which he argued was produced "by nature." More recently, however, scholars argue that property rights are always socially constructed. Thus the laboring small investors—both those who succeed and those who fail—are critical figures for converting the value of land.

22.   Domestic investors were often labeled "speculators" (*đầu cơ*) because their transactions were not intended to increase the productive capacity of firms but to generate profit. Many of these domestic investors purchased commodities—gold, lumber, coffee, and increasingly, land—solely to resell for a profit. Yet whether they carried the label of speculator or investor, their labor was critical in creating new commodity forms and markets in Ho Chi Minh City.

23.   David Harvey, *The Urban Experience* (Baltimore: Johns Hopkins University Press, 1989), 167.

24.   Nguyễn Hồng Quân, the minster of construction, estimated that 80 percent of land transfers were "underground" (*ngầm*), as reported in the *Tuổi Trẻ* newspaper, September 19, 2003.

25.   Nguyen Duong, "Officials Vow to Get Tough on Illegal Land Dealings," *Vietnam Investment Review,* October 28, 2002.

26.   Jane I. Guyer, "Composites, Fictions, and Risk: Toward an Ethnography of Price," in *Market and Society: The Great Transformation Today,* ed. Chris Hann and Keith Hart (Cambridge: Cambridge University Press, 2009).

27.   Carolyn Nordstrom, "Shadows and Sovereigns," *Theory, Culture, & Society* 17, no. 4 (2000): 35–54; Akhil Gupta, "Blurred Boundaries: The Discourse of Corruption, the Culture of Politics, and the Imagined State," *American Ethnologist* 22, no. 2 (1995): 375–402.

28.   Nguyễn-Võ Thu-Hương, *The Ironies of Freedom: Sex, Culture, and Neoliberal Governance in Vietnam* (Seattle: University of Washington, 2008), 3–24; Alexei Yurchak, "Governmentality in Post-Socialist Russia," in *The New Entrepreneurs of Europe and Asia,* ed. Victoria Bonell and Thomas Gold (Armonk: M.E. Sharpe, 2002), 278–323.

29.   Katherine Verdery, *The Vanishing Hectare: Property and Value in*

Postsocialist Transylvania (Ithaca: Cornell University Press, 2003), 61–62; Ken MacLean, "The Rehabilitation."

30. Susan Bayly, *Asian Voices in a Postcolonial Age: Vietnam, India and Beyond* (New York: Cambridge University Press, 2007).

31. Đặng Phong, *Tư duy Kinh tế Việt Nam 1975–1989: Nhật ký Thời Bao cấp* (Hanoi: NXB Tri Thức, 2009).

32. See also Melanie Beresford and Đặng Phong, *Economic Transition in Vietnam: Trade and Aid in the Demise of a Centrally Planned Economy* (Northampton, UK: Edward Elgar, 2000), 72–75.

33. On the art and science of socialist planning, see Martha Lampland, *The Object of Labor: Commodification in Socialist Hungary* (Chicago: University of Chicago Press, 1995), 233–273.

34. See Kristen Ghodsee, *The Red Riviera: Gender, Tourism, and Postsocialism on the Black Sea* (Durham, NC: Duke University Press, 2005), and Dominic Boyer, *Spirit and System: Media, Intellectuals, and the Dialectic in Modern German Culture* (Chicago: University of Chicago Press, 2005).

35. The figure's name and e-mail address have been changed, and pseudonyms are used to protect her identity, virtual or otherwise.

36. Anthony R. Welch, "Internationalisation of Vietnamese Higher Education: Retrospect and Prospect," in *Reforming Higher Education in Vietnam*, ed. G. Harman et al. (Springer Science and Business Media, 2010), 202.

37. Hoai Anh Tran and Elisabeth Dalholm, "Favoured Owners, Neglected Tenants: Privatisation of State Owned Housing in Hanoi," *Housing Studies* 20, no. 6 (2005): 897–929.

38. This essay is based on research on education and ethnicity carried out in Vietnam in 2008 as part of the Young Lives study core-funded by the UK Department for International Development (www.younglives.org.uk). The views expressed are those of the author and do not necessarily reflect those of Young Lives, DFID, or other funders.

39. The World Bank, *Country Social Analysis: Ethnicity and Development in Vietnam* (Washington, D.C.: World Bank, 2009).

40. Ibid.

41. Charles F. Keyes, "The Peoples of Asia—Science and Politics in the Classification of Ethnic Groups in Thailand, China and Vietnam," *Journal of Asian Studies* 61 (winter 1997): 1163–1203.

42. Benedict Anderson, *Imagined Communities: Reflections on the Origin and Spread of Nationalism* (London: Verso, 1983).

43. Gerald Hickey, *Window on a War: An Anthropologist in the Vietnam Conflict* (Lubbock: Texas Tech University Press, 2003).

44. Oscar Salemink, *The Ethnography of Vietnam's Central Highlanders: A Historical Contextualization, 1850–1990* (Honolulu: University of Hawai'i Press, 2003).

45. Anne Fadiman, *The Spirit Catches You and You Fall Down* (New York: Farrar Strauss & Giroux, 1998).

46. Sherry B. Ortner, *Anthropology and Social Theory: Culture, Power, and the Acting Subject* (Durham, NC: Duke University Press, 2006).

47. James C. Scott, *The Art of Not Being Governed: An Anarchist History of Upland Southeast Asia* (New Haven, CT: Yale University Press, 2009), 36–37.

48. Pierre Gourou, *Indochine Française: Le Tonkin* (Paris: Mâcon, 1931), 236–237.

49. Cf. John T. McAlister Jr., "Mountain Minorities and the Viet Minh: A Key to the Indochina War," in *Southeast Asian Tribes, Minorities, and Nations*, ed. Peter Kunstadter (Princeton, NJ: Princeton University Press, 1967), 771–844.

50. Cf. Tạ Long and Ngô Thị Chính, *Sự Biến đổi nền Nông nghiệp Châu Thổ-Thái Bình ở Vùng núi Điện Biên Lai Châu* (Hanoi: NXB Nông Nghiệp, 2000).

51. Hội Nghệ Sĩ Nhiếp Ảnh Việt Nam, *Lịch Sử Nhiếp Ảnh Việt Nam (sơ thảo)* [History of Vietnamese Photography (A Rough Draft)] (Hanoi: NXB Văn Hóa-Thông Tin, 1993), 22.

52. The term has been in use at least since the postrevolutionary period. I have found it in publications from the 1950s.

53. Tô Ngọc Thanh, "Nghệ Nhân Dân Gian: Tài Sản Vô Giá Của Nền Văn Hóa Việt Nam" (Master of Folklore: An Invaluable Property of Vietnam Traditional Culture), in *Hội Văn Nghệ Dân Gian Việt Nam: Nghệ Nhân Dân Gian* (Folklore Association of Vietnam: Masters of Folklore) (Hanoi: Nhà Xuất Bản Khoa Học Xã Hội, 2007), 18.

54. As listed in the "Report Results: Compiling a List of Typical Quan Họ *Nghệ Nhân* of Bac Ninh" in *Báo Cáo Kết Quả: Xây Dựng Danh Sách Nghệ Nhân Quan Họ Tiêu Biểu Của Bắc Ninh: Report Number BC-SVHTT* (Hanoi: Sở Văn Hóa-Thông Tin, December 15, 2003). The project was conducted by the Bắc Ninh Department of Culture and Information, the Ministry of Culture and Information, and UNESCO Vietnam. The list also includes twenty-four "*nghệ nhân* with origins in the past" (Nghệ nhân nguyên xưa là các liên anh, liên chị quan họ) and thirty-four "*nghệ nhân* of the next generation of singers" (nghệ nhân là tầng lớp kế cận các lên anh, chiên chị).

55. Tô Ngọc Thanh, "Nghệ Nhân Dân Gian," 19.

56. Ibid.

57. The idea of cultural "brands" is discussed in John L. Comaroff and Jean Comaroff, *Ethnicity, Inc.* (Chicago: University of Chicago Press, 2009). To date, UNESCO has added Nhã Nhạc, Vietnamese Court Music (2008), the Bronze Gongs of the Central Highlands (2008), Quan Họ Folk Songs (2009), and Gióng Festival of Phù Đông and Sóc Temples (2010) to the Representative List of Intangible Cultural Heritage and Ca Trù Singing (2009) to the Urgent Safeguarding List.

58. Culture as "resource" is discussed in George Yúdice, *The Expediency of Culture: Uses of Culture in the Global Era* (Durham, NC: Duke University Press, 2005).

59. Erving Goffman, "Performances," in *Ritual, Play, and Performance:*

Readings in the Social Sciences/Theatre, ed. Richard Schechner and Mady Schuman (New York: Seabury Press, 1976), 92–93.

60. San Jose, California, is home to the second-largest Vietnamese community in the United States, after Orange County in the same state.

61. The United States normalized diplomatic relations with Vietnam in 1995; the U.S.–Vietnam Bilateral Trade Agreement was passed in 2001.

62. Including a five-year visa waiver for overseas Vietnamese: Vietnam Prime Ministerial Decision 135, August 2007.

63. Andrew Lam, *"Boat People" Return to Vietnam after Finding Success in America,* May 3, 2010. See following URL, accessed June 2, 2010: http://www.america.gov/st/peopleplaceenglish/ 2010/May/ 20100429163322maduobbA0.2777674.html.

64. On nonmigrants as local "spectators" within new mobile geographies, see Julie Chu, *Cosmologies of Credit: Transnational Mobility and the Politics of Destination in China* (Durham, NC: Duke University Press, 2010).

65.   James Clifford, *Routes: Travel and Translation in the Late Twentieth Century* (Cambridge, MA: Harvard University Press, 1997).

66. Immanuel Kant, *Critique of Pure Reason* (Chicago: Encyclopedia Britannica, 1955).

67. Anderson's assertion that "the nativeness of natives is always unmoored" suggests that modern flows of identities are not necessarily embodied in individual, spatial, or temporal ways but are rather contingent and phantasmagorical. Benedict Anderson, "Long Distance Nationalism," in *The Spectre of Comparisons: Nationalism, Southeast Asia, and the World* (London: Verso, 1998), 58–76.

68. Aihwa Ong discusses the important intersection of mobility, networks, and capital in her study of modern transnational Chinese subjects, *Flexible Citizenship* (Durham, NC: Duke University Press, 1999).

3 CAMBODIA

1. The government of the PRK, later renamed the State of Cambodia, was installed by Vietnam following that country's invasion of Cambodia in 1979. The invasion liberated Cambodia from the control of the Khmer Rouge regime, but the ruling party put in place by Cambodia's more powerful neighbor remained in power, with firm Vietnamese control, throughout the next decade. See Michael Vickery, *Cambodia: 1975–1982* (Boston: South End Press, 1984), 189–252; Ben Kiernan, "The Inclusion of the Khmer Rouge in the Cambodian Peace Process: Causes and Consequences," in *Genocide and Democracy in Cambodia: The Khmer Rouge, the United Nations and the International Community,* Yale University Southeast Asian Studies Monograph Series 41 (New Haven, CT: Yale University Southeast Asia Studies Program, 1993), 191–272; Steve Heder and Judy Ledgerwood, *Propaganda, Politics,*

Notes to Pages 75–84

and Violence in Cambodia: Democratic Transition under United Nations Peace-keeping (Armonk, NY: M.E. Sharpe, 1996).

2. Steve Heder, "Hun Sen's Consolidation: Death or Beginning of Reform?" *Southeast Asian Affairs* 2005 (2005): 114. Heder points out the similarity between the recent period of struggle and that which followed national independence. For an in-depth analysis of the political-economic bases for this transformation and its social implications, see Caroline Hughes and Kheang Un, eds., *Cambodia's Economic Transformation* (Copenhagen: Nordic Institute of Asian Studies Press, 2010).

3. UNHRC, *Report of the Special Representative of the Secretary-General for Human Rights in Cambodia, Yash Ghai,* A/HRC/4/36 (United Nations Human Rights Council, January 30, 2007), 22. Available at http://www.unhcr.org/refworld/docid/47e0db072.html.

4. Walter Benjamin, "Paris, Capital of the 19th Century," in *Reflections: Essays, Aphorisms, Autobiographical Writing* (New York: Schocken Books, 1986), 148.

5. Giorgio Agamben, *Homo Sacer: Sovereign Power and Bare Life* (Stanford, CA: Stanford University Press, 1998), 99. While we may join Agamben in imagining modernity to be characterized by "the camp," we needn't accept his position. For a critique of Agamben that takes issue with exactly this point, see Paul Rabinow and Nikolas Rose, "Biopower Today," *BioSocieties* 1 (2006): 195–217.

6. This is, of course, Bauman's argument about the Holocaust; see Zygmunt Bauman, *Modernity and the Holocaust* (Ithaca, NY: Cornell University Press, 1989), 4–5.

7. Bert Pijpers, *Kampuchea: Undoing the Legacy of Pol Pot's Water Control System* (Dublin: Trócaire, 1989).

8. For an example of Prime Minister Hun Sen's use of the term, see Judy Ledgerwood and Kheang Un, "Introduction," in *Cambodia Emerges from the Past: Eight Essays* (DeKalb, IL: Center for Southeast Asian Studies, Northern Illinois University, 2002), 7–8.

9. See, especially, chapter 4 in Arthur Kleinman, *What Really Matters: Living a Moral Life amidst Uncertainty and Danger* (New York: Oxford University Press, 2006).

10. As noted by Jackson in the Thai context, the term *kathoey* in Cambodia bears culturally specific meanings that cannot be easily translated into Western terminology for transgender persons. Referring to Thailand's "rich indigenous history of complex sex and gender patterns," Jackson notes that the *kathoey,* as an intermediate category, was "available to both males and females" and that "there is no single 'Thai attitude' toward homosexuality and transgenderism." There are strong parallels with the Cambodian case; see Peter A. Jackson, "Thai Research on Male Homosexuality and Transgenderism and the Cultural Limits of Foucaultian Analysis," *Journal of the History of Sexuality* 8, no. 1 (1997): 52–53.

11.   Judy Ledgerwood, *Changing Khmer Conceptions of Gender: Women, Stories, and the Social Order* (PhD diss., Cornell University, 1990), 325.
12.   Annuska Derks, *Khmer Women on the Move: Exploring Work and Life in Urban Cambodia* (Honolulu: University of Hawai'i Press, 2008).
13.   John Marston, "Clay into Stone: A Modern-Day Tapas," in *History, Buddhism, and New Religious Movements in Cambodia*, ed. John Marston and Elizabeth Guthrie (Honolulu: University of Hawai'i Press, 2004).
14.   Penny Edwards, ed., *The Buddhist Institute: A Short History* (Phnom Penh: The Buddhist Institute, 2005); Anne Ruth Hansen, *How to Behave: Buddhism and Modernity in Colonial Cambodia, 1860–1931* (Honolulu: University of Hawai'i Press, 2007).
15.   On the proliferation of human rights discourse, see Paul Rabinow, "Midst Anthropology's Problems," *Cultural Anthropology* 17, no. 2 (2002): 135–149.
16.   Judy Ledgerwood and Kheang Un, "Global Concepts and Local Meaning: Human Rights and Buddhism in Cambodia," *Journal of Human Rights* 2, no. 4 (2003): 531–549.
17.   *Lancet,* "The Trials of Tenofovir Trials," editorial in the *Lancet* 365 (2005): 1111.

4 LAOS

1.   Pál Nyíri, "Extraterritoriality," *EspacesTemps.net, Mensuelles,* November 19, 2009. See http://espacestemps.net/document7952.html, accessed March 10, 2010. The research draws on work by Chris Lyttleton and Paul T. Cohen. The *Economist* reported the casino was forced to close on May 26, 2011. See also Aihwa Ong, *Neoliberalism as Exception: Mutations in Citizenship and Sovereignty* (Durham, NC: Duke University Press, 2006).
2.   Aihwa Ong, "Graduated Sovereignty in South-East Asia," *Theory, Culture and Society* 17, no. 4 (2000): 55–75.
3.   For a discussion of the terms "contemporary" and "modern," see Paul Rabinow, *Marking Time: On the Anthropology of the Contemporary* (Princeton, NJ: Princeton University Press, 2007).
4.   Grant Evans, *A Short History of Laos: The Land in Between* (Crows Nest, Australia: Allen and Unwin, 2002), 21–25.
5.   Daniel Miller, "What Is a Mobile Phone Relationship?" in *Living the Asian Information Society,* ed. Erwin Alampay (Singapore: Institute for Southeast Asian Studies, 2009).
6.   Laurent Thevenot, "Which Road to Follow? The Moral Complexity of an 'Equipped' Humanity," in *Complexities: Social Studies of Knowledge Practices,* ed. John Law and Annemarie Mol (Durham, NC: Duke University Press, 2002), 59.
7.   Louis Dumont, *"*World Renunciation in Indian Religions,*"* in *Homo Hierarchicus: The Caste System and Its Implications* (Chicago: University of Chicago Press, 1980).

8. Max Weber, "Asceticism, Mysticism and Salvation," in *Sociology of Religion,* trans. Ephraim Fischoff (Boston: Beacon Press, 1993).

9. James Laidlaw, *Riches and Renunciation: Religion, Economy and Society among the Jains* (Oxford: Clarendon Press, 1995), 388.

10. Stanley J. Tambiah, "The Renouncer: His Individuality and His Community," *Contributions to Indian Sociology* 15 (1982): 299–320.

11. Dumont, "World Renunciation," 285.

12. Karl Polanyi, *The Great Transformation* (Boston: Beacon Press, 2001 [1944]), 79.

13. Michael Dove, "Theories of Swidden Agriculture, and the Political Economy of Ignorance," *Agroforestry Systems* 1 (1983): 85–99.

14. The *meuang* polity was a decentralized form of political organization in which local communities were symbolically subordinate to larger sovereign kingdoms even while they retained autonomy for most practical purposes. Stanley J. Tambiah, "The Galactic Polity: The Structure of Traditional Kingdoms in Southeast Asia," *Annals of the New York Academy of Sciences* 293 (1977): 69–97; Grant Evans, *Short History.*

15. Tania Murray Li, "Compromising Power: Development, Culture and Rule in Indonesia," *Cultural Anthropology* 14, no. 3 (1999): 295–322.

16. Michael Herzfeld, *Cultural Intimacy: Social Poetics in the Nation-State,* 2nd ed. (New York: Routledge, 2005).

5 THAILAND

1. Benedict Anderson, "Studies of the Thai State: The State of Thai Studies," in *The Study of Thailand: Analyses of Knowledge, Approaches, and Prospects in Anthropology, Art History, Economics, History and Political Science,* ed. Eliezer B. Ayal, Papers in International Studies, Southeast Asia Series 54 (Athens: Ohio University Center for International Studies, 1978), 198–199.

2. Hjorleifur Jonsson, "Mien Alter-Natives in Thai Modernity," *Anthropological Quarterly* 77, no. 4 (2004): 673–704.

3. John Embree, "Thailand—A Loosely Structured Social System," *American Anthropologist* 52, no. 2 (1950): 181–193.

4. Mary Beth Mills, "Contesting the Margins of Modernity: Women, Migration and Consumption in Thailand," *American Ethnologist* 24, no. 1 (1997): 41.

5. Anthony Diller, "What Makes Central Thai a National Language?" in *National Identity and Its Defenders Thailand, 1938–1989,* ed. Craig J. Reynolds (Chiang Mai: Silkworm, 1991), 87–132.

6. Mary Beth Mills, "Contesting the Margins," 43.

7. Charles F. Keyes, "Mother or Mistress but Never a Monk: Buddhist Notions of Female Gender in Rural Thailand," *American Ethnologist* 11, no. 2 (1984): 223–241.

8.   Kazuki Iwanaga, ed., *Women and Politics in Thailand: Continuity and Change* (Copenhagen, Denmark: NIAS Press, 2008).

9.   Sonia E. Alvarez, "Advocating Feminism: The Latin American Feminist NGO 'Boom,'" *International Feminist Journal of Politics* 1, no. 2 (1999): 181–209.

10. Mary Beth Mills, *Thai Women in the Global Labor Force: Consuming Desires, Contested Selves* (New Brunswick: Rutgers University Press, 1999).

11. Vichai Viratkapan and Ranjith Perera. "Slum Relocation Projects in Bangkok: What Has Contributed to Their Success or Failure," *Habitat International* 30, no. 1 (2006): 159.

12. Naruemol Bunjongjit. "Fact-Finding Study on Poverty in Urban Areas," *Journal of Social Research* 23, no. 2 (2000).

13. "Poor to Register in 8 Provinces for Dec. 6th," *The Nation (Bangkok)*, November 21, 2003.

14. Pasuk Phongpaichit and Chris Baker, "Pluto-Populism in Thailand: Business Remaking Politics," in *Populism and Reformism in Asia,* ed. John Sidel and Eva-Lotta Hedman (New Haven, CT: Yale University Press, 2005), 20–22.

15. Ibid., 3.

16. John Bowe, "Bound for America," *Mother Jones,* May–June 2010, 60–65.

17. Peter Vail, "Modern Muai Thai Mythology," *Crossroads: An Interdisciplinary Journal of Southeast Asian Studies* 12, no. 2 (1998): 75–95.

18. Pattana Kitiarsa, "Lives of Hunting Dogs: Muai Thai and the Politics of Thai Masculinities," *South East Asia Research* 13, no. 1 (March 2005): 57–90.

19. James Twitchell, *Where Men Hide* (New York: Columbia University Press, 2006), 42.

20. For an excellent overview of Thai values and the gendering of family roles, see Penny Van Esterik, *Nurturance and Reciprocity in Thai Studies: A Tribute to Lucien and Jane Hanks* (Toronto: York University Press, 1992). Suchada Thaweesit, *From Village to Factory "Girl": Shifting Narratives on Gender and Sexuality in Thailand* (PhD diss., University of Washington, 2000), provides a vivid ethnographic account of changing Thai views on the subject of gendered virtue.

21. Even white-robed nuns (*mae-chi*) are seen as pathetic figures, although they embrace the virtuous asceticism of the Buddhist temple. Sidney Brown quotes a monk on the source of the stigma: "A woman's power is in birth, and [nuns] are not exercising their power . . . they've failed at it. And that's the stereotype: heartbroken, old maids." Sidney Brown, *Gifts of Contemplation and Action: Buddhist Nuns in Thailand* (PhD diss., University of Virginia, 1997), 115.

22. Charles Hirschkind, *The Ethical Soundscape: Cassette Sermons and Islamic Counterpublics* (New York: Columbia University Press, 2006).

23. Julia Cassaniti, "Toward a Cultural Psychology of Impermanence in Thailand," *Ethos* 34, no. 1 (2006): 58–88.

24. Not unlike the Columbians described by Michael Taussig in *The Devil and*

Commodity Fetishism in South America (Chapel Hill: University of North Carolina Press, 1980).

25. Juliane Schober, "The Theravada Buddhist Engagement with Modernity in Southeast Asia: Whither the Social Paradigm of the Galactic Polity?" *Journal of Southeast Asian Studies* 26, no. 2 (1995).

26. Arjun Appadurai, *Modernity at Large: Cultural Dimensions of Globalization* (Minneapolis: University of Minnesota Press, 1996).

27. Walter Irvine, "Decline of Village Spirit Cults and Growth of Urban Spirit Mediumship: The Persistence of Spirit Beliefs, the Position of Women and Modernization," *Mankind* 14, no. 4 (1984): 315–324.

28. Pattana Kitiarsa, "You May Not Believe, but Never Offend the Spirits," in *Global Goes Local: Popular Culture in Asia,* ed. Timothy Craig and Richard King (Vancouver: University of British Columbia Press, 2002), 160–176.

6 INDONESIA

1. *Dangdut* is a wildly popular hybrid genre of Indonesian popular music, with roots in Malay, Arabic, and Hindustani music.

2. Kinanti Pinta Karana, "Julia Perez Disappointed Over Fake Certificate Allegations," *Jakarta Globe,* May 5, 2010.

3. Armando Siahaan and Dewi Kurniawati, "Julia Perez Visits Pacitan to Win Hearts and Minds," *Jakarta Globe,* April 26, 2010.

4. Zidane, "Roy Suryo, Punya Hobi Baca Buku Dikamar Mandi," 2006. See http://www.lampunginteraktif. com/depan/cetak_berita.php?kode=477, accessed October 7, 2008.

5. "Lokasinya Hotel Mulia, Kursinya Leter L: Mengungkap Skandal Rekaman Suara Mirip Baramuli-Setya Novanto," *Jateng Pos,* August 24, 1999.

6. Sigit Widodo, "Teliti dari Klise Asli 'Gus Dur-Aryanti,' Roy: Foto Bukan Hasil Rekayasa," *Detik,* September 2, 2000. See http://www.library.ohiou.edu/indopubs/2000/09/02/0071.html, accessed October 7, 2008.

7. Roy Suryo, "Fotografi, Teknologi dan Pornografi," *Kedaulatan Rakyat,* July 15, 1999. See also, "Beda, Foto Sensual dan Porno: Analisis RM Roy Suryo," *Kedaulatan Rakyat,* July 13, 1999.

8. See, for example, Dani Mamdani and Astari Yanuarti, "Seratus Kurang Satu Persen," *Gatra* 15, February 20, 2004. See http://www.gatra.com/2004–03–08/versicetak.php?id=34327, accessed August 24, 2004.

9. Nils Bubandt, "Rumors, Pamphlets, and the Politics of Paranoia in Indonesia," *Journal of Asian Studies* 67, no. 3 (2007): 789–817. See also Karen Strassler, "Material Resources of the Historical Imagination: Documents and the Future of the Past in Post-Suharto Indonesia," in *Timely Assets: Resources and their Temporalities,* ed. Elizabeth Ferry and Mandana Limbert (Santa Fe, NM: SAR Press, 2008), 217–244.

10.   James T. Siegel, *A New Criminal Type in Jakarta: Counter-Revolution Today* (Durham, NC: Duke University Press, 1998).

11.   See "RM Roy Suryo: Belajar Secara Otodidak," August 9, 2004. See http://news.indosiar.com/news_read?id=24469, accessed August 24, 2004.

12.   See Rhadon Dhelika, "Menyelami 68% Dunia Blog Indonesia," August 19, 2006. See http://selembarkertas. blogspot.com/2006/08/menyelami-68-dunia-blog-indonesia.html, accessed June 10, 2008.

13.   Ryan Koesuma, "Indonesia Raya, YouTube, Roy Suryo, and the Whole Government Bandwagon," August 7, 2007. See http://commonroom.info/2007/indonesia-raya-youtube-roy-suryo-and-the-whole-government-bandwagon/, accessed June 10, 2008. On the antagonism between bloggers and Roy Suryo, see for example, Jarar Siahaan, "Roy Suryo vs Bloger Indonesia," March 29, 2008. See http://blogberita.net/2008/03/29/roy-suryo-vs-bloger-indonesia/, accessed June 10, 2008.

14.   "Boy Surya, Pakar Multimedia dan Telematika," Sidewalk Studio, 2008, posted by Hadiprojo. See http://www.youtube.com/watch?v=w0gsuEYx3A4, accessed November 8, 2008.

15.   Dorothea Schulz, "Promises of (Im)mediate Salvation: Islam, Broadcast Media, and the Remaking of Religious Experience in Mali," *American Ethnologist* 33, no. 2 (2006): 223. See also Greg Fealy, "Consuming Islam: Commodified Religion and Aspirational Pietism in Contemporary Indonesia," in *Expressing Islam: Religious Life and Politics in Indonesia,* ed. Greg Fealy and Sally White (Singapore: Institute for Southeast Asian Studies, 2008), 15–39; and Gregory Starrett, "The Political Economy of Religious Commodities in Cairo," *American Anthropologist* 97, no. 1 (1995): 51–68.

16.   Compare with Siegel, *New Criminal Type.*

17.   C. W. Watson, "A Popular Indonesian Preacher: The Significance of Aa Gymnastiar," *Journal of the Royal Anthropological Institute* 11, no. 4 (2005): 773–792.

18.   Mara Einstein, *Brands of Faith: Marketing Religion in a Commercial Age* (New York: Routledge, 2008); Eva Illouz, *Saving the Modern Soul: Therapy, Emotions, and the Culture of Self-Help* (Berkeley: University of California Press, 2008).

19.   James Hoesterey, "Marketing Morality: The Rise, Fall, and Re-branding of Aa Gym," in Fealy and White, *Expressing Islam,* 95–112.

20.   Ariel Heryanto, "The 'Development' of Development," *Indonesia* 46 (October 1988): 1–24.

21.   For more on these programs, see Daromir Rudnyckyj, "Spiritual Economies: Islam and Neoliberalism in Contemporary Indonesia," *Cultural Anthropology* 24, no. 1 (2009): 104–141.

22.   Linda Connor and Adrian Vickers, "Crisis, Citizenship, and Cosmopolitanism: Living in a Local and Global Risk Society in Bali," *Indonesia* 75 (April 2003): 153–180.

23. Nigel Thrift refers to business success theories, leadership coaching, and self-help principles as management knowledge. See his "Rise of Soft Capitalism," in *An Unruly World? Globalisation, Governance, and Geography,* eds. Andrew Herod, Gearóid Ó Tuathail, and Susan M. Roberts (London: Routledge, 1998), 25–71.
24. The confidence exhibited by the figure of the spiritual trainer resembles that displayed by another figure of Indonesian modernity: the engineer. However, whereas the engineers described by Joshua Barker view technology as capable of resolving differences across a fractured archipelago, spiritual trainers perceive the amalgamation of Islamic ethics and popular business practices as the remedy to the economic and political crises understood to afflict the nation. See Joshua Barker, "Engineers and Political Dreams: Indonesia in the Satellite Age," *Current Anthropology* 46, no. 5 (2005): 703–727.
25. Max Weber, *The Protestant Ethic and the Spirit of Capitalism* (London: Unwin Hyman, 1990).
26. "Injecting drug user," or "IDU," is by now a common term in HIV/AIDS discourse and in much of Indonesian public culture as well. Heroin is the most common drug so injected in Indonesia.
27. Leslie Butt, "'Lipstick Girls' and 'Fallen Women': AIDS and Conspiratorial Thinking in Papua, Indonesia," *Cultural Anthropology* 20, no. 3 (2005): 412–442; and Karen Kroeger, "AIDS Rumors, Imaginary Enemies, and the Body Politic in Indonesia," *American Ethnologist* 30, no. 2 (2003): 243–257.
28. James T. Siegel, *Fetish, Recognition, Revolution* (Princeton, NJ: Princeton University Press, 1997).
29. See Benedict Anderson's important thesis on the origins and role of *pemuda* in the Indonesian Revolution, *Java in a Time of Revolution: Occupation and Resistance, 1944–1946* (Ithaca, NY: Cornell University Press, 1972). For more recent work on the reemergence of youth in conceptions of Indonesian historiography, see Karen Strassler, "Photographs and the Making of Reformasi Memory," in *Beginning to Remember,* ed. Mary S. Zurbuchen (Singapore: Singapore University Press, 2005), 278–311; and Keith Foulcher, "Sumpah Pemuda: The Making and Meaning of a Symbol of Indonesian Nationhood," *Asian Studies Review* 24, no. 3 (2000): 377–410.
30. New research on the business dealings of ex–GAM members, particularly among the leadership and commanders, can be found in Edward Aspinall, "Combatants to Contractors: The Political Economy of Peace in Aceh," *Indonesia* 87 (April 2009): 1–34.
31. The World Bank reported that 83 percent of the $7.8 billion of funds committed to Aceh for tsunami-related reconstruction had been distributed to aid projects. This makes Aceh one of the largest reconstruction endeavors in the developing world. See "Aceh Tsunami Reconstruction Expenditure Tracking Update," April 2008. See http://siteresources.worldbank.org/INTINDONESIA/Resources/226271-1176706430507/3681211-1194602678235/Aceh.Reconstruction.Finance.Update.Dec2007.pdf, accessed March 9, 2009.

32. Anna Tsing, *Friction: An Ethnography of Global Connections* (Princeton, NJ: Princeton University Press, 2005).

33. BNP2TKI (Badan Nasional Penempatan dan Perlindungan Tenaga Kerja Indonesia, The National Placement and Protection Body for the Indonesian Labor Force), "Penempatan TKI Menurut Negara Tujuan dan tempat Bekerja, Tahun 1994–2006" ("TKI Placement According to Country of Destination and Place of Work, 1994–2006"), 2009. See http://www.bnp2tki.go.id/content/view/90/87/, accessed February 1, 2009.

34. "Uang Kiriman TKI Mencapai Rp40 Triliun," *Antara News,* September 23, 2008. See http://www.antara.co.id/arc/2008/9/23/uang-kiriman-tki-mencapai-rp40-triliun, accessed February 1, 2009.

35. Barbara Ehrenreich and Arlie Hochschild, *Global Woman: Nannies, Maids, and Sex Workers in the New Economy* (New York: Metropolitan Books, 2003).

36. Katharine Gibson, Lisa Law, and Deirdre McKay, "Beyond Heroes and Victims: Filipina Contract Migrants, Economic Activism, and Class Transformations," *International Feminist Journal of Politics* 3, no. 3 (2001): 365–386; and Michele Ford, "Beyond the Femina Fantasy: The Working-Class Woman in Indonesian Discourses of Women's Work," *Review of Indonesian and Malaysian Affairs* 37, no. 2 (2003): 83–113.

37. Pei-Chia Lan, *Global Cinderellas: Migrant Domestics and Newly Rich Employers in Taiwan* (Durham, NC: Duke University Press, 2006).

38. *Petugas* literally means "a subordinate who is given an order or task," while *lapangan* means "field." Although "field agent" is not an ideal translation, arguably it is preferable to "field operative" or "field-worker," since the word "agent" highlights to a greater degree the form of brokering that the *petugas lapangan* engages in.

39. Wolf's classic article on the shifting position of brokers in colonial and post-colonial Mexico offers an important comparative starting point. See Eric Wolf, "Aspects of Group Relations in a Complex Society: Mexico," *American Anthropologist* 58, no. 6 (1956): 1065–1078.

40. Clifford Geertz, *Peddlers and Princes: Social Development and Economic Change in Two Indonesian Towns* (Chicago: University of Chicago Press, 1963).

41. Hildred Geertz, *Indonesian Cultures and Communities: A Study Guide* (New Haven, CT: HRAF Press, 1963).

42. Abidin Kusno, *Behind the Postcolonial: Architecture, Urban Space, and Political Cultures in Indonesia* (New York: Routledge, 2000).

43. Siegel, *New Criminal Type.*

44. Quoted from Sri Santuti Hariadi and Bagong Suyanto, *Anak Jalanan di Jawa Timur* (Surabaya: Airlangga University Press, 1999), xvii, my translation.

45. Quoted in I. Sandyawan Sumardi, *Perjuangan Anak Pinggiran* (Jakarta: Institut Sosial Jakarta, 1997), iii, my translation.

46. Michel Foucault, *Discipline and Punish* (New York: Vintage Books, 1979), 292 et passim.

47. Hildred Geertz, *The Javanese Family* (New York: Free Press of Glencoe, 1961).

48. The state is not invested in reformatories for *anjal,* and *anjal* are commonly expected to (and frequently do) run away from religious and NGO–sponsored programs established to keep them off the streets. A widely invoked example is the story of an Indonesian actress who took several kids into her home after they appeared together in a movie (*Daun di atas Bantal*); despite their elevation into the lap of luxury, the kids shortly ran away to live on the streets again.

49. See Onghokham, "The *Jago* in Colonial Java, Ambivalent Champion of the People," in *History and Peasant Consciousness in South East Asia,* ed. Andrew Turnton and Shigeru Tanabe (Osaka: National Museum of Ethnography, 1984); Siegel, *New Criminal Type*; Vicente L. Rafael, ed., *Figures of Criminality in Indonesia, the Philippines, and Colonial Vietnam* (Ithaca, NY: Cornell University Southeast Asia Program Publications, 1999).

50. Clifford Geertz, "The Javanese Kijaji: The Changing Role of a Cultural Broker," *Comparative Studies in Society and History* 2, no. 2 (1960): 228–249.

51. In the 1990s, Yanto and his ilk were sometimes referred to as *orang kaya baru,* or nouveau riche, a type that was evident mostly in cities but also in rural areas. See Hans Antlöv, "The New Rich and Cultural Tensions in Rural Indonesia," in *Culture and Privilege in Capitalist Asia,* ed. Michael Pinches (London: Routledge, 1999).

52. See Saya Shiraishi, *Young Heroes: The Indonesian Family in Politics* (Ithaca, NY: Cornell University Southeast Asia Program Publications, 1997); and Takashi Shiraishi, "Rewiring the Indonesian State," in *Making Indonesia,* ed. Daniel Lev and Ruth McVey (Ithaca: Cornell Southeast Asian Program Publications, 1996), 164–179.

53. Carla Jones has written in some detail about the role domestic servants play in the emotional work that sustains the middle-class Javanese household. See "Whose Stress? Emotion Work in Middle-Class Javanese Homes," *Ethnos* 69, no. 4 (2004): 509–528.

54. See Ford, "Beyond the Femina Fantasy."

55. Suzanne Brenner, "On the Public Intimacy of the New Order: Images of Women in the Popular Indonesian Print Media," *Indonesia* 67 (April 1999): 18.

56. Sumbo Tinarbuko, "Konsumtivisme dan Kriminalitas," *Kedaulatan Rakyat,* August 13, 2008.

7   MALAYSIA

1. Raymond Williams, *Culture* (London: Fontana, 1981).

2. The NEP was crafted as a consequence of "race riots" (largely between "Malays" and "Chinese") in Kuala Lumpur erupting after the results of the 1969

general elections saw a serious weakening of the ruling Alliance Party. In brief, the NEP was to generate and redistribute wealth more equitably among the ethnic groups. Particular privileges were stipulated for "Malays" and indigenous peoples of the country (that is, *bumiputeras,* literally the "princes of the soil") in order for them to achieve income levels comparable to the Malaysian Chinese middle class.

3. Shariah is a set of legal codes used to adjudicate Muslims. For details, see Michael Peletz, *Islamic Modern: Religious Courts and Cultural Politics in Malaysia* (Princeton, NJ: Princeton University Press, 2002).

4. Johan Fischer, *Proper Islamic Consumption: Shopping among the Malays in Modern Malaysia* (Copenhagen: Nordic Institute of Asian Studies, 2008).

5. Eric C. Thompson, *Unsettling Absences: Urbanism in Rural Malaysia* (Singapore: National University of Singapore Press, 2007).

6. Mahathir bin Mohamad Iskandar was born in the sultanate of Kedah in northern British Malaya in 1925. Before joining politics, he had been a medical doctor in private practice. Mahathir became a member of Parliament in 1964 and joined the cabinet of Tun Abdul Razak as minister of education in 1974 before being appointed Malaysia's fourth prime minister in 1981. Although Mahathir stepped down in 2003, he remains an active commentator on the country's political affairs.

7. Mahathir Mohamad, *The Challenge* (Petaling Jaya: Pelanduk, 1986), 47.

8. Mahathir Mohamad, "Speech Delivered at the First East Asian Young Leaders Congress on East Asian Peace, Stability and Prosperity," Kuala Lumpur, August 5, 1994, reprinted in *The Encyclopaedia of Dr. Mahathir bin Mohamad* (Kuala Lumpur: Darulfikir, 2004), vol. 9, part 1, 23–30.

9. Mahathir Mohamad, "Islam: The Misunderstood Religion," keynote address delivered at the Oxford Centre for Islamic Studies, April 16, 1996, reproduced in *The Encyclopaedia of Dr. Mahathir bin Mohamad* (Kuala Lumpur: Darulfikir, 2004), vol. 1, 187–202.

10. Mahathir Mohamad, "Islam in the Era of Globalisation," opening speech at the World Ulama Conference, Putrajaya, July 10, 2003, available from http://www.pmo.gov.my, accessed August 30, 2007.

11. Mahathir Mohamad, "Islam: The Misunderstood Religion."

12. Mahathir Mohamad, "Whither Malaysia?" speech at International Symposium organized by Keio University, Tokyo, November 11, 1983, available from http://www.pmo.gov.my, accessed August 30, 2007.

13. See "Dr. Mahathir Mohamad," Blog Homepage, available from http://chedet.co.cc/chedetblog/, accessed September 15, 2011.

14. For a full bibliography of Wan Zawawi's works and details about his illustrious career, see Wan Zawawi Ibrahim, *The Anthropology of the Malay Peasantry: Reflecting on Colonial and Indigenous Scholarship* (Kuala Lumpur: University of Malaya Press, 2009).

15. Goh Beng Lan, *Modern Dreams: An Inquiry into Power, Cultural Production,*

and the Cityscape in Contemporary Urban Penang, Malaysia (Ithaca, NY: Southeast Asia Program, Cornell University, 2002), 18.

16. Patricia Matusky and Tan Sooi Beng, *The Music of Malaysia: The Classical, Folk, and Syncretic Traditions* (Aldershot, UK: Ashgate, 2004), 414.

17. *New Straits Times*, January 23, 2005.

18. See Todd Harvey, *The Formative Dylan: Transmission and Stylistic Influences, 1961–1963* (Lanham, MA: Scarecrow Press, 2001); Leonard Cohen, "The Unbearable Panic of Being," in *Inside the Music: Conversations with Contemporary Musicians about Spirituality, Creativity, and Consciousness*, ed. Dimitri Ehrlich (Boston: Shambhala, 1997), 190–201.

19. Partha Chatterjee, *Nationalist Thought and the Colonial World: A Derivative Discourse* (Minneapolis: University of Minnesota Press, 1993), 36–53.

20. An Internet search for such an association loops back to the conspiracy story.

21. Also known as *Sejarah Melayu* (the Malay Annals).

22. *Sejarah Melayu* and *Hikayat Hang Tuah* were first committed to paper in the seventeenth century but are believed to have been documented as court text since the fifteenth century. See Leonard Andaya, "The Search for the 'Origins' of Melayu," *Journal of Southeast Asian Studies* 32, no. 3 (2001): 327–328.

23. UMNO, United Malays National Organisation, is the Malay-based ruling party in Malaysia.

24. A *keris* is short dagger traditionally used for self-defense but now largely serving a ceremonial function in Malay rites.

25. Hang Tuah's association with the Orang Asli is also discussed in Leonard Andaya, *Leaves of the Same Tree: Trade and Ethnicity in the Straits of Melaka* (Honolulu: University of Hawai'i Press, 2008), 229.

26. Alan Dundes, *Sacred Narrative: Readings in the Theory of Myth* (Berkeley: University of California Press, 1984), 1.

27. Jan Brunvand, *The Vanishing Hitchhiker: American Urban Legends and their Meanings* (New York: W.W. Norton and Company, 1989), 2.

28. *CSI* and *Bones* are American television shows—popular in Malaysia—that highlight the role of forensic science.

29. Ronald Provencher, "An Overview of Malay Humor Magazines: Significance, Origins, Contexts, Texts, and Audiences," in *Themes and Issues in Asian Cartooning: Cute, Cheap, Mad, and Sexy*, ed. John A. Lent (Bowling Green, KY: Bowling Green State University Popular Press, 1999), 12.

30. Provencher, "Overview of Malay Humor Magazines," 18.

31. Under the Internal Security Act, which allows for detention without trial, over a hundred people, including opposition leaders and social activists, were arrested.

32. The Instant Café Theatre Company homepage, "Who We Are: History," available from http://www.instantcafetheatre.com/html/main.html, accessed January 10, 2011.

33. The Publications and Printing Act, which legislates that publishing licenses have to be annually renewed, leads to self-censorship.

34. Ding Jo-Anne, "Why the government fears satire," the Nut Graph, September 20, 2010, available from http://www.thenutgraph.com/why-the-government-fears-satire/, accessed January 10, 2011.

35. Tenaga Nasional Berhad (TNB) is Malaysia's main energy provider.

36. Matthew H. Amster (writer/director), *The Internet and the Water Buffalo,* documentary film (2010), fifty-two minutes.

37. Matthew H. Amster and Johan Lindquist, "Frontiers, Sovereignty, and Marital Tactics: Comparisons from the Borneo Highlands and the Indonesia-Malaysia-Singapore Growth Triangle," *Asia Pacific Journal of Anthropology* 6, no. 1 (2005): 1–17.

38. Form Five refers to the fifth and potentially final year of secondary schooling in Malaysia; it is the critical point when students must take an exam that determines whether they will be able to continue to Form Six (pre-university).

39. Matthew H. Amster,"Borderland Tactics: Cross-border Marriage in the Highlands of Borneo," in *Borderlands: Ethnographic Approaches to Security, Power and Identity*, ed. Hastings Donnan and Thomas M. Wilson (Lantham, MD: University Press of America, 2010), 93–107.

40. Clifford Geertz, "The Javanese Kijaji: The Changing Role of a Cultural Broker," *Comparative Studies in Society and History* 2, no. 2 (1960): 237.

41. Ibid., 248.

42. The word *cukong* itself stems from Hokkien Chinese and denotes leader, chairperson, and boss. In other parts of Southeast Asia, the *cukong* or broker/entrepreneur is known as *towkai, tukai, tauke,* or *taikong.*

43. "Cerita Tentang Cukong Kayu DPO Mabes Polri," *Sinar Harapan,* October 8, 2005.

44. Edi Petebang, "Illegal Logging Rampant along Indonesian-Malaysian Border," *Jakarta Post,* May 23, 2000.

45. Craig A. Lockard, "Leadership and Power within the Chinese Community of Sarawak: A Historical Survey," *Journal of Southeast Asian Studies* 2, no. 2 (1971): 195–217.

46. R. S. Milne, "Patrons, Clients and Ethnicity: The Case of Sarawak and Sabah in Malaysia," *Asian Survey* 13, no. 10 (1973): 891–907.

8 SINGAPORE

1. Walter Benjamin, *The Arcades Project* (Cambridge: Belknap Press, 1999), 76–77.

2. Cherian George, "Singapore without Singaporeans," in *Singapore: The Air-Conditioned Nation: Essays on the Politics of Comfort and Control 1990–2000* (Singapore: Landmark Books, 2000), 159–169.

3. Quoted in C. J. W.-L. Wee, *The Asian Modern: Culture, Capitalist Development, Singapore* (Hong Kong: Hong Kong University Press, 2007), 89.

4. Rem Koolhaas, "The Past Is Too Small to Inhabit," in *The Changing Global*

Order: World Leaders Reflect, ed. Nathan Gardels (Malden: Blackwell Publishers, 1997), 171.

5. James C. Scott, *Seeing Like a State: How Certain Schemes to Improve the Human Condition Have Failed* (New Haven, CT: Yale University Press, 1998), 1.

6. Zygmunt Bauman, "Making and Unmaking of Strangers," in *The Bauman Reader,* ed. Peter Beilharz (Malden, MA: Blackwell Publishers, 2001), 201.

7. Arjun Appadurai, *Modernity at Large: Cultural Dimensions of Globalization* (Minneapolis: University of Minnesota Press, 1996), 8.

8. Veena Das, *Life and Words: Violence and the Descent into the Ordinary* (Berkeley: University of California Press, 2007).

9. Kamaludeen Mohamed Nasir, "Rethinking the 'Malay Problem' in Singapore: Image, Rhetoric and Social Realities," *Journal of Muslim Minority Affairs* 27, no. 2 (2007): 309–318.

10. "Malay Youths Want to Erase Gang Past," the *New Paper,* June 4, 2007.

11. N. Ganapathy and Lian Kwen Fee, "Policing Minority Street Corner Gangs in Singapore: A View from the Street," *Policing and Society* 12, no. 2 (2002): 139–152.

12. National Population Secretariat (NPS), 2009, "Population in Brief: 2009," a joint production by NPS and Singapore Department of Statistics, Ministry of Community Development, Young and Sports, Ministry of Home Affairs, Immigration and Checkpoints Authority, and Ministry of Manpower.

13. Md Mizanur Rahman, "Gender Dimensions of Remittances: Indonesian Domestic Workers in East and Southeast Asia," UNIFEM—East and Southeast Asia Report (Bangkok: UNIFEM East and Southeast Asia, 2009).

14. Md Mizanur Rahman, "Sending Remittances Home: The Singapore-Bangladesh Remittance Corridor," International Organization for Migration, forthcoming.

15. Brenda S. A Yeoh, "Migration, International Labour and Multicultural Policies in Singapore," Working Paper Series no. 19, Asia Research Institute, National University of Singapore, 2004.

16. Chng Nai Rui, "The Working Committees: From 'Fear' to Creative Activism," in *Renaissance Singapore? Economy, Culture and Politics,* ed. Kenneth Paul Tan (Singapore: NUS Press, 2007), 201.

17. Terence Lee, "The Politics of Civil Society in Singapore," *Asian Studies Review* 26, no. 1 (2002): 110.

18. Wee, *The Asian Modern,* 6.

19. Nirmala PuruShotam, "Women and the Middle Class in Singapore," in *Gender and Power in Affluent Asia,* eds. Krishna Sen and Maila Stivens (New York: Routledge, 1998), 160.

20. The term "peri-urban" refers to areas immediately adjoining the officially designated municipal zone, typically manifesting a semirural way of life.

21. Loh Kah Seng, "Change and Conflict at the Margins: Emergency Kampong Clearance and the Making of Modern Singapore," *Asian Studies Review* 33, no. 2 (2009): 139–159.

22. HB 1013/50 Vol. I, Memo from Chief Architect, HDB, to CEO, HDB, December 4, 1963.
23. Chua Beng Huat, "Singapore Cinema: Eric Khoo and Jack Neo—Critique from the Margins and the Mainstream," *Inter-Asia Cultural Studies* 4, no. 1 (2003): 117–125.
24. Interview with Gomedia in Mandarin (July 28, 2008).
25. Kenneth Paul Tan, *Cinema & Television in Singapore: Resistance in One Dimension* (Leiden: Brill, 2008).
26. Bryan Walsh, "Neo is the One," *Time Magazine,* April 1, 2002. Available at http://www.time.com/time/magazine/article/0,9171,501020408-221199,00 .html#ixzz0hGQ8wCVj, accessed on August 18, 2011.
27. Singapore Ministry of Finance, "Total Estimated Outlays for FY2009 by Head of Expenditure," Singapore Budget, 2009. Available at http://www.mof.gov .sg/budget_2009/revenue_expenditure/attachment/Expenditure_Estimates.pdf, accessed on August 18, 2011.
28. Singapore Ministry of Education, "FY 2009 Committee of Supply Debate: 1st Reply by Minister Dr Ng Eng Hen on Seizing Opportunities to Build a World Class Education System," Ministry of Education Speeches, 2009. Available at http://www.moe.gov.sg/media/speeches/2009/02/10/fy-2009-committee-of-supply-de.php, accessed on August 18, 2011.
29. Christopher Tremewan, *The Political Economy of Social Control in Singapore* (New York: St. Martin's Press, 1994), 75.
30. Jason Tan, "The Rise and Fall of Religious Knowledge in Singapore Secondary Schools," *Journal of Curriculum Studies* 29, no. 5 (1997): 620.
31. Ulrike Freitag, "Arab Merchants in Singapore: Attempt of a Collective Biography," in *Transcending Borders: Arabs, Politics, Trade and Islam in Southeast Asia,* eds. Huub de Jonge and Nico Kaptein (Leiden: KITLV Press, 2002), 109–142; Erik Holmberg, "Sheikh Salim bin Mohamed bin Talib," in *Hadhrami Arabs Across the Indian Ocean: Contributions to Southeast Asian Economy and Society,* ed. Syed Farid Alatas (Singapore: National Library Board, 2010), 32–37.

9 BURMA

1. Do we call the country Burma or Myanmar? It is now almost obligatory for the initial footnote in academic writings about Southeast Asia's most contentious country to clarify the relevant nomenclature. In this chapter, I have opted to retain the choices of expression and spelling of each individual essay author. Perhaps one day such ambiguity and inconsistency will no longer be required but, in the present moment, it helpfully illuminates the challenges of studying this contested political and linguistic landscape.
2. For the most famous of these anthropological studies, see Edmund R. Leach, *Political Systems of Highland Burma: A Study of Kachin Social Structures* (London: G. Bell & Son, 1954).

3.   I would like to express my gratitude to La Nga Zau La and his family for their warmth and generosity when I was researching traditional Jinghpaw spirit practices in Burma.

4.   See H. G. Tegenfeldt, *A Century of Growth: The Kachin Baptist Church of Burma* (South Pasadena, CA: William Carey Library, 1974), and E. Fischer, *Mission in Burma: The Columban Fathers' Forty-Three Years in Kachin Country* (New York: Seabury Press, 1980). Reverend N'Ngai Gam, "The Kachin Theology," *Myihtoi Ma Magazine* (Myitkyina: Nawng Nang Kachin Theological College, 1998), 165–172, gives an important alternative reading of the role of Christian missions in Kachin society from someone who was a leading Kachin theologian himself. This article, which questioned the universally positive interpretation of missionary endeavors for understandings of Kachin culture, caused a great deal of controversy within the church establishment at the time.

5.   United Nations Educational, Scientific and Cultural Organization, Myanmar, available from http://www.unesco.org/new/en/communication-and-information/themes/professional-journalistic-standards-and-code-of-ethics/southeast-asia/myanmar/, accessed December 1, 2010.

6.   U Thaung, *A Journalist, a General and an Army in Burma* (Bangkok: White Lotus, 1995), 1–3.

7.   Ibid., 22.

8.   Freedom House, *Freedom in the World Country Ratings,* no date. Available from http://www.freedomhouse.org/uploads/fiw09/CompHistData/CountryStatus&RatingsOverview1973–2009.pdf, accessed September 12, 2011.

9.   Ludu Sein Win, as quoted in Sandar Lwin, "Industry Facing Journalist Shortage," *Myanmar Times,* September 13–19, 2010.

10.   Personal communication (e-mail), December 20, 2010. Name withheld.

11.   Anna J. Allot, *Inked Over Ripped Out* (New York: PEN American Center, 1993), 6.

12.   Personal communication (e-mail), December 20, 2010.

13.   Kyaw Thu, personal communication (e-mail), December 13, 2010.

14.   Personal communication (e-mail), December 20, 2010.

15.   "Death of Ma Khaine Shun Lae Yee at SSC Special Clinic and the Media," *Weekly Eleven,* no date. Available from http://eversion.news-eleven.com/index.php?option=com_content&view=article&id=321%3Adeath-of-ma-khaine-shun-lae-yee-at-ssc-special-clinic-and-the-media&Itemid=110), accessed September 12, 2011.

16.   Kyaw Thu, personal communication (e-mail), December 17, 2010.

17.   Khin Myat, "Medical Ethics in the Spotlight," *Myanmar Times,* January 25–31, 2010. (Article censored.)

18.   Human Rights Watch, *Burma's Forgotten Prisoners* (New York: Human Rights Watch, September 2009).

19.   Mary Callahan, "Myanmar's Perpetual Junta: Solving the Riddle of the Tatmadaw's Long Reign," *New Left Review* 60 (2009): 27–63.

20. Nick Cheesman, "Thin Rule of Law or Un-Rule of Law in Myanmar," *Pacific Affairs* 82, no. 4 (2009): 597–613.

21. Min Zin, "Opposition Movements in Burma: The Question of Relevancy," in *Finding Dollars, Sense, and Legitimacy in Burma,* ed. Susan L. Levenstein (Washington, D.C.: Woodrow Wilson International Center for Scholars, Asia Program, 2010), 77–94.

22. Assistance Association for Political Prisoners, *The Darkness We See: Torture in Burma's Interrogation Centers and Prison* (Mae Sot: Assistance Association for Political Prisoners— Burma, 2005).

23. Kathleen Alden and Charles Poole et al., "Burmese Political Dissidents in Thailand: Trauma and Survival among Young Adults in Exile," *American Journal of Public Health* 86, no. 11 (1996): 1561–1569.

24. Bryant Yuan Fu Yang, "Life and Death away from the Golden Land: The Plight of Burmese Migrant Workers in Thailand," *University of Hawai'i Asian-Pacific Law & Policy Journal* 8 (2007): 485–535.

25. This research was supported by a Grant-in-Aid for Scientific Research (KAKENHI 19101010) from the Japan Society for the Promotion of Sciences (JSPS). For further information, see Koichi Fujita, Tamaki Endo, Ikuku Okamoto, Yoshihiro Nakanishi, and Miwa Yamada, "Myanmar Migrant Laborers in Ranong, Thailand," IDE Discussion Paper Series 257 (Institute of Developing Economies, JETRO, 2010).

26. There are several case studies about the working conditions of Myanmar migrants in other border towns. For example, see Dennis Arnold and Kevin Hewison, "Exploitation in Global Supply Chains: Burmese Workers in Mae Sot," *Journal of Contemporary Asia* 35, no. 3 (2005): 319–340.

27. In fact, the situation may not have changed that much considering what we find in an earlier publication: Human Rights Watch, *A Modern Form of Slavery: Trafficking of Burmese Women and Girls into Brothels in Thailand* (New York: Human Rights Watch, 1993).

28. Thomas E. Blair, ed., *Living on the Edges: Cross-Border Mobility and Sexual Exploitation in the Greater Southeast Asia Sub-Region* (Bangkok: Southeast Asian Consortium on Gender, Sexuality and Health, 2006).

29. According to Ma Aye Aye, the prices were different for Thai and Myanmar clients. It was 450 baht per person (short time) for Thais, while it was 300 baht per person for Myanmar clients.

30. Larry Jagan, "Burma's Military: Purges and Coups Prevent Progress Towards Democracy," in *Myanmar's Long Road to National Reconciliation,* ed. Trevor Wilson (Canberra: Asia Pacific Press, 2006).

31. It is accepted that the army outnumbers the navy and air force. But any such numbers must be treated with caution due to a lack of reliable sources. See, for instance, Andrew Selth, "Burma's Armed Forces: Looking Down the Barrel," Regional Outlook Paper 21 (Griffith Asia Institute, 2009), 11–12.

32. "Burma's Aung San Suu Kyi 'Has Foot Soldiers' Support,'" British

Broadcasting Corporation. Available from http://www.bbc.co.uk/news/world-asia-pacific-11775469, accessed November 17, 2010.

33.   Neil Englehart, "Is Regime Change Enough for Burma? The Problem of State Capacity," *Asian Survey* 45, no. 4 (2005): 643.

34.   The *longyi* is a skirtlike garment worn by Burmese (civilian) men.

35.   "People's Desire," the *New Light of Myanmar* 2, November 25, 2010.

36.   Justin Wintle, *Perfect Hostage: A Life of Aung San Suu Kyi* (London: Hutchinson, 2007), xxvi.

37.   Sao Sanda, *The Moon Princess: Memories of the Shan States* (Bangkok: River Books, 2008), 268.

38.   The names of people and the name of the band in this essay have been changed.

FURTHER READING

BURMA (MYANMAR)

Callahan, Mary P. *Making Enemies: War and State Building in Burma.* Ithaca, NY: Cornell University Press, 2003.

Chin, Ko-Lin. *The Golden Triangle: Inside Southeast Asia's Drug Trade.* Ithaca, NY: Cornell University Press, 2009.

Fink, Christina. *Living Silence: Burma under Military Rule.* New York: Zed Books, 2001.

Houtman, Gustaaf. *Mental Culture in Burmese Crisis Politics: Aung San Suu Kyi and the National League for Democracy.* Tokyo: Tokyo University of Foreign Studies, Institute for the Study of Languages and Cultures of Asia and Africa, 1999.

Robinne, François, and Mandy Sadan, eds. *Social Dynamics in the Highlands of South East Asia: Reconsidering* Political Systems of Highland Burma *by E. R. Leach.* Leiden: Brill, 2007.

Schober, Juliane. *Modern Buddhist Conjunctures in Myanmar: Cultural Narratives, Colonial Legacies and Civil Society.* Honolulu: University of Hawai'i Press, 2010.

Scott, James C. *The Art of Not Being Governed: An Anarchist History of Upland Southeast Asia.* New Haven, CT: Yale University Press, 2009.

Skidmore, Monique. *Karaoke Fascism: Burma and the Politics of Fear.* Philadelphia: University of Pennsylvania Press, 2004.

South, Ashley. *Ethnic Politics in Burma: States of Conflict.* Abingdon, UK: Routledge, 2008.

Thant Myint-U. *Where China Meets India: Burma and the New Crossroads of Asia.* London: Faber and Faber, 2011.

CAMBODIA

Derks, Annuska. *Khmer Women on the Move: Exploring Work and Life in Urban Cambodia.* Honolulu: University of Hawai'i Press, 2008.
Edwards, Penny. *Cambodge: The Cultivation of a Nation, 1860–1945.* Honolulu: University of Hawai'i Press, 2007.
Gottesman, Evan. *Cambodia after the Khmer Rouge.* New Haven, CT: Yale University Press, 2004.
Hansen, Anne Ruth. *How to Behave: Buddhism and Modernity in Colonial Cambodia, 1860–1930.* Honolulu: University of Hawai'i Press, 2007.
Hinton, Alexander Laban. *Why Did They Kill? Cambodia in the Shadow of Genocide.* Berkeley: University of California Press, 2004.
Hughes, Caroline. *The Political Economy of Cambodia's Transition, 1991–2001.* New York: Routledge, 2003.
Hughes, Caroline, and Kheang Un, eds. *Cambodia's Economic Transformation.* Copenhagen: Nordic Institute of Asian Studies Press, 2011.
Ledgerwood, Judy. *Cambodia Emerges from the Past: Eight Essays.* DeKalb: Northern Illinois University Center for Southeast Asia Publications, 2002.
Marston, John, ed. *Anthropology and Community in Cambodia: Reflections on the Work of May Ebihara.* Monash Papers on Southeast Asia 70. Melbourne: Monash Asia Institute, 2011.
Ollier, Leakthina Chan-Pech, and Tim Winter. *Expressions of Cambodia: The Politics of Tradition, Identity and Change.* New York: Routledge, 2006.

INDONESIA

Adams, Kathleen. *Art as Politics: Re-crafting Identities, Tourism, and Power in Tana Toraja, Indonesia.* Honolulu: University of Hawai'i Press, 2006.
Aspinall, Edward. *Islam and Nation: Separatist Rebellion in Aceh, Indonesia.* Stanford, CA: Stanford University Press, 2009.
Baulch, Emma. *Making Scenes: Reggae, Punk, and Death Metal in 1990s Bali.* Durham, NC: Duke University Press, 2007.
Boellstorff, Tom. *The Gay Archipelago: Sexuality and Nation in Indonesia.* Princeton, NJ: Princeton University Press, 2005.
Kusno, Abidin. *The Appearances of Memory: Mnemonic Practices of Architecture and Urban Form in Indonesia.* Durham, NC: Duke University Press, 2010.
Li, Tania Murray. *The Will to Improve: Governmentality, Development, and the Practice of Politics.* Durham, NC: Duke University Press, 2007.
Lindquist, Johan. *The Anxieties of Mobility: Development and Migration in the Indonesian Borderlands.* Honolulu: University of Hawai'i Press, 2009.
Rudnyckyj, Daromir. *Spiritual Economies: Islam, Globalization, and the Afterlife of Development.* Ithaca, NY: Cornell University Press, 2010.

Rutherford, Danilyn. *Raiding the Land of the Foreigners.* Princeton, NJ: Princeton University Press, 2003.
Stasch, Rupert. *Society of Others: Kinship and Mourning in a West Papuan Place.* Berkeley: University of California Press, 2009.
Strassler, Karen. *Refracted Visions: Popular Photography and National Modernity in Java.* Durham, NC: Duke University Pres, 2010.
Tsing, Anna Lowenhaupt. *Friction: An Ethnography of Global Connection.* Princeton, NJ: Princeton University Press, 2005.

LAOS

Baird, Ian G. "Different Views of History: Shades of Irredentism along the Laos-Cambodia Border." *Journal of Southeast Asian Studies* 41, no. 2 (2010): 187–213.
Goscha, Christopher, and Soren Ivarsson, eds. *Contesting Visions of the Lao Past: Lao Historiography at the Crossroads.* London: Taylor & Francis, 2003.
High, Holly. "Ethnographic Exposures: Motivations for Donations in the South of Laos (and Beyond)." *American Ethnologist* 37, no. 2 (2010): 308–322.
Holt, John. *Spirits of the Place: Buddhism and Lao Religious Culture.* Honolulu: University of Hawai'i Press, 2009.
Ladwig, Patrice. "Narrative Ethics: The Excess of Giving and Moral Ambiguity in the Lao Vessantara-Jataka." In Monika Heintz, ed., *The Anthropology of Moralities* (New York: Berghahn, 2009), 136–158.
Singh, Sarinda. "Bureaucratic Migrants and the Potential of Prosperity in Upland Laos." *Journal of Southeast Asian Studies* 42, no. 2 (2011): 211–231.
Vatthana, Pholsena. *Post-War Laos: The Politics of Culture, History, and Identity.* Ithaca, NY: Cornell University Press, 2006.
Walker, Andrew. *The Legend of the Golden Boat: Regulation, Trade and Traders in the Borderlands of Laos, Thailand, China, and Burma.* Honolulu: University of Hawai'i Press, 1999.
Whitington, Jerome. "Intervention, Management, Technological Error." *Parallax* 14, no. 3 (2008): 48–61.

MALAYSIA

Baxstrom, Richard. *Houses in Motion: The Experience of Place and the Problem of Belief in Urban Malaysia.* Stanford, CA: Stanford University Press, 2008.
Bunnell, Tim. *Malaysia, Modernity and the Multi-media Super Corridor: A Critical Geography of Intelligent Spaces.* London: RoutledgeCurzon, 2004.
DeBernardi, Jean. *Rites of Belonging: Memory, Modernity and Identity in a Chinese Community.* Stanford, CA: Stanford University Press, 2004.
Fischer, Johan. *Proper Islamic Consumption: Shopping among the Malays in Modern Malaysia.* Copenhagen: Nordic Institute of Asian Studies, 2008.

Kahn, Joel. *Other Malays: Nationalism and Cosmopolitanism in the Modern Malay World.* Singapore: NUS Press, 2006.

Khoo, Gaik-Cheng. *Reclaiming Adat: Contemporary Malaysian Film and Literature.* Vancouver: University of British Columbia Press, 2006.

King, Ross. *Kuala Lumpur and Putrajaya: Negotiating Urban Space in Malaysia.* Singapore: NUS Press, 2008.

Peletz, Michael. *Islamic Modern: Religious Courts and Cultural Politics in Malaysia.* Princeton, NJ: Princeton University Press, 2002.

Postill, John. *Media and Nation Building: How the Iban Became Malaysian.* Oxford: Berghahn, 2008.

Thompson, Eric C. *Unsettling Absences: Urbanism in Rural Malaysia.* Singapore: NUS Press, 2007.

Wain, Barry. *Malaysian Maverick: Mahathir Mohamad in Turbulent Times.* Basingstoke, UK: Palgrave Macmillan, 2009.

Willford, Andrew. *Cage of Freedom: Tamil Identity and the Ethnic Fetish in Malaysia.* Ann Arbor: University of Michigan Press, 2006.

PHILIPPINES

Abinales, Patricio. *The Joys of Dislocation: Mindanao, Nation, and Region.* Mandaluyong, Philippines: Anvil, 2008.

Bryant, Raymond. *Nongovernmental Organizations in Environmental Struggles: Politics and the Making of Moral Capital in the Philippines.* New Haven, CT: Yale University Press, 2005.

Cannell, Fenella. *Power and Intimacy in the Christian Philippines.* New York: Cambridge University Press, 1999.

Faier, Lieba. *Intimate Encounters: Filipina Women and the Remaking of Rural Japan.* Berkeley: University of California, 2009.

Hedman, Eva-Lotta, and John Sidel. *Philippine Politics and Society in the Twentieth Century: Colonial Legacies, Post-Colonial Trajectories.* New York: Routledge, 2001.

Kramer, Paul. *The Blood of Government: Race, Empire, the United States, and the Philippines.* Chapel Hill: University of North Carolina Press, 2006.

McCoy, Alfred W. *Lives at the Margin: Biography of Filipinos Obscure, Ordinary, and Heroic.* Madison: University of Wisconsin–Madison Center for Southeast Asian Studies, 2004.

Parreñas, Rhacel. *Servants of Globalization: Women, Migration, and Domestic Work.* Stanford, CA: Stanford University Press, 2001.

Rafael, Vicente. *White Love and Other Events in Filipino History.* Durham, NC: Duke University Press, 2000.

Tadiar, Neferti. *Things Fall Away: Philippine Historical Experience and the Makings of Globalization.* Durham, NC: Duke University Press, 2009.

SINGAPORE

Chong, Terence, ed. *The AWARE Saga: Civil Society and Public Morality in Singapore*. Singapore: NUS Press, 2011.

Chong, Terence. *The Theatre and the State in Singapore: Orthodoxy and Resistance*. London: Routledge, 2009.

Göransson, Kristina. *The Binding Tie: Chinese Intergenerational Relations in Modern Singapore*. Honolulu: University of Hawai'i Press, 2009.

Maznah, Mohamed, and Syed Muhd Khairudin Aljunied, eds. *Melayu: The Politics, Poetics and Paradoxes of Malayness*. Singapore: NUS Press, 2011.

Nasir, Kamaludeen Mohamed, Alexius A. Pereira, and Bryan S. Turner. *Muslims in Singapore: Piety, Politics and Policies*. London: Routledge, 2010.

Ortmann, Stephan. *Politics and Change in Singapore and Hong Kong: Containing Contention*. London: Routledge, 2010.

Tan, Kenneth-Paul. *Cinema and Television in Singapore: Resistance in One Dimension*. Leiden: Brill, 2008.

Teo, Youyenn. *Neoliberal Morality in Singapore: How Family Policies Make State and Society*. London: Routledge, 2011.

Trocki, Carl A. *Singapore: Wealth, Power and the Culture of Control*. London: Routledge, 2006.

Yao, Souchou. *Singapore: The State and the Culture of Excess*. London: Routledge, 2007.

THAILAND

Eberhardt, Nancy. *Imagining the Course of Life: Self-Transformation in a Shan Buddhist Community*. Honolulu: University of Hawai'i Press, 2006.

Jonsson, Hjorleifur. *Mien Relations: Mountain People and State Control in Thailand*. Ithaca, NY: Cornell University Press, 2005.

Kiong, Tong Chee, and Chan Kwok Bun, eds. *Alternate Identities: The Chinese of Contemporary Thailand*. Singapore: Times Academic Press, 2001.

Klima, Alan. *The Funeral Casino: Meditation, Massacre, and Exchange with the Dead in Thailand*. Princeton, NJ: Princeton University Press, 2002.

Morris, Rosalind C. *In the Place of Origins: Modernity and Its Mediums in Northern Thailand*. Durham, NC: Duke University Press, 2000.

Pattana Kitiarsa. *Religious Commodifications in Asia*. London: Routledge, 2008.

Sinnott, Megan. *Toms and Dees: Transgender Identity and Female Same-Sex Relationships in Thailand*. Honolulu: University of Hawai'i Press, 2004.

Tanabe, Shigaharu, and Charles Keyes, eds. *Cultural Crisis and Social Memory: Modernity and Identity in Thailand and Laos*. Honolulu: University of Hawai'i Press, 2002.

Walker, Andrew, ed. *Tai Lands and Thailand: Community and the State in Southeast Asia*. Copenhagen: NIAS Press, 2009.

Wilson, Ara. *The Intimate Economies of Bangkok: Tomboys, Tycoons, and Avon Ladies in the Global City.* Berkeley: University of California Press, 2004.

VIETNAM

Harms, Erik. *Saigon's Edge: On the Margins of Ho Chi Minh City.* Minneapolis: University of Minnesota Press, 2011.
Kwon, Heonik. *Ghosts of War in Vietnam.* Cambridge: Cambridge University Press, 2008.
Luong, Hy V. *Tradition, Revolution, and Market Economy in a North Vietnamese Village, 1925–2006.* Honolulu: University of Hawai'i Press, 2010.
Malarney, Shawn K. *Culture, Ritual and Revolution in Vietnam.* New York: RoutledgeCurzon, 2002.
Norton, Barley. *Songs for the Spirits: Music and Mediums in Modern Vietnam.* Urbana: University of Illinois Press, 2009.
Pettus, Ashley. *Between Sacrifice and Desire: National Identity and the Governing of Femininity in Vietnam.* New York: Routledge, 2003.
Pham Quynh Phuong. *Hero and Deity: Tran Hung Dao and the Resurgence of Popular Religion in Vietnam.* Chiang Mai, Thailand: Mekong Press/Silkworm Books, 2009.
Rydstrøm, Helle. *Embodying Morality: Growing up in Rural Northern Vietnam.* Honolulu: University of Hawai'i Press, 2003.
Schwenkel, Christina. *The American War in Contemporary Vietnam: Transnational Remembrance and Representation.* Bloomington: Indiana University Press, 2009.
Taylor, Philip. *Fragments of the Present: Searching for Modernity in Vietnam's South.* Honolulu: University of Hawai'i Press, 2001.
———, ed. *Modernity and Re-Enchantment: Religion in Post-Revolutionary Vietnam.* Lanham, MD: Lexington Books, 2007.

CONTRIBUTORS

PROLOGUE

ULF HANNERZ is professor emeritus of social anthropology at Stockholm University. His books include *Foreign News: Exploring the World of Foreign Correspondents* (Chicago: University of Chicago Press, 2004) and *Anthropology's World: Life in a Twenty-First Century Discipline* (London: Pluto Press, 2010).

THE PHILIPPINES

JOSÉ B. CAPINO is associate professor of English at the University of Illinois–Urbana-Champaign and is the author of *Dream Factories of a Former Colony: American Fantasies, Philippine Cinema* (Minneapolis: University of Minnesota Press, 2010).

RICHARD T. CHU is Five College Associate Professor of History at the University of Massachusetts–Amherst and is the author of *Chinese and Chinese Mestizos of Manila: Family, Identity, and Culture 1860s-1930* (Leiden: Brill, 2010) and *Chinese Merchants of Binondo in the Nineteenth Century* (Manila: University of Santo Tomás Press, 2010).

DEIRDRE DE LA CRUZ is an assistant professor in the Departments of Asian Languages and Cultures and History at the University of Michigan.

KALE BANTIGUE FAJARDO is an assistant professor of American Studies and Asian American Studies at the University of Minnesota–Twin Cities and is the author of *Filipino Crosscurrents: Oceanographies of Seafaring, Masculinities and Globalization* (Minneapolis: University of Minnesota Press, 2011).

ANNA ROMINA GUEVARRA is an associate professor of Asian American studies, sociology, and gender and women's studies at the University of Illinois–Chicago.

ORLANDO DE GUZMAN is a Bangkok-based documentary filmmaker focusing on human rights, social change, and political upheaval in Southeast Asia.

SMITA LAHIRI is a researcher affiliated with the Anthropology Department at Harvard University, where she was a member of the faculty between 2002 and 2011.

ADAM LUKASIEWICZ is a PhD candidate with the Department of Geography at York University, Canada.

MARTIN F. MANALANSAN is associate professor of anthropology and Asian American studies and Conrad Humanities Professorial Scholar at the University of Illinois–Urbana-Champaign.

JAN M. PADIOS is assistant professor of American Studies at the University of Maryland College Park, where she is completing a book on customer service call centers in the Philippines.

MAI M. TAQUEBAN has worked in human rights law and advocacy and currently teaches anthropology at the University of the Philippines.

T. RUANNI F. TUPAS is senior lecturer at the Centre for English Language Communication, National University of Singapore.

VIETNAM

ERIK HARMS is assistant professor of anthropology and international and area studies at Yale University. He is the author of *Saigon's Edge: On the Margins of Ho Chi Minh City* (Minneapolis: University of Minnesota Press, 2011).

NINA HIEN is a visual anthropologist and assistant professor/faculty fellow in the John W. Draper Program at New York University.

CHRISTIAN C. LENTZ is assistant professor in the Department of Geography at the University of North Carolina–Chapel Hill. He earned his PhD in development sociology from Cornell University in January 2011.

ANN MARIE LESHKOWICH is associate professor of anthropology at the College of the Holy Cross. Her publications have focused on gender, entrepreneurship, middle classes, neoliberalism, and fashion in Vietnam.

KEN MACLEAN is an assistant professor of international development and social change at Clark University. His most recent publication on Vietnam is "The Collected Works of the Communist Party: The Possibilities and Limits of Official Representations of Actually Existing Government," *Journal of Vietnamese Studies* 5, no. 2 (2010): 195–207.

LAUREN MEEKER is assistant professor of anthropology at State University of New York–New Paltz. She is the author of "How Much for a Song? Local and National Representations of Quan Họ Folk Song," *Journal of Vietnamese Studies* 5, no. 1 (2010): 125–161.

CHRISTOPHE ROBERT is a cultural anthropologist with a PhD from Cornell University

(2005). He taught at Princeton, Yale, and City University of Hong Kong. He lives and writes in Saigon.

CHRISTINA SCHWENKEL is an associate professor of anthropology at the University of California–Riverside. She is the author of *The American War in Contemporary Vietnam: Transnational Remembrance and Representation* (Bloomington: Indiana University Press, 2009).

IVAN SMALL is a PhD candidate in cultural anthropology at Cornell University. His field research in Vietnam from 2007–2008 was conducted on a Fulbright-Hays grant.

ALLISON TRUITT is an assistant professor of anthropology at Tulane University. She is the author of several journal articles and coeditor of the book *Money: Ethnographic Encounters* (Berg, 2007).

TRUONG HUYEN CHI holds a PhD in social/cultural anthropology from the University of Toronto (2001) and is an independent researcher interested in societies in transition, narrative and memories, and K-12 education. She taught at Vietnam National University–Hanoi and served as lead qualitative researcher in a sub-study of young lives (University of Oxford) in Vietnam.

CAMBODIA

ERIK DAVIS is assistant professor of religious studies at Macalester College. His research focuses on Buddhism, ritual, and religious interactions in Cambodia and mainland Southeast Asia.

ANNUSKA DERKS is a Swiss National Science Foundation Research Fellow affiliated with the Institute for Social Anthropology of Bern University and the Center for Asian Studies at the Graduate Institute for International and Development Studies in Geneva; and a visiting lecturer on the faculty of sociology of the Vietnam National University, Hanoi.

JENNA GRANT is a doctoral candidate in cultural anthropology at the University of Iowa whose research examines the cultural politics of biomedicine—most recently, medical imaging and clinical trials—in Phnom Penh.

STEPHEN MAMULA is an ethnomusicologist specializing in Cambodia's musical culture and particularly its regeneration following the Khmer Rouge genocide.

JONATHAN PADWE is an assistant professor of anthropology at the University of Hawai'i–Manoa, where he conducts research on postwar environmental and social change among highland ethnic minorities of Cambodia and Vietnam.

ALBERTO PÉREZ-PEREIRO is a PhD candidate at Arizona State University researching ethnic and religious identity among the Cham Muslims of Cambodia.

EVE ZUCKER is an anthropologist whose work focuses on the topics of morality, memory, and social change in southwest upland Cambodia and beyond.

LAOS

MICHAEL DWYER'S dissertation, "Territorial Affairs: Turning Battlefields into Marketplaces in Postwar Laos," from U.C. Berkeley's Energy and Resources Group, is based on fieldwork conducted in Laos from 2006 to 2008.

N. J. ENFIELD is professor of ethnolinguistics at the Max Planck Institute and Radboud University–Nijmegen and is author of many works on Lao language and culture, including *A Grammar of Lao* (Tübingen: Mouton de Gruyter, 2007) and *The Anatomy of Meaning* (Cambridge: Cambridge University Press, 2009).

HOLLY HIGH is an anthropologist—trained at the Australian National University, fieldwork in the south of Laos, lecturer at the University of Sydney, and fellow of Clare Hall, Cambridge—who specializes in the intersection of fantasy, desire, and aspiration with politics and economy.

PATRICE LADWIG obtained his PhD in social anthropology from the University of Cambridge (2008) and is currently research fellow at the Max Planck Institute for Social Anthropology (Halle, Germany).

JEROME WHITINGTON is a research fellow at the National University of Singapore, where he is finishing a project on risk management in Lao hydropower while initiating an ethnographic project on new regimes to manage climate change in Asia and beyond.

THAILAND

JULIA CASSANITI received her PhD from the University of Chicago's Department of Comparative Development for her research on the psychology of Buddhism in northern Thailand and is currently a postdoctoral scholar in the Anthropology Department at Stanford University.

LEERAY M. COSTA teaches anthropology and gender and women's studies at Hollins University, and her research and teaching interests include gender, activism and social justice, feminist theory, narrative methodology, and feminist pedagogy.

PILAPA ESARA obtained her PhD in anthropology from Brown University and teaches at the College at Brockport, State University of New York.

JANE M. FERGUSON holds a PhD from Cornell University (2008) and currently teaches courses on mainland Southeast Asian studies at the Australian National University.

ANDREW JOHNSON, a cultural anthropologist, is currently a postdoctoral fellow in the Asian Urbanisms research cluster at the National University of Singapore's Asia Research Institute.

TRACY PILAR JOHNSON holds a PhD from Columbia University (2005), is research director at the Context-based Research Group, an ethnographic consulting firm, and has lived and worked throughout South and Southeast Asia for many years.

PATTANA KITIARSA is a Thai ethnographer and currently teaches in the Southeast Asian Studies Department, National University of Singapore.

SUDARAT MUSIKAWONG is assistant professor of sociology at Siena College, with research in transnational labor, citizenship, nationalism, and memory.

EMILY ZEAMER holds a PhD from Harvard (2008), is a social anthropologist with a current research focus on Buddhist modernities in contemporary Thailand, and her research interests more broadly include the anthropological study of knowledge and the senses, technology and technique, religion and secularism, and the history and theory of ethnographic film and media.

INDONESIA

JOSHUA BARKER is associate professor in the Department of Anthropology at the University of Toronto. He is contributing editor for the journal *Indonesia* and coedited the volume *State of Authority: State in Society in Indonesia* (Ithaca, NY: Cornell Southeast Asia Program Publications, 2009).

TOM BOELLSTORFF is professor in the Department of Anthropology at the University of California–Irvine and editor-in-chief of *American Anthropologist.* He is the author of *The Gay Archipelago: Sexuality and Nation in Indonesia* (Princeton, NJ: Princeton University Press, 2005); *A Coincidence of Desires: Anthropology, Queer Studies, Indonesia* (Durham, NC: Duke University Press, 2007); and *Coming of Age in Second Life: An Anthropologist Explores the Virtually Human* (Princeton University Press, 2008).

CHRIS BROWN recently completed a PhD in anthropology at the University of Washington. His dissertation is about streets and children in Surabaya.

ARYO DANUSIRI is a nonfiction filmmaker at Ragam in Jakarta and a PhD candidate in the Department of Anthropology at Harvard University, with a secondary field in critical media practice. Currently he is working on his dissertation project about the urban circulatory forms of the Tariqa Alawiya youth movement in Jakarta.

DADI DARMADI is a researcher at the Center for the Study of Islam and Society at Universitas Islam Negeri Syarif Hidayatullah in Jakarta and a PhD candidate in the Department of Anthropology at Harvard University.

SHERI GIBBINGS is a Social Science and Humanities Research Council of Canada Postdoctoral Fellow at the Institute of Asian Research, University of British Columbia. Her current research examines the political organizing of street vendors as they confront problems of urbanization and state-organized resettlement, while also encountering the new social imaginaries of democracy and transparency.

JESSE GRAYMAN is a PhD candidate in social anthropology at Harvard University. He is writing his dissertation about postconflict recovery issues in Aceh.

JAMES HOESTEREY is the ACLS New Faculty Fellow at the Center for Southeast Asian Studies at the University of Michigan. He has held postdoctoral fellowships at Stanford University and Lake Forest College and is currently completing a book about Islam, popular culture, and public piety in Indonesia.

CARLA JONES is associate professor of anthropology at the University of Colorado–Boulder. Her research is on the intersection of gender and class, analyzing the anxieties and cultural politics of femininity, middle-class propriety, and consumption in urban Indonesia.

DOREEN LEE is assistant professor of anthropology at Northeastern University. In addition to her work on memory, politics, and youth activism in Indonesia, she is now conducting research on street art, new art markets, and communities in Indonesia.

JOHAN LINDQUIST is associate professor of social anthropology at Stockholm University in Sweden. He is the author of *The Anxieties of Mobility: Development and Migration in the Indonesian Borderlands* (Honolulu: University of Hawai'i Press, 2009), and his documentary film *B.A.T.A.M.* is available from Documentary Educational Resources. His current research deals with labor recruitment on the Indonesian island of Lombok.

DAROMIR RUDNYCKYJ is assistant professor in the Department of Pacific and Asian Studies at the University of Victoria, British Columbia, Canada. He is the author of *Spiritual Economies: Islam, Globalization, and the Afterlife of Development* (Ithaca, NY: Cornell University Press, 2010). His current research project, "Malaysia and the Globalization of Islamic Finance," examines efforts to make Kuala Lumpur the "New York of the Muslim World."

RACHEL SILVEY is associate professor in the Department of Geography at the University of Toronto. She is the author of articles published in the *Annals of the Association of American Geography, Political Geography, Global Networks, Progress in Human Geography,* and *Gender, Place and Culture.* Her most recent research focuses on the regulation of transnational migration as it intersects with religion.

KAREN STRASSLER is associate professor of anthropology at Queens College and the CUNY Graduate Center. Her book on popular photography in Java, *Refracted Visions,* was published in 2010 by Duke University Press. Her current research focuses on media and political communication in post-Suharto Indonesia.

MALAYSIA

SYED MUHD KHAIRUDIN ALJUNIED is assistant professor in the Department of Malay Studies, National University of Singapore. He is the author of *Colonialism, Violence and Muslims in Southeast Asia: The Maria Hertogh Controversy and Its Aftermath* (London: Routledge, 2009).

MATTHEW AMSTER is associate professor of anthropology at Gettysburg College in Pennsylvania. His ethnographic research in Malaysia has been among the Kelabit of Sarawak.

KHOO GAIK CHENG lectures in gender, sexuality, and culture at the Australian National University and researches independent filmmaking, food, identity, and cosmopolitanism in Malaysia.

MICHAEL EILENBERG is assistant professor of anthropology at Aarhus University. He is the author of *At the Edge of States: Dynamics of State Formation in the Indonesian Borderlands* (Leiden: KITLV Press, 2012).

GERHARD HOFFSTAEDTER is research fellow at the Institute for Human Security at La Trobe University. He is the author of *Modern Muslim Identities: Negotiating Religion and Ethnicity in Malaysia* (Copenhagen: NIAS Press, 2011).

JULIAN C. H. LEE is lecturer in international studies at RMIT University. He is the author of *Policing Sexuality: Sex, Society and the State* (London: Zed Books, 2011).

RUSASLINA IDRUS is a social anthropologist and visiting research fellow at the Institute of Southeast Asian Studies in Singapore.

SVEN ALEXANDER SCHOTTMANN is research associate at the Centre for Dialogue, La Trobe University.

YEOH SENG GUAN is senior lecturer at the School of Arts and Social Sciences, Monash University–Sunway Campus. He is editor of *Media, Culture and Society in Malaysia* (London: Routledge, 2010).

SINGAPORE

SYED MUHD KHAIRUDIN ALJUNIED is assistant professor in the Department of Malay Studies, National University of Singapore. He is the author of *Colonialism, Violence and Muslims in Southeast Asia: The Maria Hertogh Controversy and its Aftermath* (London: Routledge, 2009).

ERIK HOLMBERG has been fascinated by the history of Singapore since he moved there in 1999, and in recent years he has learned about Singapore's Arab minority community. He is the author of "Sheikh Salim bin Mohamed bin Talib," in *Hadhrami Arabs across the Indian Ocean: Contributions to Southeast Asian Economy and Society,* ed. Syed Farid Alatas (Singapore: National Library Board, 2010), 32–37.

ADELINE KOH is assistant professor of literature at Richard Stockton College. She works in comparative race studies and in African and southeast African literatures. She recently coedited *Rethinking Third Cinema: The Role of Anti-Colonial Media and Aesthetics in Postmodernity* (Berlin: Lit Verlag, 2011).

LIEW KAI KHIUN is assistant professor at the Wee Kim Wee School of Communication and Information, Nanyang Technological University. His main research interests are in East Asian film and television dramas, popular music, and Malayan history. He is coeditor of *The Makers and Keepers of Singapore History* (Singapore: Ethos Books & Singapore Heritage Society, 2010).

LOH KAH SENG is an independent scholar. He is coeditor of *The Makers and Keepers of Singapore History* (Singapore: Ethos Books & Singapore Heritage Society, 2010) and author of *Making and Unmaking the Asylum: Leprosy and Modernity in Singapore and Malaysia* (Kuala Lumpur: Strategic Information, Research and Development Centre, 2009).

KAMALUDEEN MOHAMED NASIR is a Lee Kong Chian Fellow at the National Library of Singapore. His research interests are in minority studies, social theory, sociology of religion, and sociology of Islam. He is coauthor of *Muslims in Singapore: Piety, Politics and Policies* (New York: Routledge, 2010).

MD MIZANUR RAHMAN is a research fellow at the Institute of South Asian Studies, National University of Singapore. His articles have appeared in journals such as *International Migration, Population, Space and Place, Journal of International Migration and Integration,* and *Asian Population Studies.* He is the author of *In Quest of Golden Deer: Bangladeshi Transient Migrants Overseas* (Saarbrücken: VDM Verlag, 2004).

YU-MEI BALASINGAMCHOW is a writer and independent scholar in Singapore. She is the coauthor of *Singapore: A Biography* (Singapore: National Museum of Singapore/ Editions Didier Millet, 2009) and the coeditor of the forthcoming volume of essays, *Troublesome Women in Asia: The Politics of Women, Gender and Sexuality in Singapore and Malaysia.*

BURMA

AUNG NAING THU works for a nongovernmental organization focusing on poverty reduction and rural development based in Yangon, Myanmar.

AUNG SI is a PhD candidate in the Department of Linguistics at the Australian National University, Canberra.

VIOLET CHO is an independent journalist who recently completed a Bachelor of Communication Studies (Honours) at Auckland University of Technology.

NICHOLAS FARRELLY is a research fellow in the College of Asia and the Pacific at the Australian National University, Canberra.

DAVID GILBERT is a PhD candidate in the College of Asia and the Pacific at the Australian National University, Canberra.

THOMAS KEAN is the editor of the English-language edition of the *Myanmar Times.*

DAVID SCOTT MATHIESON is a senior researcher in the Asia Division of Human Rights Watch.

JACQUELINE MENAGER is a PhD candidate in the College of Asia and the Pacific at the Australian National University, Canberra.

IKUKO OKAMOTO is a senior research fellow at the Institute of Developing Economies–JETRO, Japan.

MANDY SADAN is a lecturer at the School of Oriental and African Studies, University of London.

EPILOGUE

BENEDICT ANDERSON is Aaron L. Binenkorp Professor of International Studies Emeritus at Cornell University. His books include *Imagined Communities: Reflections on the Origin and Spread of Nationalism* (London: Verso, 2006, Rev. ed.) and *The Spectre of Comparisons: Nationalism, Southeast Asia, and the World* (London: Verso, 1998).

THEMATIC INDEX

The purpose of this index is to provide readers with alternative ways of navigating the book. If read from front to back, the book presents a country-based mode of understanding the Southeast Asian region. But the book can be read differently. Readers may wish to read the book by following particular themes, such as "Globalization" in Southeast Asia, "Gender" in Southeast Asia, and so forth. In this index, we present a list of such themes, each of which provides the reader with a unique path through the book and through the region.

BODY

Philippines: *Bakla* Returnee, 36; Community
    Health Worker, 41
Vietnam: Prostitute, 52; Photo Retoucher, 67
Cambodia: Broken Woman, 84
Laos: Miss Beer Lao, 95
Thailand: Kickboxer, 119
Indonesia: Person with HIV/AIDS, 141
Singapore: Malay Gangster, 198
Burma: Sex Worker in Thailand, 227

BROKERS

Philippines: Domestic Helper, 23; Public
    Manager, 29; Community Health
    Worker, 41
Vietnam: Domestic Investor, 54; Vietnamese
    Transnational(s), 72
Cambodia: Cham Modernizer, 78; World
    Musician, 80; Government Official,
    89
Laos: Mitigation Expert, 99; Beleaguered
    Village Leader, 104
Thailand: Bangkok Slum Leader, 113;
    Transnational Farmworker, 115; Rural
    DJ, 123; Spirit Medium, 125
Indonesia: Telecommunications and
    Multimedia Expert, 133; Muslim
    Television Preacher, 136; Spiritual
    Trainer, 138; Ex-Combatant, 146; NGO
    Worker, 148; Field Agent, 154
Malaysia: Returning Urbanite, 190; Timber
    Entrepreneur, 192
Singapore: Bangladeshi Worker, 200;
    The People's Filmmaker, 207;
    Schoolteacher, 209; Social
    Entrepreneur, 211
Burma: Urban *Dumsa*, 218; Journalist, 220;
    Political Prisoner, 222; Exile, 225;
    Entrepreneur, 234; Indie Musician,
    236

BUDDHISM
(SEE ALSO RELIGION)

Cambodia: (Buddhist) Ascetic, 86
Laos: Mobile Phone Monk, 97
Burma: Urban *Dumsa,* 218

BUREAUCRACY

Philippines: Public Manager, 29; Community
    Health Worker, 41

Vietnam: Domestic Investor, 54; Enterprising
    Cadre, 56; Soviet-Trained Scientist, 59;
    Mountain Village Head, 65; Cultural
    Expert, 70
Cambodia: Government Official, 89
Laos: Mitigation Expert, 99; Beleaguered
    Village Leader, 104
Thailand: Grassroots Woman Leader,
    110; Bangkok Slum Leader, 113;
    Transnational Farmworker, 115
Indonesia: Ex-Combatant, 146; Overseas
    Female Labor Migrant, 152; Street
    Kid(s), 159
Singapore: Schoolteacher, 209
Burma: Tatmadaw Officer, 229

CAPITALISM AND CLASS

Philippines: Domestic Helper, 23;
    Agriculturalist, 34; Call Center Agent,
    38; Beauty Contestant, 43
Vietnam: Petty Trader, 49; Prostitute, 52;
    Domestic Investor, 54; Enterprising
    Cadre, 56; Soviet-Trained Scientist,
    59; Mountain Village Head, 65;
    Photo Retoucher, 67; Vietnamese
    Transnational(s), 72
Laos: Miss Beer Lao, 95
Thailand: Bangkok Slum Leader, 113;
    Transnational Farmworker, 115; Thai
    Airways Flight Attendant, 117; Single
    Woman, 121
Indonesia: Muslim Television Preacher, 136;
    Spiritual Trainer, 138; Overseas Female
    Labor Migrant, 152; Field Agent, 154;
    Street Vendor, 156; Street Kid(s), 159;
    Mr. Hajj, 162; Rich Person, 165; Career
    Woman, 167
Malaysia: National Leader, 174; Squatter,
    188; Timber Entrepreneur, 192
Singapore: Bangladeshi Worker, 200; Woman
    Activist, 203; Peri-Urban Tenant,
    205; The People's Filmmaker, 207;
    Schoolteacher, 209
Burma: Sex Worker in Thailand, 227;
    Entrepreneur, 234

CHRISTIANITY
(SEE ALSO RELIGION)

Philippines: Community Health Worker, 41
Burma: Urban *Dumsa,* 218; Tatmadaw
    Officer, 229

Female Labor Migrant, 152; Field
Agent, 154; Street Vendor, 156; Street
Kid(s), 159; Rich Person, 165
Malaysia: Returning Urbanite, 190
Singapore: Bangladeshi Worker, 200; Peri-
Urban Tenant, 205; Schoolteacher, 209
Burma: Urban *Dumsa,* 218; Sex Worker in
Thailand, 227

LAW

Philippines: Public Manager, 29; Lawless
Element, 32
Vietnam: Domestic Investor, 54; Enterprising
Cadre, 56
Thailand: Grassroots Woman Leader, 110
Malaysia: Reactionary, 176; Timber
Entrepreneur, 192
Singapore: Malay Gangster, 198
Burma: Journalist, 220; Political Prisoner,
222

MAGIC

Vietnam: Cham H'Roi Girl, 63; Photo
Retoucher, 67
Laos: Mobile Phone Monk, 97
Thailand: Spirit Medium, 125

MEDIA AND TECHNOLOGY

Philippines: Call Center Agent, 38
Vietnam: Aspiring Overseas Student, 61;
Cham H'Roi Girl, 63; Photo Retoucher,
67; Cultural Expert, 70; Vietnamese
Transnational(s), 72
Laos: Miss Beer Lao, 95; Mobile Phone
Monk, 97
Thailand: Rural DJ, 123
Indonesia: Multimedia Expert, 133; Muslim
Television Preacher, 136; Spiritual
Trainer, 138
Malaysia: Hang Tuah, Revisited, 181;
Political Satirist, 185
Singapore: The People's Filmmaker, 207
Burma: Journalist, 220; Korean Soap Opera
Junkie, 232

MIGRATION AND MOBILITIES

Philippines: Chinese Mestizo, 25; Filipino
Seaman, 27; Public Manager, 29;
Agriculturalist, 34; *Bakla* Returnee, 36
Vietnam: Soviet-Trained Scientist, 59;

Aspiring Overseas Student, 61;
Vietnamese Transnational(s), 72
Thailand: Transnational Farmworker, 115;
Thai Airways Flight Attendant, 117
Indonesia: Overseas Female Labor Migrant,
152; Field Agent, 154; Street Vendor, 156
Malaysia: Returning Urbanite, 190
Singapore: Bangladeshi Worker, 200; Social
Entrepreneur, 211
Burma: Sex Worker in Thailand, 227

MILITARY

Philippines: Lawless Element, 32;
Community Health Worker, 41
Indonesia: Ex-Combatant, 146
Burma: Political Prisoner, 222; Exile, 225;
Tatmadaw Officer, 229; Entrepreneur,
234

MORALITY AND ETHICS

Vietnam: Petty Trader, 49; Prostitute, 52;
Enterprising Cadre, 56; Mountain
Village Head, 65
Cambodia: Village Police Chief, 82; Broken
Woman, 84; (Buddhist) Ascetic, 86;
Government Official, 89
Laos: Miss Beer Lao, 95
Indonesia: Muslim Television Preacher, 136;
Spiritual Trainer, 138; Career Woman,
167
Malaysia: Reactionary, 176

NATIONALISM

Philippines: Chinese Mestizo, 25; Filipino
Seaman, 27
Vietnam: Enterprising Cadre, 56; Soviet-
Trained Scientist, 59; Cultural Expert,
70; Vietnamese Transnational(s), 72
Cambodia: Cham Modernizer, 78; (Buddhist)
Ascetic, 86
Laos: Miss Beer Lao, 95
Indonesia: Ex-Combatant, 146
Malaysia: National Leader, 174; Reactionary,
176

NEOLIBERALISM

Philippines: Public Manager, 29; Call Center
Agent, 38
Vietnam: Petty Trader, 49; Prostitute, 52;
Domestic Investor, 54; Enterprising

Production Notes for...
Barker / *Figures of Southeast Asian Modernity*
Cover design by Julie Matsuo-Chun
Interior design and composition by Julie Matsuo-Chun
with display type in Engravers MT and text in Times New Roman
Printing and binding by Sheridan Books, Inc.
Printed on 50# House White, 514 ppi